A DEATH AT CROOKED CREEK

A DEATH AT CROOKED CREEK

THE CASE OF THE COWBOY,
THE CIGARMAKER,
AND THE LOVE LETTER

 MARIANNE WESSON

NEW YORK UNIVERSITY PRESS
New York and London

NEW YORK UNIVERSITY PRESS
New York and London
www.nyupress.org
© 2013 by NYU Press
All rights reserved

LIBRARY OF CONGRESS CATALOGING-IN-PUBLICATION DATA
Wesson, Marianne.
A death at Crooked Creek : the case of the cowboy, the cigarmaker, and the love letter /
Marianne Wesson.
pages cm.
Includes bibliographical references and index.
ISBN 978-0-8147-8456-3 (cloth : alk. paper)
1. Hillmon, Sallie E.—Trials, litigation, etc. 2. Mutual Life Insurance Company of New
York—Trials, litigation, etc. 3. Trials—Kansas—History—19th century. 4. Insurance
crimes—Kansas—History—19th century—Cases. 5. Evidence, Hearsay—United States—
History—19th century—Cases. I. Title.
KF228.H543.W47 2013
346.73'08632—dc23   2012048184

New York University Press books are printed on acid-free paper,
and their binding materials are chosen for strength and durability.
We strive to use environmentally responsible suppliers and materials
to the greatest extent possible in publishing our books.

Manufactured in the United States of America
10 9 8 7 6 5 4 3 2 1

If [the dead] should speak, what revelations there would be!
MARK TWAIN, "THE PRIVILEGE OF THE GRAVE" (1905)

† † †

Some circumstantial evidence is very strong, as when you find a trout in the milk.
HENRY DAVID THOREAU

AUTHOR'S NOTES

The volume that follows is a work of both history and imagination. Portions of the narrative, those told from the point of view of one or another of the characters in the Hillmon story, necessarily contain some invention; nobody memorialized the sorts of conversations that surely took place in parlors and courthouse vestibules, nor did Sallie Hillmon or any of the other actors, apart from John Hillmon, leave behind for us a journal or diary that recorded her or his thoughts. Notes at the end of each of these scenes inform the reader which aspects represent documented history, and which parts are invented.

Imagination is hardly a steady beacon, of course, and at times as I researched and wrote, mine led me off the straight path. New information and reconsideration many times compelled me to revise my theories, and these moments came to form their own narrative.

The remaining portions of the book are as accurate historically as I could make them. All newspaper stories in the text are rendered verbatim as in the originals. Other sources are documented in the endnotes. When inventing, I did my best to hew to the historical record as I discovered it. Nothing herein is contradicted by the evidence to which I had access, and I have made an effort to treat the case evenhandedly. The reader must judge whether I have succeeded.

CONTENTS

Contents

IMPORTANT CHARACTERS IN THE STORY OF THE HILLMON CASE

THE HILLMONS AND FAMILY OF LAWRENCE, KANSAS, AND ENVIRONS:

Sallie Quinn Hillmon, the plaintiff. Waitress and seamstress.

John Wesley Hillmon, her first husband. Civil War veteran and cowboy.

Levi Baldwin, her cousin. Rancher.

James Smith, her second husband. Traveling salesman.

THE WALTERS FAMILY OF FORT MADISON, IOWA, AND ELSEWHERE:

Frederick Adolph Walters, itinerant cigarmaker.

Mr. and Mrs. Daniel Walters, his parents.

Fannie and Anna Walters and Elizabeth Walters Rieffenach, his sisters.

C.R. Walters of Missouri, his brother.

Alvina Kasten of Fort Madison, Frederick Adolph's fiancée.

FRIENDS AND ACQUAINTANCES OF THE HILLMONS:

Mr. and Mrs. Arthur Judson, the Hillmons' landlords.

John Brown, John Hillmon's former employee and occasional traveling companion.

THE INSURANCE COMPANIES' AGENTS AND INVESTIGATORS:

A.L. Selig, agent. Later Mayor of Lawrence.

G.W.E. Griffith, agent.

H.B. Munn, agent.

C.E. Tillinghast, investigator.

Samuel ("Colonel") Walker, investigator.

Theodore ("Major") Wiseman, investigator.

CORONERS:

George Paddock, Medicine Lodge, Kansas.

Richard Morris, Lawrence, Kansas.

EXAMINING PHYSICIANS:

Dr. J.H. Stewart.

Dr. G.G. Miller.

Dr. Charles V. Mottram.

LAWYERS FOR SALLIE HILLMON:

E.O. Borgalthaus (the Lawrence inquest).

Lysander Wheat (all six trials).

Samuel Riggs (all six trials).

John Hutchings (second and third trials).

Charles Hutchings, brother of John (fourth through sixth trials)

John Atwood (sixth trial).

LAWYERS FOR THE INSURANCE COMPANIES:

James Woods Green (all six trials). Also at one time County Attorney of Douglas County, and at all pertinent times Dean of the University of Kansas Law School.

George Barker (all six trials). Also at one time Assistant County Attorney for Douglas County.

W.H. Buchan, Kansas State Senator. No trial appearances, except as witness. Also claimed to represent John Brown.

Charles Gleed (second through sixth trials). Also businessman, occasional journalist, and eventual owner of the *Kansas City Journal.*

Eugene Ware (fourth through sixth trials). Also known as the poet "Ironquill."

Edward Isham (fifth and sixth trials). From Chicago law firm of Isham, Lincoln, and Beale; law partner to Abraham Lincoln's son Robert.

ASSORTED WITNESSES:

W.H. Lamon, photographer.

Reuben Brown, John's brother.

James Crew, banker.

W.W. Nichols, buffalo hunter and brother-in-law to John Hillmon.

William Hillmon and Mrs. George Nichols, brother and sister to John Hillmon.

Dr. Patterson, dentist.

Patrick Heely, agent for railroad excursion tickets.

Alva Baldwin, Levi's brother.

Arthur Simmons, cigar factory owner.

Various citizens of Lawrence and Fort Madison.

Many others.

KANSAS OFFICIALS:

S.H. Snider, Superintendent of Insurance (1893–1894).

Webb McNall, Superintendent of Insurance (1897–1899).

FEDERAL TRIAL JUDGES:

Judge Cassius Foster (first trial).

Judge David Brewer (second trial).

Judge Oliver P. Shiras (third trial) (visiting from Iowa).

Judge Alfred D. Thomas (fourth trial) (visiting from North Dakota).

Judge John A. Williams (fifth trial) (visiting from Arkansas).

Judge William C. Hook (sixth trial).

IN THE UNITED STATES SUPREME COURT:

Justice Horace Gray, author of the Court's 1892 Hillmon opinion.

Ezra Ripley Thayer, law secretary to Justice Gray, later Dean of the Harvard Law School.

Justice Henry Brown, author of the Court's 1903 Hillmon opinion.

Justice David Brewer, presiding judge in second trial, later elevated to the Supreme Court. Dissented from the Court's ruling in the 1903 Hillmon decision.

TIMELINE OF EVENTS IMPORTANT TO THE HILLMON LITIGATION

OCTOBER 3, 1878: John Hillmon and Sallie Quinn marry in Lawrence, Kansas.

DECEMBER 1878: John Hillmon leaves Lawrence, meets John Brown in Wichita, and the two travel west.

FEBRUARY 1879: After being driven back home to Lawrence by cold weather, Hillmon leaves home again to reunite with Brown and recommence the journey west.

MARCH 17, 1879: John Brown knocks on door of a rural resident near Crooked Creek, Kansas, and reports that his traveling companion, John Hillmon, has been killed in a firearm accident.

MARCH 1879: Coroner's jury at Medicine Lodge, Kansas, concludes that the death at Crooked Creek was accidental.

APRIL 1879: Coroner's jury in Lawrence, Kansas, returns verdict that death was felonious and victim was not John Hillmon.

SEPTEMBER 1879: John Brown signs affidavit at urging of attorney and State Senator W.J. Buchan.

JANUARY 1880: Insurance company attorneys contact Walters family of Fort Madison, Iowa, who identify the corpse from photographs as Frederick Adolph Walters.

JULY 1880: Sallie Hillmon files lawsuits against the Mutual Life Insurance Company of New York, the New York Life Insurance Company, and the Connecticut Mutual Life Insurance Company.

JUNE 1881: Alvina Kasten sits for a deposition taken by the insurance companies' attorneys.

DECEMBER 1881–FEBRUARY 1882: John Brown sits for a deposition taken by the insurance companies' attorneys.

JUNE 1882: First trial of *Hillmon v. Mutual Life Insurance Company et al.*

JULY 4, 1882: First jury reports itself unable to decide; mistrial declared.

JUNE 1885: Second trial of *Hillmon v. Mutual Life Insurance Company et al.*

JUNE 24, 1885: Second jury reports itself unable to decide; mistrial declared

FEBRUARY–MARCH 1888: Third trial of *Hillmon v. Mutual Life Insurance Company et al.*

MARCH 22, 1888: Third jury returns a verdict for Sallie Hillmon.

MAY 16, 1892: United States Supreme Court overturns verdict, remands Hillmon case for retrial.

JANUARY–MARCH 1895: Fourth trial of *Hillmon v. Mutual Life Insurance Company et al.*

MARCH 23, 1895: Fourth jury reports itself unable to decide; mistrial declared.

MARCH–APRIL 1896: Fifth trial of *Hillmon v. Mutual Life Insurance Company et al.*

APRIL 3, 1896: Fifth jury reports itself unable to decide; mistrial declared.

MARCH 1897: Kansas Insurance Commissioner Webb McNall declines to renew business licenses of all three insurance companies.

SEPTEMBER 1897: Judge Williams enjoins McNall from interfering with insurance companies' business in the state.

JANUARY 12, 1898: Kansas Supreme Court affirms McNall's authority to ban the companies.

JANUARY 20 (APPROX.), 1898: New York Life Insurance Company settles with Sallie Hillmon.

OCTOBER–NOVEMBER 1899: Sixth trial of *Hillmon v. Mutual Life Insurance Company et al.*

NOVEMBER 18, 1899: Sixth jury returns a verdict in favor of Sallie Hillmon against the two remaining life insurance companies.

AUGUST 1900: Mutual Life Insurance Company of New York settles with Sallie Hillmon.

APRIL 3, 1901: Court of Appeals for the Eight Circuit affirms the verdict in favor of Sallie Hillmon.

JANUARY 2, 1903: United States Supreme Court reverses the verdict in favor of Sallie Hillmon and remands the case for another trial.

JULY 1903: Settlement is reported between Sallie Hillmon and the Connecticut Mutual Life Insurance Company.

PROLOGUE

It's not yet eight in the morning, but even so heat rises in shimmering waves from the grass-carpeted floor of the graveyard. The earlier months of this spring brought drenching rains to eastern Kansas, and the saturated green of the cemetery hurts my drought-accustomed Colorado eyes.

The neon color scheme extends to a coffin-sized rectangular outline of Day-Glo orange that glistens on the grass amid a jumble of old headstones. The grave that interests us has no stone or monument, but Mitch Young, the cemetery supervisor, has marked its boundaries with spray paint. Even after all these years, he is confident that their records allow him to identify its location with precision. I have seen the entry: *John W. Hillman, 04/05/1879, grave number 555, lot ID 0000421.* The spelling is wrong—it's Hillmon—but the rest of the name and the date are correct. This is the place, all right.

Mitch sits in the cab of his backhoe, and everyone else stands gathered a few yards away, expectant—anthropologist Dennis Van Gerven and his graduate student Paul Sandberg, my husband, Ben Herr, Ernesto Acevedo-Muñoz and his documentary film crew, a small crowd of journalists kept mercilessly at bay by the city's communication officer. They're waiting for me to give the signal to begin, and any further delay would be pointless: it has taken us more than a year and considerable trouble to achieve permission to disinter the body below the ground, and we're not going home until we do. I know, moreover, that we are not the first to disturb the dead man's repose. Even so, the ancient prohibition against violating a final resting place pushes back with surprising force against my determined intentions. I mumble a few awkward words in the direction of the ground—something about apologizing to the man below for the intrusion, and thanking him for what he will allow us to learn—but they do not vanquish the dread, which will remain with me all day.

I nod to Mitch and he fires up the backhoe's engine, maneuvers its corrugated iron teeth into the ground, and begins to strip off the top layer of earth between the orange boundaries. The raw turned soil beneath the blade sends up a bracing scent of minerals mingled with decay.

Dennis, my partner in this venture, is a colleague at the University, a physical anthropologist—an unlikely Indiana Jones, short and bald, but dashing and unflappable nevertheless. He consorts habitually with dead people; I do not. I believe in cremation and memorial services and avoid funerals.

Dennis, on the other hand, has made a name for himself with his research on mummies. As a matter of professional necessity, he regards the dead as reasonably good company. I am of course familiar with the rumors about curses and the like, so I imagine he's had to develop a matter-of-fact attitude toward his work. I recruited him to this investigation even before I realized it would entail digging a body out of the ground, but as matters have turned out I am very grateful for the participation of someone who has done this sort of thing before. I appreciate his calm and his experience, because as far as I am concerned this situation, despite the brightness of the day and the clutch of onlookers and crew, invites the presence of irrational anxieties and the occasional apparition.

Sallie Hillmon, for example, John's wife—she's haunted my thinking for many months now, and it would not be at all difficult for me to believe that I've caught a glimpse of her, wearing a long calico dress, over there in the shade beneath a stand of oak trees. I know she stood near here once, in 1879, the first time they put the body into this grave that Mitch is now busy uncovering. I've learned quite a bit about her, actually, and as for the rest, I find it dangerously easy to imagine. Sometimes the things I've discovered and those I imagine collude to persuade me that I know her, that I understand her as well as I do my friends and colleagues. I appreciate that this is an illusion, but it is at certain moments an irresistible one.

There is of course one thing that I don't know about Sallie: What was she thinking when she looked on the body that we will disinter today? "Oh my dear, I will miss you so very much"? Or perhaps more like "Dear God, I hope we get away with this"? That is, did she recognize her husband immediately, as she would claim in every public forum? Or did she gaze on a corpse that she knew was not John Hillmon's but another's, as the insurance companies would later maintain? Or was she perhaps in doubt, confounded by the changes the corpse had gone through during the month since life had left it? I cannot be sure; I can only hope that what we learn from Dennis's examination will bring us closer to knowing. This uncertainty, however, does not seem greatly to impede my imagination.

I press my back against the trunk of a massive oak and watch the backhoe tear up the thick grass, trying to calm my unruly pulse by reflecting on the events that have brought me here. Some of them happened quite a long time ago.

On May 16, 1892, the United States Supreme Court announced its decision in the case of *Mutual Life Insurance Company v. Hillmon*. More than a century later the case remains one of the most influential decisions in the American law of evidence. This corner of the law comprises a set of rules designed to answer one question: what information is allowed as proof in a court of law? One of the most important of those rules originated in the Hillmon case.[1]

The Hillmon lawsuit arose out of a dispute concerning the identity of a corpse, and its macabre subject matter had brought the case a great deal of attention even before the nation's highest court agreed to hear it. The suit was one for enforcement of a contract of life insurance: Sallie

Hillmon, a young woman of Lawrence, Kansas, claimed that her husband, John, had been killed, in the late winter of 1879, by a firearm accident at a desolate campsite in western Kansas called Crooked Creek. The three insurance companies that had issued policies on John Hillmon's life disputed the claim, maintaining that Hillmon was still alive, so in 1880 Sallie sued the companies for the policy proceeds. The case had been tried three times before reaching the Supreme Court; the first two trials ended in hung juries, but the third had produced a verdict for Sallie Hillmon.

Just as today, getting a case on the Supreme Court's docket required a certain procedural diligence. To prosecute their appeal before the Supreme Court, and there to argue for a new trial, the insurance companies were required to identify the errors that they claimed the trial court had committed (in the third trial, the one they lost). To this end they had filed a compendium, or "assignment," of errors they alleged, a lengthy list of eighty-eight items. The eighty-sixth error on the companies' list was the trial court's refusal to allow the jury to see a certain exhibit offered as evidence by the insurance companies: a letter. It was a document in some ways as common as a Kansas windstorm, a love letter from a young man who had been traveling about the country addressed to his sweetheart back home.[2]

The placement of the letter's exclusion from evidence so far down the insurance companies' designated error list suggests that the lawyers did not put much stock in this particular claim, for every appellate advocate knows to put your best arguments in the front of your papers and leave the less convincing for the end. The letter is charming, however: a handwritten epistle postmarked Wichita, Kansas, March 2, 1879. Its author, a young cigarmaker originally of Fort Madison, Iowa, who on this date has been away from his birthplace plying his trade for nearly a year, has written it to his fiancée back home, a Miss Alvina Kasten. His letter contains both some awkward endearments and some news. The trifling endearments provide most of the missive's charm, but the news is less whimsical. Indeed, the information the letter supplies is very significant, or at least the insurance companies would so later claim: the young man reports that he has met "a man named Hillmon." Moreover, he writes, this Hillmon has promised him higher wages than he can make in any other pursuit if only the cigarmaker will come along as hired help on Hillmon's travels out west, where (as the letter says) "he hopes to start a sheep ranch." (Or sheep *range*, perhaps—the handwriting is a bit spidery.) The letter writer reports to his sweetheart that he has decided to accept Hillmon's offer.[3]

Alvina Kasten and the young man's family would later swear that this was the last letter any of them ever had from the cigarmaker, whose name was Frederick Adolph Walters. Indeed, they would testify that they never saw him again. It was this letter that was offered by the companies as proof that Hillmon was not dead at all, but quite alive. The body belonged instead, they insisted, to the young itinerant Walters, whom Hillmon and an accomplice had inveigled along on their journey, and then killed and dressed up in Hillmon's clothes and boots in a diabolical effort to use his corpse to commit life insurance fraud.[4]

The cigarmaker's love letter, almost a footnote to the insurance companies' case on appeal, would become the unexpected centerpiece of the Supreme Court's opinion. The Justices ruled unanimously that Frederick Adolph Walters' letter to Miss Alvina Kasten should have been admitted in evidence. In order to arrive at this conclusion the Court would create an entirely new piece of the law of evidence, and the insurance companies thus would win the new trial they desired. But these events constitute only the beginning of a story marked by complexity and persistent mystery, as well as great legal importance. For the Court's opinion in the Hillmon case was to become not only a famous decision but also a highly consequential one: the rule it announced is now written into the law of evidence in nearly every jurisdiction in the United States.[5]

The trial judge whom the Supreme Court implicitly rebuked in its Hillmon opinion was a distinguished jurist named O.P. Shiras. Judge Shiras had kept the letter away from the jury by sustaining an objection from Sallie Hillmon's lawyers, who argued that the letter was hearsay. The hearsay variety of evidence was generally forbidden in American courts from colonial times, although the rule was always subject to a number of exceptions. Hearsay is a showing of what someone said or wrote outside the trial, put forward to prove the proposition said or written. The out-of-court speaker or writer is known to the law as the *declarant*. Since the hearsay declarant ordinarily does not come to court, hearsay evidence lacks the protections against falsehood and mistake that sworn testimony by an in-court witness enjoys: the oath, an opportunity for the jury to size up the person making the statement, and the rigors of cross-examination by the opposing party. Accordingly, the law of evidence forbids the use of hearsay as evidence, except in certain limited circumstances known as the *exceptions* to the hearsay rule.[6]

Frederick Adolph Walters's letter, in which he said more or less "I plan to travel out west with John Hillmon," was undeniably hearsay, as it was offered in evidence to prove that the cigarmaker had this intention (and hence that he carried it out, which in turn would contribute to the likelihood that it was he rather than John Hillmon who died at the Crooked Creek campground). Judge Shiras's ruling excluding the letter thus seems in retrospect clearly correct, indeed unavoidable. The more surprising circumstance is that Sallie Hillmon's lawyers did not make the hearsay objection at either of the first two trials, the ones that ended in hung juries; it seems not to have occurred to them until the third.

The law did recognize various exceptions to the hearsay rule at the time the Hillmon case was tried. These exceptions could operate to make an out-of-court statement admissible even if it was put forward, as lawyers say, "to prove the truth of the matter asserted." Most of the hearsay exceptions were designed to accommodate evidence of statements made outside of court when there were reasons to believe they were true and reliable. Dying declarations, for example—statements made by a person on his deathbed, knowing that he was about to die— were deemed admissible on the premise that "no man would meet his Maker with a lie upon his lips." Statements against the speaker's interest—for example, a confession to an act of wrongdoing, or the acknowledgment of a debt—were generally regarded as an exception, because it was understood that only a desire to tell the truth would account for a human being's open presentation of a statement that could not advance, but only harm, her interests. Written business records, if kept and maintained in a regular and reliable fashion, were deemed admissible despite their hearsay nature: this exception rested on a recognition that the exigencies of business would require a merchant or banker to keep accurate records or fail. Startled utterances describing some exciting or alarming event that had just happened were admitted on account of the excited state of the declarant and the immediacy of the outburst, for these circumstances were thought to provide some warranty against prevarication.

The lawyers for the three insurance companies appear to have been blindsided by the Hillmon attorneys' belated invocation of the hearsay rule during the third trial. No doubt they ran through the various exceptions to the hearsay rule in their minds, desperately seeking to recall and invoke one that would suit Frederick Adolph Walters's letter to Alvina Kasten. With little time to reflect on the matter, they argued that the letter was a business record. But this was desperate indeed, for the letter resembled no business record that the court had ever seen, and so Judge Shiras rejected this suggestion and ruled that the letter, undeniably hearsay, was subject to no recognized exception to the hearsay rule and was thus inadmissible.

Between the jury's verdict against them in 1888 and the argument of their case before the Supreme Court in 1892, the insurance companies' lawyers had a great deal more leisure to perfect their advocacy for the admissibility of the letter. They were impressive lawyers, but regarding the letter they could formulate no proposal any better than the one the trial judge had already rejected: in their appellate briefs they argued again that it was a business record.

The Supreme Court was plainly eager to rule for the insurance companies, and began its opinion by declaring that Judge Shiras had not allowed the defendants to remove a sufficient number of prospective jurors without cause. The opinion could have stopped there and sent the case back to be retried on the basis of that error, but Justice Horace Gray, writing for the Court, seemed bent on addressing the question of the Walters–Kasten letter. He and his brethren could not, however, endorse the proposition that the letter was a business record. Nor did any of the other generally recognized hearsay exceptions seem to fit Frederick Adolph Walters's correspondence with his betrothed.

Nevertheless, the insurance companies won their argument about the letter: the Court simply invented a new piece of law in order to make it admissible and thus to thwart Sallie Hillmon's efforts to claim the insurance proceeds. But it was not the custom of the United States Supreme Court in that century (nor is it now) to acknowledge that it makes the law to suit the facts, or its view of them. Justice Gray's language and logic in the Hillmon decision are designed to persuade the reader that the Court is discovering, not creating, a legal rule. Accordingly, the opinion does not announce that a new rule is being devised to make a cigarmaker's love letter admissible in evidence. Instead it pronounces that there is a well-recognized exception to the hearsay rule for out-of-court statements that describe the *intentions* of the declarant. Since the Walters letter described young Frederick Adolph's intention to travel west with a man named Hillmon, it was, the Court said, admissible, and Judge Shiras had erred in keeping it from the jury.

But as we shall see, there was no such well-recognized exception to the hearsay rule. If there had been, the insurance companies would have identified it and argued for it in their appellate papers, but they did not. The small shreds of history that are preserved about the Court's decision-making process suggest that the rule they rested their decision on was a new one, invented for the occasion. It is a curious rule as well, for unlike statements recognized by other hearsay exceptions, the things we say about our intentions are not trustworthy guides to the truth of what we might actually intend. Such statements rest on nothing like the psychological underpinnings of dying declarations or statements against interest, varieties of speech that are genuinely unlikely to be uttered or written unless they are true. Indeed, there is almost nothing so easy to lie about as one's intentions. Yet the proposition that statements of intention carry with them some guarantee of accuracy is all the Supreme Court's Hillmon opinion can claim to rest on, at least as a matter of reason. Reason so flimsy demands that we look for another explanation for what the Court did.[7]

The great jurist Oliver Wendell Holmes, who would later succeed Horace Gray on the Supreme Court, famously observed that the life of the law has not been logic, but experience—a statement that encapsulated his belief in the primacy of human factors over strict reason in the law's creation. Over time I have concluded that the law of evidence was indeed altered by the Supreme Court in the Hillmon case for reasons less logical than human, although a certain inescapable logic played its part as well.[8]

I have come to believe that the Justices (having seen the famous love letter) were certain that John Hillmon had murdered Frederick Adolph Walters to perpetrate insurance fraud, and was probably hiding out somewhere until the proceeds were paid. They could not bring themselves to let Hillmon get away with this crime, as he would if his wife were to succeed in obtaining the life insurance proceeds. The only way to prevent this outcome was to ensure that the jury in a new trial saw the letter. But the letter was undeniably hearsay, and hearsay was not admissible unless it conformed to some exception to the hearsay rule. No generally recognized hearsay exception made the letter admissible. There was but one inexorable solution to this puzzle: the Court must invent a new exception to the hearsay rule, one that would by its terms apply to Frederick Adolph Walters's letter to his fiancée. And that is precisely what the Court proceeded to do.

The case was not over with the Court's decision, of course; it was sent back to be retried. Later events and circumstances prolonged it for more than another decade, and cast both more light and more shadow on the truth of what happened at Crooked Creek in 1897. It was 1903 before the Hillmon case was finally settled.

The story of the Hillmon affair, from its origins in a wintertime journey taken by a newlywed Civil War veteran to its eventual conclusion nearly a quarter of a century later, is the subject of this book. It would be a worthy tale even if it had affected only its parties, in my opinion, for it teems with remarkable characters and offers a window into American history, law, politics, and culture during the transformational era that was the final quarter of the nineteenth century. But its legacy surpasses even this narrative interest, for the Hillmon rule of evidence, created in the Court's first opinion in the case, is not only embedded in the law of nearly every American jurisdiction; it has been exported to England and Australia as well, strictly on the prestige of Justice Horace Gray's opinion for the Court. Not many nineteenth-century Supreme Court precedents have proved as durable and influential.[9]

The evidence about the identity of the body at Crooked Creek, developed in the course of six separate trials, was by no means all on one side. The famous letter from the cigarmaker to his sweetheart was joined by other strong evidence that the corpse was not Hillmon's; but it was also opposed by some convincing evidence, offered by Sallie Hillmon's lawyers, that the body indeed belonged to her husband. Suppose, as I have argued, the Supreme Court did invent the Hillmon rule to make the outcome of the case as they understood it—that is, as one of murder and fraud—a proper one. Wouldn't some inquiry into whether they got the facts right be useful in arriving at history's judgment of the Court's work? What might such an investigation disclose? And might twenty-first-century science and technology allow us to arrive at a more confident judgment about the corpse's identity than nineteenth-century forensics would permit? These questions are taken up in the pages that follow.

A WINTER JOURNEY
LEADS TO AN INQUEST

1879

LAWRENCE, KANSAS | APRIL 1879

Sarah Ellen Quinn Hillmon pronounces exactly those four words, practicing. She has had very few occasions to say all the names together and stumbles slightly. Regarding herself reproachfully in the cloudy glass she tries again, this time with more success. She is certain she will be asked at the very outset to state her name and does not wish to be flustered by the task. Nor will she allow herself to weep when she says *Hillmon*, the name that has been hers for such a short time.

Then there is another ground for worry: she ironed the calico dress, her only fine one, into crisp respectability the night before, but already the damp air has softened its finish and left it limp. It really should be black under the circumstances, but she owns no dress of that color, and the ancient bombazine Mrs. Judson offered to lend her was far too large and smelt of mothballs. Turning, she attempts to see how the dress looks from behind, but the glass is too small and the light too dim to reveal much. Being in the Judsons' chamber makes her anxious anyway, as she rarely visits this room at the rear of the house, despite her friendship with the couple and her tenancy of the second floor bedroom. It is kind of Mrs. Judson to allow her to come in to inspect her appearance this morning.

Outside the window five or six girls, the same ones who congregate on the sidewalk nearly every day, are jumping rope. Sallie has even jumped with them a few evenings on her way home from the hotel where she works, enjoying their cries of admiration for her still-nimble movements. The girls have a new chant, Sallie realizes as she listens.

> John Wesley HILL-A-MAN
> Said that he might KILL-A-MAN
> Is he a CORPSE NOW
> Or do you think he's STILL-A-MAN?

> Sadie Quinn HILL-A-MAN
> Says he wouldn't KILL-A-MAN
> Will she tell the TRUTH NOW
> And is her love a KILLER MAN?

Little savages. What do they know? She's never gone by Sadie; it's common. And the name doesn't end with *man*, although the newspapers keep getting it wrong.

With her forefinger she worries the burn on her thumb, a souvenir of her inexperience with the Judson's heavy flatiron. She hopes it will not blister. Waitressing is hard enough without a raw thumb, and her mother will be annoyed if she does not appear at the hotel's dining room tomorrow in time to help serve breakfast.

Sallie knows that her mother was not overfond of John Hillmon. Candice Quinn thinks herself a shrewd judge of male character from her many years in the restaurant business, and by the time she met Hillmon she had fed too many cattlemen to be impressed with one who had no ranch of his own. When Sallie told her that she and John were to be married, the older woman said only, "I reckoned I had taught you better."

Sallie has indeed learned much about men from her mother, including the concealment of her feelings and the maintenance of an air of indifference to gibes and compliments alike. Moreover, she can spot a lecher or a rake quicker than most. She was sure at the time that her mother was mistaken about John, whose only shortcoming as Sallie saw it was a lifelong partnership with mildly bad luck.

Mrs. Judson looks into the room, her straw hat already askew. "Ready to go, Sallie? Arthur has brought the wagon around to the front."

Sallie is thankful for the pressure of Mrs. Judson's gloved hand on her own as they share the splintery backseat. Mr. Judson drives the team himself, as a driver would be an extravagance. The Judsons are not much better off than she and John are (*were*, she corrects herself; she must learn to speak of him in the past tense), but they have always been generous. The wagon's sudden sway nearly robs her of balance on the narrow seat, and she looks at Mrs. Judson with surprise as the conveyance swings onto New Hampshire Street.

"Isn't the inquest at the courthouse?"

"Yes, my dear, but Arthur thinks that you ought to go by Bailey and Smith's before. To take a look at the body."

Sallie shakes her head quickly. "It's no use. They wouldn't allow me to see it yesterday."

She has never before seen Mrs. Judson's motherly gaze grow so flinty. "Who prevented you?"

"That Mr. Selig from the insurance company, and the other. Griffith. They said I should remember him as he was. Anyway, I know it's him. Arthur says so, and he knew John as well as any man. I don't want to see him in a coffin."

Mrs. Judson holds her hand even more tightly and Sallie flinches; her friend has unknowingly rubbed the burn. "You must, Sallie. You will insist on being admitted. Arthur has learned that numerous persons have been let into the room to view the body. He was your husband and you have a right to see him. I am sure Arthur is right that it is John, but if you do not see for yourself they will say it's because you know it isn't John but have not the gumption to tell a lie."

After a moment's reflection, which takes in the jump rope chant, Sallie can see that this is true. She nods; it will have to be done.[1]

Sallie would have been astonished at this early moment to learn that her name would be given to one of the most famous and lengthy pieces of litigation in American law, a lawsuit sometimes described as an American *Jarndyce v. Jarndyce*. That fictitious lawsuit at the center of Charles Dickens's *Bleak House* consumed its parties like a succubus; countless babies were born into it, and for generations its unhappy litigants could escape only in death. Sallie's suit was not quite so long, nor quite so fatal. Nevertheless, a nation of observers attached their own loyalties and opinions to the dispute, and its duration spanned at least one generation; it supplied plenty of epic drama in its time, drama quite suited by its subject and parties to stand in for the struggles that preoccupied its spectators when they weren't watching or reading about the Hillmon trials.

Kansas, at the edge of the American frontier in the years of Sallie Hillmon's lawsuit, harbored disputation from the beginning of its written history. The former Territory of Kansas had been admitted to the Union as a free state on the eve of the Civil War, after a decade of bloody struggle, and by the seventies the worst violence occasioned by the slavery question lay in its past. But the bitter conflicts that had once earned the Territory the label "Bleeding Kansas" lingered in collective memory, as the old resentments were reinvested in new divisions: urban against rural, agricultural versus mercantile, prohibitionists against their opponents, white settler against Native American, the religious against the freethinker. The controversy over the Hillmon case took root in this troubled ground.

John Wesley Hillmon, who was born in Indiana in 1848 and served in the Union Army as a very young man, moved with his parents and siblings to a Kansas township called Grasshopper Springs in the late 1860s. This northeastern portion of Kansas close to the Missouri border was more thickly settled and easily traveled than the outlying sections, where the weather was harsher and the land less fertile. It was also safer than the lands farther west and south, where bloody battles took place well into the 1870s between the settlers, backed up by their military protectors, and the native peoples they saw as their enemies.[2]

Even after the Treaty of Medicine Lodge in 1867, a few bands of the plains tribes resisted the peace that agreement sought to impose on the region. They suffered much loss of life from both privation and assault, and their warriors sometimes took revenge on settlers as well as sol-diers. Indeed, mere weeks before John Wesley Hillmon first applied for life insurance, a band of Northern Cheyenne people seeking to return from Indian Territory to their homeland in Montana clashed with Kansas homesteaders; there were many deaths among both groups.[3]

Nevertheless, thousands of homesteaders from the eastern and middle Atlantic states braved the dangers and the elements to stake out their one hundred sixty acres and hunker down in sod houses or rude cabins, hoping to endure long enough to acquire title, make enough money to pay for their claims, and become what they never could have been where they came from: landowners. Homesteaders who learned enough to survive their first hazardous winter found that if they could manage to raise a crop of any size, they could use the newly built railroad to ship their produce to distant markets where it would command a good price. For a time after the Civil War the partnership of farmers and railroad was a happy one, with enough profit for both, although later this alliance would unravel in bitter fashion. But the cultivation of food crops was always difficult in Kansas, especially as one moved westward into the arid regions, because of the harsh weather and uncertain precipitation. Many men instead tried to make a living in the livestock business. Cattle were raised in great numbers in New Mexico and Texas and driven via the great Santa Fe and Chisholm Trails to the cow towns of western Kansas, often trampling some homesteader's fields along the way. From thence they could be loaded onto railroad cars and transported to the markets back east.

Like many young soldiers released from service after the Civil War, John Hillmon tried out various occupations. He worked in 1874 as a foreman at the Quartzville mine near what is now Fairplay, Colorado, and then moved on to Central City, where he worked in both mining and brickmaking. But before long he drifted back to Kansas, and into the cattle business. Hillmon was skilled on a mount from his time in the military, so he worked as a cowboy for men who bought and sold cattle, sometimes investing in his own small herd. Occasionally he dealt in buffalo hides; he was one of the many hunters and traders responsible for reducing the great bison hordes of the plains from a population of millions in 1870 to near extinction by 1890. His cattle dealing took him to Texas and back, and not everyone who dealt with him had praise for his business ethics: in 1879 the sheriff at Lawrence reported darkly that he had received "inquiries" from parties in Texas who had business complaints against Hillmon.

In the mid-1870s Hillmon worked off and on with a cattle rancher named Levi Baldwin who owned property in Tonganoxie, not far from Lawrence. Baldwin was sometimes Hillmon's employer, sometimes his partner in certain ventures. The rancher had a cousin named Sarah Quinn, called Sallie, whom he introduced to Hillmon during this time. Sallie and John Hillmon were married after an acquaintance of several years, in October 1878, and the couple thereafter set up housekeeping in a Lawrence, renting a room in the home of a couple named Judson. John was thirty at the time; Sallie was several years younger.[4]

An ambitious cattleman like John Hillmon might reflect that a Kansan who could find the land on which to raise his own livestock, as Baldwin had, would enjoy a great advantage in proximity to the new train lines and thus to the markets. But the land around Lawrence was mostly occupied by the time John Hillmon started to speak of staking out his own claim. For homesteading one had to go farther south or west, where the government was selling land, much of it available as the result of broken treaties. The price was $1.25 to $2.50 an acre if one would settle on the land for six months (and in some places cultivate it, although that requirement was not much enforced). Land was available for purchase from the railroads in some places as well, for they had been granted outright several millions of acres as right of way for their roads, and were free to sell any acreage they had no need to use. Their prices were often as cheap as the government's, for they saw every trackside settlement as a source of endless future shipping and travel revenues.

There were plenty of buyers, too, especially as the idea took hold that "rain follows the plow." This early version of a belief in human-induced climate change proposed that cultivation activity could literally modify the weather, and that the skies west of the hundredth meridian thus would be made to shed moisture onto the ground by the farmers who moved westward, turned the soil, and transformed the plains into fields. It was an appealing notion; many aspiring homesteaders were persuaded. But later events would not bear out the idea that rainfall followed human settlement, and it would prove the undoing of many.[5]

Even without cultivation, the native grasses could provide some nourishment for livestock, but for most of the nineteenth century cattle ranching, as distinct from cattle driving, had been practically impossible in western Kansas. The difficulties included not only the hostilities between the would-be ranchers and the native peoples who lived on the plains, but also the unavailability of the materials needed to create enclosures for cattle: there was no stone, and insufficient hardwood timber for sawed boards. The 1867 Treaty of Medicine Lodge, however, imposed at least a theoretical peace on the prairie, and the invention of barbed wire in the 1870s solved the fencing problem. Homesteading a ranch on the prairie, somewhere between Wichita and the Territory of Colorado, had become by 1878 a possibility to which a reasonably enterprising man could aspire.[6]

John Hillmon told Sallie shortly after their wedding that he was planning to set out on a journey, accompanied by a man named John Brown. Brown was an old sidekick of his; Hillmon had supervised him at the Quartzville mines and knocked around Colorado with him a bit. The two men had run into each other again by accident at the Kansas City train station in 1876, and Hillmon had recruited Brown on the spot to join an expedition to Texas to hunt buffalo and carry on some trade in the hides. But according to Sallie, Hillmon promised her that the trip he was about to embark on with Brown in 1878 had a purpose more suitable to a married man: he would look for a place where he might start a ranch of his own. It is not known how or whether he explained his reasons for departing in the bitter midst of a Kansas winter, but Sallie Hillmon's lawyers would later argue that it was necessary because cold-season feeding of cattle was a great expense, and a place would bear consideration only if, upon inspection, its winter range appeared sufficient to the sustenance of a herd.[7]

Thus the two Johns, Hillmon and Brown, set out for the first time shortly before Christmas 1878, taking the train as far as Wichita and then procuring a wagon and team of horses. The pair got as far as the frontier hamlet of Medicine Lodge, where they stayed for a few days and met several of the local men before striking out westward, But within a day or two, cold weather drove them home—back to Wichita together, and then Hillmon back to Lawrence and his wife for a time.

Hillmon left Sallie a second time to try the venture anew in late February 1879, traveling through Wichita to pick up Brown and heading southwest from there. After passing through Medicine Lodge again the two men camped out on the night of March 16 near a place usually called Crooked Creek—although some locals called it Spring Creek.[8]

After dark on the evening of March 17, John Brown found his way to the home of a rural neighbor named Philip Briley (or Brierly) and reported that his traveling companion, John Hillmon, had been shot dead at their campsite. The neighbor summoned the coroner from Medicine Lodge, who came to Crooked Creek and inspected the scene of the death. The next day the coroner, George Paddock, convened an inquest. John Brown testified that he had accidentally shot and killed John Hillmon when the rifle he was unloading from their wagon discharged and the bullet flew into Hillmon's head. The coroner's jury deemed the death to have been a misadventure—an accident.[9]

Violent accidental death was not uncommon on the prairie, and ordinarily this verdict would have been the end of the matter, except for burial. But it developed that there was money at stake—a great deal of money for the time—for John Hillmon, aided by a loan from Sallie's cousin Levi Baldwin, had taken out $25,000 in life insurance shortly before his departure from Lawrence. This sum, equivalent to nearly half a million early twenty-first-century dollars, was so great that no single company would issue Hillmon a policy for the entire amount; there were four policies from three different companies, one for $10,000 and three for $5,000. The three insurance companies, New York and Connecticut corporations, employed representatives in Lawrence, and once word of the death made its way back to that city their agents reacted with swift suspicion. Within days the companies had taken the position that they would not pay out on any claims against John Hillmon's life insurance policies because the dead man was not John Hillmon but someone else. Within a few months they claimed to have discovered the identity of the corpse: a young Iowan named Frederick Adolph Walters.

More than a century later, the mystery of the dead man's identity remained unsolved. I had become obsessed with it in 2003, ordering up hundreds of pages of photocopies, documents, and microfilmed newspaper accounts to pore over. One postprandial evening at home, as I mounted the steps to my paper-strewn office, my husband observed gently that it was a bit difficult to compete with a fellow who'd been dead for over a hundred years.

"I think she's the one I'm interested in, actually," I said.

"What, the wife?"

I nodded. "Sallie. But I can't figure her out unless I know what happened to him."

Ben knew the story. "I can see that," he said, his voice carefully neutral.

"Perhaps someday you can help me with all this," I suggested.

"I don't see how, exactly. Unless you want me to dig the guy up for you."

I laughed. "I don't think they'd let us do that. But thanks for the offer. Look, I'll be back down in an hour or so."

Ben nodded and went back to his newspaper.

OAK HILL CEMETERY | LAWRENCE, KANSAS | MAY 19, 2006

I walk over to Dennis, who is watching serenely, ready to begin digging by hand once the backhoe and its metal teeth have removed a couple of feet of soil. The old newspaper accounts I've shown him do not leave him confident that the remains were necessarily buried six feet below the surface; it's not unusual, he has told me, to find that the gravediggers cheated a bit, especially if the ground was hard or the dead man poor. Ben, Paul, Ernesto, and the rest of the crew stand calmly nearby, all prepared to pursue their tasks, but it's not clear what mine is. My hands are restless, insufficiently occupied by periodic efforts to hold back the untidy hair that keeps falling across my face and obscuring my vision, as I seem always to be looking down. This old section of the graveyard is so crowded that it's impossible to avoid walking on some other grave. I've been stumbling all morning over the tombstones that lean this way and that like crooked teeth. On many of them the inscriptions have been effaced by time and weather; some are unreadable.

Dennis appears utterly at ease, a man who knows what he's about and has no doubt he commands the right skills to perform his task. But there is nothing useful for me to do. It is painful to feel so superfluous and I turn away, barely avoiding stepping on a stone set flush to the ground: *Capt. Wm. Murch, born May 8, 1800, died Dec. 6, 1881.* The inscription on this stone has survived much better than most, as has the small anchor carved above it. Captain Murch must have been pretty sturdy, too: he enjoyed a very long life for those times. He outlived John Hillmon by two years—unless the insurance companies were right.

† † †

There is a brief stir as Sallie and the Judsons enter the courtroom an hour later, many heads turning in their direction. Sallie surveys the large room, taking in the scene quickly. Of the six men in the jury box she knows only one, the grocer E.B. Good. He does not return her nod, but he wears spectacles; perhaps he cannot see so far as the back of the courtroom, where it is dim anyway. The man seated behind the high judge's bench applies a gavel timidly to the wooden surface before him. He looks ill at ease up there, an unsteady captain trying to command his ship from the crow's nest.

"What is the judge's name?" Sallie whispers to Arthur Judson.

"He's not a judge, Sallie, he is the coroner, Dr. Morris. This is not exactly a trial. It is a coroner's inquest."

Morris gavels the bench again and says, "Let's get on with it, Mr. Green." The six men in the jury box return their attention to the man on the witness stand. It is Brown, she can see, miserably attired in a tattered coat that he must have borrowed, for it is much too small for him. If he was going to borrow a coat, he could at least have borrowed a respectable one, but John Brown never was one to reflect on how folks would take him. When he dined once with the Hillmons, Mrs. Judson had to ask him to wash his hands. Today he holds a dirty hat in his crooked fingers.

An elegantly dressed bald man of about her John's age seems to be asking the questions. "And so, Mr. Brown, this stranger you mentioned, where did he join up with you and John Hillmon?"

Brown clears his throat before speaking. "Outside a Wichita, like I said. Matter of a few miles."

"And would you describe him please?" The bald gentleman seems to be enjoying himself.

"Who is that man asking the questions?" Sallie whispers again. The coroner frowns in her direction.

"That's Mr. J.W. Green, the County Attorney," says Arthur. "Come now, we must be seated."

Once she and the Judsons are settled in the third row, Sallie has a chance to note the other spectators. The public gallery is nearly full, mostly with gentlemen. She feels the pressure of a hand on her shoulder and turns to see her cousin Levi Baldwin. "Levi!" she whispers with relief, experiencing the reassurance that his solid presence always seems to generate.

"Morning, Sallie," he says, taking the seat next to her on the other side from Mrs. Judson, nodding at several of the men seated in the row behind. "Don't worry about all this folderol. It's just the insurance boys putting on a little show for their bosses back east. I reckon these jurors will do the right thing when the time comes." Sallie notices for the first time that another man has come in behind her cousin and seated himself to his left. "This is Mr. Borgalthaus, Sallie. I asked him to be here to keep an eye on things for us."

The man extends his hand and Sallie takes it, reaching across Levi's chest. She does not altogether understand what there is to keep an eye on, but she does not care for the manner of the man named Green and is glad to have another ally.

Brown continues his account of the stranger, prodded by Mr. Green's questions.

"Would you have us believe, Mr. Brown, under oath as you are, that this stranger joined you three or four miles outside of Wichita, traveled with you another *three* or *four* miles, said he was looking for work, and that the three of you camped together there about *eight miles* outside of Wichita for *three days*, and then once you were on the move again, he took his *leave* of you, and further that in all this camping and discussion and the like, you never once learned his *name* or where he was *from*?"

It is clear to Sallie that Brown cannot not keep track of the twisting and turning of this question, but in her experience he never could admit to being confused, and today is no exception. Instead he twists his soiled hat in his hands and says, "More or less the case, sir."

"Well, what part more and what part less, Mr. Brown? This jury is entitled to your truthful testimony, no more and no less."

"That's about right. Best a my recollection." He lifts his gaze from the hat and his eyes find Sallie, then slide away.

Sallie has grown irritated during the halting colloquy. "What is the point of all these questions about some stranger?" she asks Levi softly.

"It is merely Mr. Green trying to confuse the jurors," her cousin replies.

"But why? I mean to what end?"

"I am not sure, but I believe he means to make something sinister out of John's allowing an occasional stranger to travel alongside them for a time," says Levi. "Now hush, Sallie, and listen."

Sallie does, and decides that she definitely does not care for Mr. Green; his questions have an insinuating lilt to them, playing with Brown as though everyone finds the witness's awkward attempts at language as amusing as he does. She knows that John Brown is not a man of pretty words, for she once had a letter of him. She remembers every word of it.

MEDICINE LODGE, KAN. MARCH 19, 1879

Mrs. S.E. Hillmon: Am sorry to state the news that I have to state to you. John was shot and killed accidentally by a gun as I was about to take it out of the wagon, about fifteen miles north of this place. I had him dressed in his best clothes and buried in Medicine Lodge graveyard. I shall wait here until Mr. Morris hears from you. If you will leave me to take charge of the team, I will dispose of them to the best advantage, and take the proceeds, and when I get back to Lawrence I will relate the sad news. Probably you have heard of it before you get this. Yours truly,

John H. Brown

"Are you all right, my dear?"

Sallie starts, then nods at Mrs. Judson's anxious face and turns her attention back to the courtroom, where Green is speaking again.

"And this stranger, was he the *last* stranger that you and Mr. Hillmon took into your traveling party after leaving Wichita?"

"No, sir. There was the one other."

Green sketches a satisfied grin, seemingly for the benefit of the jurymen. "Please tell the jury about this *other* stranger."

"He were a small man, sandy complected. Not near as big as the first one. Said he'd been herding cattle up to Salt Creek, and he stayed with us just the one night, not too far from Medicine. Didn't catch his name neither. We never did see him again."

"I take it by 'Medicine' you mean Medicine Lodge?" A nod. "So, after leaving this second mysterious stranger behind, where did you and Mr. Hillmon next make camp?"

"I guess the place is called Crooked Creek, but I didn't know it at the time. It was just a place to camp. I could draw it for you if you want. Like a map I mean."

Green aims a look of vast entertainment toward the jurors, two of whom grin back. "If you would be so kind, Mr. Brown."

The little man who is taking notes below the coroner fetches a piece of paper and pencil for Brown, who applies himself to the task with what seems like relief. Green's assistant then displays Brown's drawing to the jury. Then there is a rustling and, to her surprise, Borgalthaus is rising to his feet.

"*Doctor* Morris," he says, loudly enough to be heard by the coroner, who looks back toward him in annoyance, squinting into the darkness that prevails in the spectator section. "Might it be possible for me to have a look at the exhibit?"

"And who might you be, sir?" says Morris irritably.

"A.B. Borgalthaus, sir. A citizen of Douglas County and member of the Bar."

Green, standing in the well of the courtroom, inclines his head toward the jurors. "Ah, so the lady has come to this inquest with an attorney."

"I do not represent the lady today," says Borgalthaus, walking through the swinging gate into the well. Sallie turns toward Levi again, confused, but he looks forward and with a slight pressure of his arm against hers seems to suggest that she do the same, so she does. "I represent the citizens of this county," the lawyer continues, "some of whom object to this proceeding as an unnecessary burden on public monies, sir. But surely Mr. Green is not suggesting that there would be something untoward about Mrs. Hillmon being represented, under the circumstances. His clients are, after all, trying to deprive her of a large sum of money to which she is apparently entitled."

It is J.W. Green's turn to be angry, or to pretend to be. "My clients! My only client is the County of Douglas, sir, and my only interest is in the truth. A man is dead, and it is incumbent on the authorities to ensure that no crime goes unanswered within our purview."

"I am surprised, Mr. Green, if you are correct about your true client, that it has any interest at all in this matter, as the death happened within the jurisdiction of the authorities at Medicine Lodge, Barbour County, to be precise. Moreover, I believe they satisfied themselves that the death resulted from misadventure, and no crime."

The coroner looks at Green inquiringly. "Sir," Green says, "the inquest conducted at Medicine Lodge was an ignorant and shockingly managed affair, and rendered its over-hasty verdict without a thorough examination of the many facts that have since come to light, chiefly the circumstance that John Hillmon contracted for twenty-five thousand dollars in life insurance a short time before leaving home for the mysterious journey on which this witness accompanied him. As the deceased was a resident of Lawrence and the body is now located in this county, it is altogether correct that the inquest you quite properly convened here, Dr. Morris, should go forward without any more interruption!"

Morris looks as though he is about to say something but Borgalthaus speaks up again. "I am most apologetic, Mr. Green, for this interruption, but did I understand you to say that the deceased was a resident of Lawrence?"

Sallie looks quickly at Green, but he is unembarrassed. "I said *claimed* deceased," he pronounces. But he didn't, she is sure of it.

Borgalthaus smiles, and this time it is he who looks at the jurors, although they stare back at him stonily for the most part. "I take it there is no dispute that there *is* a deceased that is the subject of this inquest," he says. "May I inquire where *your* client says the deceased came from?"

Morris bangs the gavel hard this time and stands up, the better to see over the tall bench. "Sit down, Mr. Borgalthaus. You are out of order. I have convened this inquest and I will see it conducted properly. You may examine the witness's map if you wish, then return to your seat."

"And may I make objections, sir, if called for, on behalf of myself and other citizens with an interest in this proceeding?"

"What sort of objections?" says Green, before the coroner can speak.

"Why I don't know, Mr. Green, for it will depend on you and your witnesses, and whether you do anything objectionable." Borgalthaus makes this sound quite reasonable, Sallie thinks, but Green is plainly annoyed.

"What d'you mean? Like hearsay, for example?"

"Perhaps."

Green shakes his head with disgust and looks toward the coroner, who bangs the gavel one last time before resuming his seat heavily. "There will be no objections, Mr. Borgalthaus. This is not a law court, and we'll have no quarreling in here about hearsay this and that. Sit down, sir, and do not try my patience."[10]

† † †

Even in settings where the hearsay rule was enforced (as it was not in Dr. Morris's inquest), the law of the nineteenth century recognized many exceptions to the rule—about twenty to thirty, depending on how one counted. Unless an exception could be found to apply, however, the hearsay rule prohibited the use of written as well as spoken statements—it could apply to, among other writings, a letter. If the coroner had been enforcing the rules of evidence, then the letter that Sallie Hillmon received from John Brown, for example, would have been inadmissible if it had been offered into evidence—at least inadmissible to prove that the account it gave of John Hillmon's death was true. But it seems the coroner was not enforcing the rules, possibly because he was no lawyer and could not be expected to understand them. And in any event, Brown's awkward message of condolence was not offered at the inquest.

As we now know, it would be another letter altogether that would make the Hillmon case famous. But that would be later—years later. The companies had a different strategy in mind during the early weeks of the Hillmon affair, a strategy that they hoped would discourage Sallie Hillmon from pursuing her claims in a court of law. Their plan depended on the inquest, and the effect they expected its outcome would have on John Brown, and in turn on Sallie.

† † †

It is not very comfortable on the hard wooden bench outside the "joint" where Levi and Mr. Borgalthaus have gone to take some midday refreshment. Governor St. John has recently called on the Legislature to make such establishments against the law in Kansas, together with the refreshments they serve, but for now this place seems quite popular. Perhaps folks are simply enjoying themselves while they have the opportunity. There are even some ladies within, in a manner of speaking, but after a quick look through the swinging doors Sallie has decided that she does not wish to be taken for one of them, and Levi has confirmed that it would be best if she were to wait for him on the bench.

It is warm despite the shade. Sallie loosens her hat a bit to allow the breeze to find its way beneath, and reflects on her morning.

It had been chilly in the room into which she was shown at Bailey and Smith's, or perhaps it was her errand that had made it seem so. Nobody tried to stop her this time, but someone must have informed Smith the undertaker of her presence, because he and the insurance men Selig and Griffith were all standing outside the room when she emerged. She was prepared; she had rehearsed the concealment of her feelings. Each man looked at the other, as though none wished to be the one to ask her the question that was on everyone's mind, and she took advantage of this respite to walk right by them, without saying anything. She had pretended not to hear Smith's voice calling after her, and pressed her handkerchief to her mouth, hiding her face, as she fled through the reception area back outside, where the Judsons' carriage was waiting for her at the curb. She had recovered herself well enough, she believes, by the time they reached the courthouse.

A slender young man with whiskers on his cheeks and chin takes a seat beside her on the bench outside the saloon. "I expect this is very hard for you, Mrs. Hillmon," he says. She nods uncertainly. "I suppose one thing that has left a number of folks skeptical is the rather large sum of insurance your husband took," says the man in a friendly manner.

"I suppose," she says faintly. The man briefly fingers a pencil sticking out of the breast pocket of his jacket.

"Perhaps you have some explanation," he suggests. She shakes her head slightly and looks away down the street, just as Levi and Borgalthaus emerge through the swinging doors, their boots clattering on the wooden porch. Levi takes note of the man with the pencil, and is at once displeased by his presence.

"You get the GD hell away from this lady, Gleed," he says, his voice low but carrying an unmistakable note of menace. The smaller man is not intimidated, however.

"I believe I have as much right to sit in this pleasant spot as the lady does," he says coolly. But he then rises and, with a mocking nod to Sallie, walks away.

"Don't ever talk to him, Sallie," says Mr. Borgalthaus. "He will pretend to be your friend, but he is not."

"But who is he?" she says.

Levi spits into the street. "Gleed. A journalist. Worse than that, really, a journalist who aspires to become a lawyer."

"Lowest of the low," agrees Borgalthaus, and then both men laugh rather too loud. Sallie can smell the whiskey on them. Oh dear, she thinks.

The crowd in the back of the courtroom has grown since the morning; apparently word has gotten about that the proceedings are not routine, and many citizens of Lawrence not otherwise occupied have come to observe them. Quite a few of them seem to have spent the noon hour in the same manner as Levi and Mr. Borgalthaus. Dr. Morris's exasperation is growing, and he makes frequent percussions of the gavel to admonish the spectators to be quiet. Sallie has resettled herself in the next to last row. Seated just in front of her, Gleed and several other young men are marking up their notebooks with alacrity.

Sallie does not know where John Brown spent the recess, but it has not improved his appearance or his demeanor. Hangdog is the word Sallie would use, and she thinks he is bound to make a poor impression. The questioning has been taken over by Mr. Green's assistant, whose name seems to be Barker.

Mr. Barker is a younger man than Mr. Green, heavier to the eye and softer to the ear. Perhaps because he has not so much experience, he does not treat his witness quite so scornfully. He is a bit monotonous, in truth, and John Brown testifies in rather a droning voice, and despite the circumstance that this part of his account is the more important and dramatic, Sallie nevertheless finds herself growing drowsy in the warm room. Her attention seems to function only in fits and starts, but of course, she has heard John Brown's story before. Later when she recalls his afternoon testimony, it will resemble almost perfectly the account she reads of it that evening in the *Daily Tribune*.

† † †

LAWRENCE DAILY TRIBUNE, APRIL 4, 1879

Testimony of Brown continued: . . . on the second day (17th) after supper, about sundown the accident occurred; of the shooting had no weapon except the needle gun, about three feet long; Hillman was using the gun in the afternoon; shot once or twice afterward put it back in the wagon; the gun was with the breach down in the bed, and the muzzle sticking out between the sheet and the bed, the bed is about 15 or 18 inches deep; I went to the wagon to take quilt and bedding out of the wagon; threw the quilt on hind wheel; as I was taking blankets out saw the gun and went to take the gun out of the way; I raised it out of the wagon; the deceased was standing between me and the fire, while moving the gun it was discharged; did not know the gun was loaded; I took hold of the barrel with the right hand, and took it out of the wagon; I could not say where I took hold; as soon as the gun was discharged I dropped it on the ground; do not know whether the gun fell out of my hand or out of the wagon; whirled round and saw Hillmon was struck, and put my hands out to keep him out of the fire; caught him about the body; do not know that I got any blood on me; never thought of it; he fell pretty near straight; discovered blood on his face; did not look to see where he was hit; he made no outcry that I heard; went to a house nearby and called for help.

At this time we go to press.[11]

I do not know for certain that Charles Gleed reported the Hillmon inquest for one of the Lawrence newspapers—the articles are unsigned, in the manner of the time. But it seems likely: Gleed's fingerprints are all over the Hillmon litigation, from its earliest days when he was a recent law student until its eventual end when he was well past middle age. The only mark that appears on it more clearly is that of Gleed's mentor, James W. Green.

In the spring of 1879, when the inquest into the Crooked Creek death had become the central public preoccupation of the town of Lawrence, Gleed had just finished a year of law study at the University of Kansas in that city, under the tutelage of its founding Dean and only faculty member, James Woods Green. The School of Law was new in the fall of 1878, and Gleed was one of the thirteen members of its first class. He was likely a great admirer of Green, one of many young men who looked up to "Uncle Jimmy," as he was called by his students. But Gleed left the formal study of law after a single year, at just about the time the Hillmon inquest came to town. His real interest was journalism. He had founded the student newspaper as an undergraduate at the University, and during his year of law study he had filed stories for several newspapers.[12]

Gleed was already covering Lawrence affairs for out-of-town newspapers, and seems a likely author of the Hillmon case coverage in the *Lawrence Standard*. Indeed some years later, writing about the Hillmon case, Gleed boasted that "apart from [my] knowledge of the case as an attorney, [I] was one of the first newspaper reporters to become familiar with [the facts]."[13]

Whether it was Gleed or some other reporter who wrote it, the *Standard's* reportage displays an evenhandedness at first, acknowledging that John Brown's story of accidental death seems plausible, and coupling an observation that $25,000 is a large amount of life insurance for an ordinary man to carry, with one that life insurance companies "will insure a poor man as well as a rich one, but they more readily and successfully fight payments to the heirs of a poor man." Of Sallie Hillmon and her husband, the *Standard's* early accounts of the inquest report that "her grief, because of his death, has all the appearance of being genuine and heartfelt."[14]

On the other hand, the *Standard*'s journalist is evidently a fan of James W. Green. He reports, for example, that "County Attorney Green has the faculty of asking a question in a way that one cannot but consider it a privilege to answer." And as the inquest progresses, the reporter's asides become more partisan. At one point he chastises those citizens of Lawrence who have suggested that the insurance companies are behind the second inquest. "The mistake is made by some," one story says, "of supposing that the inquest now being held is managed by the representatives of the insurance companies. The inquest is, of course, by the State to determine whether the body brought here is that of Hillmon, and the manner of that death. County Attorney Green and Geo. J. Barker represent the State and not the insurance companies in the examination now being held."[15]

This representation may have been reassuring to the citizens of Lawrence. It did not, however, happen to be true. Sixteen years later, during the fourth trial of Sallie Hillmon's lawsuit against the insurance companies, the coroner Morris admitted that he had received his pay for conducting the inquest from the insurance companies, that he believed the witnesses and jurors had been compensated from the same source, and that "as far as he knew the coroner's inquest had not cost the county of Douglas a single dollar." He also recalled "the fact of the examination of witnesses being conducted by [Green's assistant] George J. Barker in behalf of the insurance companies." Testifying in the same trial, the companies' agent Major Theo. Wiseman corroborated this account: he said that he had "employed Mr. Barker at the time of the inquest to assist him in establishing the fact that the body was not Hillmon's."[16]

As for the *Standard*'s reporter, before the inquest was finished he abandoned all pretense of objectivity about Mrs. Hillmon's disputed widowhood, and added his speculations to the others in circulation about the identity of the dead man. "It is probable," he wrote, "that before many days some man will be missing whose appearance will correspond to that of the dead body. Or, possibly, the man came down in the southwest, where men lead a rambling life, and one would not be missed."[17]

Gleed never did return to law school, but he would later become a lawyer after all, not by achieving a law degree but by "reading law" as an apprentice. Six years later, as the Hillmon case was to be tried for the second time, the list of lawyers serving as counsel of record for the insurance companies contained the name Charles Gleed. He would remain on the case for nearly twenty years.

At the end of the day's proceedings, Arthur Judson reappears to convey Sallie and Levi to the undertakers to retrieve the coffin. The cousins walk ahead on foot as Mr. Judson drives the team and wagon, carrying the now-closed coffin slowly through the streets to the Oak Hill Cemetery. Candice Quinn and Levi's daughter Mary accompany them, walking a few yards apart. "I have made certain that John will be buried as who he was," Levi says to Sallie, steadying her as she stumbles briefly on the uneven street. "No matter what the inquest decides, his grave will be marked with his name, and no other man's."

"Have you ordered a marker then? I should like to have some say . . . "

"Not yet, cousin," interrupts Levi. "When we come into some funds we will purchase one, and you and I together shall decide what it should say."

The procession leaves Sallie tired and empty, and the scene at the graveside is unceremonious. No preacher says words over John's grave, and this seems proper to Sallie at the time, as John was no churchgoer. Upon later reflection, though, she will come to think that a few words of some sort would have been a comfort.

Levi has returned to the Judsons with Sallie and Arthur and consented to take supper with them. "I don't much like that business about the vaccination," Levi says as they eat. "I think those doctors will say near anything to keep the insurance companies' business."

"What do they say about it?" says Mrs. Judson. "I remember when John took that smallpox scratch on the shoulder because the insurance doctors said that he must have it to get the insurance. I can tell them that much."

"You are kind, Mrs. Judson," says Levi. "But they do not deny that he had the vaccination. And they cannot escape the fact that the body has one, too, on the same spot where John received it. Instead the doctors who saw the body say that the scar was too fresh to be from the vaccination that John had in February; they say it was still angry and red and so must have been administered many days later." He keeps an eye on Sallie as he says this, for she has not heard of this matter before. She has several times picked up her fork and set it down again without finding her mouth.

"They are liars," she says finally.

"Lawyers, liars," says Levi. "Six and a half dozen."

She is bewildered by their laughter, and an unsteady feeling is stealing over her. No doubt it is from fatigue, and the lingering feelings of the afternoon. She had held back her tears then, but now they press insistently against her eyes from behind. "Please excuse me," she says, pushing her chair quietly back from the Judson's dining table and heading for the stairs.

"Let her grieve," she hears Levi say softly to the Judsons. "She's still just a girl, after all. Let her go." And she does, but she is careful to take the newspaper with her.

In her bedroom, after a brief crying spell, she carefully scissors out the *Daily Tribune*'s story to be pasted into her scrapbook with the others. She leafs through the book, passing dried flowers and valentines and camp meeting fliers until she reaches the clipping that a kind soul has mailed to her from the Medicine Lodge newspaper of March 20: *We ascertained from his books and papers that he was a gentleman of taste and culture. He leaves a young wife at Lawrence, Kansas, who will sadly mourn his loss.* She turns the page, examines the rectangle from the *Lawrence Standard*, March 24, tracing its rough surface with her finger until she finds the sentence she is looking for: *Mrs. Hillman receives the earnest sympathy of her friends in this city, in this sad and unexpected bereavement.* Then she leafs back, to the picture she had of him. His solemn face regards her above the unaccustomed jacket and tie.

Sallie twists the narrow ring that surrounds her fourth finger. She is glad to have it, for those jackals at the undertaker's would surely have stolen it had John been wearing it. It is not a valuable ring, of course, but nevertheless John had not given it up easily. She had been required to cajole it from him, before he left her for the second time, telling him playfully that he had better give his wife a ring if he was not going to be around to protect her from the restaurant customers. It was too small for him anyway; he had struggled to remove it from his smallest finger.

But it had been his for a long time, and John Hillmon was not a man who easily gave up what was his.

"Oh John," she says aloud. "How could you leave me alone with all this?"

The next morning, Sallie is called to the witness stand. Mr. J.W. Green has lost much of his sarcastic manner and examines her respectfully, almost tenderly. She states her name, all four pieces of it, without hesitation or stammering, and from there he leads her past her age, twenty-three, and her previous acquaintance with her husband. He does seem to dwell a bit on the date of their marriage the previous autumn and the length of their courtship and how much time she spent with her mother after they were married. He professes to be puzzled by the circumstance that she continued to waitress after she was married. He admits to surprise that she and John had known each other since '71 or '72, which they had (as he was often at Levi's on business or sometimes to work for her cousin) and yet had not married until October of '78. Sallie considers retorting that she does not know what could be considered disreputable about getting to know one's husband well before marriage, but she thinks better of it and states instead that Rev. Henning married them. This is entirely truthful, if not altogether in answer to Green's insinuations, and nothing she is asked seems to require her to add that the ceremony had taken place in the Judsons' parlor because John had refused to go to church. She becomes tearful only when she is describing the last letter she had of him, and the County Attorney is not so relentless that he fails to give her a moment to recover herself.

She is asked to describe John's appearance, which takes her by surprise, but she does the best she can. Amid a somewhat sentimental account of his hair and mustache, she is taken aback when Green interrupts her to ask, "What was his height?" and replies she does not know. She informs Mr. Green that she recognized her husband in the room at Bailey and Smith's by his general appearance, rather than by any particular feature, and says that he did not use tobacco that she knew of. Then it is over, and she sees that some of the ladies in the back of the courtroom dab their handkerchiefs at their eyes and she thinks that she has perhaps done well enough.

Her cousin is next, and she thinks he cuts a fine figure in the witness chair. George Barker examines him, and the young lawyer is washy and quibblesome by comparison, in her opinion. Levi Baldwin explains his circumstances, a prosperous ranch near Tonganoxie, a lively cattle trading business, his acquaintance over the years with John Hillmon, who had sometimes been his employee, sometimes his partner, and whom he had introduced to his cousin Sallie. John Brown comes into Levi's account, too, and the plan that the two Johns had described to him to go west in search of a place to start a cattle ranch. Sallie could have told Mr. Green about this plan if he had asked her, and had indeed been prepared to do so, but he hadn't asked. No doubt these lawyers think it is not a woman's place to speak of her man's business, she thinks with annoyance, but in fairness she has to acknowledge that she had not known as much as she might have about John's affairs. It is not the custom, in Lawrence, for wives to be troubled overmuch by business matters.[18]

Even as the Hillmon inquest was occurring in Lawrence, its citizens were embroiled in a civic controversy that had its roots in the Civil War and the ensuing emancipation of the slaves. They were challenged to respond to the unexpected arrival in April 1879 of hundreds of "Exodusters," former slaves from southern states who had been drawn by the stories they had heard about John Brown and Free Soil to embark for Kansas as an escape from continuing persecution at home. Arriving at Kansas's Missouri River ports from St. Louis by the boatload, many brought with them bedding, plows, household utensils, even livestock. Scores of these migrants ended up in Lawrence temporarily, where they found sympathy and charity in the hearts of many citizens.[19]

Many—but not all. For there was in 1879 another strain of civic thinking coming into prominence, a conviction that the world was changing, that old battles should be left in the past, that Kansas should shed its youthful reputation for extravagant contrarian thought and behavior and devote itself to the pursuit of economic prosperity. None other than Charles Gleed, journalist and lawyer for insurance companies and railroads, explained the matter thus to his fellow citizens a few years later:

> We are compared to the people of Mexico, and the suggestion is freely offered that we be annexed to that turbulent republic. We are done up in satire, stung all over with barbed wit, and blistered with abuse. We are described as cranks, fad chasers, and political unaccountables generally.
>
> Ours is called the home of the hobby and the land of the ism. It is wondered if we are never to quit "bleeding"—and if our hemorrhage is uncurable. It is remembered against us that every social or political opinion ever known since Kansas has been a state has been noisily played with by its disciples, whether few or many. It is flung at us that we have always been puritanical in our opinions, intemperate in our enthusiasms, and violent in our methods.[20]

Against these suspicions, achieving mercantile respectability in the eyes of financiers and corporations would require persuading them that Lawrence, although a frontier town, was not a lawless enclave like Dodge City or Cimarron—that its institutions were stable, its legal system up-to-date, its citizens creditworthy, and its deadbeats and miscreants dealt with efficiently. There would be little room in such a vision for the accommodation of hundreds of impoverished former slaves. Nor was it compatible with any tolerance for frauds perpetrated on venerable financial institutions by wily frontier outlaws.

Toward the end of the afternoon the inquest adjourns for the day. While Levi is occupied talking with Mr. Borgalthaus in the vestibule, Sallie slips out. There is time for her to walk to Oak Hill and stand for a while by the raw clots of earth over the grave before venturing back to the Judson's for supper.

She has stayed in the cemetery longer than she realized, or walked back more slowly, for by the time she returns to the house Levi is there, with two newspapers. The Judsons have never taken the newspapers before, but now they seem to be arriving at the house with regularity. Levi and the couple are examining these in the fore-parlor with something akin to jubilation.

"Listen to this, Sallie!" exclaims Levi. "This is the *Tribune*." And he reads aloud:

> Some considerable discussion is going on in this community as to the authority or rightfulness of the coroner's inquest now being held at the court house, upon the body alleged to be that of J.W. Hillman, from the fact that the death took place in another county—Barber—and that a coroner's inquest was duly held in that county. Nobody objects to having the facts of the case sifted out, no matter how carefully, but the people—very many of them—do object to having the expense foisted upon Douglas county! The proceedings here are instituted, we understand, by the Insurance companies who have $25,000 at stake, and it is claimed to be simply a matter of justice that they should foot the bills, instead of our over-burthened taxpayers. Insurance companies are proverbially sharp and if they can fight their battles at the expense of Douglas county, it will be a smart dodge. How many inquests are necessary? We hope the county board will examine into this matter before paying any bills.

"It is Borgalthaus who has made this appear," says Levi with satisfaction. "He has been after the reporters for three days to note this aspect of the matter. This will give Green the conniption-fits!"

"Splendid," says Sallie. "Do you think they will stop the inquest then?"

A brief silence; Levi turns his attention back to the paper. It is Arthur Judson who finally speaks. "I do not think so, Sallie. The companies have gone too far to turn back, and the coroner appears to be in their pocket. But it does appear they may have to pony up some funds."

"Funds! They have endless funds to spend to defeat a widow!" She flounces down onto the settee in exasperation. "What good does all this do? The companies are going to deny that it is John in that grave, are they not? They will call John a criminal, and me his accessory or something like, and refuse to pay the money!"

Levi walks over to touch her on the shoulder. "You must not despair so soon," he says. "It is not over yet."

"And when *will* it be over?" Sallie thinks she has never been so tired.

"Not yet, Sallie. You'd better go take off your dress and let Mrs. Judson wash it out for you, so it will dry by morning. I do not think they are finished with us."

The next morning the condition of John Hillmon's teeth begins to assume far more importance in death than it ever had during his life. County Attorney Green questions Levi Baldwin at such length about these features that Sallie, sitting in back beside Mr. Borgalthaus, starts to grow restive. Why had they not asked her about the teeth? She was after all the man's wife, was she not? She has never known a man other than a dentist who paid any meaningful attention to someone else's teeth, any more than to shoes or hats or any such, and her cousin is no exception. Levi repeats again and again that Hillmon's teeth were excellent, perfect, and Sallie knows that this is not quite right: one of John's upper side teeth was somewhat shorter than its mate on the other side, giving the appearance of a gap when he bestowed a slight smile. With his usual full grin the tooth would be revealed, and the observer unlikely to notice the difference. No doubt John was usually smiling broadly, if at all, when in Levi's company, as the two men were friendly. Sallie wonders if she ought to offer to explain this misunderstanding, and with this in mind she turns to Borgalthaus and whispers that she needs to speak to him. He nods at once and rises, taking her arm as the two of them leave the courtroom by the rear door.

The lawyer directs her to an alcove just off the courthouse vestibule, and the two are seated on a worn bench. Sallie explains her concern and Borgalthaus pulls on his upper lip thoughtfully. "I don't believe you need say anything," he offers finally. "There are to be other witnesses on the question of the teeth, from what I have been hearing."

"I just think the truth should be told," she explains, although she will be glad not to have to get back into the witness box.

Borgalthaus's attention is diverted for a moment by the need to nod at another gentleman passing by; the man examines the pair curiously, then reverses direction and walks back toward the courtroom. "Mrs. Hillmon," says Mr. Borgalthaus, "Levi has told you, has he not, that the inquest is unlikely to be the end of the matter? Most likely there will be a trial before these matters are finally settled."

"What do you mean? What sort of trial?"

"No matter what this coroner's jury says, the companies are unlikely to pay your claims. You will have to sue them."

"But I can't! I have no money to hire lawyers, or to sue anyone!"

Borgalthaus touches her arm sympathetically. "Do not worry about that. Some portion of your expectation will be sufficient to motivate a good lawyer. I do not care for litigation myself, but I have already begun inquiries."

But Sallie is still unsatisfied. "If the inquest is not to be a sufficient determination, why go on with it? Mr. Judson said the companies have gone too far to turn back. I do not understand why they would insist on this proceeding if it is to have no consequence."

Borgalthaus shakes his head slightly. "I do not know, Mrs. Hillmon. I only know that they are very determined, and have something up their sleeves. Mr. Green and Mr. Barker have been burning the midnight oil, conferring with the companies' men. I am afraid that some of our fellow citizens may be susceptible to their persuasions. You must not lose heart if you hear some things you know to be untrue. I don't mean from Levi, of course. From others."

"But these witnesses are under oath before the living God to tell the truth!"

The lawyer nods. "These are hard times, Mrs. Hillmon. And some men are wicked. Now we'd better go back into the courtroom. But do not despair, your cousin is doing very well."

When they return, Levi is explaining the trip he took to Medicine Lodge, at Sallie's request, to accompany the body back to Lawrence. "I did not think it proper that the body should travel without the company of anyone who knew John Hillmon in life," he is saying.

"And yet you and Mrs. Hillmon were quite willing for the body to remain buried in Medicine Lodge, far from the man's home and family," observes J.W. Green.

"That is so," Levi acknowledges. "The misfortune was fresh in our minds and we had not the heart to require the good citizens of Medicine Lodge to dig up the body they had so kindly buried. But when we heard that Colonel Walker and Mr. Tillinghast and Major Wiseman—the insurance companies' men, you know—had prevailed on the Medicine Lodge authorities to permit them to do just that, I thought that my brother and I ought to get there and escort the body back."

"Did you have occasion to view the body in Medicine Lodge before you commenced your journey to bring it home?"

"Yes. It was John Hillmon." Green seems about to interject something here but Levi rather cleverly keeps talking without leaving the sort of pause that would make an interruption convenient; the jurors are watching him closely. "Of course there was some damage to the body, especially the face around the eyes, and he did not look exactly like the man who had taken his leave of me a month or so earlier. Still, it was Hillmon. I am quite certain."

Green hesitates, then turns away, toward the coroner. "Nothing further from this witness, Mr. Coroner. We will call next Mr. Arthur Judson."

Judson's testimony is brief and straightforward. He describes his relationship to the Hillmons, and manages to mention that John Hillmon had eaten breakfast and supper across the table from him many times. He has never noticed any defect in Hillmon's teeth. Not saying they were perfect, mind you, but he has never noticed any flaw in them. Yes, he saw the cadaver at Smith and Bailey's. It was his boarder John Hillmon, not a doubt of it.

Brown is then recalled, looking more feckless than ever, to identify the Sharps rifle that fired the fatal shot. Sallie begins to feel a bit faint, but is set on staying through it all. The rifle is passed around to the jurymen, who feel for some reason that it will aid them in their decision if each is to test its heft, aim it, and sight along its barrel. By the time Brown is finished with this coda to his testimony, Levi has rejoined Sallie.

"We would next call Dr. Fuller," says Green. Levi suggests that Sallie might wish to step outside, perhaps even go home for the day, as Dr. Fuller is one of the autopsy physicians; his testimony may be upsetting. Sallie agrees, for she is queasy and anxious, and also she knows that the newspapers will have quite a complete account of the doctor's testimony.

Walking back to the Judson's Sallie reflects on the information Mr. Borgalthaus gave her earlier in the day, and is surprised to find that the prospect of a lawsuit does not seem quite so intimidating as it was when he first mentioned it. Why should not a woman, a citizen, have a perfect right to pursue her legal remedies when her adversaries refuse to do what is right? Especially when they are greedy eastern corporations of the sort that are bleeding Kansas dry? Let a real Kansas jury, and not those whey-faced coroner's marionettes, decide whether she would fail to recognize her own husband in his coffin.

"Sarah Ellen Quinn Hillmon," she says softly, "versus the Mutual Life Insurance Company of New York, the Connecticut Mutual Life Insurance Company, and . . . " She frowns; she has forgotten the name of the other. No matter, her lawyer will know it. And she will go by Sallie, she decides. Nobody knows her as Sarah.

Over the ensuing days Sallie has more than one occasion to be grateful for Mr. Borgalthaus's advice that the outcome of the inquest will not seal the fate of her insurance claims. Otherwise her peace of mind should be sorely tested, for it is at just about this time that matters before that tribunal go from ill to dire. The next day's first witness is another physician who participated in the autopsy, Dr. Miller. Sworn to tell the truth, he is confident about the height of the cadaver: five feet eleven inches. But this man of medicine then testifies to several propositions that Sallie doubts the truth of, or in some cases knows to be untrue: that he knew John Hillmon well in life; that Hillmon had at least one, possibly two, broken incisors among his teeth; that the body he examined was not that of John Hillmon and bore no resemblance to him.

Most implausibly, Miller admits that when John Hillmon first came to him to be examined for the life insurance, her husband reported his height as five feet eleven inches (for so the application paper originally recorded), but the doctor claims that John returned a few days later to advise that he had been mistaken about his own height, and in fact stood only five feet nine inches. On this second occasion, the physician says solemnly, he measured the man and found that the shorter height was correct, recording this discovery in the ledger book, which otherwise contained his records of patient accounts. Sallie almost laughs aloud, but Levi's cautioning arm reminds her to be discreet and so she must convert the noise into a sort of cough.

Then there are two of the insurance companies' agents, Mr. Selig and Mr. Wiseman, who is referred to by all as "Major." Each man sold John one of the insurance policies, one on behalf of the New York Life and the other from the Connecticut Mutual. Wiseman complains that Hillmon had come straight to him to apply for the policy, which he says is not the way things are done: ordinarily an agent will solicit a customer and not the other way around. Sallie begins to whisper to Levi that this is the only time she has ever heard a salesman complain about a buyer's aggressions, but her cousin shushes her again.

Selig also reports that John had objected to the first policy offered him because it contained a condition that he could not race on a mount; he pointed out that he was in the cattle business and riding fast was sometimes required. Selig testifies that he then offered another company's policy, which was not so restricted. Sallie wishes *she* could query the witness, for she would ask why John would have protested about this condition if his only plan were to disappear after a trip by wagon and thus defraud the insurance companies. She is wondering why the illogic of the companies' position does not seem so plain to everyone else as it does to her when she hears her name called out by Mr. Green.

She is not pleased to be required to resume the witness chair, but at least she is wearing a new dress, which she has been able to purchase with part of the twenty-five dollars that Levi tucked into her pocket the previous Friday evening. "To keep you for a while," her cousin had said. Fortunately Sallie is a standard size, and no alterations were required.

She has not quite reached the witness stand when the coroner's voice booms out officiously, "Mrs. Hillmon, I am required to remind you that you are still under oath." The little man has become quite taken with himself, she thinks, and although she knows she ought only to nod her head respectfully, instead she speaks.

"That," she says, "is quite unnecessary," and seats herself in the hard chair.

It seems she is called back only to examine a couple of tintypes, which she recognizes instantly, for they once were hers, kept in her own small box of photographs. Two days before she had given them to Levi; her cousin must have passed them on to the coroner, or perhaps to Mr.

Green. One is of John, although not a very good likeness. The second depicts John Brown and her husband, on some occasion while both men were still single. They are standing side by side, dressed very formally in dark frock coats and pants. Both look very solemn, and John Hillmon is wearing a most unattractive pointy sort of beard that she had requested him to remove once they were married. She remembers, indeed, the night he shaved it off, using his straight razor and the mirror in their bedroom at the Judsons'. About this, however, she is not asked; she is only requested to identify the men.

"Thank you, Mrs. Hillmon," says Green after she has done so, but she does not deign to reply, and matters are adjourned for the day.

Just before supper Sallie's cousin takes advantage of Mr. Judson's absence and Mrs. Judson's preoccupation with meal preparations to take her to task. "I know the behavior of these prevaricators is exasperating," he says, "but you cannot allow your feelings to show. You must keep your own counsel, and maintain a steady and detached demeanor at all times."

"Why must I, Levi?" she protests. "It is so tiresome."

"I know it is. But if you must express yourself, do so to me only, or to Borgalthaus, when we are alone. Do not trust anybody else, except for the Judsons," he advises. "The companies are playing a deep game, and it may be many months before this matter is settled."

"Tell me this, Levi," she says. "If they say the body is not John's, whose do they claim it is? It must belong to someone."

Levi rubs both hands over his head rapidly, disarranging his hair badly. "That is another mystery, Sallie, and not the only one. I am also puzzled what they hope to gain by prolonging this inquest, but I believe they hope to discourage you somehow."

"I will never be discouraged," she says stoutly.

He smiles kindly. "Oh yes you will, my dear. Many times, before it is over. But so long as you do nothing without consulting me, your discouragement will not harm you."

She considers this and returns to the other subject. "So whose is the body?

Levi only shakes his rumpled head. "It is John's, of course."

"Yes, but whose do they say it is?"

"They have not said yet, but I believe they will have to eventually."

"That," says Sallie, "will be most interesting."[21]

Apparently complaints about the impropriety of the inquest continued, to the point that the *Standard*'s reporter felt the need to remonstrate with his fellow citizens.

LAWRENCE STANDARD, APRIL 10, 1879

The attempt to belittle the case is, of course, a failure. A human life was sacrificed under such circumstances that it becomes the duty of the proper authorities to thoroughly investigate the matter. It is known that the Coroner's inquest in Barbour County was a harried and ignorantly-managed affair.

According to Levi Baldwin's own testimony, the first coroner's jury summoned in Barbour County did not know how to render a verdict, and another was summoned, and after a brief and hasty consideration of the matter, based entirely on Brown's testimony, gave a verdict of accidental killing. Subsequent facts that came to light, rendering it absolutely imperative that the strange and unaccountable performance that caused the death of a citizen of Douglas county (or a purported citizen) should be thoroughly looked into, and every fact connected with it brought to the surface, so that the calcium light of truth may shine in upon what seems to be a cowardly and murderous transaction. If all parties are innocent, no one should object to an investigation, and those who do object to it may find themselves upon the side of thieves and murderers.

One cannot really blame the insurance company executives for their suspicions when news of the death at Crooked Creek reached them. In the years after the Civil War everyone in the insurance industry understood fraud to be a serious problem, and often a fraudulent life insurance scheme turned on mistaken identity. The underworld of life insurance fraud had become so colorful and so worrying by the 1870s that it merited extended treatment in a book called *Remarkable*

Stratagems and Conspiracies: An Authentic Record of Surprising Attempts to Defraud Life Insurance Companies. This vivid treatise was coauthored by two physicians who worked for the insurance industry, one as an adjuster and "consulting surgeon," and the other as editor of a publication called the *Baltimore Underwriter.* Their book's numerous accounts suggest that many notorious life insurance swindles were accomplished by means that bore a certain resemblance to aspects of the Hillmon affair. Among the cases the authors recount is one that arose in Wichita, Kansas, where in 1873 a house contractor named A.N. Winner is said to have schemed to insure a friend of his named McNutt for $5,000, and then collect the proceeds after faking McNutt's death by fire (although the nominal policy beneficiary was a young woman whom McNutt had recently married as part of the scheme). A body was needed for the plan to succeed, of course, and McNutt later confessed to luring a victim from Kansas City to Wichita by promising him a job, and then murdering him in gruesome fashion.

An even more notorious attempt at life insurance fraud was undertaken in Baltimore in 1872 by two confederates, William Udderzook and Winfield Scott Goss. After insuring Goss's life for $25,000 altogether, through four different companies, the men obtained a corpse from a medical supplier, placed the cadaver in Goss's rented house, and staged a kerosene lamp explosion. The burned corpse was then claimed to belong to Goss (who, it was explained, had been "experimenting" with certain processes involving India rubber). But the insurance companies refused to pay. One of the chief origins of their suspicion was a disparity between the teeth of the corpse and those of the living Goss. In a reversal of the later dental dispute in Hillmon, the insurers claimed that Goss had strikingly good teeth but that the corpse, whom they arranged to be exhumed a year after burial, had a severely decayed set. William Udderzook apparently became alarmed by the vigor of the companies' investigations, which included the widespread circulation of photographs of Goss inquiring whether anyone had seen the living man. He decided that Goss, who was in hiding in New Jersey and had a weakness for liquor, could not be trusted to remain out of sight, so he lured him to some nearby woods and murdered him. Udderzook was hanged for Goss's murder in 1874.[22]

Thus the similarities between some features of the Hillmon case and certain details of spectacular frauds in the companies' recent memories were notable: the multiple insurance policies totaling $25,000 in Goss–Udderzook, the Wichita connection, as well as the recent marriage of the alleged deceased and the policy beneficiary in Winner–McNutt. One of the Hillmon defendants, the Mutual Life Insurance Company of New York, had even been a party to the Goss–Udderzook litigation, which had resulted in a verdict for Goss's purported widow that was overturned only after Udderzook was convicted of murdering Goss. So of course they were suspicious about Hillmon's alleged death, and desperate for evidence to confirm their suspicions. They devoutly hoped for an opportunity to identify the body as belonging to someone else—some man of about the right age and size who had recently been missed by his loved ones. Even as the Lawrence inquest was in progress, the companies' agents were trying hard to turn up a candidate for this role.

A tremendous pounding at the Judson's front door rouses Sallie from her sleep. She can make out Arthur's voice, and then another's, followed by her landlord's heavy steps on the stairs and a tentative knock on her bedroom door.

"Come in," she calls as she sits up, for she has been sleeping in one of John's shirts and it is modest enough.

Arthur stands uncomfortably in the door, candle in hand. "I thought I should tell you, Sallie, although I do not think you should leave the house. I wish Levi were here to advise us."

This is most uninformative, she thinks impatiently. "Tell me what?"

"It seems they are digging up the grave. Some woman has appeared saying the body may belong to her missing brother, and they are digging it up to see if she can recognize it."

Rage shakes her fully awake. "They are going to desecrate my husband's grave because some silly woman cannot find her brother?"

Arthur nods. "It is an evil deed, but I do not see how we can stop it. I have sent for Borgalthaus. He may have some idea. It is nearly morning, so there is no point to sending for Levi. He will be here soon in any event."

"I will get dressed and come down to wait for Borgalthaus," she says, and Judson nods and closes the door. She does dress, in the light of the candle on her nightstand, but not for company. Instead she dons an old pair of John's pants, which she must tie about the waist with the sash of her new dress, and a waistcoat left behind at the hotel by a customer who never returned for it. She then slips out the back door of the Judson's and walks to Oak Hill, drawing her cloak tight about her against the chill. The walk takes her nearly half an hour, past darkened houses and a stable. She can see torches and hear voices as she approaches the cemetery, and a bit closer can smell pipe tobacco and fresh earth. One of the voices she knows: it belongs to George Barker, Green's assistant.

Sallie lingers in the shadows afforded by the grove of oak trees, and listens. There are three white men, smoking and stamping their feet occasionally against the cold, and two black men, digging. Little is said for long moments, so the predominant sounds are the striking of shovels against stones, the hitching scratch of a lucifer as one of the men relights his pipe, and the grunting of the diggers. Finally, after a shovel makes a ringing sound, one of the diggers calls out, "Think we hit a rock, boss!"

"Dig it out, then!" says one of the white men, and as he turns to whisper to another she sees his face in profile: Colonel Walker, who has been at the inquest every day but has neither testified nor said anything. He was one of those, Sallie recalls, who went to Medicine Lodge to insist that the body be taken from its grave there and brought to Lawrence. Ghoul! she thinks with furious dislike, and she steps forward into the flickering light of the torches.

"Colonel Walker," she says, "how many times must you dig my husband up before you allow him to rest in peace?"

The three men all turn toward her voice. Barker looks startled, as does the third white man, whom she now recognizes as the newspaper reporter Gleed, but Walker is not at all discomfited. "You'd better go home, Mrs. Hillmon," he says, grinning. "Unless you want to jump down there into the grave and be buried yourself. I hear that's what widows do in India." He takes her arm above the elbow and holds it firmly, but she does not flinch. She has endured this and worse from customers at the hotel, and anyway Walker is an ignorant man if he does not even know that corpses in India are burned instead of buried. She will not allow herself to be afraid of such a blustering fool.

The two colored men are staring up from the excavation, interest overborne by apprehension in their faces. Gleed, too, seems unhappy about the turn matters have taken. "You'd best let her go, Colonel," suggests the little newspaperman.

Sallie nods. "Yes, you'd better, sir, unless you want this gentleman of the press reporting that you assaulted a widow at her husband's gravesite."

Walker laughs shortly. "I don't think I'm too worried about what Mr. Gleed here will write," he says, nodding toward the smaller man. "I think he might write that you come here and tried to interfere with a proper effort to identify a corpse, because you was afraid that the lady who looks at it tomorrow will prove that you ain't a widow, and that this ain't the gravesite of your husband but of some poor bas—some poor fool he murdered."

Colonel Walker looks at Gleed as though expecting him to confirm this journalistic prediction, but Gleed avoids his eyes. Barker, who has stayed at the edge of the light until now, comes forward and puts a hand on Walker's shoulder. "Come, Colonel," he says, "let us conclude our business here, and allow Mrs. Hillmon to return to her home. Mrs. Hillmon, this excavation is being accomplished by order of the coroner. There is nothing you can do to prevent it. We expect to have the body taken up by afternoon. You had best get some sleep, for tomorrow's proceedings will be important, and you will no doubt wish to be present."

Walker releases her arm, but not before giving it a cruel squeeze. "Do you and your cousin and your husband really think you can fool us forever? Winner and McNutt are in prison, Goss is dead and Udderzook was hanged, and they was much better criminals than you. You had best give up your claims, and then mebbe this could be forgotten. Mebbe God will even forgive your lies, and this poor soul in the coffin can have his rest."

"I do not know those individuals, sir," says Sallie, rubbing her arm. "And I am no criminal."

"Go home, Mrs. Hillmon," says Barker wearily, and then he turns back to the dark declivity in the earth and bids the diggers continue.

Sallie considers, and concludes there is little point in remaining. Dawn is just creeping into the sky as she arrives back at the boardinghouse.

The Judsons and Mr. Borgalthaus, who is with them, are greatly relieved when she returns, for they had been alarmed after discovering her absence. She describes her errand briefly and without elaboration, and after ascertaining that she is unharmed they suggest that she take some tea to warm herself, and perhaps wash her face. Her cousin, however, is very angry when he arrives and hears what has occurred, nearly as much at Sallie as at Walker, Barker, and Gleed. But after breakfast, as they walk together to the courthouse, he seems to forget his displeasure in favor of insisting that she recount her conversations at the graveside with particularity.

"Who are Winner and McNutt and Goss and Udderzook?" she asks after telling him all she can remember.

"Criminals," says Levi shortly. "Men who tried to defraud insurance companies and were caught. It is in detecting such matters that Colonel Walker made his name."

"Insurance fraud," says Sallie glumly. "That is what they say we are doing."

"I know, but they will not persuade a real jury of it."

Sallie hesitates, then speaks the question that has been stalking her thoughts. "Levi, that is not what we are doing, is it?"

"Of course not, Sallie," says her cousin. "How can you think so?"

"No," says Sallie. "Of course not. I saw that body and it was John's, was it not?"

"Certainly it was. You have no doubt, have you?" Levi is studying her face closely.

"No, no. Only—he was so very changed, of course. His poor face . . ." Here Sallie begins to weep, and is mortified, for they are approaching the door to the courthouse.

"We'd better go in," says Levi. "Stay near me and, Sallie," he takes her arm just at the spot where Colonel Walker had bruised it a few hours before, "say *nothing*, do you understand me? I pray you have not already done us damage. No matter what you hear, show no feeling toward it."

"Yes," says Sallie meekly, smarting from his words as well as from his grip, and wipes the sleeve of her new dress across her face before any of the ladies have a chance to observe her.[23]

Mrs. Lowell, wife of M.L. Lowell, of this city, has a brother who left here on the 5th of last March, for Wichita, and to go from there southwest, and return to Independence and Humboldt.

She has not heard of him since he went away, although it was customary for him to write to her often. From the description of the dead body, she thought it was that of her brother. Yesterday afternoon the body was taken up, and Mrs. Lowell saw it, but could not identify it as that of her brother.

It was reported yesterday that a young man of Indiana saw the body brought here, and recognized it as that of a friend who left Indiana some time ago, for Wichita, and has not since been heard of. Many wild rumors are afloat, but as yet there has been nothing definite learned concerning him.

Brown has not been heard from since he left so mysteriously yesterday morning, nor is his whereabouts known. It was supposed that he went to Wyandotte to visit his family, but such is not the case. Brown should not have been allowed to leave the city until the inquest was closed, especially as such damaging testimony against him had been brought out.

The body was photographed by W.H. Lamon, when it was exhumed yesterday.

W.H. Lamon's photographs endure; they were received as exhibits in each of the six trials of the Hillmon case. While the cadaver was aboveground during this brief adjournment of the inquest the photographer took two shots of it, one from the side and one head-on. In the second shot, the coffin must have been propped up a bit for us to see the face as well as we can, although the angle of view is a low one. The photographs look gruesome to most modern eyes, but the photographing of corpses was a respectable Victorian practice, although ordinarily the reasons for it were more sentimental than, as in this case, forensic. In both photographs of the dead man one can see the damage to the eye area and the shrinking of the flesh around the nose, but on the whole the corpse looks remarkably lifelike considering the adventures it has undergone. Even before this disinterment it had been dug up once before, after being buried at Medicine Lodge, to be transported by rail and wagon back to Lawrence. In the weather for its journey it was fortunate, if that description can be applied to a corpse, because March in central Kansas is still very chilly—this circumstance no doubt spared it a certain amount of decomposition.

After Mr. Lamon took the coffin photographs, and Mrs. Lowell said that the corpse did not resemble her brother, the body was reburied in Oak Hill Cemetery. Those who had taken an interest in the Hillmon matter were left to await the verdict of the coroner's jury.

LAWRENCE DAILY TRIBUNE, APRIL 10, 1879
The jury in the case returned a sealed verdict which has not yet been made public.

There is an unreasonable curiosity on the part of our citizens with regard to the verdict of the coroner's jury in the Hillman case. We say that the curiosity is unreasonable, in the sense that it is unseemly to be curious about that which does not concern us. In fact it is none of our business. It is a private matter and hence we have no right to be too inquisitive. We do not say this ironically, but in sober earnest. It is not county or city business; we do not pay the bills; we did not encourage or justify the official action; we have no right to ask any questions. If justice be meted out well and good. We might guess, but we deny our right to hazard guesses about somebody else's business, when by our surmises we may defeat their plans. Good people be patient.

Those able to take this advice found their patience rewarded the next day, when the *Tribune* reproduced the verdict of the coroner's jury.

LAWRENCE DAILY TRIBUNE, APRIL 11, 1879
STATE OF KANSAS | DOUGLAS COUNTY

An inquisition, holden at Lawrence, in Douglas County, on the fourth, fifth, seventh, eighth, and ninth days of April, A.D. 1879, before me, Dr. R. Morris, coroner of said county, on the body of an unknown man there lying dead, by the jurors whose names are hereunto subscribed. The said jurors on their oaths do say, that the unknown body before us, came by his death on the seventeenth day of March, A.D. 1879, by a gunshot wound through the head. Said wound was caused by a gun, held in the hands of John H. Brown; we further believe it was feloniously. In testimony whereof, the said jurors have hereunto set their hands the day last and year aforesaid.

W.O. Humble	E.B. Good
O.D. Pickens	J.W. Adams
G.W. Adams	Andrew Tosh

Attest: R. Morris, Coroner, Douglas County, Kansas

† † †

Levi and Sallie are in Mr. Borgalthaus's office, the one smoking while studying a chessboard that Borgalthaus has laid out on a table near the window and the other looking at some law books, which are full of gibberish in her opinion, when the scrivener who has been dispatched to the courthouse brings in a copy of the verdict. The lawyer has been scribbling busily on a stack of foolscap, but stops when the boy arrives and pushes the papers aside in order to spread the verdict across his desk. They have already heard what it reports, but still the three of them crowd around the desk to read it.

"It's only what we expected, Sallie," says Levi after they have perused it. "You cannot be discouraged. We will find a good lawyer for you, and he will file suit, and the companies will see that you are not so easily pushed off. It is not as easy to buy a jury as it is to purchase the loyalty of a gaggle of rustics."

Sallie is furious, and also perplexed. "If the companies really controlled all this as you say, why would the verdict say that John Brown was the killer? If they claim that my husband is still alive, why do they not get the jurors to charge him with murder, instead of John Brown?"

"That is a good question." Levi taps the shoulder of Borgalthaus, who has gone back to his writing.

"Hmm?" says the lawyer absently. "Oh, yes. A good question, yes. I am not sure. But we must keep a close eye on Brown, Levi. He cannot be resting too easily just now, even across the border in Missouri."

Levi nods grimly. "I will."

"Here, Mrs. Hillmon," says Borgalthaus, pushing some paper and a pen across the table toward her. "I have a task for you."

"We'll file right away, then?" says Levi eagerly.

The lawyer looks into the distance. "Not immediately, I think. Some efforts at negotiation might be fruitful. But I've found that it strengthens one's position with an adversary to have the complaint in hand."

"I understand," nods Levi. "I'll be in touch with Colonel Walker."

"I think it possible that Mrs. Hillmon might have more success."

"Sallie?" Levi begins to chuckle then seems to think better of it.

"She might surprise you. Meantime, we should not make our opening move until we have given some thought to those that will come after." He moves his eyes in the direction of his chessboard, and Sallie's follow. "In the meantime, Mrs. Hillmon, will you write down what I will read off to you?" The lawyer scrutinizes a sheaf of untidy notes he has been making, and clears his throat. "Please begin, in capital letters, sallie q. hillmon versus the mutual life insurance company of new york."

"Just a moment, then." Sallie walks to the writing stand against the wall, where she locates a pen and a blank sheet of foolscap. As she begins to write, she experiences the momentary dizzying illusion that she has lived this moment before.[24]

News of the second Hillmon inquest traveled slowly to the farther reaches of the state, the delay sometimes amounting to a week or two between the events in Lawrence and their retelling in distant Kansas newspapers. These accounts were often highly colored by the newspaper's own political bent, which no editor of the time thought necessary to confine to the editorial page.

The journalists of Medicine Lodge had a particular, one might say proprietary, interest in the Hillmon matter. Their editorial inclinations differed considerably from those of the Lawrence newspapers, and they displayed an indignant suspicion that one subtext of the Lawrence inquiry was a certain contempt for their rural community.

MEDICINE LODGE CRESSET, APRIL 17, 1879

Many of our readers will remember the brief account we gave four weeks ago, of the fatal accident on Spring Creek, whereby John W. Hillman, a resident of Lawrence, Kansas, came to a violent death by the accidental discharge of a gun, in the hands of one J.H. Brown. Hillman was buried in the graveyard at Medicine Lodge, where for ten days he lay at peace with all mankind. The sad news of his death traveled on swift wings to the grief stricken friends and heart broken widow, and mourned over the loss of a friend and husband.

Meanwhile the fact was discovered that Hillman had his life insured, in three different companies, aggregating 25,000 dollars, and parties were sent to this place to identify the body and take it home. And now comes forward divers and sundry medical experts, versed in the intricacies of insurance swindling, and propose to choke down our throat the monstrous falsehood, that Mrs. Sadie E. Hillman and the man J.H. Brown are accomplices in a matter of selling human life and human blood for money. The legal and medical twisting shows an evident strain on the part of the Insurance departments, to establish by quack doctors, old women, and hack drivers, that Hillman was not Hillman, but that some poor unfortunate soul has been sent to eternity, and his body to do duty as a dead man in Hillman's boots. At last account (the Lawrence Standard) a party was enroute to the cemetery, to unearth the dead man that he might be recognized by a Mrs. Lowell, a lady who has not heard from a long lost brother, who went to the south-west part of Kansas. We would kindly suggest to the lady in question, that she search the penitentiary, as these silent brothers are more likely to turn up there or on a cotton-wood tree, than in the grave of a respectable citizen.

The whole affair is claimed to be wrapped in deep mystery. A shade of suspicion hangs on the fact that the transaction took place (as the Lawrence Standard gives it) "away down on the wilds of Barbour county." It might have added, where the "Lion roareth and the Whangdoodle mourneth for its first-born."

But so far as our researches have gone, we find instead of a deep plot laid in blood, the mysteries are on the part of the Insurance companies, who have availed themselves of some cheap testimony, to disprove the identity of J.W. Hillman. The friends of Mrs. Hillman have, as yet, made no showing, and we predict that hundreds who have examined the body can be found willing to make the necessary identification. The whole affair will be thoroughly sifted and the light of calcium truth be permitted to shine through the dark and infamous swindle which the Insurance companies propose to so coolly carry out.

Back in Lawrence, the failures of the earlier attempts to identify the corpse as Mrs. Lowell's brother, the young unnamed man of Indiana, or (as another rumor had suggested) a Mr. Willey of Illinois, did not discourage further journalistic speculation. A hypothesis put forward toward the end of June seemed to be supported by the most persuasive confirmation: the statements of the candidate, just prior to his disappearance, that he had contracted to travel with John Hillmon and John Brown.

LAWRENCE STANDARD, JUNE 26, 1879

If the body was not that of Hillman, whose was it? To this arduous task Major Wiseman applied himself in good earnest. . . . Armed with the photographs of Hillman, Brown, and the dead man, the Major went to Wichita and found a number of persons who knew Hillman and Brown, and who recognized the photograph of the dead man as that of Frank Nichols, sometimes

called "Arkansaw." . . . At Wichita the Major found the baggage
of Frank Nichols in pawn for an $18 board bill. A sketch of Frank
Nichols' life was obtained by inquiry, and by reading the letters
and memoranda found in his baggage. . . . He was raised by some
charitable people in New Orleans, and after growing to manhood, he wandered over the country . . . for the past three years
he had lived in the vicinity of Wichita, a part of the time working on a farm, and when not so employed, would generally stop
in Wichita. He boarded at the same hotel as that Hillman and
Brown stopped at, and became quite intimate with them. He left
Wichita on March 2nd and went to Oxford, 35 miles south, to collect some money due for work, stating to some of his friends that
he intended to herd cattle for hillman and brown at $20 a month.
. . . His friends advised him to accept the situation offered, and
he told them afterwards that he had, and before leaving Wichita,
promised to write to them, but, up to date, they have never
received any letter from him. . . . Certain things that transpired
after the three men met near Wellington cannot be related here.
Suffice it to say that one of the party left and the other two traveled together. . . . In a lovely place fourteen miles north of Medicine Lodge, the shooting took place. . . .

It is stated that Brown sent word from Missouri that he himself
did not do the killing as he claimed in his testimony before the
coroner's jury, and that if assured protection, he is ready to turn
State's evidence.

The statements that the *Standard* attributed to the missing Frank
"Arkansaw" Nichols, about his understanding with Hillmon and Brown,
were of course hearsay, having been apparently related to the journalist
by friends of the gentleman rather than by Arkansaw himself. But journalists, like coroners, are not bound by the rules of evidence; their profession has its own rules. In any event, despite these rather spectacular
revelations, Frank "Arkansaw" Nichols turned up quite alive not many
weeks later. But the insurance companies, if they were disappointed
by his resurrection, would not have remained so for long. Soon their
agents would find still another candidate, a new name to attach to the
thrice-buried body: Frederick Adolph Walters. [25]

Before turning to this development, however, let us consider the question of ethics in the legal profession. Lawyers and their ethical choices strongly influenced the behavior of the Hillmon case principals—throughout the litigation, but never more strongly than in the weeks after the Lawrence coroner's jury returned its verdict that the death at Crooked Creek was caused "feloniously" by a "gunshot wound to the head," that the deceased was a "person unknown," and that the gun had been held in the hand of John H. Brown.

Today, some of the most complex rules of professional conduct for lawyers fall under the heading of conflict of interest. The rules now in force require, at a minimum, full disclosure of what client or clients an attorney represents in a public tribunal. But these standards were not well developed in the nineteenth century; we have already seen that attorneys on both sides of the Hillmon dispute, including J.B. Green, his assistant George Barker, and Mr. E.B. Borgalthaus, displayed a lack of candor about who their real clients were during the Lawrence inquest. It would seem that many lawyers of that time engaged in practices that would today violate the profession's conflict of interest regulations. The beleaguered John H. Brown, whom the *Standard*'s writer reported to be "ready to turn State's evidence," would soon acquire the advice of such an attorney.

◁ 2 ▷

THE PARTIES READY
THEIR CASES FOR TRIAL

1879–1882

FULTON'S MILL | PARKVILLE, MISSOURI | SEPTEMBER 1879

The mill owner Fulton has a daughter Polly, a bitty freckled girl too young for school who runs all over the place like a wild Injun, and it is she who comes to tell John Brown that there is a man at the office to see him. He doesn't see her coming because his attention is elsewhere: he is straining to load a bundle of four-by-fours onto a wagon that is hitched to a balky mule. The animal has already startled once, spilling the load, and so he is using language not suitable for even such an unruly child to hear. Having no regard at the moment for anything much but the mule and the four-by-fours and his profane opinion of them, he nearly jumps when he feels the tug at his pants leg and looks down to see the young'un there.

"Your name John Brown?" she says, her head tilted. A front tooth is out and curls of wood shaving cling to the top of her head.

"Who wants to know?" he asks.

"*I* don't know. Some city man is all, in the office. Has a lawman with him, too. My daddy says take you a break and see what he wants." She spins and runs back toward the creek and the cottonwood trees and the house and office that Fulton has built in their shade.

He can't leave his task just then, as the mule's owner is waiting for his load to be finished so he can get home with it. The two men will have to cool their heels. He thinks he knows who they are anyway, at least one of them, and sure enough looking toward the stables he believes he recognizes Buchan's horse, tied beside another in the yard. The man has pursued him from one workplace to another for the last two months, but Brown had lately started to hope that he had given up. No such luck.

When he gets to the office a quarter of an hour later it is just as he thought. W.J. Buchan is standing there in the door; the lawyer is fanning himself with a hat to keep the flies from landing on his head. "This is Deputy Ward," Buchan says without being asked, pointing the hat toward his companion, who leans against the wall and returns Brown's glance with a nod. Ward has a no-account look to him, but he does wear a tarnished star pinned onto his jacket, and a sidearm in a holster. "From Wyandotte," Buchan adds. "He has his orders, John, but I'm trying to make him see that there might be another way to handle this matter. There can't be any more putting it off, though. It has to be settled today."

Fulton looks up from the desk, where he is figuring and marking up some papers. "I can't have this, Brown, folks bringing the law down here to get after my employees. You have off the rest of the day and take care of this thing or else don't bother to come back." The miller returns to his papers, slashing through some figures.

Brown looks from one man to the other, then beckons to Buchan. The lawyer follows him outside, over to the shade of a big cottonwood. "I thought I told you when you come after me last time that you better leave me alone," Brown says. "I told my story in Lawrence and then I signed a paper for Mr. Riggs that said again how it happened. I don't mean to have anything more to do with lawyers."

"You did indeed tell me that," says Buchan. "Your father told me something different, though, Mr. Brown. That kind old man told me, 'Don't let them send my boy to the penitentiary.'"

"The hell you say. You stay away from my old man, don't you worry him."

The lawyer seems not to hear this. "Your father is getting old to be living alone in Kansas while you and your brother stay here across the river in Missouri. He wishes to see you. I would like to be able to carry out his wishes, but I can't do it without your help."

"I think you're a liar. I think I'll ask him myself if he told you that."

"By all means. But possibly it would not be a very good idea for you to show yourself on the other side of the river just now, John. As I advised you before, there is a warrant out for your arrest ever since the coroner's jury declared that you murdered that poor soul at Crooked Creek."

"You know I didn't do that."

"Yes I do, John. It is too bad the coroner's jury saw it that way. But they did, and that is why you need the services of a lawyer such as myself."

Brown does not trust this man but cannot resist seeking his advice anyway. "I'm safe as long as I stay on the Missouri side, ain't I?" The point is one that has troubled his sleep many nights.

"I would have thought so, yes. I have thought so. But," the lawyer tilts his head in the direction of the deputy, who blinks, "it seems that Ward has been advised he has authority as long as he is within a hundred miles of the site of the warrant's issuance, no matter what state lines may intervene. I have tried to dissuade him from this belief, but apparently Mr. Green has encouraged him in it. And Green is, as you know, the County Attorney." He looks toward the Ward, who nods in agreement. Buchan then assumes a sorrowful mien. "The insurance men want you badly, John. They want someone to blame for the death that threatens to cost them so much money, and they seem to care but little whether they punish the criminal Hillmon or his innocent companion."

Like most poor men who ever showed a bit of enterprise, Brown has seen the inside of a jail. He has eaten buggy food and sweltered without water and bunked below a man who coughs all night from the grippe and shivered with the fever he caught from him and sworn never to go back into a cell. He looks up to the yellow late summer sky. Buchan takes this as an encouraging sign.

"If you sign this, you need never be a witness, John. I know you don't want to go against Mrs. Hillmon in a courtroom. But when she sees this paper, she will give up her claims. She will never file her case when she sees that you have told the truth."

At *truth* Brown's eyes flare briefly, but then he sighs. "We'd better go to my brother's. I'll walk and meet you there. The sign says Reuben Brown, it's just . . . "

"I know where it is." Buchan smiles. "Good man. I'll be working on Ward as we ride over. I'm certain I can make him see the light."

John Brown walks through the cooling afternoon to his brother's farm, a quarter mile south from Fulton's mill, reflecting on Reuben's reactions should John lose the job his brother obtained for him. His mounting anger is not cooled by the sight that greets him as he approaches Reuben's gate: Ward and Buchan, their horses tethered to the fence, chatting with Reuben at the big wooden outdoor table and sipping on glasses of what looks like his sister-in-law Eliza's lemonade. There is a roll of paper, a pen, and an ink bottle on the table beside the pitcher. The three men look up at the sound of his steps, and Reuben directs a significant look toward the other two as he rises to greet his brother. Beyond the table Eliza stands at the door to her kitchen, shaking out a cloth but also watching to see what happens. She's been none too pleased to have her brother-in-law as a free boarder these last few weeks. The brothers meet halfway down the lane, and John can smell Reuben's breath: the lemonade has hardened well. He would like a glass himself.

"John," says Reuben, taking his elbow and leading him a little aside, beyond the hearing of the other two. "I know what you think. But maybe his way is the best. You don't owe that Hillmon woman nothing, far as I can figure, and you could get quit of this thing, and they say they'll pay off the board you owe us and a little more to boot. You can stop worrying and sleep better, and go back to Kansas if you want to. Back to the cattle trade. You can go see Dad in Wyandotte, see if he's all right. Senator Buchan says he seems lonely."

John Brown has never read a word by William Shakespeare, and so his next words are not a reference to anything but the weary state of his soul. "You too, Reuben?" he says.

"I just think . . . ," Reuben begins.

But Brown shakes his head and holds up his hand. "Never mind," he says to his brother. "Get me a glass of that lemonade. And then take me to that damn paper."

† † †

JOHN H. BROWN, of lawful age, being first duly sworn according to law, deposes and says: "My name is John H. Brown, my age thirty years, I am acquainted with John W. Hillmon also Mrs. S.E. Hillmon and Levi Baldwin of Douglas county, Kansas; have known John W. Hillmon for about five years, have been with him a good deal for the past two years, was with him last March at Wichita, and on the trip from there to and around Medicine Lodge in Barber county, Kansas, where it is claimed that I killed him on the 17th of March, 1879. Along about the 10th of December, 1878, John W. Hillmon, Levi Baldwin talked about and entered into a conspiracy to defraud the New York Life Insurance Company and the Mutual Life of New York out of some money, to be obtained by means of effecting a policy or policies on the life of said John W. Hillmon; Baldwin was to furnish the money to pay the premiums and to keep up the policies in case they had to be renewed. Our original arrangement was to get Hillmon's life insured for fifteen thousand, but it was afterward changed to twenty-five thousand dollars. Hillmon and myself were to go off southwest from Wichita, Kansas, ostensibly to locate a stock ranch, but in fact, to in some way find a subject to pass off as the body of John W. Hillmon for the purpose of obtaining the insurance money aforesaid. We had no definite plan of getting a subject, but to in some manner get one, the final termination of the matter was the last idea thought of. Our first trip out from Wichita the last days of December while the snow was on the ground we expected to find a subject that would appear to be Hillmon, frozen to death, and that not be identified only by the clothes and papers found on it, and so I could pass off as Hillmon. We went from Wichita to Medicine Lodge, then direct to Sun City, from there to Kinsley, from there to Great Bend on the Santa Fe road, then to Larned, and on to Wichita via Hutchinson.

Hillmon and myself were entirely alone on this trip. Iliff of Medicine Lodge saw Hillmon on this trip; we put up at his stable. I then stayed in Wichita until the 4th of March. Hillmon in the meantime went up to Lawrence to see his wife and to get some more money; he returned about the first of March, and on the fifth we left on our second trip. We went due west to Cow Skin creek, then west to Harper City, then to Medicine Lodge, on by Sun City and beyond some miles, then we turned northeast down Medicine river to a camp on Elm creek, about eighteen miles north of Medicine Lodge, where Hillmon is claimed to have been killed. We got there about an hour before sundown and stayed in camp until the next evening. We overtook a stranger on this trip the first day out from Wichita, about two or two and one-half miles from town, who Hillmon invited to get in and ride and who he (Hillmon) proposed to hire and work for him on the ranch as proposed to be located; this man was with us during all this trip. Hillmon proposed to me that this man would do for a subject to pass for him. I told him and contended with him that the man would not do to pass off for him, giving him various reasons why the man would not answer his description, and complained and objected because his proposition was to take the man's life, and I protested and said that was going beyond what we had agreed and something I had never before thought of, and was beyond my grit entirely. But Hillmon seemed to get more deeply determined and more and more desperate in the matter; pains were taken not to have more than two of us seen together in the wagon, sometimes one and then the other would be kept back out of sight. On this trip up to Lawrence Hillmon was vaccinated; his arm was quite bad. Hillmon kept at that man until he let him vaccinate him, which he did, taking his pocket knife and using virus in his own arm for the purpose. He also traded clothes with him, Hillmon first giving him a change of underclothing, then traded suits, the one he was killed in; the suit he was buried in was a suit Hillmon traded with Baldwin for. This man appeared to be a stranger in the country, a sort of easy-go-long fellow; and not suspicious or very attentive to anything; his arm became very sore and he got quite stupid and dull. He said his name was either Berkley or Burgis or something sounding like that; we always called him Joe. He said he had been around Fort Scott awhile and also had worked about Wellington or Arkansas City. I don't know where he was from nor where his home nor friends were. I did not see him at Wichita that I know of. I had but very little to say to the man and less to do with him; he was taken in charge by Hillmon and yielded willingly to his will. I dreaded what I thought was to be done, and kept out of having any more to do with him than possible. I frequently remonstrated with Hillmon, and tried to deter him from carrying out his intentions of killing the man. The next evening after we got to the camp last named, the man Joe was sitting by the fire, I was at the hind end of the wagon either putting feed in the box for the horses or taking a sack of corn out when I heard a gun go off; I looked around and saw the man was shot, and Hillmon was pulling him away around to keep him out of the fire. Hillmon changed a day-book from his own coat to Joe's, and said to me everything was all right and in shape just as he wanted it, and that I need not be afraid but it would be all right. He told me to get on a pony and go down to a ranch about three-quarters of a mile and get some one to come up. He took Joe's valise and started north; this was about sundown. We had no arrangements about communicating with each other; he first proposed to do so, but I told him I did not want to know where he was, that in case I should I might find him out in some other way. I have never heard a word from him since; at Lawrence Mrs. Hillmon gave me to understand that she knew where Hillmon was and that he was all right. The man over whom an inquest was held at camp, afterward at Medicine Lodge, and at Lawrence, Kansas, was the man Joe Burgis or Berkley, killed by Hillmon, as related above, and John W. Hillmon I believe to be still alive, at least he left our camp and went north as stated above after killing Joe. Hillmon said he would assume the name of William Marshall. Baldwin's wife and Mrs. Hillmon know all about this. In my testimony at Lawrence I stated the route taken as above described, but the man who I described as being in camp with us, and who I said went off with some wagons, was Joe the man killed. I afterwards, sometime in August, 1879, made four affidavits, under great importunities from Baldwin who came after me three different times, the last time persuading me to go with him to Kansas City, where Honorable Samuel Riggs insisted on my signing them. I don't think Mr. Riggs is aware of the facts in this case, nor the other counsel in the case. I make the above statement in this Hillmon case, as the full and true facts in the case, regretting the part that I have taken in the affair."

† † †

Reuben nods encouragement, and John Brown picks up the pen and writes.

John H. Brown

"Now will you leave me alone?" he says to the lawyer, who has been standing over him anxiously as he reads and finally signs the strange paper. The deputy Ward is lounging negligently in the shade, his eyes drooping. Eliza's lemonade has partnered with the heat of the day to wilt the starch out of him.

"Nearly so," says Buchan. "Here is one more paper. This one you must write over in your own hand before you sign it. But it is not long."

Brown reads over the cobwebby writing he is asked to copy. "What is this for? She won't answer this. She'll know it's from you."

"Don't concern yourself," says Buchan. "It is not necessary that she answer it, nor even receive it." Brown claims the small satisfaction of spitting a large tobacco clot close to the man's feet before taking up the pen again.

MRS. SALLIE HILLMON

C/O ARTHUR JUDSON

LAWRENCE, KANSAS

I would like to know where John is, and how that business is, and what should I do, if anything. Let me know through my father.

Yours truly, John H. Brown

"Very good," says Buchan, placing the missive neatly between two clean sheets to blot it. "You have done well for yourself, and your family,

Mr. Brown. Now you must just ride over to Parkville with me to get that affidavit notarized."

Brown rubs his hands on his pants in disgust. "Let's go then," he says. Eliza, at the kitchen window, bestows a rare smile on him as he walks by on his way to get the horse.[1]

That summer after the Lawrence inquest, while attorney W.J. Buchan pursued his reluctant client John Brown from hamlet to hamlet in Missouri, back in Lawrence the insurance men were still searching for a ghost: a young man who had gone missing to his friends and kin. To that point their most promising candidate had been Frank "Arkansaw" Nichols, but Arkansaw had disappointed them by turning up alive not long after it was suggested that he might have been Hillmon's victim. There was, however, no shortage of anxious frontier families whose young men had left home and neglected to correspond, and it was here the companies' hopes lay. They hoped to hear of some fellow of about the right age who might have been footloose enough to fall in with Hillmon and Brown and agree to accompany them on the trail, and inexperienced and trusting enough to have met his death at the campground near Crooked Creek. Or they needed to find John Hillmon, alive.[2]

Either discovery, they must have thought, would suffice to persuade Sallie Hillmon not to pursue lawsuits against the companies for the insurance proceeds. She was the named beneficiary of the insurance policies; the decision whether to sue would be hers alone. And whether she was a co-conspirator or an innocent participant (for they suspected that Levi Baldwin might have been the mastermind), surely she would not go forward if they could show her the futility of trying to persuade a jury that her husband was dead.[3]

To these ends, their agents and scouts made inquiries through the channels of communication they thought likely to yield leads. Several times over that summer Major Theodore Wiseman, agent for the Mutual Life Insurance Company of New York, visited a banker he knew in Wichita. He showed the banker W.L. Lamon's photographs of the corpse, and asked him if he knew anything concerning the whereabouts of John Hillmon.

The banker did not, but later in the fall he received a letter in his capacity as secretary of the Wichita Masonic Lodge. The missive was from his counterpart at the lodge in Fort Madison, Iowa, and it inquired whether any of the Wichita Masons might have information about a young cigarmaker from Fort Madison who had traveled recently in Kansas. The young man's family had stopped receiving correspondence from him in early March, and was worried. The cigarmaker's name was Frederick Adolph Walters.

This inquiry reminded the banker of his conversations with Wiseman, but he was not certain how to reach the insurance agent, other than recalling that he seemed to live in Lawrence. He remembered the corpse photos, however, and that they had come from an inquest, so the banker took the letter of inquiry he had received and forwarded it to the coroner at Lawrence, Dr. Richard Morris, together with a request that Morris forward it in turn to Wiseman. Dr. Morris obligingly passed the letter on to the Major. Wiseman would later testify at one of the trials that the letter from Fort Madison said, in substance, "I am inquiring for a lost son who wrote home last that he was going west with a man by the name of Hillmon to herd sheep for him." But the letter could not be produced.[4]

There seems no doubt, however, that there had been some letter. Daniel Walters, a Swiss immigrant to Iowa and the patriarch of a healthy family of seven children, would testify in an 1881 deposition that he had asked the secretary of his local Masonic Lodge to correspond with other lodges in nearby states about his missing son. But the father did not mention the name Hillmon.[5]

Whatever the twice-forwarded letter from Daniel Walters may have said, when Major Wiseman received it he made immediate arrangements to visit the Walters family in Iowa. Having first sent ahead one of the corpse photographs, Wiseman traveled to Fort Madison with another insurance company agent named Tillinghast, and asked to meet with as many members of the family as could be assembled. This group included Daniel Walters, his wife, and the three daughters who still lived at home: Anna, Fannie, and Elizabeth. Fannie Walters would later testify that she and her parents and sisters examined the photos at the Walters home in January 1880. Fannie said that she was sure the pictures were of her brother; Elizabeth would say the same. Mrs. Walters never appeared in court, but in the fourth and fifth trials, Fannie was allowed to testify that when shown the coffin photographs, her mother had exclaimed, "That's my boy."[6]

The idea of hearsay (like any number of unfamiliar ideas to which one might be introduced) has a way of colonizing the new initiate's perceptions, at least for a while. Having been unaware of the notion for all my life, I found that when it was explained to me as a law student I quickly became incapable of listening to any account or reading any narrative without noticing that there was a great deal of hearsay going on. *Hearsay!* my mind would object while I was reading the newspaper or listening to my friends talk about their weekends. This was not a useful mental habit, and I seem to have recovered from it to some degree in the intervening years.

But perhaps my reader has had the same experience just now. How, you might be wondering, was Fannie Walters permitted to testify to what her mother said upon seeing Mr. Lamon's photos of the Crooked Creek corpse? Wouldn't that be hearsay? An excellent question, and one not answered with complete clarity by the available records. But probably Mrs. Walter's anguished cry was made under circumstances that qualified it as a long-recognized exception to the hearsay rule, the exception for excited, or startled, utterances.[7]

The hearsay issue, however, does not exhaust the problematic nature of using Mrs. Walters's statement as evidence. For how reliable could such an identification be, under the circumstances? Photographs were new enough as evidence in 1880 that the courts were just beginning to sort out whether and how they might be employed. But in the ensuing decades it came to be accepted among lawyers and judges that eyewitness testimony in which a witness matches a photo to her memory of an individual she has seen is subject to a certain infirmity: the witness may be easily influenced by the manner of presenting the photograph. This objection would be pursued with some notable success by mid-twentieth-century criminal lawyers whose clients were identified by eyewitnesses who had been shown their photographs.

It seems likely that even before seeing the photographs, the Walters family had come to believe that their son and brother was the man killed at Crooked Creek: Daniel Walters would later testify that "he had learned the fate of his son" from the master of his Masonic Lodge. The news that men were coming with photographs of the corpse must have created a stir of bereaved expectation in the Walters household. And expectation is one of the most potent antagonists to accuracy in identification. From the perspective of the Supreme Court's later rulings on identification evidence, the procedure that led to Mrs. Daniel Walters's outburst suffered from at least two defects: the pressure of a group procedure (what family member would deny the identification after hearing the grieving mother speak?), and the absence of any choice beyond yes and no. The last defect would have been hard to remedy even if the insurance companies had been interested in doing so (unless Lamon could have been persuaded to photograph a number of other corpses). But the first is troubling, and could have been avoided if the companies had presented the corpse photos in a more considered way—for example, by asking the family members one at a time to examine the photographs, perhaps in a separate room, and to confide their opinions. Such delicacy, however, would not have served the companies' interest in obtaining unanimous positive identifications of the corpse as someone other than Hillmon.[8]

Apparently something like these doubts took hold in the mind of Judge William C. Hook, who was to preside many years later over the sixth and last Hillmon trial; he would take a stricter view than had his predecessors and rule out any testimony about the mother's reaction to the photographs. "So far as the pictures would affect the mother," he would explain, "they would naturally have the effect they did. She was aged and had long mourned her son as dead. The picture of any cadaver would have much the same effect."[9]

In none of the six trials, however, were the other Walters family members prevented from testifying to their certainty that the corpse pictured in the photographs was that of their missing son or brother. Moreover, numerous friends and acquaintances of Frederick Adolph were shown the Lamon pictures, and later came to court to swear that they depicted the man they knew. The record does not show us the circumstances under which all these identifications were first made; but very likely these witnesses, before being invited to come to court by the insurance company lawyers, were shown the corpse photographs and asked whether they thought the dead man was Walters—a classic single-suspect photographic display of the sort much later condemned by the Supreme Court.[10]

Of course, the Court's decisions lay three quarters of a century in the future, and in any event they have no bearing on the trial of civil cases. But a good lawyer, even in the nineteenth century, could cast considerable doubt on these family and acquaintance identifications by appealing to a jury's common sense. From the outset the insurance company's men must have perceived the likelihood that the testimony of witnesses who claimed that the corpse in the photographs was Frederick Adolph Walters would not be enough to discourage Sallie Hillmon, nor by itself sufficient to defeat her lawsuits if she were to bring them. Nor would the affidavit signed by John Brown at the instance of the lawyer Buchan have much effect on Sallie, for as we shall see presently, Brown renounced the affidavit nearly as soon as he signed it. The insurance companies would need more if they were to intimidate Sallie, or defeat her at trial.

It was probably someone in the Walters family who suggested to Major Wiseman and Mr. Tillinghast that they ought to talk to Frederick Adolph's fiancée, Miss Alvina Kasten. It was these overtures to the cigarmaker's betrothed that again elevated the insurance lawyers' hopes, and led to the piece of evidence for which the Hillmon case is remembered by lawyers and judges throughout the Anglo-American legal world.

FORT MADISON, IOWA | JUNE 1881

"You need not be concerned in the least," says Mr. Tillinghast, as he takes her arm above the elbow to aid her up the steps into the courthouse. "This is not a trial, nothing like it. A deposition, we call it."

"Mr. Green said there would be no judge." The young woman who accompanies him slips his grasp once they have achieved the top of the stairs and entered the dim building. "I told him I should not agree to appear before a judge."

"No judge at all," says the insurance man reassuringly. "Just a few lawyers to ask you some questions. And a notary, a Mr. Casey, to take the words down. You will do quite well if you merely remember the things we have discussed, Miss Kasten. I give you my word you will never have to testify before a judge, and you will not be required to travel to Kansas at all. After today you may put this unhappy matter aside and try to go forward with your young life."

"I scarcely think that will be possible, sir, under the circumstances," says Alvina Kasten, her chin set at an obtuse angle. The lightness of head that has been troubling her for the past few days is worsened by the abrupt transition from sunlight to dimness.

"Of course," says Tillinghast distractedly, "of course." But he is already looking about the dark corridor. A slim man wearing a shirt and collar but no jacket steps out of a door near the end, his appearance relieving Tillinghast's frown. "Ah, Casey. There you are. This is Miss Alvina Kasten."

"Come then, young lady," says the slim man. "The lawyers are assembled." He vanishes back into the room.

"Will Mrs. Hillmon be there?" asks Alvina, resisting slightly the pressure of her companion's hand on her back as the pair walk toward the door from which this Casey had appeared.

"No, my dear, I am told she did not make the journey. Only one or two of her lawyers will be present. You need not fear seeing her."

Alvina, her heart beginning to vibrate most unpleasantly inside her chest, steps away from the man's touch and sits down abruptly on the long bench that lines the corridor wall. "What do you mean? I wish to see her! I am determined to tell her that I hate her and her wicked husband for killing my Dolph!"

Tillinghast looks about hastily, then sits beside her and takes her hands in his. "What you are about to do, Miss Kasten, will accomplish more to revenge the death of your young man than anything you could say to Mrs. Hillmon in person. Do you understand? The letter, my dear. It is the proof, the unmistakable token of your loss, and their guilt of it. Your Dolph's last epistle, the one he meant for you. We are all of us devoted to the same cause now, to thwarting their crime by denying them the fruits of it. You need only remember what we have discussed, answer the questions, and identify the letter. The letter will do the rest. They will find it quite useless to question your veracity because there is no denying that the letter is in the handwriting of your—of Mr. Walters. Mr. Casey will record everything you say and produce a transcript. And we believe, my colleagues and I, that Mrs. Hillmon will see the impossibility of her position once she reads what you will say today."

She rubs her gloved hands over her eyes. "Give me a moment, Mr. Tillinghast. If you would be so kind."

He nods and moved a few feet away, but keeps his eyes on her the whole time.

† † †

EXCERPTS FROM THE TRANSCRIPT

DEPOSITION OF MISS ALVINA KASTEN, TAKEN JUNE 1881

FILED IN THE CASE OF HILLMON VS. MUTUAL LIFE INS. CO. ET AL.

Miss Alvina D. Kasten, a witness of lawful age, produced by defendant, being duly sworn, testified as follows:

Q.1.   State your name, age and place of residence?

A.   Alvina D. Kasten. My age is twenty-one; reside at Fort Madison, Iowa.

Q.2.   How long have you resided in Fort Madison?

A.   I was born and raised right in this place.

Q.3.   State if at any time you were acquainted with one Frederick Adolph Walters, and if so, please state where he was residing at the time of that acquaintance.

A.   Well, as long as I knew him he had been living on Second street where they now live in Fort Madison, Iowa.

Q.4.   When did you last see Frederick Adolph Walters?

A.   It was on the 24th of March, 1878, at Fort Madison at the Kasten house.

Q.5.   You may state whether or not he has been residing in Fort Madison since.

A.   He has not.

Q.6.   State whether or not he left Fort Madison about that time.

A.   To my knowledge he did.

Q.7.   State if you please if at any time after he left Fort Madison you heard from him, and if so, in what manner?

A.   I received a letter two weeks after he was gone.

Q.8.   Did you received other letters from him, and if so, please state.

A.   I have; I have received letters most every two weeks, generally every two weeks, or a week and a half.

Q.9.   How long did this correspondence between you and Mr. Walters last?

A.   I received letters until the 3d of March, 1879, was the last one I received.

Q.10. State whether or not you know the handwriting of Frederick Adolph Walters?

A.   Well, I think I would.

Q.11. Look at the letter now shown you by J.W. Green and state if you know in whose handwriting the body of the letter is in, and whose signature is affixed thereto?

A.   The handwriting is that of F.A. Walters; I recognize the letter as one I have given to Mr. Tillinghast. The signature is in the handwriting of F.A. Walters. It is his signature.

Q.12. State whether or not you ever saw this letter before, and if so, please state about when you first saw it?

A.   When I first saw it was on the 3d of March, Monday evening in 1879.

Q.13. Where did you first see it?

A.   The letter was handed to me at the post office.

Q.14. State whether or not by a person connected with the post office?

A.   The letter was handed to me personally by the postmaster.

Q.15. How many letters, if any, did you receive after this letter shown you?

A.   Not any.

Q. 16. Had your correspondence with F.A. Walters been regular from the time that he left Fort Madison up to the receipt of this last letter, if so, please state?

A.   Yes, sir, it had.

Q.17. Will you please state to the notary what appears on the face of the envelope written and printed?

A.   Miss Alvina Kasten. Fort Madison, Iowa, Lee County, postmarked, Wichita, March 2nd.

Q.18. State if you know in whose handwriting is the address on the letter?

A.   F.A. Walters.

Q.19. State to whom that letter was addressed if you know?

A.   To myself, of course.

Q.20. You may state if this is the letter that you referred to as being the last letter received by you from Frederick Adolph Walters, and as having been received about March 3rd, 1879?

A.   Yes, sir.

SABERT M. CASEY,

NOTARY PUBLIC

WICHITA, KAS., MAR. 1ST, '79

DEAREST ALVINA:

Your kind and ever welcome letter was received yesterday afternoon about an hour before I left Emporia so I did not have time to answer it at Emporia. I will stay here until the fore part of next week & then will leave here to see a part of the Country that I never expected to see when I left home as I am going with a man by the name of Hillmon who intends to start a sheep range and as he promised me more wages than I could make at anything else I Concluded to take it for a while at least until I strike something better. There is so many folks in this country that have got the Leadville Feaver, & and if I would not of got the situation that I have got now I would have went there myself but as it is at present I will get to see the best portion of Kansas Indian Territory Colorado & Mexico the route we intend to take would Cost a man to travel from $150 to $200. but it will not cost me a cent. Besides I get good Wages. I will drop you a letter occasionally until I get settled down then I want you to answer it. (You bet Honey.) Don't it? So you can see that I will not get home for a few months yet, but cannot tell how soon I will get back, I am about as Anxious to see you as you are to see me. But I do not want to get back there without a sent of money for that is not what I left for (you know). When I get back you will get to see me in about the way we parted (You bet)!? If any one asks what I am doing tell them that you were not Informed for it is none of their Business and an other thing don't ask me to write long letters for I would

without being told if I could find the Words when I write as I
am generaly Busy when I receive a letter from my (Old Woman)
Sweet Little Girl. But you know how that is without being told so
I will not have to waist any more paper on that cubject (at present). I will have to come to a close before long or I will have to do
as that Other Fellow write 2 Sheets & swindle the P. Master out
of 3 cents and you know that I don't like to do that. (Pet) Please
give compliments to enquiring Friends and all the love that you
can embrace for yourself & no body else. I will close for this time
Love, to let you hear from me soon again.

Yours as ever,
F.A. Walter

P.S. Much obliged for that Poetry & I done as you said (thought
of you when I read it.)[11]

† † †

I first read the Dearest Alvina letter when I was a second-year law student, preparing for my evidence class. The professor had assigned the
1892 decision of the United States Supreme Court in Sallie Hillmon's
case against the insurance companies—the case in which the Court
decided, thirteen years after the date of Mr. Walters's letter to his sweetheart, that it was admissible evidence despite its undeniable hearsay
character. The appearance of this letter in an assigned reading was
unforgettable to a very young woman whose dreams about the romance
of the law had by then acquired some tattered edges. Law school is—
there's no getting around this—often very tedious. One reads almost
nothing but cases, reports of how lawsuits were decided. Disagreements
between corporations about how the profits or losses from transactions should be divided seem to alternate with consideration of whether
one state's court or another's has jurisdiction over a particular dispute.
Human interest is mostly lacking, except in the course on criminal law,
where it is present but extremely dispiriting: the cases feature a dismal
parade of child molesters and inebriated morons whose conception of
dispute resolution involves firearms.

I am sure I had never encountered a love letter in a law school read-ing assignment until I read the Court's decision in *Hillmon v. Mutual Life Insurance Company*. The Court didn't recite the entire letter, but quoted enough of it to have an immediate effect: I was enchanted. The casebook mentioned that an article about the case could be found in a 1968 edition of *American Heritage* magazine, and the next day I went to the main library at the University of Texas to find it, and made a copy. The whole letter was reproduced there, including the postscript. My imagination, starved for material in the desert of legal education, went to work at once picturing the sturdy cigarmaker, the shy fiancée (just about my age at the time), their separation while the young man sought his fortune, the agonizing sorrow of his failure to return. My heart's sympathies flew out to them. As for the insured, John Hillmon, all I knew about him was the suspiciously large amount of life insurance that he purchased, and the inconsistent and sometimes incriminating stories told by his traveling companion, John Brown.[12]

I was glad to read that the Court had not let the verdict for Sallie Hill-mon stand. It seemed very likely that her husband had killed Frederick Adolph Walters and that she had been part of the criminal scheme. I wrote a few sentences in my case brief for use in class the next day, and went on to the next case. It was something about the admissibility of business records, much less interesting. I read it dutifully but my mind kept going back to the Hillmon decision, and the letter. *Much obliged for that Poetry & I done as you said (thought of you when I read it.)* The rustic but romantic cigarmaker and his disappointed fiancée were still on my mind more than thirty years later.

NATIONAL ARCHIVES AND RECORDS ADMINISTRATION

CENTRAL PLAINS REGION, KANSAS CITY, MISSOURI

OCTOBER 31, 2003

The original pleadings, orders, transcripts, and exhibits to the six trials of the Hillmon case are now housed in an official government deposi-tory in Kansas City. The first day I went there to visit them, it was Halloween, 2003. Six enormous boxes of documents had been pulled from their resting place and shelved on a cart for my examination. I opened the first box with some trepidation, for I could see that the papers stuffed inside were old and discolored. Gingerly I tried to pull one folded sheaf out from the center; it crackled as it came, and a small shower of flakes fell back into the box. It was folded twice, like a business letter, and more fragments crumbled and fell as I unfolded it. The papers resisted opening, the fibers returning to their familiar bends unless I held them in place.

"Oh!" I exclaimed in dismay as the document slid from my hands and collided with the side of the box, an occasion for a new explosion of flakes. "This document really doesn't want me to read it."

"Next time you come, we'll humidify the box for a few days beforehand," said Barbara Larsen, the librarian who was assisting me. "But it's okay. Just be careful. I'll be back in a while to see how you're getting along. And come have some cake, if you like." The archive staff, although their assistance was stunningly professional, had obviously decided to celebrate the holiday in style; there were homemade refreshments and everyone but me was dressed in costume.

After a couple of hours I had learned a few techniques for minimizing damage to the documents that I examined, although their fragility and their lively defiance of my efforts to unfold them continued to daunt me. I found the original complaints—three of them, for Sallie Hillmon had sued each of the insurance companies separately at first. I came across the order signed by Judge Foster of the Circuit Court in Leavenworth, the first of the six trial judges to preside over the case, ordering that the three cases be consolidated. All these documents were written by hand, for the widespread adoption of the still-new typewriter lay a few years into the future. The three complaints (identical except for where each one named the defendant or specified the amount of the policy or policies it had issued on John Hillmon's life) were copied and attested in the same careful, rounded script: Sallie Hillmon had written them out herself.

The papers were not stored in any sort of chronological order; court orders from 1898 rested alongside deposition transcripts made in 1880. By the mid-eighties some of the documents were typewritten; apparently the earliest typing machines could make only uppercase letters, but the familiar upper- and lowercase style began to appear in some of the documents dated 1887 or 1888.

Finding that letter to Miss Alvina Kasten from Frederick Adolph Walters was my chief desire as I struggled to progress methodically through the six cartons. I wanted to hold the original letter in my hands. I had read the text of the letter in the Supreme Court's microfilm records of the case, but I thought the original could tell me something that the printed transcription of it could not. Certain aspects of it still bemused me. Did the writer have some intimation of the danger to which he was exposing himself? What accounted for the rather stern way he instructed Alvina not to disclose too much about his plans to others?

The materials in the cartons were not organized by any discernable principle, so I decided to examine the documents in the order they appeared, trying to keep notes so I could find important things again. In the second of the six boxes, between a "Judgment nunc pro tunc" dated 1890 and a set of "Plaintiff's Requested Jury Instructions" from 1885, I found the letter. Its slanted script filled three sheets of long paper, and I scanned it eagerly, scrutinizing the cigarmaker's handwriting for clues. Surprisingly, it was a very legible and professional copperplate, the hand of a person who writes a good deal.

Only what was this? At the top was inscribed "Copy-1." It then said "Exhibit C. Sabert M. Casey, Notary Public" before the familiar place ("Wichita, Kas.") and date ("Mar. 1st, '79") were given. And below the notary's name was this notation: "(Seal)." I know from reading Alvina Kasten's deposition that the notary had taken the letter from her (or from the lawyers) and made an exhibit of it, but this was rather obviously not the original letter—for that would have an actual seal on it, not the word "Seal." I scanned the rest of the letter, looking for an explanation, and at the bottom I found one:

Received June 24, 1881 a letter of which the above is a true copy.

A copy! I blinked at the signature below these words, eying it with puzzlement for a moment until my eye could decode it.

J. W. Green, Atty. For Deft.

Green. I paged back quickly to my earlier notes: Kasten had given her deposition in June 1881, the day unspecified. Within days then (perhaps that very same day), James W. Green had been permitted to take custody of the letter and envelope, and substitute a copy. It was, of course, not a facsimile or anything we would today call a copy, as the technology required for that process was nearly nonexistent then—it was a *handwritten* copy. So the handwriting in which this copy was written (which looked to me like that of Green himself, as evidenced by his signature) was not the same as the handwriting of the original. This was very disappointing, though I nonetheless I made a photocopy of the handwritten copy at the machine in the corner of the document examination room. I turned back to the remaining boxes with a sigh. After several hours I had accumulated a small pile of copied documents.

The room was windowless, but I noted from glancing at the clock that the afternoon was drawing to a close: nearly time to stop. Fatigued in body and mind, I reached wearily back into the box. In a tattered envelope wedged between some trivial documents, my fingers encountered some smaller but more substantial, thicker papers. I spilled them out of their ragged container and adrenaline jolted through my heart as I saw what they were. Photographs: Two of Frederick Adolph Walters.

Photographer unknown. Courtesy National
Archives and Records Administration.

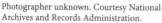

Three of John Hillmon.

Photographer unknown. Courtesy National
Archives and Records Administration.

And, most thrillingly but also disturbingly, W.H. Lamon's photographs of the corpse.

Photographer W.H. Lamon. Courtesy National
Archives and Records Administration.

I had only a few minutes to look at them; the archive was about to close for the day, and I had booked a flight back home for the next morning. I arranged to have digital images of the photographs sent to me, since the copy machine would be inadequate to capture their nuances, and then reluctantly had to leave them behind. I bade farewell to the archive's staff and stumbled out of the building into dazzling sunshine, holding my briefcase in one hand and a piece of Halloween cake edged with orange frosting in the other, disoriented from my daylong excursion. My body was in twenty-first-century Kansas City, navigating its way through a parking lot filled with glittering vehicles, but my mind lingered in dusty nineteenth-century Lawrence.

In my shabby hotel room that evening I pulled the Alvina letter—the photocopy I'd made at the archive—out of my briefcase and looked at it again. By now I was past the disappointment of not having found the original, and I had become accustomed to the hand of the copymaker, so I could pay attention to the words. I had read them before, but somehow they looked different written by hand, even if it wasn't Walters's hand. Puzzled, I riffled back through my files to find my copy of John Brown's affidavit—the one the lawyer Buchan had persuaded him to sign in Parkville, Missouri, that September after the death at Crooked Creek. These two items, the letter and the affidavit, were the strongest evidence the insurance companies had for their claim that the body belonged not to Hillmon, but to Walters. I knew that Brown had later repudiated the affidavit, and gone back to his original story; even so, to my mind his affidavit was lent some weight by its correspondence with the letter. But now when I looked at them together, something wasn't right.

There was that odd name the affidavit gave for the young man Brown said Hillmon had killed: "Berkley or Burgis, but we always called him Joe." Joe Berkley does not sound very much like Frederick Adolph Walters, I mused, but perhaps the young man was for some reason traveling under an alias. Brown's affidavit went on to say that the fellow had spoken of working in Fort Scott, Wellington, and Arkansas City. Hadn't Alvina Kasten's deposition mentioned the places from which her fiancé had written her during the year of his absence? I scattered papers all over the slippery motel bedspread until I found the transcript of her deposition.

Q. 30. State the different places where you received letters from?

A.   I received some from Alladin, Kansas. I received one from Kansas City.
I don't remember whether it was one or two from Holden, Missouri.
I received some from Paola, Kansas. Most of them were I think from
Emporia, Kansas, and the rest from Wichita.[13]

Alvina Kasten's fiancé had gotten around quite a bit during his travels,
but he did not seem to have stayed in the same places as "Joe Burgis." I
turned back to the letter. It all seemed so convincing: Walters's description of the meeting in Wichita around March 1 and his new acquaintance's offer to pay him "more wages" to accompany him out west than
the cigarmaker could make in any other way. It did mention Hillmon's plan to start a "sheep ranch" instead of a cattle ranch, which was
what Hillmon had told Sallie, but that seemed a trivial difference. The
date and place were right—it appeared to be undisputed that Hillmon
and Brown were in Wichita on March 1. The name Hillmon was even
spelled correctly with an *o*, although it was elsewhere almost universally misspelled.

The letter didn't mention Brown, however, although he had been in
Wichita with Hillmon. I turned back to the affidavit to see how Brown,
for his part, had described his first meeting with "Joe."

We overtook a stranger on this trip the first day out from Wichita, about two or two and one-half miles from town, who Hillmon invited to get in and ride and who he (Hillmon) proposed
to hire and work for him on the ranch as proposed to be located;
this man was with us during all this trip. Hillmon proposed to me
that this man would do for a subject to pass for him.[14]

My puzzlement was beginning to acquire a shape. How could Walters have written a letter headed "Wichita" (and postmarked in Wichita)
mentioning a meeting with Hillmon, if Hillmon and Brown didn't meet
him until two and one-half miles outside Wichita, headed west away
from that town? I turned this over in my mind for a long time, without
conclusion. It seemed like a discrepancy between Brown's affidavit and
the Dearest Alvina letter. But so what? What did it prove? If the letter
were a forgery, wouldn't Sallie Hillmon's lawyers have been suspicious,

and sought to compare it to other letters Walters had written? And why would Miss Alvina Kasten, a respectable young woman, lie and say that the letter was one she had received in the mail? It didn't make sense.

Maybe Walters had actually written the letter on the trail, after meeting up with Brown and Hillmon, and just headed it "Wichita" because that was the nearest city? Then perhaps he handed it to some traveler he met going the opposite direction and asked that it be posted in Wichita? This still didn't seem quite right to me, as the letter said "I will stay here until the fore part of next week & then will leave here," but I couldn't think of a better explanation.

My plane would leave early so I set the gimcrack clock radio on the bedside for five-thirty, but I needn't have. I was already awake when the cool jazz station clicked on, my head full of Sallie and her antagonists, trying to think of ways to unravel the mystery of how her husband had died.

I was burning up with the desire to know—not just who had died at Crooked Creek, but who Sallie Hillmon was. Grieving widow, easily led girl, spunky proto-feminist, cool conspirator at murder? Or something more nuanced than any of these identities? I promised myself that I would learn the answer before I was finished, and in the meantime try to restrain my imagination from outrunning the evidence.

LEAVENWORTH, KANSAS | SEPTEMBER 1879

Senator W.J. Buchan is a patient man, but he is becoming exasperated. Will the GD train never appear? Buchan has better business to attend to than cooling his heels in this train depot, waiting for a representative of the fairer sex who may or may not appear. Give him a straightforward fool like John Brown any day, over this vacillating waitress. He looks at his watch, not for the first time in this quarter hour. The train is eight minutes late.

"Are you certain she said she would come?" he asks his companion.

Brown is sitting uncomfortably on a bench, elbows on his knees in a way that requires him to hang his head in a most aggravating fashion. "It's what she told me last night," he says.

Brown seems to be resigned to her arriving or not, which irritates Buchan further. "I trust you recall that the companies' forbearance is conditioned on a successful conclusion to this negotiation."

"So you say," Brown mutters, and the lawyer looks up sharply at the slight note of defiance in this reply. Senator W.J. Buchan does not intend to be associated with a repetition of the Goss–Udderzook matter. He cannot afford to have this fool threatening to jump ship.

"Your father—" he begins, but then there is the rising clatter of the tracks, precluding further conversation, and in a few minutes the train has arrived. The lady steps off the car lightly, a basket over her arm. Seeing John Brown, who has risen from his seat, she approaches him with a smile and begins to relate some trifling detail of her journey, taking his arm as she does so. As though she needs any more assistance in taking care of herself, thinks Buchan with disgust. He has learned that she has incurred the advice not only of that meddler E.B. Borgalthaus in Lawrence, but of another lawyer as well, the insufferable Lysander B. Wheat of this town. He is relieved that she is not accompanied by one of these shysters today; perhaps she has seen that her interests do not lie with theirs.

"Good day, Mr. Buchan," she says finally, turning toward him. Her hat is trimmed with black, another detail he notes with annoyance. Has she not come to sign a paper that acknowledges her husband is not where the crepe suggests but in hiding above the ground?

He smiles and says, "Good day, Mrs. Hillmon. It is good to see you again. Will you come with us to the Planter's House and take some supper?"

She looks not at him, but again at Brown. "I will come with you," she says.

But there follows the most infuriating train of events Senator Buchan, who is not accustomed to such treatment, has ever experienced. Upon arriving at the Planter's he takes her to the parlor that he has engaged, and signals to Brown to make the declaration they have practiced. Brown harrumphs and then tells Mrs. Hillmon that he has signed a statement saying that the dead man was not her husband but a stranger they killed for the insurance money. She does not seem surprised, saying rather coolly to Brown (but looking somewhat sideways at Buchan), "Do you really think, John, that I would not know my own husband's body when I see it?" She then feigns fatigue and illness and declines to break bread with them in favor of resting in the parlor, so he must tolerate the undiluted company of Brown for the entirety of a meal.

When he and Brown return to the parlor at about six o'clock, Buchan briefly believes that his patience is to be rewarded, for Sallie Hillmon surprises him by rising from the davenport and saying she will sign the papers he has prepared releasing the insurance companies from her claims. And she does sign, but when he asks her for the policies (for he had most particularly instructed Brown to tell her to bring them along) she says she does not have the policy papers, that they rest in the keeping of attorney Wheat.

Buchan considers it possible that a court will not enforce the releases unless she has also surrendered the policies. So there follows a search for attorney Wheat, who is sent for at home and sends back word that he will meet Senator Buchan and Mrs. Hillmon at his office.

The stubborn old pettifogger does not appear pleased to have been sent for so late in the evening, but he is civil enough. Mrs. Hillmon instructs him to give Buchan the policies, but in an odd tone of voice. And when Wheat asks her for what reason she wishes him to restore the policies to her possession, she says quietly, "No reason, sir."

"In that case," Wheat says, "I must decline." He declares that he has a lien on the policies on account of having worked on Mrs. Hillmon's case. Buchan must hold his hands behind his back to prevent them from shaking with anger while he tries to reason with Wheat and his client. "How much work can you have done, sir?" he asks. "I believe it is mere weeks since you first learnt the names John and Sallie Hillmon, and you have filed no papers of any sort as far as I know." But Wheat merely smiles and nods and murmurs of the privilege between attorney and client, and puts out his hand, which Buchan is compelled to take.

"And now, sir, I ask your leave to rejoin my family," says Wheat, and Mrs. Hillmon and Buchan are forced to return to the street. She walks silently back to the Planter's House by his side as though this is all in a day's work for her, which perhaps it is. Buchan is forced to pay for a room for her as well as for himself, as the last trains to Lawrence and Wyandotte have left. But he does succeed in persuading the lady that she should come with him to his office in Wyandotte the next day, so she may see for herself the statement that John Brown has signed, and perhaps understand the futility of Mr. Wheat's resistance to the surrender of her claims.

Brown meets them again the next morning at Buchan's offices in Wyandotte, and Mrs. Hillmon is shown the paper that her friend has signed. It is a chilly morning, but Buchan's assistant has earlier laid a fire in the stove; the heated metal still casts a little warmth, although the flames have died out. Sallie Hillmon occupies some little time, sitting at Buchan's desk, in reading the affidavit, and when she has finished she is as cool as February.

"Why would you say such things, John?" she says, handing the document not to Buchan but to Brown, who appears to have grown somewhat afraid in the face of her composure.

"I aim to stick to it, Mrs. Hillmon," he says, but there is no conviction in his voice.

The lady continues to look at him evenly, saying again that she wonders why anyone would doubt her when she says the body she saw belonged to her husband. And then in a sort of spasm the wretch Brown crumples the affidavit and thrusts it into the stove!

"There!" he expostulates, with a ferocious grimace toward Buchan. "It did not work, and so I've burnt it up! You and your companies will have to do your worst, Senator, for I've had enough." He is in a spitting rage, and in his ire he has overestimated the ardor of the fire, although Buchan does not see that it is necessary to point this out. The lawyer says nothing, indeed, as he reckons further persuasion is unlikely at this moment. It is thus not long before Brown and the diabolical woman leave together and Buchan is able to retrieve the document from the stove, not too much the worse for the abuse it has sustained.

Buchan has earlier taken the precaution of having his scrivener make a copy, but he knows that the time may come when the original is demanded, and he does not mean to fail in what has been required of him. He smooths the creases absently, seeing that the paper is only a little scorched at the edges. A very useful document, despite its misadventure, he reflects. The companies will pay him well for his work even though he has failed through no fault of his own to obtain the policies. And why should they not? His other client does not seem to feel the proper gratitude, and in any event has not the means to compensate him at an appropriate rate.[15]

† † †

I find I have a certain sympathy for Buchan. He is a shifty character, but Sallie's behavior on these occasions is not precisely what one might expect from an innocent young widow. Nevertheless, as I yield more and more to obsession with the Hillmon case, I find my youthful loyalties toward Alvina Kasten and her lost fiancé somewhat overborne. My sympathies begin to lean toward Sallie Hillmon, yet still I am torn. It isn't only Sallie's inconstant behavior; I am bothered by the implausibility of certain items among her claims about John Hillmon's death. At one point I begin a list:

- Sallie's lawyers maintained (as they more or less had to) that Hillmon's motives for taking out such a large amount of life insurance were no more than the reasons that might prompt any married man to do the same. But skeptics noted that the amount of the insurance, nearly half a million dollars in today's currency, was vastly out of proportion to Hillmon's economic value as a spouse, and so expensive that he had to borrow money to pay the first year's premium.
- John Brown's narrative about the fatal accident at Crooked Creek depended entirely on his claim of mishap, but how likely was it that the Sharps rifle could have discharged accidentally upon being removed from the wagon?
- The story given about Hillmon's reasons for leaving home in the middle of the winter was that he wished to find a place to start a ranch of his own, but this would have been a risky and dangerous proposition. What would drive a married man (if the marriage was a real one) to take such chances, when he enjoyed a decent steady income working for other men, including Sallie's cousin Levi Baldwin?

The magnitude of the insurance policies was troublesome to many contemporaneous observers—so much so that T.A. McNeal, a thoughtful observer who acknowledged there were strong reasons to believe that the dead man was Hillmon, was nevertheless driven to the conclusion that Hillmon and Baldwin had connived to commit insurance fraud. McNeal, who lived in Medicine Lodge and published its newspaper, the *Cresset*, knew more than most about the inquest that was held there before the body was disinterred and shipped back to Lawrence. The death at Crooked Creek coincided almost perfectly with the beginning of his venture of newspaper publishing; it was his new paper's first big story. Many years later he wrote about the Hillmon case in his memoir *When Kansas Was Young*:

> The attorneys for Mrs. Hillman produced several reputable witnesses in Medicine Lodge, who declared that Hillman had visited the Lodge several weeks before the killing, and was detained there during a storm which lasted several days. These witnesses declared that the man who visited the Lodge on the prior occasion and the man who was shot were one and the same. Knowing these men well, I can not doubt their honesty, and it is hard to believe that they were mistaken.[16]

But there were also countervailing signs, as McNeal saw them:

> On the other hand, the circumstances were exceedingly suspicious, the taking out of a $25,000 life insurance by a common laborer, the burial of the body in an unmarked grave, with apparently no intention of removing it to his home at Lawrence, the giving of notes instead of cash for the payment of the first premiums on the policies, the confession of Brown, all tended to make a strong *prima facie* case for the insurance companies.[17]

McNeal was plainly impressed by "Brown's confession," apparently unaware that Brown had recanted. But it was chiefly the circumstances of the policies' purchase that left him so deeply suspicious. He could account for all the evidence only with a somewhat unusual hypothesis:

> If Hillman was not killed, he was never heard from again; if the man who was killed was not Walters then there was another remarkable disappearance. I have little doubt that taking out the policies of insurance was part of a conspiracy to defraud the insurance companies, but I have thought there was a failure of the plan, at least so far as Hillman was concerned, and that he was really killed at the lonesome camp on Spring Creek.[18]

It was McNeal's ornate hypothesis that John Hillmon, although a conspirator at fraud and murder, ended up dead himself in some unexplained miscalculation. But was the journalist justified in finding John Hillmon's decision to insure his life so irregular? Sallie Hillmon's lawyers would later argue that there was nothing surprising about a man protecting his wife by taking out life insurance before sojourning to barely inhabited lands, still the site of occasional Indian raids, in the chill of winter, but that proposition sounds as extravagant as McNeal's solution.

What came to seem less unlikely, to me, is that Hillmon and Baldwin did have an understanding in advance about the life insurance, an agreement that would explain why Baldwin provided at least some of the premium. For it was not uncommon in the history of life insurance for men to employ it not strictly as a business practice, but as a sort of wager.

In the late nineteenth century life insurance supplanted another form of contractual arrangement in which death was the operative contingency: the tontine. Tontines, invented in Europe hundreds of years earlier, rested on a simple model. Each member would pay a sum into the tontine, and the funds would be invested. When a member died, his or her share would be reinvested for the benefit of the surviving members. The process continued until only one member survived, at which time he or she could liquidate the investment. The tontine represented an unapologetic gamble: one member would be the big winner, and the more short-lived participants would never recover their original investments (although in some cases tontine members were paid dividends during their lives).[19]

The tontines were objectionable to many nineteenth-century moralists, for each investor's rational wish would necessarily be for his fellow investors to die—and soon. Preachers deemed this alignment of fortune and ill will to be hazardous to man's spiritual health, and they moralized against the tontines, condemning them as grotesque wagers.[20]

The widespread replacement of tontines with life insurance did not avert this hazard, for even a policy of life insurance could align a person's interest with the death of another. And early in the history of life insurance, many such contracts constituted nothing more than a bet against the survival of some identified person, not necessarily related to the policyholder. In eighteenth-century England, speculation with the lives of others was a near-mania, with royalty and rulers the most common objects. *Harper's New Monthly Magazine* reported in 1859 that "[w]hen Lord Nithsdale escaped from the tower [of London, in 1715] . . . the wretches who had periled money on his life and to whom his impending execution would have been a profit, were noisy in their own complaints."[21]

The stigma of gambling clung to life insurance well into the late nineteenth century; as late as 1895, a Lutheran minister denounced it as "money speculation," and many prospective customers declined to purchase it on moral grounds. Life insurance companies were forced, in their sales strategies, to insist on distinctions between insurance and gambling, as in this article in the *Insurance Gazette*: "Life insurance contracts do not partake in the least of the nature of lotteries, or games of chance as some erroneously affirm, nor are they wager contracts." The purveyors of life insurance attempted to recast the purchase of their product as the mark of a domestic hero, the symbol of a successful man who not only took care of his wife and children in life, but cared enough (and was prosperous enough) to make arrangements for their support if he should die before them. This marketing campaign was largely successful.[22]

Another innovation that rescued life insurance from unseemliness was the requirement, first appearing in eighteenth-century England, that the beneficiary of a life insurance policy have an "insurable interest" in the life of the insured person. Although it proved somewhat difficult to define (did parents have an "insurable interest" in the lives of their children?), the doctrine of insurable interest at least discouraged gamblers from speculating on the lives of monarchs and other strangers. Moreover, it might discourage some attempts at fraud, for multi-actor life insurance schemes like that of Goss and Udderzook could not be successful unless one of the conspirators had an insurable interest in the life of another. Of course, if the named insured were a married man they might be able to recruit his wife to the conspiracy. And if he were single, they could perhaps find some young woman willing to enter into a sham marriage in exchange for a share of the eventual proceeds of the crime.[23]

These reflections naturally led to others. Was John Hillmon's purchase of such a robust amount of insurance part of such a scheme, in which his very recent bride Sallie served as willing accomplice to the fraud? Or was there a conspiracy, perhaps encompassing Hillmon and Baldwin and Brown, of which Sallie was innocent? Or—a third hypothesis—did Levi Baldwin perceive, in the plans of his friend and former employee to embark on a reckless sojourn into the heart of the winter wilderness, an opportunity to make a fine wager? Perhaps Baldwin was a gambler at heart; after all, he was a cattleman, a decidedly speculative occupation. Possibly he reasoned that for the price of a single premium payment he could purchase a chance at winning $25,000 (or more likely some portion of it, for Sallie must be taken care of) in the not unlikely event that John Hillmon met his death during his travels.

We cannot know for sure why the bachelor Hillmon became so suddenly a family man and provided so extravagantly for his new wife. But if the arrangement represented a wagering opportunity for Baldwin, in which Hillmon was for his own reasons willing to participate, it is not hard to imagine why the two men would have kept their agreement secret. Life insurance had become respectable in most quarters by 1878, but only when its wagering-on-death aspects were disguised by such stipulations as the insurable interest requirement. Levi probably would not have been permitted to buy insurance on John Hillmon's life with himself as beneficiary; but naming Sallie as beneficiary (with the understanding that she and Levi would share any proceeds according to some formula) would have solved that difficulty. There is some evidence for this hypothesis in the testimony at the third Hillmon trial of a man named J.S. Crew, a banker. Crew said that in March 1879, after the putative death of Hillmon had been announced, he was attempting to foreclose a mortgage his bank held on some of Levi Baldwin's property. Baldwin, Crew said, asked him to forebear briefly, saying that he would soon come into $10,000 of the Hillmon life insurance policy proceeds. But when the insurance companies refused to pay, Crew moved forward and foreclosed on the property.[24]

If such an arrangement between Hillmon and Baldwin accounted for the purchase of the insurance policies, the two men would have been guilty of a certain amount of misrepresentation, but not the murderous fraud imputed to them by the companies. It occurred to me, however, that the question of whether Sallie's sudden accession to wealth would benefit Levi would have to depend on the relationship between them, and of that I was able to discover very little.

3

THE HILLMON CASE
IS TRIED BEFORE A JURY

1882

LEAVENWORTH TIMES, JUNE 13, 1882 | THE HILLMON CASES
These celebrated insurance cases will be called up to-morrow, and if they proceed to trial, which it is almost certain they will, they will occupy all of two weeks with night sessions as almost a certainty. It is calculated that it will take almost a week to read the depositions, beside the testimony to be taken. It was stated yesterday that during the course of the trial Judge Foster would hold night session from 7 to 11 o'clock each night. Pity the judge, the jury, the lawyers, the spectators, and the—newspaper man.

† † †

Sallie thinks she has acquired some patience over the last two years, a quality she now sees she had not properly valued in her youth, but even so she finds the waiting difficult, as well as the continual announcements and predictions about when matters will occur in the court-house, not one of which has been accurate so far. She and Borgalthaus have prepared the document (it is an affidavit, a piece of vocabulary she would never have acquired but for this court case) to persuade the judge, Foster is his name, to permit her to go forward with her suits (or suit, for already he has ruled that they must be united into a single case) without the need for posting a bond, which means merely a sum of money deposited with the court, which sum she cannot command. Sallie has noticed in recent months that her speech and even her thoughts have begun to employ the serpentine rhythms of the law and make use of its mysterious terms, and she rather likes this discovery. She sometimes thinks it a pity that women are not permitted to be lawyers, a rule the United States Supreme Court not long ago affirmed as a fair one—a decision Sallie has read and about which she has some doubts, though remaining quite certain that it is important, as the Court said, for married women to give their highest loyalty to their husbands and families. She is in any event sure that a woman's lot would not be pleasant among the pestering and overbearing fellows who overpopulate this stately building and pollute its grandeur with their harsh conversations and sudden barking laughter, but notes however that waitressing also had its distasteful aspects. She examines these last thoughts and finds evidence of the same tendency previously noted, then exhales deeply to calm her mind, and attempts to ignore those who frankly scrutinize her as she sits on the bench and waits for Mr. Wheat to summon her for the moment when he will read the affidavit to Judge Foster and they will learn whether matters must end here, or go forward to trial.

Mr. Wheat finally appears and says that the judge has called their case. The courtly lawyer ushers her into the courtroom, a chamber of such great size that she is momentarily taken aback. But Wheat gestures that she should walk toward a seat behind the rail, between him and her new lawyer Samuel Riggs. "Call the case of Sallie E. Hillmon versus the Mutual Life Insurance Company et al.," pronounces Judge Foster, and Sallie crosses the barrier and takes a seat before the bar, with her lawyers on either side, and she smiles but only to herself, and thinks, Now it begins.

Levi Baldwin paces to and fro in the vestibule of the courtroom, waiting for the bailiff to step out and call his name. Mr. Riggs has asked that the judge require the witnesses apart from the parties to wait outside the courtroom until they are ready to be sworn, a questionable and exasperating decision about which Levi was not consulted, and the judge has obligingly made this order. Levi will be having words with

Riggs at the end of the day, but until then he must endure. Most of the other witnesses have been sent to wait in a room across the hall, but the rancher has a distaste for sitting. He sees that one other witness has also deserted the witness room—John Brown, who stands in a corner, leaning against the wall. Baldwin knows they may not converse today, as this, too, is one of the strictures the judge has imposed on the witnesses, but he notes with approval Brown's respectable jacket and clean-shaven face. Perhaps his transaction with the fellow two weeks ago was successful after all.

The prohibitions on his behavior annoy Levi a great deal. He is not an ordinary witness; it is not as though he has no stake in this matter. He recalls every detail of his last conversation with John Hillmon.

"It's a pretty good investment, Levi," his old friend had said. "What with the cold and the Indians, nobody could be very surprised if I didn't come back."

"Not to mention what with the marksmanship of John Brown," added Levi, and both men had laughed.

"I'm in your debt," said Hillmon. "That has to be acknowledged. And not just for the premiums, but for all the rest."

"I'm not worried," Levi said. "I know you're good for it."

"Just as long as Sallie is taken care of."

"Goes without saying."

Hillmon had then directed a harder look his way. "But we're saying it. If I don't return, the greater part is to be hers."

"Course. Be careful, John."

"Good-bye then," said Hillmon, and they had shaken hands. Briefly each man tried for the stronger grip, but they quit the effort simultaneously. They had known each other too long for that.

Dean James Woods Green surveys the courtroom with satisfaction. Perhaps an ignorant observer would think that he had little cause for comfort in the proceedings thus far. Judge Foster seems inclined to permit Sallie Hillmon to proceed without posting a bond, as she has pleaded poverty, and Green has also lost his objection to consolidating the three cases. But the Dean is undismayed; these rulings have gone as he expected, and will be held in reserve as claimed errors on which to base an appeal—in the unlikely event this jury is persuaded by the

Hillmon woman's implausible case. He is well pleased with this jury, twelve solid fellows. All white, goes without saying. He does not think they will fall for sentimental appeals to the sorrows of widowhood, but if so, well, he has his own widow (or as good as) to display to them. Not in person, for Alvina Kasten has made clear her disinclination to travel to Kansas and appear as a witness; but they have her deposition for the jury to read, and when it comes time to argue, he believes he can conjure the bereaved fiancée up with words about as well as any man might, and better than most.

He is watching the judge for signs of partiality, but has seen none so far.

Sallie Hillmon sits with her lawyers, Samuel Riggs and Lysander B. Wheat, and some others who come and go and whose names are not yet familiar to her. She watches as the jurors are questioned and seated, one by one, and assays each with her waitress's eye as their number grows toward twelve (or thirteen, she corrects herself, for the judge has said there is to be an alternate). She cannot think that on the whole they would be very generous in calculating a tip, and one or two seem the sort who might complain of the fare, but she believes none of the men would attempt to exit through the window in order to avoid settling his bill. What these estimates might portend for their verdict she has no idea, but surely Messrs. Wheat and Riggs know some method for arriving at the judgments they are required to make, for they seem to be permitted to exclude some candidates simply by indicating their disapproval. She senses that the number of such opportunities is limited, for the lawyers confer quietly but with great intensity before making any such indication.

At length the jury is seated and the judge has administered an oath to them, requiring them to well and truly try the matter. Mr. Wheat and then Mr. Green make brief speeches (Green merely saying, in a cagey but flowery way, that the jurors should wait until they have heard all the evidence before making up their minds). When these are concluded and Wheat has been instructed to call his first witness Sallie smooths her skirt with her hands, but Wheat stands and says, "Plaintiff will call E.B. Borgalthaus, Your Honor." Really, Sallie will never understand the law, and why this attorney of very small involvement in the matter should testify before she does. But presently she sees that this was a very good plan, for after taking the oath Borgalthaus is able to explain how the inquest in Lawrence was all bought and paid for by the insurance companies, and relates how he was not permitted to make objections or question witnesses, and best of all makes a point of letting the jurors know that it was Mr. Green, who now sits before them, who was County Attorney during those days and who along with Mr. Geo. Barker piously pretended that their only interest in the matter was that of the County, a lie so large and brazen that Sallie is certain that every juror must be shocked to hear it, although they do not seem to be near so scandalized as they ought to be judging from their casual postures. Green seems altogether unembarrassed. She believes she sees him actually wink at one of the jurors, although the man does not appear to take note of it. He asks no questions of Mr. Borgalthaus on cross-examination.

The courtroom door opens and the bailiff beckons to Levi. "You are summoned, sir."[1]

From time to time I returned to my list of the implausibilities of Sallie Hillmon's claims. Concerning Brown's account of his accidental shooting of Hillmon, I had difficulty formulating a research method. I knew from the newspaper accounts that the weapon was a Sharps rifle, and learned that this particular gun had been important in the history of Kansas. These firearms became known as "Beecher's Bibles" after the famed abolitionist Henry Ward Beecher opined in a news article that there was more moral power in such a gun than in a hundred Bibles, since "you might just as well . . . read the Bible to Buffaloes as to those [proslavery] fellows . . . but they have a supreme respect for the logic that is embodied in Sharp's rifle." The rifles were shipped from New England to abolitionist settlers of prewar Kansas in large numbers, perhaps nine hundred to one thousand all told, and often packed in crates marked "Books"—or "Bibles."[2]

But none of this interesting information aided in evaluating the claim that the firing mechanism of Hillmon and Brown's Sharps rifle had caught on a blanket as Brown removed the rifle from their wagon, and discharged its round into Hillmon's head as he tended the fire. Or at least, that some part of the gun had—but it would have to be the trigger, wouldn't it? My ignorance of firearms was nearly total.

I found pictures of the Sharps rifle at various websites, and saw one displayed behind glass at the Kansas State Historical Society. The trigger curved comma-like inside a semi-elliptical metal guard; it looked to me as though it would not be very easy for the trigger to catch accidentally on an external object—not impossible, but not likely either. Such an accident would have to be, I thought, freakish. I understood why the insurance companies had been skeptical of Brown's account.

Then in early 2006 I was lucky enough to strike up an e-mail correspondence with Jerry Ferrin, a gifted amateur historian—amateur in the best sense—who maintains a historical website about Barber (in the nineteenth century called Barbour) County, Kansas, location of Medicine Lodge and Crooked Creek. Actually it was Jerry who did the striking—he wrote after reading a newspaper account of the impending exhumation in Lawrence. He sent me enormous amounts of helpful information, but some of the most useful pertained to accidental shootings in and around Medicine Lodge. In one message he wrote, "It seems that being killed by a gun, esp. a shotgun, being accidently fired was generally accepted as a plausible explanation for a death in earlier days, tho' . . . there was suspicion if a third party was involved. I know little to nothing about firearms, but it's notable that so many of the anecdotes . . . refer to the hammer getting caught on something and causing the firearm to discharge."

Later Jerry collected at his website a large number of accounts of accidental shooting; quite a few described firearms accidents resulting from a gun's transportation in a wagon or conveyance. Two in particular struck me.

THE MEDICINE LODGE CHIEF, SEPTEMBER 9, 1887

Died: A young man named Harrison Jones, 20 years old, living six or seven miles northwest of town on the Walker farm, while hunting plover on last Saturday week, was accidentally shot and died on Thursday of last week. It seems that he was in a wagon with a friend or two and standing behind the spring seat, with the breech of the gun resting on the way box, the seat struck the lock, discharging the contents of the gun into his right breast, inflicting a terrible wound. No blame seemingly can be attached to anyone, unless it would be carelessness on the part of the young man in carrying a loaded gun in such a position.

THE MEDICINE LODGE HERALD, DECEMBER 27, 1890

Died: A Fatal Accident—A very sad and distressing accident, which resulted in the death of Mr. Frank Robinson, of Hazelton, Barber county, occurred near that city Friday evening last. From residents of the immediate locality, the Herald's correspondent learns that Mr. F.S. Smith and the deceased were out hunting and while riding together in a road cart, approached the residence of Mr. James O'Connell, with whom they stopped and exchanged the civilities of the day. The deceased's gun was resting on the slats of the cart with the muzzle resting against his shoulder. After leaving Mr. O'Connell's, they had proceeded but a few paces when the cart gave a sudden lurch, by which the gun was thrown forward and coming in contact with some hard substance. Its contents were discharged into the deceased's side, ranging upward. Upon hearing the report, and before realizing that he had been shot, Mr. Robinson jumped from the vehicle and after reaching the ground, clasped his hands to his breast and exclaimed, "My God, see what I have done," and instantly expired.[3]

Had I been too skeptical about the story that John Brown had told? I would have to learn more about Sharps rifles, if I could. I found entries in various encyclopedias, but they used terms unfamiliar to the firearms-averse (falling block action? pelleted primers?) and I knew I required some expert assistance. Even Ben, who was a Marine Corps sharpshooter, found the technical language daunting; he suggested we visit a gun store for advice. So it was that the next weekend we found ourselves at Gunsport in Boulder.

The store was busy with customers buying ammunition and inspecting the assorted weapons. But Steve, a long-haired guy who identified himself as the shop's gunsmith, was lunching on a large sandwich when we arrived, and he was willing to talk to us while he ate.

After I explained my errand, he got interested and showed me a couple of Sharps from the shop's inventory. "What model was the one in that case of yours?" he asked.

"There's more than one model?"

"Dozens," he said. I couldn't remember ever reading anything about the particular model of Hillmon's rifle. Between bites, Steve pointed out the difference between an internal-hammer and external-hammer mechanism, and then slid the external hammer on one of the Sharps weapons to the cocked position. "If this hammer were to fall forward, it could cause the weapon to discharge," he advised.

"You mean even without pulling the trigger?"

He nodded. "But, you know, it probably wouldn't happen. The hammer shouldn't move even if it's bumped." To illustrate, he banged the weapon lightly against the rack from which he had removed it.

The hammer dislodged itself and flew forward, and the gun issued an authoritative report. The rifle wasn't loaded, of course, so no bullet flew out. I believe what it did is called a "dry fire." Even so, the bang was enough to cause most of the customers in the store to turn and look.

"Hmm." Steve put his sandwich down to examine the gun with both hands. "That shouldn't have happened."

† † †

OAK HILL CEMETERY | LAWRENCE, KANSAS | MAY 19, 2006

The digging crew consists of Dennis, Ben, Dennis's graduate student Paul Sandberg, and Sarah Garner, a University of Kansas student who has volunteered to help us. They work with shovels for a couple of hours, as the sun and the temperature climb. Soon they are all filthy, and even at some distance from the excavation I have acquired a film of mud as the flying dirt hits my perspiring skin.

There is a little joking—Ben reminds everyone that when measuring the depth of the excavation they should avoid saying things like "That's a foot" in favor of the less alarming "That's twelve inches"—but on the whole it is surprisingly quiet. Ernesto and his film crew move around the site with their mics and cameras, and several television and newspaper crew circle the site as well, although the latter are mercilessly shushed and kept about twenty-five feet away by enforcers of the City of Lawrence's plan for managing the media. Some foresighted journalist has brought what looks like an eight-foot ladder, and every so often a photographer will climb to the top of it for a shot into the excavation.

At about 8:45 Dennis pauses and says, "I'm afraid of the shovel from here on in." He is worried about the fragility of the remains, and so the shovels are exchanged for trowels. Time expands and contracts at random as the work proceeds without much by way of punctuation. Sometimes when I check my watch I am surprised at how much time has passed, other times shocked by how little.

At 11:20 Paul's fingers find a coffin nail, and we are all cheered momentarily by the idea that the crew must be getting close to the skeleton. But the nail cannot tell us anything about which guy has been occupying the coffin, of course, and after this first discovery long minutes drag on without any more findings. The soil grows wetter and stickier as the diggers burrow down, until at about four feet below ground they encounter liquid water, an underground spring of the sort Mitch, the cemetery superintendent, had warned us about. It quickly forms a pool in the bottom of the excavation, like a vat of nasty chocolate milk. This is very bad news, I know, as Dennis has warned me that water is the enemy of preservation when it comes to human remains. It must be my discouraged mental state that induces the illusion that near silence has fallen on the cemetery; activity continues, but none of it seems to generate any sound. I can discern only an occasional faint oath emanating from the hole, as Dennis quietly and repeatedly takes the name of sexual intercourse in vain.

The crew continues to dig, those at the bottom of the pit handing out buckets of sloppy muck to be emptied. But an undeniable steamy gloom has blanketed the proceedings. The sun has grown very hot, and the breeze has died; even nearly motionless in the shade I am sweating by the quart, and small midwestern bugs are discovering the backs of my knees. I know the diggers must be growing exhausted and dehydrated. I catch a glimpse of Dennis sitting down inside the grave, looking dejected and dazed. Mud smears his face and shirt, and coats the expensive watch that he did not remove before climbing into the ground. He motions me over to the lip of the excavation.

"There's not going to be any skull," he says, his voice hoarse. "I could feel it from the inside, and then it just dissolved against my fingers. I'm sorry, buddy. It's the bastard water."

"It's okay, partner," I reassure him, but I have no idea whether this is true. It's all down to the DNA, I think, if they can even find anything to extract it from. Maybe the water has dissolved all of the bones. I peer into the pit and see that the water is actually moving, flowing slowly into the excavation.

"Yeah," says Dennis. "We've damn near got current in here."

Although I believe I have prepared myself for the possibility that we will learn nothing, a wave of disappointment crashes over me. I sink onto the ground, leaning my back against someone's headstone and considering how things will go from here. Can this exhumation enterprise be redeemed somehow, or have we disturbed someone's final repose for nothing?

The hole is deep enough by now that I cannot see, from my seat on the grass, anything that might be going on inside. Flushed and gritty, eyes stinging from the drops of sweat that have meandered down from my scalp, I sink into a state of torpid despair that seems likely to persist for eternity.

At 12:34, Dennis says something from the bottom of the excavation; even sitting ten feet away I can hear excitement in his voice. I jump up and run to the side of the hole, where Ben crouches looking in. From the media area I hear the shutters of a dozen cameras nicking like a flight of grasshoppers. "What did he say?" I demand of Ben. "What?"

Ben turns his head toward me, sweat dripping from his hatband onto his shirt. "It's a bone," he says, grinning. "He said it's a bone."

Dennis and Paul are examining a gritty piece of matter that looks like a twig. "Yup, it's bone," I hear Paul say, Paul being one of the calmest guys I have ever met, and that's when I know that we are not going home empty-handed.

The bones keep coming after that, and then some teeth. Paul and Dennis hand them out to Sarah Garner, who bags them after gently wiping some of the mud off. By 2:15, there are about twenty of them, and a couple of teeth. There is also an acrid odor near the pit, where Dennis continues to lie on his belly, his face nearly in the murky water.

Once when he raises his head for a moment to hand out a fragment of bone, I see a miasmic cloud rising from the surface of the liquid.

"What's *that*?"

Nobody answers. I am still crouched over the excavation watching the diggers hand their small treasures out to Sarah when the City's press officer beckons me. I leave the hole and walk over to where she stands in the shade.

"Time to leave for the press conference," she says. The City has exacted a promise that we will hold a news conference at three on the University of Kansas campus, a measure designed to lure the press contingent away from Oak Hill Cemetery. I wish desperately that we had not made this agreement. For one thing, I have to be the filthiest, sweatiest person to ever appear in the history of press conferences. For another, I am worried about that smoky cloud coming out of the excavation. But the main source of my reluctance to leave the cemetery is that Leray and Sandra Hillmon have not yet shown up.

It is pure good luck that I am in touch with Leray Hillmon at all. The genealogist I hired to trace the ancestry of both John Hillmon and Frederick Adolph Walters did not find Leray's branch of the Hillmon family. Until about a month before the exhumation, I had believed that John Hillmon's family had no living male descendants. This negative finding by the genealogist had been a serious disappointment, even though we had discovered a living male descendant in Frederick Adolph Walters's family. In fact we had been in touch with the man, Dan Davis of Spokane, Washington, and he had been kind enough not only to give us written consent to the exhumation, but also to supply Dennis with a sample of his DNA, a swirl of his spit in a cup of preservative that he had shipped to us weeks earlier. He was sorry that he would not be able to attend the disinterment, he had written me; he was ninety-one and did not travel much anymore.

Dan Davis's generosity was welcome, but his DNA sample was unlikely to help us identify the remains. Davis was born into a mixed male–female line of descent from F.A. Walters's brother C.R. Walters, who was Dan Davis's maternal grandfather. Accordingly, Dennis had instructed me, there was no possibility that Davis's DNA and that of Frederick Adolph Walters would exhibit any identical chromosomes. If Davis had been in a straight male line of descent, then his Y chromosome and Walters's would be identical, meaning that his Y would match the body's if and only if the body belonged to Walters (or another male descendant from the same family, a possibility that could safely be ruled out). This configuration might have produced an elegant and certain solution to our problem, but the mixture of male and female in Davis's bloodlines as they reached back to the Iowa cigarmaker left it out of reach.

I remember being crestfallen when Dennis explained this. "So with no male ancestors on the Hillmon side, and only Dan Davis on the Walters side, does it even make sense to try to do a DNA analysis?" I had asked him. "It's not like we've found a hairbrush or a bloodstain that belonged to Walters or Hillmon. Dan Davis is all we have."

Dennis said that the DNA work would not be pointless, because there was a small and unpredictable possibility that some unusual genetic sequence would be found in both Dan Davis's DNA and in the corpse's. "If that happens, we'll know to some degree of likelihood that the body is Walters," he told me.

"But if there's no such resemblance, that tells us nothing one way or the other?" I asked.

"Right."

"And even if the corpse belongs to Walters, the chance of finding that sort of a match is small."

"Also right." He must have seen my look of dismay. "Don't worry, partner. I don't like this DNA stuff anyway; I'm going for the old-fashioned evidence. We're going to lift that skull right out of the ground, and I'm going to show you how to make it look like the guy who once lived in it. And then we compare it to the pictures we have."

"Okay," I had said. "I like that."

But now, watching the tiny shards of bone that Dennis and the crew are pulling delicately from the muck, I know that nobody is going to be reconstructing a skull from the remains in this grave. Still, I do not think that all is lost. In April 2006, with the exhumation scheduled for less than a month away, I had found this message awaiting my attention in my e-mail inbox:

I'm writing you at the suggestion of Kim Fowles. Kim saw my genealogy chart on ancestry.com and saw that we have a John Wesley Hillman b. 1848 and she e-mailed me.

Since then we have made contact and she encouraged me to write you.

My husband's [Leray] father's father was George Benjamin Hillmon. Son of Benjamin and Louisa Hillman of Grasshopper Falls, KS.

The information I have shows that George Benj. Hillmon was 1/2 brother to John Wesley Hillman (Hillmon).

This summer's project was to locate descendants of Benjamin and Elizabeth Hillman, to see if they had any ancestry information.

From reading your information on the John W. Hillman case, it appears that it would be fruitless to pursue.

I understand that you have received permission to exhume the body of "John W."

We would like to be kept informed as to when this would take place as it might be possible to arrange to be present.[4]

I had read this missive three times, my hands unsteady, and then printed it. I pulled out a blank sheet of paper and diagrammed Leray Hillmon's genealogy, as described by Sandra. Then I reached for the phone to call Dennis's office. I had my mouth all set to leave a message, but he picked up right away and I was momentarily befuddled, unprepared for the opportunity to talk to a real person.

"Oh, Dennis. Oh. I didn't think you'd be there."

"Yeah, well you were wrong. I'm here. What's up?"

"Um. Tell me this, buddy. If John Hillmon's father had a son who had a son who had a son, would that last guy have the same Y chromosome as John Hillmon?"

"Say it again," said Dennis, and I could tell he was drawing it, too, at his end. I repeated my question, and there was a long pause.

"Tell me that this is not what you lawyers call a hypothetical question," Dennis had said finally. "Do we have our Y's?"

"I think so. The DNA might solve our case after all."

Leray and Sandra are the proprietors of a mom-and-pop trucking business. They own their own gleaming rig, and work the Internet assiduously from their home in Montana, strategizing a schedule of pickups and deliveries that will allow them to make a living at a time when the price of fuel eats hungrily into a trucker's profits. They had managed to put together a route that had them dropping off a load in Kentucky and would allow them, if all went well, to be in Lawrence for the disinterment of the grave that was registered to Leray's great-uncle John Wesley Hillmon. But they have missed the morning's events because they are driving around Lawrence trying to find a place to leave the rig. I've been in touch with them by cell phone during the morning and know they are nearby, but I am too unfamiliar with Lawrence to give them much helpful advice about the parking issue. The last couple of times I've tried to call, nobody has answered; I am worried they have given up and headed back to Montana. With the possibility of skull reconstruction gone, I know that Leray's DNA offers nearly our only hope for an identification. I hate for the Hillmons to miss the day's events, but there is more to it than that. I need some of Leray's spit—badly.

I nod to the press officer and then go over to speak to Ben at the side of the grave. "If the Hillmons arrive," I tell him, "ask them to go to the University Center. I know the press will want to meet him."

"Okay," he says, "but they may not show up—don't wait for them."

I learn later that eventually Leray and Sandra had found the local Wal-Mart and parked the semitrailer and cab in the shade at the end of the store's massive parking lot, ensuring that the two dachshunds that travel with them would be able to stay cool. Then they had hitched a ride to the University of Kansas, and found the room where the press conference was to be held, just as it began.

I am checking out the microphones at the podium table and trying not to drop too much grimy sweat on the white paper tablecloth beneath them, when I look up to see a couple arriving through the double doors across the room. I don't need to be told who they are. Leray Hillmon, a tall handsome white-haired man, is a ringer for his great-uncle. We barely have time for introductions before the City's press officer calls the conference to order.

"Come on up to the podium with me," I urge Leray. "They'll want to meet you." It doesn't seem right to present him with the spit cup right then; we have barely met. Most of the journalists in attendance have followed the story for months and know quite a bit about it, so not much needs to be said by way of preliminaries. I tell only a little of the backstory before describing the remains that have been located so far, emphasizing that the work is still in progress as we speak. The press officer frowns at me; I know she doesn't want me to encourage anyone to race back to the cemetery after the conference. I introduce Leray and explain who he is, then ask for questions. Charlie Brennan from the *Rocky Mountain News*, who has written about the story from the beginning, asks if there are any findings from the work so far.

"Only from the teeth," I say. "Dennis showed me that the teeth he found so far don't seem to have any roots, or almost none. That suggests they came from a younger person."

"Which man is younger?" asks somebody.

"Walters," I confess. "Walters was twenty-four when the death occurred. Hillmon was thirty-one."

"That means it's probably him instead of Hillmon."

"Maybe," I say. "We'll have to wait for the final results." But I know these findings are not promising for the theory that the corpse is John Hillmon's after all, and I find this prospect curiously dismaying. I'm not really ready to think out loud about it. "Perhaps you all have some questions for Mr. Hillmon," I suggest.

A brief general silence ensues as the press corps tries to think of a question to ask John Hillmon's great-nephew. Finally one fellow speaks up.

"What do you think of the possibility that your ancestor was a fraud and a murderer?"

Jesus, I think. What a rude jerk. But Leray is more than equal to the moment.

"I don't know about that," he says quietly. "I understand that remains an open question. But in any event, it's got nothing to do with who I am. It's interesting, but I'm myself, Leray Hillmon. An honest man."

† † †

Sallie writes a few reminders on the foolscap that Mr. Riggs has given her for making notes. Her cousin Levi is the next witness and as usual acquits himself well. After he gives his familiar account of his part in the matter Wheat asks him a curious question: Did he ever ask a woman named Mrs. Carr not to say anything about Hillmon's teeth? Levi acknowledges that he is acquainted with the lady, who is a neighbor of his, but looks puzzled about the remainder of the question and says that he did not. Sallie understands immediately that Wheat has learned that Mrs. Carr—a lady with whom Sallie is acquainted, and with whom she has exchanged a few pleasant words earlier in the vestibule—will come to court later and testify otherwise. No doubt she will say as well that John's teeth were rotten or some such rubbish. Levi says that he never measured John Hillmon but that Hillmon was the taller of the two, and Levi claims for himself five feet nine inches. And he tells the jurors that the corpse, when it reached Lawrence, had its shirtsleeves torn open to reveal a smallpox vaccination scar on the arm. Sallie observes that several of the jurors appear to be most interested in this detail, and she writes this down as well, in case Mr. Wheat has not noticed.

Arthur Judson is next, and at first Sallie cannot believe that any juror could find it in his heart to disbelieve her landlord, whose white head nods as he answers Wheat's questions. He explains how Sallie asked him to go to the depot to meet the train that was bringing the body, and to convey it back to the house, but some man he did not know was there and directed that the body be taken instead to Bailey and Smith's. He looks directly at the jurymen when he says that he saw the body twice and has no doubt that it belonged to his boarder. Sallie can tell that Wheat has practiced these answers with Arthur and judges that he has taken his instruction well, but mightn't some of the jurors think this fluent recital a bit suspicious? She starts to make another note, but as she writes Arthur says something that stills her fingers: he swears that one evening during the winter before Hillmon left, the Hillmons and the Judsons measured one another for entertainment, and that the marks of their stature remain on his bedroom door frame. All three of the others measured John, says Arthur, and made the mark in the same spot. Then Arthur says that he recently remembered this event because Sallie asked him about it. He had until then forgotten about it, he says, which is why he did not mention it at the inquest. When he went back to measure John Hillmon's mark, he found it was five feet eleven inches above the floor.

Sallie's fingers are quite frozen now, although her face feels danger-ously warm. She gazes down, certain some of the jurors are looking at her. She does not remember any evening of playful measurement, and she certainly did not recently say anything to Arthur Judson about such a thing. Sallie thinks this testimony a most unpleasant surprise. Arthur is now saying, quite truthfully, that John's teeth were as sound as those of any other man, and Sallie trusts herself enough to raise her head. Nobody is watching her; all eyes are on her landlord. She does not know what the proper thing to do might be, but then Mr. Wheat, seated next to her, presses her hand with kindness and whispers to ask if she is quite well, and she understands that this sort of thing must be part of the law's halting journey toward justice, and that she must come to accept it in silence if she is to be victorious over the old men who would deny her the money to which she is, for all of her worry and suffering, entitled.

Just before he is permitted to leave the witness chair, Arthur is shown a photograph: one of the pictures of John that she had attached to her complaint so many months before when she took it to the courthouse and asked the clerk to file it.

"Yes," he says. "That is my friend John Hillmon." And this is so absolutely true and indisputable that the tears sting Sallie's eyes. She must drop her head again, this time to allow the salty drops to fall unhindered onto her paper where they dissolve the inked letters of her last line of notes into unreadable ciphers.[5]

For photographs to be received in evidence in the Hillmon case, they had to be admissible according to the rules of evidence. For a time after the invention of photography in the mid-nineteenth century, American courts of law struggled to decide whether this new form of evidence should be allowed at all, for there was little precedent to guide them. The rules of evidence were at the time nowhere written in the form of an integrated set of commands and prohibitions, as they are now; they were rather to be found in the decisions of the various courts of the states, and in the federal courts. It was possible for the law of evidence to differ from state to state, and in some particulars it did, although there was a drive toward uniformity; and of course the lower courts were subject to having their decisions overruled by the higher ones. It was thus not always easy to discover or predict how a particular court would treat photographic evidence. But courts have always been inherently cautious in their embrace of the probative uses of new technologies, as they were a century after *Hillmon* in their halting recognition of the admissibility of DNA evidence. "The law of the land is a wary old fox," wrote one scholar of photographic evidence in 1879, "and scrutinizes a new invention a long time before extending a paw to appropriate it."[6]

All federal judges, including those who presided over the Hillmon trials, had to take their cues concerning the law of evidence from the United States Supreme Court, and that Court had suggested twenty years before the Hillmon disappearance that photographs were useful, especially facsimiles of documents that enabled the comparison of genuine and disputed signatures and the like. The Court had even referred to photography as "the beautiful art." But some legal observers remained dubious: was not a photograph a form of hearsay, a claim made by an inanimate object (which could of course not be cross-examined) that something that had appeared before it looked *thus*? "[H]earsay of the sun," one skeptical opponent dubbed photographic evidence. This argument was not altogether implausible, but did not usually prevail. A widely read article published in 1869 observed that photography "differs from hearsay . . . in one essential particular; it is wholly free from the infirmity which causes the rejection of hearsay evidence, namely, the uncertainty whether or not it is an exact repetition of what was said. . . . In the picture we have before us, at the trial, precisely what the apparatus did say."[7]

Probably most lawyers and judges of the time, never having heard of Adobe Photoshop, would have nodded in agreement with this proposition. Soon the view that photographs are not hearsay won the day. In 1871, for example, a New York judge affirmed the murder conviction of a man named Edward Ruloff, which had been based partly on witness identifications of photographs that had been taken of Ruloff's accomplices' corpses. The judge in that case remarked that one might as well "deny the use of the compass to the surveyor or the mariner" as rule out the use of photographs as evidence. Later decisions were in accord, and when the Federal Rules of Evidence were adopted more than a century later, their definition of hearsay as an out-of-court statement made by a "person" reflected this victorious view: a camera not being a "person," photographs are not hearsay.[8]

The only precondition to the admissibility of a photograph in today's courts is the testimony of some witness, not necessarily the photographer, that the photograph "fairly and adequately depicts" some relevant scene or object that the witness once saw. This foundation will even be adequate if the photograph has been retouched or manipulated, so long as the essential accuracy of the image is not damaged. The photographer Lamon admitted that his photographs of the corpse "may have been touched up a little to bring out imperfections in the negative." But nobody seems to have objected to the coffin photos based on this confession. Retouching in the darkroom, however at odds with the idea of photography as a transparent depiction of the truth, was not uncommon; one historian says that the practice is "almost as old as photography itself." Apparently aware that the trend in the courts was to approve of the admissibility of photographs, the lawyers on both sides of the Hillmon litigation seem to have acquiesced in the admission of all those offered in evidence—the two of the corpse in its coffin, and the several of Hillmon and Walters while alive. There was thus not much quarrel over the admissibility of the various photographs offered into evidence in the Hillmon case, but naturally much debate about what precisely they proved.[9]

I have shown the photographs to many audiences, and opinion has been divided on which man the corpse more resembles. Even though our judgments may differ on this point, however, all contemporary viewers share the experience of having seen thousands, probably millions, of photographic images during our lives. But reproduced images were far more of a novelty in the nineteenth century, and in 1882 in a frontier town they would still have carried a sort of magic or mystery about them. Is it possible for us to imagine how those seventy-two jurors and unnumbered bystanders may have seen and interpreted the photographs that played a role in the Hillmon trials?

The principal purpose of the photographic evidence in the Hillmon trials was to facilitate comparisons between the appearance of the corpse and that of the two men. But the belief that character could be read in a face was deeply cherished in the late nineteenth century; one scholar had asserted in 1869 that a photograph of a person is "direct and original evidence *of the kind of man he was.*" Another wrote that photography ensures "that men shall ultimately be known for what they are. In vain do the profligate, the base, the wicked, and the selfish mimic those outward indications which pertain naturally to the pure, the good, and the generous." If these beliefs prevailed, I thought it likely that the jurors (and the spectators, or some of them) had scrutinized the images of John Hillmon and Frederick Adolph Walters for evidence of other truths as well, truths about the qualities of the two men in life. What had they seen?[10]

On the question of identity, each side of the Hillmon controversy claimed the photographs as proof of its claims, by promoting comparisons between the coffin photographs and the living men. These comparisons were of two sorts. Many persons who had known one man or the other while alive testified that the coffin photographs were (or were not) of the man the witness had known. And the jurors were allowed to form their own opinions, by direct examination of the coffin pictures alongside portraits of the two men.

There is reason to doubt that the identifications made by witnesses who knew one man or the other could be relied on, for expectation and sorrow play a large role in any such matter. An influential nineteenth-century American treatise on "medical jurisprudence" recounts the case in which the body of an unidentified man was found in the cupboard of an English house. The discovery having been publicized, the house was swarmed by "a crowd of persons, most of them bringing photographs . . . to see if the features corresponded with those of missing friends." Numbers of such witnesses claimed to see in the body the corporeal remains of their friends, although they were by no means all the same friend. The *London Spectator* remarked that the case illustrated "the uncertainty of all human testimony on questions of personal identity."[11]

The chief identification evidence of the defendants consisted of the claims of several witnesses who had seen the corpse photos that they recognized in them their friend Frederick Adolph Walters. The insurance companies did in addition call many acquaintances of John Hillmon's to say that the dead man was not Hillmon; most of these witnesses had actually seen the body, while it rested (if that is the word for such an over-scheduled cadaver) in the Bailey and Smith's undertaking establishment. But accusations that many of the companies' witnesses had been "bought" seethed barely below the surface in all the trials and sometimes emerged explicitly, to be made or indignantly denied in the lawyers' summations.

Mrs. Hillmon's side, although they presented a few witnesses who had seen the body and said it was Hillmon's, emphasized a different sort of evidence. Her lawyers suggested that the jurors would do better to ignore all testimony on the question of identification, and instead decide for themselves: they urged the jurors to examine each of the photographs, and consider on that basis which man more resembled the corpse. They asked the jurors to note, for example, that it was a "fact" that Walters's temples were absolutely bare, while those of Hillmon were shown by the photographs to have hair corresponding to that on the cadaver's. They argued that the postmortem notes of the surgeons who autopsied the body at Bailey and Smith's documented that the eyebrows of the corpse met over the nose, a "peculiarity very striking in the picture of Hillmon, the reverse being equally striking in the picture of Walters."[12]

The defendants' lawyers were scornful of this sort of argument, probably because their identification witnesses greatly outnumbered the plaintiff's and they did not want to yield any advantage this preponderance might supply. Yet they felt they must meet the plaintiff's case on this ground as well, and so Green argued in the fourth trial that a comparison of the three sets of pictures must support the conclusion that the dead man was Walters.

> Look at Hillmon's nose. See, how it runs straight into the forehead. How thin it is at the base of the frontal bone. Now look at the cadaver; see how the nose does not run straight into the forehead; how it arches off and runs into the eyebrows; how it shows a half circle, and look how thick the nose is where it joins the forehead as compared with the thinness of Hillmon's nose. . . . Look again at the photograph of Hillmon. How close the eyebrows come together over the nose. Now look at the photograph of Walters and the cadaver and you will find the distance in both of them is fully double the distance in that of Hillmon.[13]

None of these arguments rested on any scientific measurements or tests of the features displayed in the various photographs. Nor is there reason to think that any of the jurors brought a scientifically trained eye to the examination of the pictures.

I wondered what such an eye might detect. The first request I ever made of Dennis Van Gerven, two years before we gained permission to exhume the remains, was that he examine the photographs of both men and of the corpse. Here is what he wrote to me after he did so:

What we need to focus on are soft tissue features that overlie bone closely and are also distinctive of individuals. Two of these are relevant here. One is the shape (actually depth) of the nasal root and the other is the shape of the bony portion of the nasal bridge. The nasal root is that area of the base of the nose where the nasal bones articulate with the frontal bone of the skull. It is the area approximately between the eyes and typically flanked by and just below the upper margin of the eye orbits. It is also the area between the eye brows. The bony bridge of the nose is formed by the suture line of the left and right nasal bones as they extend outward and downward from nasal root until they meet the cartilage that forms the latter third or so of the nose. The union can be felt as the point where the nose along its bridge stops being stiff and becomes flexible. In short, these two features form an area that in life is near the surface with little overlying tissue. It is also an area that gives the face a distinctive recognizable quality that we tend to recognize. And the form in life conforms very closely to the form in death—that is on the skull.

It is not at all surprising to me that this area is addressed in the lawyer's arguments. Green argued "look at Hillman's nose. See, how it runs straight to the forehead. How thin it is at the base of the frontal bone." Green is directing the jury to the right place but I fail to see what he saw. Indeed I see the opposite. Hillman's nasal root forms a deep saddle and the nasal bones are strongly elevated above that saddle as they form the bridge of the nose. This gives Hillman's nose a strong so-called "beaky" appearance in profile. This is precisely the form seen on the corpse—particularly in profile. On the contrary, Walters' profile is quite different. There is no depressed nasal root to be seen. Indeed the nasal profile extends directly from the bridge of the nose to the juncture of the nasals and frontal bone with very little depression at the root. In other words the line of the nose in profile appears virtually straight from the bridge to the forehead.

So here I must disagree with Green but fortunately our dis-agreement can be resolved. We can find these features easily on the preserved skull and make a close and detailed comparison under controlled conditions with the surviving photos.

Dennis was suggesting that an examination of the skeleton would be the best method of investigation, and he was not the first. A few months earlier I had been asked to speak at a gathering of the Retired Faculty Association of the University of Colorado, and had told the fine minds assembled about my work in progress on the Hillmon case. The evidence I described to them comprised documents, old newspapers, and legal mate-rials; that was all I had. I told them that I had come to doubt the received wisdom of the case, that the body belonged to the cigarmaker. But I could not be sure, I said, and my research was ongoing. During the question and answer period, I recognized a small woman in the back row, and she rose to ask her question: why didn't I dig the body up and see whose it was?

I don't remember how I answered her. I was nonplussed by the ques-tion, for I had never considered a research method so far beyond my experience and capabilities. Like the woman with a hammer who sees every problem as a nail, I had assumed that the Hillmon mystery was susceptible only to such investigations as I knew how to carry out. But exhuming a body? How exactly was I going to accomplish that? I had no idea how one obtained permission to dig up a body, buried in a cem-etery, to which I had no family relationship. I doubted that it could be done; the world regards the disruption of a dead body's rest as a form of desecration, a grave robbery.

And even if I somehow succeeded in lawfully exhuming the remains, how would I know what to look for once they were out of the ground? Dennis's memo answered that question, at least: I would ask him to take charge from that moment. But would a court really allow us to dig up a grave to satisfy our historical curiosity? I was certain exhumation could be accomplished lawfully for some purpose related to law enforcement; surely I had read of such cases. But exhumation to solve a mystery more than a century old, because some academic was acquiring a dim sense that a piece of the law of evidence may have rested on certain mistaken assumptions about the solution? I asked my research assistant to look into the law of exhumation in Kansas.

Once his testimony is over, Levi is permitted to remain in the court-room, and the remainder of the day is taken up by the testimony of various good citizens of Medicine Lodge, most of them members of the inquest jury that the coroner of that city had convened within a day of the shooting. Several of those—the lawyer Harvey Davis, day laborer Clark Gillmore, clerk E.M. Byerly, and hotelkeeper Derrick Updegraff—swear that they were certain the dead man who lay before them during their deliberations was Hillmon. They could be so certain, they said, because they had met Hillmon and Brown when the pair had traveled through Medicine Lodge in December, on their first venture to look for land. The corpse, each man avers, was surely the same John Hillmon in whose company they had passed some time a few months earlier.

Hah! Levi thinks this is all very fine, and by the time Judge Foster gavels the court to adjournment he has forgotten his ire toward Samuel Riggs.[14]

Of course nobody knew that the first trial of the Hillmon case would one day be remembered as the first of several. No doubt everyone engaged in the matter, participant and onlooker, thought it would be the only trial. And in its general contours it originated the pattern that the others five would follow with some degree of fidelity, although each of the six trials had its novelties, omissions, and surprises.

As the trial progressed, another Hillmon friend named John Eldredge testified; he said he had recognized the corpse as Hillmon's, and that in life John Hillmon had been about five feet eleven inches tall. Then the oath was taken by the witness about whom all were most curious (or in the case of the parties, apprehensive): John Brown. The *Leavenworth Times* described him as "not a bad looking man," adding that "he has a brown moustache, several shades lighter than his hair, which is inclined to be black; is rather well-proportioned, and is plainly but neatly dressed in a dark suit." The reporter opined that Brown's testimony would be of great importance, "as it is alleged the last few days of the dead man's life was passed in his company, with no others about, not to consider that he freely avers having done the shooting."[15]

This would be John Brown's only live appearance as a trial witness in the Hillmon case. In the later trials, the parties would employ a transcript either of this testimony, or of Brown's pretrial deposition. The constant and vexed theme of John Brown's testimony would be, of course, the two very different accounts he had given of the shooting: the accident that he described at both inquests, versus the version narrated in the affidavit he had signed, saying that Hillmon had persuaded the hapless young man known as "Joe Berkely or Burgis" to join their party, and shot him to death at the campsite so that his body might be used to defraud the insurance companies. Since Sallie was the plaintiff, her lawyers called Brown to the stand first, and began by eliciting the familiar story of the accident. The newspaper's report, in its accustomed highly semicoloned style, made short work of the crucial moment in his direct testimony:

> when I went to the wagon to get the bedding the gun was there, with the breech on the bedclothes; the gun went off and shot Hillmon in the head; he was behind me, between me and the fire; when the gun went off I turned and grabbed at Hillmon, who was falling, to keep him from falling in the fire; he was falling when I caught him; as soon as I laid him down I rode after help; . . . [16]

But this account of the shooting formed a small portion of Brown's direct testimony, for Riggs and Wheat knew that on cross-examination their witness would be taxed with the alternative version found in the affidavit, which he had signed under oath. Hence they tried to blunt the effect of this anticipated cross-examination by eliciting from their witness, in vivid terms, the story of his pursuit by W.J. Buchan. He described, for the better part of a day on the stand, his efforts to resist the lawyer's blandishments and threats; he explained his eventual capitulation after Buchan appeared at his place of work with the sheriff's deputy and prompted Brown's own brother to suggest that he had better do as the Senator said. He testified that he had reluctantly signed the affidavit, and gone to the notary with Buchan for it to be attested, and that Buchan had told him that he (Buchan) would be "paid for it, and paid big" by the insurance companies. Brown also swore that he had been reassured by Buchan that the document's only purpose was to persuade Sallie Hillmon to relinquish her claims, and he told the jury of tearing the affidavit and throwing it into the fire when he saw that Sallie Hillmon was steadfast in maintaining that the dead man was her husband. "I don't know whether there was fire in the stove," he told them. "I don't know what became of the pieces of paper." It reads like a plaintive and convincing account, but when court adjourned for the afternoon, John Brown had yet to face the cross-examination of Mr. George Barker.[17]

Barker, the next day, took Brown back over the details of the affidavit, making sure to emphasize for the jurors the seeming coherence of the very different story that document told: the young man called Joe persuaded to join their journey, Hillmon playing on the fellow's credulity and persuading him to submit to a vaccination on the shoulder with the virus from the older man's arm, Brown's reluctance when he realized the plan (protesting that he "had not the grit" to carry it out), Hillmon's implacable determination. At every opportunity Brown answered that he had not told Buchan any such thing, that Buchan had invented the events in the affidavit. But to the reader a century later it seems that this cross-examination must have succeeded in portraying the affidavit's version of events as at least a plausible alternative to Brown's account on direct examination, and possibly the more convincing narrative altogether.

Then Barker turned to another incriminating document, a letter written in Brown's own hand: "Mrs. Hillmon: I would like to know where John is, and how that business is, and what I should do, if anything. Let me know through my father. Yours truly, John H. Brown."[18]

"Buchan told me what to write," was Brown's explanation. Barker suggested that the witness had waited quite a while before telling anyone that he had made a false statement, and Brown said he could not remember about that. The judge there gaveled the day's session to a close. The insurance companies' lawyers would have the evening for strategizing about how to conclude their cross-examination of John Brown.[19]

This was not their first chance to question Brown under oath. They had required him to sit for a deposition beginning on the last day of 1881, and it was no brief ordeal: it went on for so long that it encroached on Valentine's Day, 1882. Despite this protracted opportunity to recruit

Brown back to their cause, or at least to catch him in a contradiction, they had never managed to accomplish either. The affidavit (and, implicitly, the letter to Sallie Hillmon) represented the only written evidence the companies ever acquired in which Brown told the story they wanted the jury to believe.

Barker went back at John Brown the next morning with renewed energy (leavened, if the newspaper accounts convey the matter truly, with considerable indignation on Barker's part, genuine or simulated). But Brown did not back down, and before noon the defense had to let him go. They had several witnesses of their own, of course, but it was still the plaintiff's case in chief, and so after releasing John Brown from the stand they were compelled to listen to the testimony of his brother Reuben. And Reuben Brown, once their ally in achieving his brother's cooperation, had become a powerful witness for Sallie Hillmon. He related the frequency of Buchan's importunings, the lawyer's arrival at his home with a deputy sheriff, his brother's resistance to signing a paper that he said was not true, Buchan's authorship of the affidavit, and Reuben's own role in persuading John to sign the paper. In return for the latter, Reuben acknowledged, he had been paid the sum of fifteen dollars toward John's board with him and his family. In his final answer, he summed up the months of negotiations: "Buchan told me he wanted John to say it was not Hillmon who was killed."[20]

Then Wheat called the next and final witness to their case in chief: Sallie Hillmon, the purported widow. The trial had by then been in progress for five days, and the citizens of Leavenworth were able to read about its curiosities every day in their newspaper. Sallie must have been the witness some had been waiting to hear from; the *Times* reported that attendance was "better than it has been since the commencement of the Hillmon cases."[21]

It is doubtful that many in the spectator section were there for reasons of personal interest; Leavenworth is nearly forty miles from Lawrence, and most acquaintances of the parties and witnesses would not have found it convenient to attend. Instead it was the citizens of Leavenworth who came—for the entertainment. Already the matter was becoming a cause célèbre, a form of diversion in a place where electronic amusements did not exist and the theater could not be expected to come to town very often. But its notoriety was still in its infancy, for that grew in proportion to its length, and of course nobody could then know how long the case would endure.

Sallie has quite given up worrying about when she will be called to the witness stand, and has devoted herself to the project of recording various features of the proceedings for later discussion with her attorneys, with whom she spends at least two hours every evening after supper. Her hands have been sullied with ink at the end of every day so far, marks that her evening ablutions cannot quite remove, but she finds that she does not mind this so much as perhaps she ought.

She has learnt a great deal, not all of it encouraging. Sallie has come to understand that certain aspects of the case that seem to her extremely significant are not so regarded by the law. And vice versa, for much of the testimony she hears seems to her inconsequential, although when she raises this point with Mr. Wheat he advises her that she should accustom herself to the sensation, for as he puts it, "You have never yet seen such a rubbish of irrelevance as you will confront when Mr. Green begins to present his case." All of this thinking has kept her mind disordered and her body wakeful for long hours in the lumpy bed at her boardinghouse, but she does not feel tired.

She is now writing some observations about Reuben Brown's testimony, which overall she thinks was quite helpful and extremely relevant, when Mr. Wheat touches her sleeve to get her attention before rising to pronounce her name to the judge. She understands his meaning immediately and stands to walk to the witness stand and take the oath. Facing the spectator gallery for the first time today she is shocked to see that every seat is filled, and a double row of citizens stands behind the last row of benches. To judge by their bobbing some of the smaller ones are trying to stand on their toes, evidently from their great desire to see her. Not long ago this attention would have caused her distress, but today it does not. Let them gawk, thinks Sallie. I am the one who will have $25,000 at the end of this matter—possibly plus interest (for she has learned about interest in her study).

Mr. Wheat takes Sallie crisply through her marriage to John, and his purchase of the insurance policies. She describes how she once, after

John had left home, tried to retrieve the premium that had been paid on two of the policies, telling Mr. Selig and Mr. Griffith that they had decided to carry only half the insurance after all. But Selig told her that it was too late to cancel, and Griffith insisted that they should above all not drop his company's policy because his corporation was the best, worth $90 million. Sallie can see Selig and Griffith, seated with attorneys Green and Barker, waxing indignant at this and pulling at the lawyers' sleeves, and she knows that she must not smile at this and does not.

She speaks of the last time she saw John, about February 26 or 28 three years before, and of learning of his death in March, and seeing his body at Bailey and Smith's in early April. She understands how she must comport herself, that she must not cry but that she may otherwise convey her dignified grief, and she believes she does so with some success. She identifies the letter that Selig dispatched to her on April 2, inviting her to come to his office so he can aid her in applying for the payment of the proceeds. And she recounts how when she appeared, the agent then took the opportunity to demand that she describe her husband, refusing to relent even when she reminded him that he had himself met John Hillmon more than once. And that when she said her husband was five feet eleven and one half inches tall, Selig exclaimed, "Oh, no!" and also demurred when she said his hair was brown. But he told Sallie that he would send to New York, and she would have her money in two weeks. There is another stir at the defense table, more subdued this time.

Then she moves on to the most difficult part, the part she and Wheat had practiced the evening before, each carefully looking elsewhere so their eyes had not met. Yes, she replies to his query, she was present when Arthur Judson measured her husband. All three were measured by one another, she says calmly, and the marks were made on the door frame. She does not know when Judson returned to the door to measure the distance between John's mark and the floor, but she did so herself not long ago, when certain persons started saying that John was not so tall as she knew him to be. The measure was five feet eleven inches and a half.

She then tells the jurors about her summons to meet with W.J. Buchan, and finding him in the company of John Brown, and how

Buchan prompted Brown to tell her that he had signed a paper saying that the corpse was not John Hillmon, and that her husband had murdered the dead man. And she recounts that she had despaired and felt herself alone in the world of sharp dealers and liars, and had signed the papers abandoning her claims that Buchan had thrust at her, and she tells how Mr. Wheat had saved her from this foolish mistake by refusing to turn the policies over to Buchan. At this juncture she smiles at Wheat, who is sitting at the plaintiff's table behind his stack of documents, and he sketches a little seated bow toward her.

She describes the next day, when John Brown pushed the paper he had signed into the stove (she knows its correct name, affidavit, but she calls it a paper for the benefit of any of the jurors who may not know the less common term). When she speaks of Buchan she turns slightly in her chair to face the jury, for she wants them to see her sincerity then, and every word she has to say about him is impeccably true. The Senator had told her that if she pursued her claims she would not only lose in court but incur a large bill of expense; he had said that Colonel Walker and the insurance man Munn knew where her husband was, and that the dead man was Frank Nichols and they could prove it. He had claimed he was acting for Brown, although Brown seemed more afraid of him than any other thing. This part of her account is washed in the clear light of truth, and Sallie feels that the jurors cannot but apprehend this.

When George Barker stands to cross-examine her she experiences a flash of fear, but straightens her back against it and looks at him in his face. And it is not so difficult as she had expected, for all that Barker must hop from one subject to the next, and sometimes interrupt before she is quite finished with her answer. And then when he seems to be about done, Mr. Green arises and says that he has a few questions! Mr. Wheat protests this double persecution but to no avail, and she is obliged to answer to Green as well, although not at such great length. Then Mr. Wheat asks her a few more questions by way of clarification, and it is over.

When she is permitted to return to her seat she attempts to write down notes of what she was asked and how she replied but finds it curiously difficult to remember. She knows she was questioned about when she came to Kansas, and how and when she met John, and much about his two departures in December and again February, and with what he was measured by herself and Mr. Judson. As she writes this last, she thinks but does not record that she is rather proud that her face had not reddened at all while she replied that the measure was made with a rule that folds up to be carried in the pocket; she knows there is one she has seen Mr. Judson use many times and that he could surely produce if required.

She was shown the release papers that she signed for Buchan and asked whether it was not her signature on them; of course it was, a matter she has never denied. Green asked whether it wasn't true that she had said at the inquest she could not state her husband's height, and she denied that she had said any such thing (for, as she had swiftly reasoned, had she not just before said that she and Judson had measured John shortly before he left home?). Only, writing it now, Sallie wonders whether perhaps she might have said something like it, as she dimly recollects thinking irritably during the inquest that she was not one to be measuring things all the time, and answering accordingly. She remembers that a man was recording the inquest by stenography, and her hand falters a bit and a small blot of ink falls onto the cuff of her dress, a matter she makes worse by rubbing it. Perhaps things have not gone so well after all. She casts a questioning look at Mr. Wheat, but both he and Mr. Riggs are preoccupied with the lady named Mrs. Carr who is now taking the witness chair, having been summoned at the instance of Mr. Green.[22]

After Sallie's cross-examination, it was the turn of the defense to produce its witnesses. In this early part of their case they aimed at contrasting the undisputed excellence of the corpse's teeth with the deficiencies of John Hillmon's. Levi Baldwin's neighbor Mary Carr testified, as expected, that she knew the Hillmons, and that John Hillmon had a tooth "out" on the upper left side of his mouth. Mrs. Carr was followed by several other witnesses who said they had known Hillmon and noticed a defect in his teeth, although there were certain incompatibilities in their testimony.[23]

One said the tooth had been knocked out by a kicking horse in 1872; another that the tooth was not out, but blackened, and that he had seen it in 1878. Jackson Hogan, a witness who said the tooth was black, testified that he had last seen Hillmon when both of them were nine years old. Charles Snow said that he had once watched Hillmon pick his teeth and that he had "two teeth out." Claude Holliday said that one of Hillmon's teeth was "broken." All conceded that they had not given much thought to the matter of Hillmon's teeth until Mr. Barker, Mr. Green, or one of the other insurance men came around asking about them.[24]

It is unrecorded whether the jurors began to grow weary of the tooth testimony, but regardless, they were in for more of it. The next day Major Theodore Wiseman, one of the Mutual Life Insurance Company's most energetic agents, took the stand. He made clear that when the body was taken up from its briefly occupied grave in Medicine Lodge, he knew immediately that it was not Hillmon. By Wiseman's account, in life John Hillmon did have one defective tooth, but it was not black or missing, merely "shorter than the others."[25]

There was one other curious feature of Wiseman's testimony, unrelated to dentition. The Major recounted that when he ran into John Hillmon in February, shortly before his departure from Lawrence, Hillmon had inquired "what was necessary for a wife to do to prove the death of her husband," adding that "he was going to a country where there was little law and a man must fight."[26]

Mrs. Charles Dart of Dallas, Texas, was brought in over the many miles from that city to say that she had met John Hillmon once for an hour in 1878, and that he had (as the newspaper recorded it) a "bad tooth; looked like a tooth out." Josiah B. Brown had not seen Hillmon for ten or eleven years, but remembered from that time that he had a tooth gone—the second tooth on the right side. Yes, he repeated, he was quite certain it was the right side. (Both Mary Carr and Major Wiseman had said the imperfect tooth was on the left side of Hillmon's mouth.) W.S. Angell had heard Hillmon talk once in 1874, for two or three minutes. It seemed to him that "one tooth was shorter than the others, or broken off." On reflection he thought it was just shorter.[27]

Apart from the tooth dispute, another familiar theme was developing in the defense narrative: Hillmon's efforts to recruit other possible victims to travel the fatal trail of his companionship. H.D. Marshall of Wichita testified that in February 1879 he assisted Hillmon and Brown in buying their horses, wagon, and harnesses for their journey. Thereafter, said Marshall, Hillmon attempted to persuade him to accompany them and assist in their plan to capture wild horses; but Marshall said he would require $500 in cash before embarking on such a venture, and Hillmon had only $300. The witness testified that he had "thought of the matter since, after I saw Wiseman." He now regarded it as suspicious that Hillmon could not catch wild horses on his own, and seemed to believe that he had made a near escape from peril.[28]

A different perspective on the affair was supplied by the testimony of Senator W.J. Buchan. Called by the insurance companies, on direct examination the lawyer recounted his efforts to assist John Brown, a young man Buchan had believed to be the dupe of a crafty criminal and cold-blooded murderer. Begged by John Brown's father to represent his son, who was in trouble since being named a murderer by a coroner's jury in Lawrence, Buchan said he had located the younger Brown across the river in Missouri and spoken to him several times over the summer of 1879. Once when he went to visit with Brown, he encountered Levi Baldwin, who had come to have Brown sign a paper saying that Hillmon was dead. But Brown, according to Buchan, had refused to sign Levi Baldwin's paper.[29]

Brown was initially suspicious of him, according to Buchan, but by midsummer he had come to trust his attorney and to confide what had really happened: Hillmon's scheme to defraud the companies, the two men's encounter outside of Wichita with "Joe Berkley or Burgis," Hillmon's persuasion of the young man to join their party, the exchange of smallpox virus along the trail, the camp at Crooked Creek, the murder of "Joe," and Hillmon's disappearance. Brown had told him, said the Senator, that the last time he saw Hillmon was at the campsite, heading north toward the railroad with a satchel in his hand.[30]

Meanwhile, Buchan said, representatives of the insurance companies had sought him out to inquire what his client would say if Sallie Hillmon were to sue for the policy proceeds. They had also demanded to know where Brown was, and threatened to have him arrested. The lawyer testified with pride about the solution he had managed to negotiate to his client's difficulties: he had written up an affidavit based on what Brown had told him about the death at Crooked Creek, which his client had signed on September 4. That document had satisfied the companies and led them to abandon their desire to see Brown prosecuted for murder, so long as Brown agreed that that he would testify for them if necessary should Sallie Hillmon bring suit. (Even in those days it would not have been entirely up to the insurance companies to decide whether John Brown should be prosecuted for murder, but Buchan's contact on behalf of the insurance companies was George Barker, who was also at the time Assistant County Attorney. Barker's convenient mantle of official authority apparently enabled him to make representations about the intentions of the legal authorities as well as those of the insurance companies.)[31]

By Buchan's account, once Sallie Hillmon learned that Brown had spilled the beans to Buchan she was quick to agree that she would surrender any claim on the insurance policies, and at Leavenworth in September, after Brown told her face-to-face that he was going to stick with the story in the affidavit, she had signed releases so signifying. Contrary to Brown's account, Buchan said that he (thinking the matter thus concluded) had himself destroyed Brown's affidavit in the fire in his office. But there followed an unsuccessful attempt to obtain the policies themselves from Mr. Wheat, who refused to turn them over even when Sallie asked, and there was considerable consequent uncertainty about whether the releases she had signed in Leavenworth were really valid.[32]

Cross-examination by Sallie's lawyers ensued. The theme of this interrogation would be, of course, Buchan's alleged duplicity in claiming to represent Brown while he pursued the insurance companies' interests. Buchan was shown a "paper": an authorization, signed by Brown, for Buchan to "make arrangements, if he can, with the insurance companies, for a settlement of the Hillmon case by them stopping all pursuit and prosecution of myself and John W. Hillmon if suit for the money is stopped, and policies surrendered to the companies." It was dated Parkville, Missouri, September 4, the same place and date as the "Joe Burgis" affidavit.[33]

Then another paper was shown to the witness and identified. Dated the next day, September 5, it was signed by H.B. Munn, representative of all three insurance companies. It read, "I hereby authorize and employ you to procure the surrender of the policies of insurance on the life of John W. Hillmon." Yes, Senator Buchan agreed, he had been paid by the insurance companies for his work in obtaining the affidavit from John Brown. The original that he destroyed in the fire in his office wasn't the only copy, was it? No, he acknowledged, he had made a copy of the affidavit and taken it to the insurance companies' lawyers the day after it was signed. He agreed as well that the original itself had not really been destroyed: the fire was not hot enough. Buchan confessed that he had recovered that torn and singed document from the stove, pieced it back together, then saved it for use if necessary in any trial. (An evidentiary rule of long standing, known as the best evidence rule, usually required the production of original documents rather than handwritten copies.) The cross-examination was beginning to have some effect: in particular, this last confession accorded uneasily with the lawyer's earlier claim that he himself had thrown the affidavit into the fire.[34]

Buchan was then asked about another document; the newspaper does not say which, but it is apparently the letter to Sallie Hillmon from Brown, saying "I would like to know where John is, and how that business is, and what I should do, if anything." Buchan at first pointed out that it was written in John Brown's hand, but then had to agree that it was on his own letterhead. He admitted that he had "had the letter written by Brown." Did he have it sent to Mrs. Hillmon then? No, he "did not mail it to her; never showed the letter to anyone until last winter; gave it to the insurance companies."[35]

How about those visits he had had with his client over the summer, before Brown capitulated and the affidavit was signed. Had he been alone? No, on one visit he had been accompanied by Colonel Sam Walker, a former sheriff and a marshal who carried a warrant for John Brown's arrest. Later, on the occasion of the signing of the affidavit, he had been driven over to Missouri by Dave Ward, a deputy sheriff of Wyandotte County. But that, the lawyer insisted, was mere coincidence: he had hired the sheriff's team of horses and Ward had just come along with them. Buchan acknowledged that he had a horse of his own that he could have driven. He said he did not remember telling John Brown's father that the Brown family owed him nothing because "the insurance companies would pay me amply."[36]

On his redirect examination, George Barker attempted to undo some of the damage inflicted on Buchan by the cross-examination, but without conspicuous success. He revisited the troubled matter of the "Joe Burgis" affidavit, its purpose, and its sojourn in the witness's office stove. Buchan still insisted that *he* had thrown the paper into the stove, but he admitted that there was no fire in it. Then he adopted the passive voice: "it was taken out of the stove the same day or the day after; it was sealed in an envelope and was not opened until the depositions were taken." Buchan had, however, "previously furnished a copy to Mr. Green."[37]

Why the copy then? he was asked. He said there was an understanding that "upon the surrender of the policies I was to get back the copy," and that "they [that is, the insurance company men] would deliver the copy to me." He suggested that he, too, had been misled by the insurance lawyers, for "they had a copy [apparently a *second* copy] of which I knew nothing." Buchan seems to have been excused in his own eyes for disloyalty toward his client's interests by this perfidy of the insurance company lawyers.[38]

Not that Buchan is incapable of embarrassment; on the contrary he seems quite concerned about his professional reputation. For he also states in his testimony that one of the reasons for his retention of the original affidavit was his desire to show it, at some point, to Samuel Riggs, apparently to prove to Riggs that he had a good reason for offering John Brown as a witness for the insurance companies. He did not want Mr. Riggs, he testified, to think he had "acted unprofessionally." And he also testified that he "felt indignant" toward Brown when it seemed that his client had "inveigle[d] me into making a statement, and [gone] back on it without saying anything to me."[39]

As proof of his loyalty to Brown, Buchan recounted a conversation he had with Mr. Munn, who was an agent of the insurance companies but not a lawyer. After allowing Munn to peruse the affidavit, Buchan testified, he was angry when Munn said that the two men, Brown and Hillmon, ought to be prosecuted for murder. He took the affidavit away from Munn, put it into his pocket, and said that "if he was going to talk that way, he was not going to get testimony to prosecute Brown from me." He identified a letter he received from Brown, about two weeks after the signing of the affidavit, saying "I hope you will succeed in getting the policies without trouble." And also, "Be careful about the papers you got from me."[40]

As a final flourish to his redirect examination, Barker returned his witness to a theme hinted at earlier: that Sallie Hillmon seemed to be afraid of her own attorneys, and of her cousin. It was so, Buchan suggested. Throughout the fall and winter of 1879–80, he said, she prevailed on him to finance the purchase of numerous railway tickets that enabled her to travel about and so evade any pressure from Wheat and Baldwin to pursue the lawsuit. Buchan identified a piece of their correspondence during this period. Dated January 3, 1880, it read, "I am ready to go to Colorado as soon as you send the tickets and money. Can't stay here much longer as parties in Lawrence are making inquiries and it won't do for me to stay here; please send as soon as you get this. I am living in fear all the time." It also said, "I hope you had no trouble with B_____ in convincing him he would be doing what is right." The postscript instructed, "Direct S.E. Hillmon, Tonganoxie, Leavenworth County, Kansas."[41]

When I first studied the reports of the 1882 trial in the *Leavenworth Times*, squinting at the blurred microfilm printouts, I paused to reread this letter. It certainly conjured a picture of its author quite at odds with the portrait of a helpless unsophisticated woman Sallie Hillmon's attorneys had been busy creating. It appeared that for some months after Brown's dramatic signing and immediate renunciation of the affidavit, Sallie had been winkling railway tickets and money out of the insurance companies' lawyers while they waited on tenterhooks for her decision about whether she would pursue her lawsuit. Even the suggestion that they correspond with her at Tonganoxie, where Baldwin lived on his ranch, seemed to be designed to inflame their fears about the cousin's baleful influence while suggesting that she was merely a hapless young woman who must take succor where she can find it. And who was the "B_____" of whom she wrote? Had I underestimated Sallie Hillmon's capacity for mercenary manipulation? As for Buchan, could it be that he was simply a lawyer doing his best, at the urging of a concerned father, to keep a headstrong and perhaps excessively loyal young man out of trouble?

These reflections reminded me that I had once believed it implausible that John Hillmon would marry in October 1878 and almost immediately, indeed shortly before Christmas, set out to find a place in the middle of nowhere to start a ranch. What would prompt a newlywed man with steady, if not munificent, employment to expose himself to the perils of the winter trail and leave his wife behind, the best hope ahead of him a hard hazardous life of risk and worry? Did not the prospect of failure haunt the bridegroom?

And yet I had learned that contentment with one's lot in life was not the prevailing ethic of the United States once the devastation of the Civil War receded into memory. The satisfactions of home, hearth, and steady employment came to be perceived as debilitating; risk and exposure were the only road to success—and to manhood. As Andrew Delbanco reminds us, "The installation of ambition as the one common good was the great transformation of nineteenth-century American life." Scott A. Sandage, a scholar of the law of bankruptcy in the nineteenth century, agrees: "Ambition was the holy host in the religion of American enterprise." De Tocqueville called it the "universal feeling" of America. Nor was making money by steady work and gradual accumulation thought to be an adequate performance of success: a real man was "go-ahead," displaying a willingness to take chances, to court disaster in his quest for brilliance. He was also, perhaps, a bit of a trickster. No less sober an institution than the *New York Times* suggested that flimflam and achievement were necessarily mingled in the successful man, by offering this description of the self-described "Prince of Humbug," P.T. Barnum: "Barnum is the embodiment and impersonation of success."[42]

John Hillmon's professed reasons for leaving home to travel west in pursuit of a risky venture were plausible. But that did not mean they were true.

† † †

After Buchan left the stand, a couple more tooth witnesses said that they knew Hillmon and he had a tooth out (or black, or broken). Green and Barker then called Dr. J.H. Stewart to the stand. Stewart knew a great deal of interest: he had examined John Hillmon for the insurance companies before the policies were issued, had vaccinated John Hillmon for smallpox at the insistence of the companies' representative A.L. Selig, had participated in the autopsy of the corpse, and he had (or claimed) professional expertise about several matters. On the matter of height, he was most informative. He and John Hillmon, he said, had together filled out the usual forms when Hillmon applied for the insurance. Some of the values they wrote into the blanks came from the physician's measurements (like pulse rate); others (like height, given as five feet eleven inches) Hillmon simply told Stewart and the doctor recorded. But after the forms were filled out, the doctor said, Selig and Hillmon came back to his office to "see about a misstatement" as to Hillmon's height. Someone then (not the physician himself) then measured John Hillmon and found him to be "five feet nine inches instead of five feet eleven inches." Dr. Stewart also said that he had examined Hillmon's smallpox vaccination site on February 25, 1879, about five days after he had administered the vaccine, and "found it satisfactory."[43]

About the 2nd or 3rd of April, Dr. Stewart was asked to examine the corpse that had been brought back from Crooked Creek via Medicine Lodge, and apparently inspected it minutely. Among other measurements, he found it to be five feet eleven and five-eighths inches tall. It had a smallpox vaccination scar in two places, the same places where he had vaccinated John Hillmon, but he said that the appearance of the marks on the corpse suggested the vaccine had been administered about fourteen days earlier (that is, about the first week of March). For these reasons and others related to general appearance he was sure the corpse did not belong to John Hillmon.[44]

He had removed the two vaccination marks and the flesh surrounding them from the corpse, and placed them into a bottle of water with some chloral. He did not know the present whereabouts of these specimens, for they had been left behind when he moved away.[45]

Dr. Stewart also testified that the teeth of the corpse were "fine and perfect; white in color." And he examined the hands, with a magnifying glass, detecting no scars on them. (As is often the case with a passing moment of testimony, the significance of this observation would only later become apparent.)[46]

After the intervening testimony of a hack driver, who had met Hillmon a few times observed the corpse after it was brought to Lawrence, and was certain the body was not Hillmon's, a second man of medicine took the oath. Dr. G.G. Miller, an examining physician for the Mutual Life Insurance of New York, gave testimony remarkably similar to that of Dr. J.H. Stewart. Dr. Miller, too, had been asked to examine Hillmon for the issuance of a life insurance policy, and he, too, had failed to measure Hillmon's height. But some days later, he said, he had a return visit from Hillmon, who reported that he had made a mistake in stating his height and that he was really only five feet nine inches. Miller also affirmed that it was he himself who had suggested that Dr. Stewart remove the smallpox vaccination lesions on the corpse's upper arm, for further study.[47]

The third physician who had attended the autopsy of the corpse also testified. Dr. Mottram said nothing about John Hillmon's height, but he did affirm the height of the corpse: nearly six feet. He added three matters of expert opinion that tended toward the discrediting of John Brown's story. First, Dr. Mottram asserted, he placed the age of the corpse at about twenty-four. (John Hillmon would have been thirty-one on the date of the events at Crooked Creek; F.A. Walters was seven years younger.) Second, a person shot as the corpse had been could not have reeled or spun as John Brown claimed: the body would have fallen straight to the ground. Moreover, the corpse's owner had not (as Brown said Hillmon had) consumed coffee and bacon shortly before death, because its stomach was empty and digestion ceases at death. On cross-examination, however, Mottram backed away from this last opinion and agreed that gastric acid in the stomach could effect continuing digestion after death.[48]

Attending a trial can be a disorienting experience, for while the drama of the courtroom preoccupies the spectator's attention, events in the world outside do not slow their pace. No doubt even those absorbed by the first Hillmon trial would have been aware of the terrible storm that roared through Leavenworth on Saturday, June 17, while John Brown was on the stand, blowing off the roofs of buildings all over town before flooding them with rain. The state courthouse was badly damaged by water, as was the Planter's House. But the storm spared the federal courthouse any harm, and the Hillmon trial was unaffected.[49]

Larger and less local events also roiled in the background, some notorious and others less renowned. Probably few Kansans took great notice when in December 1881, six months before Sallie Hillmon's trials began,

President Chester A. Arthur nominated Horace Gray of Massachusetts to the United States Supreme Court. Gray was confirmed immediately; ten years later he would write the opinion of the Supreme Court in *Mutual Life Insurance Company v. Hillmon*.[50]

Nor did events in the state of Kansas stand still as the Hillmon case went forward. During the first trial, the Kansas Republican Party was organizing for its state convention in nearby Topeka. The organizing committee members found a number of disputes in which to invest their taste for political combat. The chief hinge of division was a member of their own party: Governor John St. John, who had occupied that office since 1879. St. John was a religious man, and understood his mission to be the promotion of morality in his frontier state. He employed both eloquent oratory and political skill to promote the successful passage of an 1880 amendment to the Kansas constitution prohibiting the sale of alcohol anywhere in the state. Some Kansans saw St. John as a champion of sobriety, women's rights, and domestic peace: many women, including the early suffragists, understood alcohol to be a principal cause of intrafamily violence. Prohibition was derided by others, however, as a monument to hypocrisy and religious zealotry. These divisions infected the state organizing committee, and led to both spirited speechmaking and nefarious backroom dealmaking on the subject of whether the controversial St. John should be nominated for a third term, and whether his wish that the party platform include an endorsement of prohibition should be respected.[51]

After two days of wrangling, all challenges to the credentials of delegates had been resolved and a platform of proposed resolutions approved. The chair of the Credentials Committee was Senator W.J. Buchan, fresh from his testimony at the Hillmon trial. The *Topeka Commonwealth*'s reporter names Buchan along with six others as the "big men" and "brainy politicians" in attendance.[52]

Apart from Buchan (and George Barker, who would be named to the Republican Party's state committee) the political events in Topeka do not seem to have personally touched any of the case's characters, but they did afford a role to two men who would later become important, in quite different ways, to Sallie Hillmon's lawsuit. One delegate to the convention was a young man named Webb McNall, who would a decade later become the Insurance Commissioner of Kansas and strike a bold (if ultimately unsuccessful) blow for Sallie Hillmon's right to the proceeds of her husband's life insurance policies.[53]

In addition, the convention nominated David J. Brewer of Leavenworth, without opposition, to be Associate Justice of the Kansas Supreme Court. The son of missionaries and a Yale graduate, Brewer had been a member of the state's highest court since 1870; the convention's nomination was necessary merely to secure his retention on the bench, which does not seem to have been in doubt. Two years later, in 1884, Brewer would be appointed a federal judge, and not long thereafter preside over the second trial of the Hillmon case.[54]

Despite the weighty events going forward outside the courtroom in Leavenworth, inside the preoccupying matter was still teeth. Several more witnesses, including John Hillmon's sister Mary Elizabeth and her husband, testified that Hillmon had a tooth missing, on the upper left side. But the brother-in-law, G.E. Nichols, was the first witness to add another observation of interest: when last he saw Hillmon, he testified, his wife's brother had a serious scar on his right hand, between the thumb and forefinger. Nichols said he asked about the scar, and Hillmon explained that he had been trying to load a gun when the ammunition had exploded in his hand and caused the injury. (Hearsay! I exclaim when I first read the blurry newsprint.)[55]

Mary Elizabeth said she had overheard this conversation, although she did not see the scar. W.W. Nichols, G.E.'s brother, swore that he had been nearby when an accident with a gun injured Hillmon's hand in 1875. The significance of Dr. Stewart's testimony about the unscarred character of the corpse's hand thus became more apparent. All three Nicholses admitted on cross-examination to having been paid their travel and accommodation costs by Mr. Green and his assistants, but of course such reimbursement would not be improper if limited to actual expenses.[56]

Another, cleverer line of cross-examination employed by Sallie's lawyers may have had more success: almost every witness who testified about John Hillmon's missing (or blackened, or broken) tooth was asked to describe the dental appearance of various other individuals to whom the witness enjoyed a much closer acquaintance than he or she had with John Hillmon. In nearly every case the witness was unable to do so with any confidence. A Mr. James A. Adams, for example, after saying that he had noted Hillmon's missing tooth, agreed with Sallie's lawyer Samuel Riggs that he had known Riggs for twenty-five years, had talked to him "a great many hundred times," and could say nothing with confidence about his teeth.[57]

Among the tooth witnesses appeared two individuals who had some-what more to contribute to the dispute. William Layman or Lamon of Lawrence was the photographer who had taken the two photographs of the corpse, on the occasion when it was dug up from the Oak Hill Cemetery during the Lawrence inquest to permit Mrs. M.I. Lowell to determine whether it might belong to her missing younger brother (it did not). He claimed also to have taken a tintype portrait of Hillmon about a year before his departure from Lawrence, which he identified. Based on this acquaintance with both the living man and the corpse, the photographer testified to his certainty that they were not the same. He readily agreed that he had retouched the negatives of the corpse photographs, and that in one of the pictures the nose of the dead man had been "pressed down." He could not remember who had done the pressing down, but by his account the only persons present at the cem-etery were insurance company doctors and agents.[58]

Colonel Samuel Walker added a new note of doubt about the candor of the Baldwin–Hillmon family. He testified that on the occasion when the corpse was lifted out of its first place of brief repose, in Medicine Lodge, Levi Baldwin's brother Alva was present, and said when the cof-fin was opened, "It ain't him." Again I urgently wanted to reach back over the years, tug the sleeve of Mr. Riggs or Mr. Atwood, and whisper the suggestion "Hearsay!" It would not be the last time in this trial that Sallie's attorneys seemed to forget the existence of the hearsay rule.[59]

While admitting that he had accepted payment of about $150 from the insurance companies for his work on the Hillmon matter, Colonel Walker did not like to be characterized as a mercenary. "Whenever I hear of a crime," he testified, "I try to ferret out as a public-spirited citi-zen." He added, however, "This time I thought I had a good paymaster behind me." Soon after, court was adjourned for the day.[60]

The case had, according to one observer, become "tedious," but on the morrow the insurance lawyers had plans for a bit of an evidentiary bombshell. It was preceded, however, by more routine witnesses. A.L. Selig, agent for the New York Life Insurance Company, corroborated the story told by Dr. Miller about Hillmon's return visit for his height to be measured, and the discovery that he had misreported his height when he first applied for the policy. And Selig repeated a claim he had made at the Lawrence inquest: that when John Hillmon's death was reported, Selig and another agent, G.W.E. Griffith, had asked Sallie Hillmon to come in for a meeting, and had there requested that she give a description of her husband. She was, Selig testified, unable to do so: she said she did not know "his height, the color of his hair, or about his teeth," although she could say he had a moustache. Griffith would testify later in the day about this meeting as well, although by his account Sallie "said she thought his hair was brown, but was not certain about his height."[61]

There was also the testimony of banker James S. Crew, who said that Levi Baldwin had been indebted to his bank, and had not paid on time and was facing arrest. But Crew said that Baldwin had promised him repayment after John Hillmon's death was announced, saying that he was to get $10,000 of the policy money. This may have been mildly of interest, but seemed a flimsy foundation for an accusation of murder, which is what the companies' case came to. Their lawyers undoubtedly put more stock in the anticipated impact of that day's central surprise: the deposition of a witness named, according to the *Times*, "Elvira D. Caston."[62]

Normally, attorneys for a party would desire a witness who has dramatic or important testimony favoring that party to appear in person. A deposition is a statement made under oath by a witness prior to trial, recorded by a court reporter; attorneys for all parties are allowed to be present and to ask questions, and the result is transformed into a written transcript. Reading a deposition to a jury, no matter the dramatic skills of the reader, cannot match the impact of a live appearance by a witness. Much later, videotaped depositions would come into common use; their visual aspect and ability to record the actual voice of the witness made them more satisfactory substitutes for live testimony. But even today every trial lawyer prefers live testimony, if the witness is one that can help his client.

Alvina Kasten (for the deposition was hers) certainly qualified as one of the most important witnesses the insurance companies could summon in support of the proposition that it was Frederick Adolph Walters, and not John Hillmon, who had died at Crooked Creek. But she did not travel to Kansas to testify for them; the transcript would have to do. Her deposition, as the rules allowed, had an exhibit attached to it: the indelible letter. From the reading of Miss Kasten's deposition, the jurors would have heard that on the third day of March, 1879, she was handed at the post office a letter addressed to her. It was from her fiancé, Frederick Adolph Walters, who had left Iowa to seek his fortune about a year before, and written to her every couple of weeks. This particular letter, however, was the last one she ever received from him, and Alvina Kasten said she had never seen her betrothed again. The letter apparently was read aloud to the jury as well. It was the missive we have seen before, in which among the courtship pleasantries and reflections on the state of the world are embedded the crucial words: *I am going with a man by the name of Hillmon who intends to start a sheep ranch and as he promised me more wages than I could make at anything else I Concluded to take it for a while at least until I strike something better.*[63]

Had this letter not been received in evidence, the Hillmon case would be forgotten. It conferred on the case not only drama—missing fiancé, brokenhearted sweetheart, nefarious murder—but an enduring place in the law of evidence. Even so, on the day it was disclosed to the jurors and spectators it may have proved a disappointment to Green and his colleagues, for there is no suggestion that the Kasten deposition was received with breathless surprise, or endowed with great significance. The newspaper editor who wrote the headline for the *Times'* coverage of that day in court seemed to believe that Frederick Adolph Walters was simply the latest in a parade of young men whom the insurance companies had tried to identify with the corpse. "more mystery," said the headline: "john, joe, fred, or frank?"[64]

Perhaps the necessity of presenting the disappointed fiancée's story through the lifeless vehicle of a transcript robbed it of its theatrical potential; perhaps the jurors were by then fatigued and irritable, ready for the trial to end. Nevertheless, the defendants' failure to bring Alvina

Kasten into the courtroom seems a remarkable shortcoming in their presentation. True, she could not be compelled to attend, since the reach of the federal court's subpoena power encompassed only an area of a hundred miles surrounding the court. But the insurance companies were free to use such persuasions as they had at their disposal to bring witnesses to Leavenworth, and those were sufficient to induce at least fourteen witnesses who lived in Fort Madison to appear and take the oath during the following day of trial. Most testified briefly that they had known Frederick Adolph Walters, and that they recognized Walters in the corpse photos taken by William Lamon. These identifications were made with varying degrees of confidence, and indeed (unless the newspaper's reporter suffered a serious lapse of transcription), one witness seems to have said unexpectedly that he was sure the picture shown him was not Walters. One of Walters's sisters identified his handwriting on the envelope of the Alvina Kasten letter, and a brother, C.R. Walters of Missouri, claimed to have received a similar letter saying that Frederick Adolph planned to travel with a man named Hillmon, although he could not produce it.[65]

I had to wonder: why would the defense lawyers go to the expense of bringing in so many repetitive and marginally persuasive witnesses, and not Alvina? It seemed unlikely that this was a strategic choice. Nor, I thought, if Alvina Kasten had died in the interim, would they have failed to enlist the court's sympathy by saying so. I could conceive of only one reason: Alvina Kasten had refused to testify live in the Hillmon case.

After the close of the defense case there was a bit of rebuttal evidence— witnesses Sallie's lawyers were permitted to call to counter various aspects of the defense case. Two physicians testified that digestion can proceed after death, and one opined that a man shot as the corpse was could have staggered before falling. A third doctor testified that a meal of bacon, bread, and coffee could be digested in two hours or less, and after death. Mrs. Judson, Sallie and John's landlady, related that the two insurance agents Selig and Griffith had tried to prevent Sallie from seeing the corpse, and added that she was aware of no scars on John Hillmon's hands. Several of Sallie's relatives testified that they knew John Hillmon and had never seen a scar on his hands. Several of these witnesses identified one of the corpse photos as Hillmon, some saying it was "a good picture of John Hillmon." There was dueling testimony about whether one of Sallie's relatives had told an acquaintance that John Hillmon was "no more dead than he was"; the acquaintance said yes, the relative denied it. Like most trials, this one shuffled to a close rather than concluding with any great revelation.[66]

When the court next convened, it was to allow the attorneys to address their closing remarks to the jurors. George Barker for the defendants had declared his willingness to allow the case to go to the jury without argument, but Sallie Hillmon's lawyers were unwilling to acquiesce in this proposal, whereupon it was agreed that each side should have four hours to argue its case. This seems a prodigious amount of time by today's standards, but such lengthy arguments were common in the Victorian era. These may have been wonderfully eloquent, or they may have been stupefying; there is no way to know. The newspaper, otherwise so minute in its transcription, did not describe them, and no transcript remains.[67]

By contrast, the judge's summing-up was reported in such excellent detail that one must conclude that the reporter was given the advantage of a written copy. The most notable features of Judge Cassius Foster's instructions were their disposition of the defendants' argument that Sallie Hillmon had surrendered her claim when she signed the releases, and their discussion of the significance of John Brown and his testimony. As to the former, Judge Foster was unambiguous: "In my view of the law," he told the jurors, "these releases cut no figure in these cases and do not estop the plaintiff maintaining her suits." The reason was not the one that had worried Buchan—Sallie's failure to hand over the written policies. It was, rather, what lawyers call "lack of consideration": Sallie had received nothing back for the releases, and they were therefore invalid. (Every later judge to hear the Hillmon trial seemed to regard this matter as the "law of the case," that is as having been finally settled by Judge Foster's ruling. The companies would continue to urge the defense of surrender at every trial, but they never succeeded with it.)[68]

Concerning John Brown and the various accounts he had given, the judge was rather severe. Brown, he observed, was "the one person, of all the witnesses, who has within his personal knowledge the real facts of the transaction." And yet, the judge continued, "[t]his witness has placed himself in such an equivocal position as casts a cloud of doubt over his evidence." Noting that John Brown's live testimony at the trial was contradicted by the affidavit that he signed for W.J. Buchan, Judge Foster acknowledged that Brown "seeks to break the force of this confession by swearing it was not voluntarily made" but instead given in fear of the grave accusations made against him and the persuasions of Buchan. Nevertheless, pronounced the judge, "whether we contemplate the man in either role he has thus himself assumed, a conspirator to cheat and defraud the insurance companies and in furtherance thereof an accessory to shedding the blood of an innocent man, or in the role of one who sought to rob the woman whom he had made a widow, of her just dues and blacken and traduce the name of her dead husband and his own friend, sent to an untimely grave by his own hand, in any view of it stamps this man Brown with infamy that time can never erase."[69]

It is not known whether John Brown sat in the courtroom as these words were uttered. Sallie Hillmon's lawyers objected to certain of the judge's remarks, but to no effect; having delivered his harsh judgment about the character of Sallie Hillmon's principal witness, Judge Foster turned the case over to the twelve men sitting in the jury box.[70]

The jury's deliberations were arduous. They began at eleven in the morning, and continued through the afternoon after a break for the midday meal. Seven ballots were taken without producing agreement, whereupon one of the jurors was stricken with illness and compelled to lie down on a "lounge, which was furnished him by the attendants." This misfortune did not, however, interrupt the jury's attempts to reach a verdict, which continued through the night.[71]

LEAVENWORTH TIMES, JULY 4, 1882, P. 2

THE HILLMON CASES

The celebrated Hillmon cases, consolidated for the purpose of trial, have ended by the disagreement of the jury. The Times is free to state that the matter bears the marks of fraud from its inception. The policies were obtained by fraud. Then murder and perjury were resorted to obtain the insurance. The jury has been worn out by the great mass of testimony placed before it, but if it was able to see the same in the light which it has been daily presented to the public the result could not well have been other than a verdict for the defense. It is one of the boldest frauds on record.

LEAVENWORTH TIMES, JULY 4, 1882, P. 4
CITY NEWS

The jury in the Hillmon case, after being out twenty-one hours, sent for Judge Foster Sunday morning after breakfast, at 8 o'clock, and through their foreman, Hon. Leonard Bradbury, reported that they could not agree. They had had seven ballots. The judge asked them if there was no possibility of an agreement and was informed there was no possibility whatever. The judge stated that he regretted that it had been necessary for him to keep the jury confined during the night, and also the fact that they could not agree on a verdict. They were then discharged, and after being paid off, left for their homes on the morning trains. The vote of the jurors was seven for the insurance companies and five for Mrs. Hillmon. There is no question, from the evidence, but that the entire case against the insurance companies was a fraud from its inception, in order to get money from the insurance companies.

Dean James Woods Green must pass a number of the Law Department's pupils as he returns to his office on the campus that Monday morning. A pair of them call out "Uncle Jimmy!" and he waves with a deliberate grin as he hastens past. His popularity among the young is a source of great and enduring satisfaction to him, but on this particular morning he would as soon forego the accustomed jovial conversations with his acolytes. He knows that he is running late, and that the men he has invited to meet him in his office are not in a sanguine frame of mind. Green nods perfunctorily to the secretary in his outer office and asks him who is within, for he can see figures moving about beyond the frosted glass.

"Mr. Barker. Mr., or rather Colonel, I believe it is, Walker. A Major Wiseman, I believe he said. Mr. Munn. Mr. Selig. Oh yes, a delightful young man who was a student here, do you remember?" says his secretary. "Mr. Gleed?"

Sure enough, he sees the profile of Charles Gleed among the others. Gesturing clownishly, nearly coaxing a laugh from the dour Munn; a poor student, as Green recalls. Inattentive, although not unintelligent, the sort of young man who can make himself quite useful if his loyalty is engaged. Gleed has been writing newspaper accounts of the trial, excellent overall, especially toward the end. But the Dean has not issued an invitation for him to attend this meeting. He considers the significance of his former pupil's presence in this gathering and how he will handle the matter before he settles his shoulders, turns the knob, and enters the inner chamber.

He greets each man by name, and invites each to sit in a chair or on the sofa that he has recently purchased for his office, before himself settling in behind his handsome burled walnut desk. George Barker, who was never slender but whose girth has grown alarmingly since Green first made his acquaintance, settles into the sofa alone; there is not much room left for a second occupant.

Green turns his attention to Charles Gleed, who is among those who have remained on their feet. "Mr. Gleed, I did not invite you to this gathering," he says severely.

"No sir, it was Mr. Munn did. He and I have spoken together quite a bit these last four weeks, while the trial was going on, and he thought. . . . "

"You were ever inattentive to your lessons, Mr. Gleed. This is a meeting between an attorney and representatives of his clients. Accordingly, anything spoken here would be within the privilege for communications between lawyer and client. It is possible, however, for this privilege to be lost, is it not, sir? I wonder if you can tell me, Mr. Gleed, one or more of the conditions under which a privileged communication can lose its confidential status?"

Gleed is scratching his head comically and casting a look at George Barker as if soliciting a rescue raft. Precisely as he used to do with the other students in class, Green recalls. Barker seems to want to speak, and Green decides to allow it, nodding at him.

"Young Gleed says he has some information for us," says Barker. "Munn and I told him to come along, but he's to leave as soon as he gives it over, isn't that right, son?"

Gleed hesitates for a moment, frowning and studying the hat on his lap, before looking up to meet Green's gaze. "The privilege between attorney and client may be lost if communications are made in the presence of a third party," he recites. "However, the attorney may enjoy the assistance of members of his staff, who may be present without compromising the privilege."

The young fellow seems to have paid some attention after all. "That is correct," says Green. "Now suppose you tell us what you came here to convey."

Gleed holds James Green's eye with a hint of challenge. "Suppose, sir, you do me the honor of appointing me a member of your legal team, whereupon I will supply the information you desire to know."

The effrontery! But Green has to admire it. "You have not yet been called to the Bar, Mr. Gleed," he says. "Your studies have not advanced so far, and need I remind you that your proficiency in them has not been great?"

"I know," says the journalist. "That is why I must be your assistant for the time being. You will need assistance, you know, for you have not had the result you hoped for. And perhaps by the time this case is tried again, I will have my license."

"Very well, then, Mr. Gleed. You are here appointed my assistant, at a salary of one dollar per year, to aid in the litigation of Mrs. Hillmon's suit against our clients. Appointment at will, which may be terminated without notice at the instance of either party. Now what have you to tell us?"

Gleed, by this time the object of every eye in the room, prolongs his moment by choosing an upholstered chair and settling himself into it. He tugs at his shirt cuff thoughtfully. "I have spoken to the jurors, or most of 'em. Some have been willing to state the points of their disagreement, although not for publication. I thought it might be useful for you to know what they were?" His expression of innocent inquiry is not particularly convincing.

"You know it would, son," says Colonel Walker, who has suffered the previous conversation in silence. "Tell what you know."

"They never could agree about how tall John Hillmon was, or whether he had a scar on his hand. They found those doctors suspicious, especially the part about cutting off that vaccination scar. They thought John Brown was a shifty son of a bitch and agreed that you couldn't put the decision off onto either one of his stories. Sallie Hillmon impressed them very much. They all thought she was a much more accomplished person than they expected, but whether accomplished at lying or merely accomplished at standing up to a bunch of big men they could not decide."

George Barker has been nodding at each point. "Not very surprising, son. We could have told you as much from the way the jurors looked at the witnesses."

Gleed's jaw stiffens slightly. "Well then here's something you mightn't a known. When I asked them what they made of that letter from the cigarmaker to his girl, they said they didn't put much stock in it."

Major Wiseman, leaning against the wall, has said nothing so far, but he is overcome with disgust at this. "What do you mean they didn't put any stock in it? Why the hell not? That was the best piece of evidence we had! Tillinghast and I broke our bones to get that letter and coax that Kasten woman to give her depo!"

Gleed nodded sagely. "I know. But these men said that without the lady coming into court, it just didn't seem right to put a lot of weight on that letter. Could have been forged or anything, a couple of them said."

Wiseman's complexion turns choleric with his fury. "Forged! Not even the Hillmon shysters ever said so! Walters's sister looked at the envelope and said he had wrote it. And anybody could look at some other letters wrote by the man and see that this one was in the same hand."

Gleed shrugs. "Don't shout at me, sir, if you don't mind. I'm just telling you what they told me."

Green and Barker exchange glances, and then Barker turns to Wiseman. "How come you could never convince Alvina Kasten to come to court, Major? That was supposed to be part of your job, too, remember?"

Wiseman rubs his cheek, defeated. "She wouldn't do it, that's all. You don't know how hard it was to get her to even give that deposition. I don't think she would have made a very good witness, anyway." Then Wiseman remembers something, and turns an accusing eye toward Green. "How come you didn't get someone to bring in some other letters from this Walters so's folks could see the writing was the same?"

"Hindsight, Major. We'll work on that for the next trial. Make a note, will you, Gleed?" says Green half humorously, but Gleed pulls a notebook and pencil from his pocket and scribbles a few words.

A.J. Selig, the insurance agent, has been watching from his chair in the corner, puffing on a pipe. He coughs slightly and the others turn, some having forgotten his presence. "I am not certain a second trial would be in the interest of the New York Life," he offers.

Brief silence ensues, then Munn nods in agreement. "Not so sure about Connecticut Life either," he says. "I'm waiting for a letter from Hartford, but the telegram says to think about a settlement offer. They're smarting over the costs of all this."

Green, who has anticipated that matters will eventually take this turn, stands from his desk chair and places his palms flat on the desk before him. He speaks deliberately and firmly, as though in the lecture hall. "Gentlemen, we cannot accept defeat at the hands of the Hillmons. Have the officers of your companies any idea of the flood of fraud and deception such a settlement would encourage? You might as well let a tiger off the leash and expect it to dine politely at your table with a fork in its paw. It will devour you! We are stewards of this region of great promise, gentlemen. We cannot go back to the days when Bleeding Kansas and her uncertainties discouraged every form of capital from investing here. We must be seen as safe, we must be known as reliable. Or else Lawrence will before long be in ashes again, or worse, covered with the dust of history."

Gleed stands from his chair. "I have to agree with my Dean, Mr. Selig. Capitulation would injure not only the insurance companies, all of them in the entire state, but every business and industry that we hope to attract and hold. It's the law on the books that must prevail, not the lawless rules of the frontier."

Green and Barker exchange half smiles. "Well said, Mr. Gleed," says Barker. "You gentlemen should listen to our young lawyer and advise your officers accordingly."

Munn and Selig exchange sour glances. Munn nods slightly and Selig speaks. "We'll do some talking, Green. And you'd best do some thinking about how to make the next jury see the case in its true light through all a the stuff that Hillmon woman is throwing out. It's a scandal this one didn't decide for us, strictly based on that cigarmaker's letter. We expect you to make sure they pay attention to it next time." He rises heavily from the leather chair and walks out through the back porch exit, thrashing his way through the shrubbery to the sidewalk. Munn hesitates then stands, inclines his head toward the Dean, and follows.[72]

Admiration for Dean James Woods Green was widespread, especially among his students; it was not, however, universal. Green's sister-in-law, the classics professor Kate Stephens, always believed that Green had stolen from her father, Nelson T. Stephens, the credit for persuading the Regents of the University of Kansas to begin a law department. Stephens, whose sister was Green's wife, penned a rather resentful memoir of her struggles against what she saw as her brother-in-law's grandiosity and narcissism. In *Truths Back of the Uncle Jimmy Myth in a State University of the Middle West*, self-published by Stephens in 1924, she describes with considerable scorn the "claque" formed by the young men who had studied under James Green, a cult of personality that promoted the legend of his greatness against the evidence that he was an ordinary person with an outsize talent for self-promotion. Stephens is not especially plausible as an unbiased narrator; every page of her book exudes bitterness. But other sources confirm her observations about Green's ability to inspire ostentatious displays of loyalty from the aspiring lawyers who studied with him and gave him the avuncular title. Charles Gleed would have been one of the first of these.[73]

LAWRENCE, KANSAS | JULY 12, 1882

Sallie Hillmon has grown weary waiting for her cousin to arrive, and so despite his instructions she has rung the bell beside the sign that proclaims this bungalow to be the Law Office of Lysander B. Wheat. The lawyer comes to the door himself and ushers her in with his courtly manners. "No Levi today?" he inquires as he guides her through the outer office into his study.

"He is late, and I did not wish to keep you waiting," says Sallie.

"Ah," says the lawyer. "Well, we shall not have a full quota in any event. Mr. Riggs is away to Topeka today, and Mr. Hutchings is also detained. His probate hearing was postponed so some fellow could be arraigned for violating Governor St. John's law. I might have voted for Mr. St. John if I had appreciated how much business his prohibition would create for our profession." He sees that she does not smile at this wit. "Are you quite well, my dear?"

Sallie drops into the chair he has indicated, and pulls off her gloves. "I am quite tired, Mr. Wheat. The trial was very exhausting, and at the end very discouraging. I am glad Levi is not here, for he might not like me to ask you this, but is there no way we could persuade the insurance companies to pay part, if we were to release them from the rest?"

Lysander Wheat steeples his fingers. "It is possible. Are you sure it is what you want?"

As she hesitates there is a commotion in the outer office and then the door to the study bangs open. Levi Baldwin, his frock coat a study in grime, stands in the doorjamb hat in hand. He surveys the scene and then looks at Sallie. "You were to wait for me, cousin."

"Mr. Baldwin," says Wheat cordially. "I see you found your way in. No need to apologize, we must not have heard you knock. Your cousin and I were just about to discuss the possibility of settling this nettlesome matter without the need for further proceedings. I think it may be productive for us to approach Mr. Barker on this matter."

Levi's eye twitches as his thin lips sketch an unpersuasive smile. "Reward those liars for their decision to cheat a poor widow out of her means of support? Is that what you had in mind, Sallie?"

Sallie pauses as if to speak, then seems to think better of it and shakes her head. Wheat observes this gesture closely, and then turns his shrewd gaze to Baldwin.

"Very well," he says. "Come in and sit down, sir. For we must discuss how to underwrite the expenses that we have incurred to date, and those that a new trial will surely bring."

Levi nods as he walks farther into the room. "Time to ante up again, Mr. Wheat? I know how this works, whether it's cards or cattle. Tell me what is required."[74]

4

THE CASE IS TRIED TWICE MORE, AND A SURPRISING OBJECTION IS MADE

1884–1888

In 1884 Gleed and his brother Willis formed their law firm, Gleed, Ware, and Gleed. Their first partner was Eugene Ware, a former member of the Kansas Legislature. In that same year Judge David Brewer, after many years of service on the Kansas Supreme Court, was appointed to the United States Circuit Court for the Eighth Circuit. The Hillmon case was eventually assigned to Judge Brewer's trial calendar. In 1885 the firm of Gleed, Ware, and Gleed was joined by George Barker, just in time for the retrial.[1]

The case of *Hillmon v. Mutual Life Insurance Company et al.* was called for trial the second time on June 6, 1885, at the same Leavenworth federal courthouse as before. The attorneys for the parties entered their appearances. For Mrs. Hillmon, S.A. Riggs, John Hutchings, and L.B. Wheat appeared; for the insurance companies, J.W. Green, George S. Barker, and C.S. Gleed. The jury selected included four men who were ex-members of the Kansas Legislature.[2]

Followers of the first trial would have found very little novelty in the evidence and testimony offered in the second. Mrs. Hillmon's lawyers apparently decided to rest their case in chief largely on the recorded testimony of various witnesses who testified at the first trial. The tedium of the proceedings led the reporters away from their usual minute reporting, in favor of descriptions of Mrs. Hillmon's appearance. According to the *Leavenworth Times*, on the first day she was "dressed plainly in black, even to her hat and trimmings, and wore no ornaments except a wide, thin gold band on the first finger of her right hand, and a pair of very small ear-rings." On the second day she wore a "neat plain suit of brown"; on the fourth she was "dressed in black, with a pointed broad-rimmed black [hat] on, trimmed with a flowing 'crush' of black crepe and wearing her front hair loose—cut short and combed down over her forehead."[3]

One of the trial's few unexpected moments arrived when Sallie's lawyers summoned a Dr. Patterson of Lawrence, who according to the newspaper report "identified a plaster cast of the teeth of Hillman." (The origins of the cast went unexplained in the report, but this small mystery would be resolved in the fourth trial, when Dr. Patterson again appeared and made clear that the cast he had taken was from the corpse, not from any living man.) Patterson seems to have been a bit of a showman, for when he was handed the cast he "turned the grinning jaws toward the audience in the court room." Mrs. Hillmon "leaned forward and looked at it intently and eagerly listened to every word that was said regarding it."[4]

The insurance companies were not satisfied to rest their case on transcripts and depositions. The newspaper reports that they called forty-three witnesses, and in addition introduced numerous depositions and transcripts of prior testimony, but nearly all the testimony reiterated aspects of the case the companies had mounted in the first trial. As before, the condition of John Hillmon's teeth received considerable attention. All the defense witnesses who had known Hillmon were united in their certainty that he had suffered from bad teeth. There was, as in the first trial, considerable variation among the witnesses as to whether the tooth/teeth were blackened, missing, or broken, whether in the upper or lower jaw, and when and how the damage first appeared.

Several witnesses praised the perfect condition of the corpse's teeth. None of this was surprising or new, but a disastrous defense witness, a Mrs. Gilmore of Lawrence, swore that she knew Walters and that the cigarmaker had bad teeth. Moreover, she identified Walters in photographs that other witnesses had said were of Hillmon, and when shown a picture of Walters said she "wouldn't swear that it was his picture."

Defense witness C.R. Walters, Frederick Adolph's brother, presented his sponsors with a few more difficulties. He identified the corpse in the photographs as his younger sibling, but he also said that his brother had a vaccination scar the last time he saw him (raising doubt that he would have allowed Hillmon to vaccinate him again, as the defense claimed), said he had a scar on his hand (defense doctors would swear the corpse had no mark at all on its hands), and admitted that in a letter he had said that his brother's teeth had fillings (the defense was by now completely committed to the unalloyed perfection of the corpse's teeth). Senator Buchan's appearance may have inflicted some damage on the defense as well: he admitted that for representing John Brown he had been paid only by the insurance companies, in the sum of five hundred to seven hundred dollars. He seemed offended by the suggestion there was anything improper in this, saying he was "in the habit of taking fees for his work."[5]

There were but a few more novelties. Attorney James Woods Green was compelled to acknowledge under oath that he had at one time custody of the fatal Sharps carbine rifle that had been an exhibit in the earlier trial, but that he could no longer produce it. The journal of John Hillmon was received in evidence. It described his travels up until March 14, 1879 (three days before the death at Crooked Creek). Some of the entries were touching, describing homesickness, and writing to and receiving letters from Sallie. Others were more rakish, like one saying "I am as apt to err as anyone," and that he did not propose to "make a memorandum" of his misdeeds while away from home. There was no doubt that the journal was found tucked inside the jacket worn by the corpse, but of course considerable dispute about how it got there.[6]

In a curious turn, the *Leavenworth Times* reported that it had learned that "there was an insurance on the life of young Walters" and that the Walters family had been paid the policy amount during the trial. It did not say whether the company that made this payment to the Walters family was one of the defendants.[7]

In the middle of the trial, the *Leavenworth Times* reporter asked Sallie Hillmon if she thought she would win her case. "There is no reason why I should not," she answered. "If right is not on my side how do I, a poor, weak woman, bear up under the strain and excitement of the trial all this time? There is not another woman in Kansas who could have borne it. The other trial stood eleven to one in my favor. I came so near winning that time, I have hope now." When asked what the outcome would turn on, she predicted in remarkably witty, adamantine language that "the teeth will be the rock on which they will split, if there is any hard question to solve."[8]

The reporter evinced some skepticism about Mrs. Hillmon and her case, reporting that "[i]t is evident that the story of the killing of Hillman was greatly exaggerated to the attorneys for the prosecution when the case was given to them, and that Mrs. Hillman was in error on many of the main points in the case. Her statement to a reporter about the jury in the other trial, was also evidently in error, when she said it was eleven to one in her favor, as it has been since learned that the jury stood seven for the plaintiff and five for the insurance companies." Greatly exaggerated—wonderful phrase! Not until 1897 would Samuel Clemens render it immortal by telegraphing from London that reports of his death were of that character. But the journalist's correction of Sallie Hillmon's claim about the previous jury's division was the opposite of exaggerated, for his own newspaper had reported at the time that on the first jury there were seven votes for the companies to five for Sallie.[9]

At the close of all the testimony, the defense offered again to allow the case to be sent to the jury without argument, but the Hillmon attorneys once more insisted on their right to address the jurors in summation. The judge then allotted each attorney (three per side) two hours, for a total of twelve hours of anticipated argument. The *Times* reporter disclosed that the evening before the summations began, "[b]ets were freely offered among attorneys . . . that the case will result in another hung jury."[10]

However prolix they may have seemed to the suffering jurors, the arguments in summation that began the next day seem succinct enough when rendered in the prose of the reporter. Mr. Wheat, whose opening speech "lasted all the forenoon," apparently offered but variations on a single point: that it had been proven that Hillmon was a victim of accidental death, and the insurance companies were trying evade payment of this just claim. In the afternoon J.W. Green (the reporter refers to him as "Judge" Green, a title often used to denote respect for an attorney of distinction) made, it seems, many "strong points," one of the best being that the only persons to swear that the body was Hillmon's were interested parties, whereas the entire Walters family, having nothing to gain from it, had come to court and sworn that the pictures depicted their son and brother Frederick Adolph. (No mention here, of course, of the reported insurance on F.A.'s life.) The second strong point attributed to Judge Green was his recital of the evidence that proved Hillmon to be only five feet nine inches, while the corpse was two inches taller.[11]

The Wheat and Green summations together occupied an entire day, and the next day was given over to those of Messrs. Gleed and Barker for the defense, and Samuel Riggs for the plaintiff. The only one of these arguments the *Times* described at all was that of Riggs, whose address the reporter praised as "scholarly and eloquent." Apparently concerned that the jurors would regard his client's husband as a man desperate for money, Samuel Riggs laid stress on the point that John Hillmon could not fairly be regarded as a poor man at the time he undertook his fatal journey; the evidence, said the lawyer, suggested that Hillmon was a successful dealer in buffalo hides, cattle, and hogs. John Hillmon had purchased life insurance, said Riggs, because "it was a historical fact that the Barbour County had been raided by Indians, and that was the county he was in when he met his death."[12]

At the end of the two days of argument, Judge Brewer summed up the evidence for the jury and gave them their instructions. Although he touched on a few matters of law (like his predecessor, he instructed that the releases signed by Sallie Hillmon were of no effect), he emphasized that the only real decision for the jury was whether John Hillmon was alive or dead. This, he mused aloud, "is one of those mysterious things that happen, or events that traverse a point where two guide boards meet. No question of law reaches it. It is a question of fact." The judge then furnished the jury with the hair samples and photographs that had been placed into evidence, together with a "strong magnifying glass." He commended them to the guidance of a Supreme Power, and released them to their deliberations.[13]

The twelve jurors discussed matters into the evening, and at nine o'clock they requested an audience with the judge and attorneys, to whom they reported that they could not agree. Judge Brewer was indisposed to declare a mistrial without further effort, and so sent them home. The next morning he sent them back to the jury room, where after lunch they took another ballot, and then reported again that they were deadlocked. The judge accepted defeat, and declared a mistrial. The vote was six to six, a division that according to the newspaper represented the unchanging view of each juror from the moment they had first retired to deliberate.[14]

Two of the jurors (they had both been in the Hillmon camp) were willing to talk to the reporter about their discussion. The foreman said that the tooth business was one of the chief obstacles to agreement, and opined they could have deliberated for another year and still not reached accord. A second member of the jury offered more detail about his logic. If John Hillmon had bad teeth, this juror reasoned, then he knew this, and realized his dental shortcomings would be the subject of identification evidence. So would he not have taken care to procure a victim whose teeth were as bad as his own, rather than one with a mouth full of perfection? Moreover, he added, the Dearest Alvina letter had "something crooked" about it. For if young Walters really had been in Wichita and had met Hillmon and Brown there, would not some witness remember his having been in that city? But no such witness was called.[15]

This juror was certain that the Walters family were sincere in saying they saw Frederick Adolph in the corpse photographs, but he thought the likelihood of mistake in this instance was great. He also said, "it was hard to tell which of [John Brown's] stories were true," but "it will be hard to make me believe but what Buchan worked him pretty hard, to get his evidence for the companies."[16]

George Barker of the defense, interviewed by the same reporter, said that he had expected a verdict for his client, but was cheered that the jury's reported even division represented a gain of one juror over the seven to five vote by the first trial jury. (He, too, seems to have forgotten that the first jury was supposed to have had seven members who voted in his clients' favor.) Barker claimed darkly that Sallie Hillmon was only able to obtain means to prosecute the case by the assistance of a "syndicate who are furnishing the funds, with the prospect of sharing the proceeds."[17]

The case would thus have to be retried yet again, this time three years hence in Topeka. But before its new judge, O.P. Shiras, applied his gavel to the bench in February 1888 Sallie Hillmon would make a surprising decision; the law firm of Gleed, Ware, and Gleed would take on many new clients; and the Kansas weather would turn catastrophically bad.

Mr. Lysander Wheat never knew John Hillmon in life, so the effect of Sallie Hillmon's visit is perhaps even more startling than she intends. She sweeps into Wheat's office dressed smartly in a stuff gown and embroidered shawl. Wheat is compelled to search for her small face under the loops of curl that frame it, and finds there a merry smile. She quite eclipses the sober-looking gentleman whose arm she holds close to her side. It is certainly not Levi Baldwin, her usual companion.

"What a joy to see you looking so well, Mrs. Hillmon," the lawyer says. "But I do not think I have had the pleasure of this gentleman's acquaintance."

"This, Mr. Wheat," she announces, "is my husband."

Wheat is aware of his visible calm as though observing it from the corner of the room, but dismay squeezes his pulse like a vise.

"I am . . . astonished, Mrs. Hillmon," he manages to say. Then, ever the lawyer, he turns and addresses himself to the man. "And perhaps even more surprised, sir, that you should show yourself so freely. The authorities will arrest you at once if you are . . . "

"It's Mrs. Smith now," says Sallie. "I have remarried, Mr. Wheat! Mr. Smith is quite safe from arrest. His only crime is association with a woman accused by certain parties of evildoing, and he says he is willing to risk the hazards of such a friendship."

"Remarried," says Wheat, releasing a profound breath. Really, what an annoying woman! He shakes the hand of Sallie's companion briefly, murmuring "Mr. Smith" as he does so. Of course, the man looks nothing like John Hillmon's photographs; he should have seen it at once.

"We have just come from the registry office," Sallie says teasingly. "You must congratulate us."

"Oh I do, Mrs. Smith, sincerely. But you might have spoken with me about this plan."

Sallie shrugs and turns to the quiet man for support. "We are impulsive, are we not, my dear?" He nods but does not speak. Evidently he is rather timid.

"There will be no way to keep this development from Mr. Green, you know. He will hear before sundown, for he has ears throughout the town."

Sallie blinks with delight. "Of course. But what good will it do him to know, Mr. Wheat? He will wish it otherwise, I am sure. Possibly he will even try to conceal it when we go to court next, for does it not prove better than any other thing could that I know John Hillmon to be dead?"

Wheat nods slowly, and considers. Yes, or perhaps you might be such a clever vixen that you know John Hillmon, even if he lives, can never hazard to show his face, and so you propose to enjoy your new marriage and the insurance money as well. The lawyer composes his face into a mask of comfortable professional neutrality. "Does Levi know of your, ah, recent union?" he asks Sallie.

"We are off to tell him, are we not, James?" she says, and with that she tugs on her husband's arm and the pair turn toward the door.

"Just a moment, Mrs. Smith," says Wheat. "As you are here, I have some documents for you to sign. The expenses are getting very high again, but Mr. Riggs and I have found an investor who thinks highly of your prospects."

She waves insouciantly. "I shall come back tomorrow, sir. This is my wedding day. No papers today."

Wheat sits heavily in his chair for a moment after they depart, then sighs and pulls a bundle of foolscap toward him. He must let Riggs and Hutchings know of this unwelcome turn. Or is it indeed unwelcome? Could Sallie Hillmon Smith be right in predicting that it will help her case? Or should it more likely cause her to lose the tender mantle of widowhood and its incomparable advantages with the jury? It is beyond his reckoning. He writes two fair copies of the same message, then calls the boy lounging in the outer office to come take and deliver them.[18]

The early years of the 1880s had been a boom time for Kansas. The weather seduced the homesteaders and farmers by providing abundant moisture for most of the decade that began in 1878. As organized weather records were nonexistent and most of the settlers were newcomers, they took this clemency as the norm. There was also the widespread belief that the rain would follow settlement, and thus that the western regions of the state would surrender their aridity as the homesteaders there pursued the practices of cultivation and irrigation. Farming in Kansas had all the appearance of a promising enterprise.[19]

The railroads, hoping to encourage the sort of settlements along their tracks that would swell their coffers with the movement of people and products, engaged in massive marketing campaigns directed at prospective settlers. A flyer produced by the Kansas City, Lawrence, and Southern Railroad in the 1880s touted "the last chance for desirable cheap homes in kansas," and claimed that 5,825,385 acres of government land in southern Kansas were available through "homestead" and "pre-emption." Another brochure, titled "The Immigrants' Guide to the Most Fertile Lands of Kansas," suggested that "[m]ultitudes in the older States can improve their condition by selling out and emigrating to these fertile fields, which can be purchased at $2.50 to $6.00 an acre on eleven years credit." Financing was readily available from the eastern capital markets, which were attracted to the frontier because farmers and ranchers were willing to pay higher interest rates than those that prevailed back east. And the investors' local agents, whose income came from commissions when new loans were written, were not excessively particular about the creditworthiness of loan applicants.[20]

The ensuing real estate boom fed the growth of many towns, especially Wichita, which grew in population from 4,911 in 1880 to about 40,000 in 1888. Wichita real estate lots increased in price tenfold during a couple of *months* in 1887. Farm acreage prices inflated dramatically, too, for those who wished to buy land outside the homestead program. By 1887, the per capita mortgage debt in Kansas was three times what it had been in 1880; by the decade's end there was one mortgage for every two people in the state.[21]

Then in January 1886 the worst series of blizzards ever recorded in Kansas struck. In some western parts of the state temperatures stayed below zero for days, with wind chill estimates of one hundred degrees below. Eighty percent of the cattle on the overgrazed prairie died, and those that survived were generally too emaciated to be sold. The cattle barons were ruined.[22]

The following summer was good for crops, however, and the rains were plentiful again, but this respite from the perfidy of the weather was short-lived. The late summer of 1887 marked the arrival of an entire decade of drought, and thus very poor crops if any. Soon the real estate boom collapsed, and many of the settlers gave up on Kansas and headed west, some in covered wagons with canvas painted to proclaim "In God We Trusted, In Kansas We Busted." Large areas of western Kansas became almost wholly depopulated, and numerous businesses were forced into bankruptcy.[23]

The law firm of Gleed, Ware, and Gleed, however, thrived. The Governor employed it in 1886 to represent the state before the United States Supreme Court in litigation that challenged the state's power to enact liquor prohibition. The Court's decision was favorable to the state, and many of the lawyers involved credited Willis Gleed's scholarly portions of the brief for this victory. Charles Gleed's contribution to the firm's success was perhaps less cerebral, but just as important: he had worked for the Santa Fe Railroad before his admission to the Bar, and that organization sent a great deal of legal business the firm's way. In 1887 Charles also became an officer and director of the Santa Fe subsidiary that owned the rail line to Chicago. He wrote many unsigned newspaper articles during this period representing the railroad's position on various matters.[24]

The Gleed firm also represented several large land mortgage companies during the time when many farmers were forced by the hard economic times to default on their mortgage payments. The defaults ruined the farmers and damaged the mortgage companies and their investors, but the Gleed brothers prospered. Charles Gleed's biographer writes that "[i]t may be that lawyers like the Gleeds were the most fortunate of all the parties who participated in the land mortgage business in Kansas during the 1880's and 1890's. They were able to collect their legal fees in spite of the financial losses being experienced by others."[25]

Still, the losses inflicted on investors troubled the Gleed brothers, for the continued prosperity of their firm depended largely on the willingness of eastern capital to invest in the state of Kansas. Willis Gleed often expressed his opposition to proposals that the Kansas Legislature take action aimed at relieving the suffering of indebted farmers, arguing that such measures "would drive up interest rates and make capital even more scarce by alarming eastern investors."[26]

This same solicitude for the needs of the investing class, including the necessity of keeping its enterprises unfettered by intrusive regulation, would mark the law firm's efforts on behalf of three eastern life insurance companies in the Hillmon litigation and elsewhere. Wise capitalists could not be expected to do business in precincts where fraud and murder were permitted to hold sway.

The third trial of the Hillmon case convened in February 1888, not in Leavenworth, where the first two had been held, but in the state capital, Topeka. The presiding judge, the Honorable Oliver P. Shiras of Dubuque, ordinarily served as the chief judge of the Northern District of Iowa, but he had agreed to aid his fellows of the Kansas federal bench by sitting on the court in Topeka for the duration of the Hillmon trial.[27]

Everyone seemed to be determined to avoid a repetition of the hung-jury scenario, starting with the court officials responsible for summoning prospective jurors. By the account of the *Topeka Daily Capital*, these officials determined that on this occasion the jury should consist not of the "the class of men who loiter about court rooms with the hope of getting an opportunity of serving," but rather of "men of intelligence and good standing." The newspaper deemed this strategy of selective jury eligibility "quite successful," and twelve highly respected white men were seated in the jury box.[28]

In the third trial, as in the second, many disputed matters were addressed by the employment of transcripts of testimony that had been given earlier, either in the first two trials or in the pretrial depositions. Sallie's lawyers chose to begin with John Brown's deposition, most of which was read to the jury over eight hours by attorney Charles S. Gleed. One hopes, for the jury's sake, that his dramatic skills surpassed his legal ones.

Sallie's team then presented several familiar live witnesses: the stalwart Reuben Brown, Mary Judson, Levi Baldwin, and John Eldridge (or Eldredge), an acquaintance of Hillmon's who testified that he had seen the corpse and was sure it belonged to his friend. Two of the Medicine

Lodge men who had seen Brown and Hillmon together on their first journey were summoned, and testified that they recognized the corpse as that of the man they knew as Hillmon.[29]

None of this was new, nor was most of Sallie Hillmon's testimony. She did address the question of her travels during the period after Mr. Wheat had refused to give Mr. Buchan the policies. Buchan, she said, had kept her at his house, and bought her tickets to travel to Trenton, Tonganoxie, and Ottawa (Kansas), but advised her to stay away from Lawrence, where she would likely fall under Mr. Wheat's influence.[30]

There is a technique in trial advocacy known as "anticipating impeachment." If one knows that one's witness is likely to be discredited or made to look untrustworthy, it is best to bring up the unhappy matter during direct examination, so as to at least gain credit for candor. This defensive tactic must have been what Sallie's lawyers had in mind when they asked her to identify a pair of letters, written from her to Mr. W.J. Buchan during the weeks after she signed the releases at his instance. One of these we have seen before, for it was introduced at the first trial: in it she tells Buchan she is willing to go to Colorado as soon as Buchan sends her the ticket and money, and refers darkly to "parties in Lawrence" who are making "[e]nquiries about me and it will never do for me to see them you know how that is don't you?" This first letter also conveys her hope that Buchan will convince someone she refers to as "B_____" to "do what is right." The second, written mere days after she signed the releases in September 1879, seems even friendlier (or perhaps more manipulative) toward Buchan. "When I started from Lawrence," she wrote, "I had very little money and I will be obliged to ask you to send me enough to bye my ticket to your city. I wrote to L. Baldwin but he had no money for me. . . . I did write that letter to Riggs & Borgalthaus, have got no answer and don't want any. I will be on the Wednesday's Train without something Offle happens."[31]

These are ambiguous documents at best, but one plausible interpretation is that Sallie remained determined to surrender her claims, even after Lysander Wheat refused to turn the policies over to Buchan. One could read them further as evidence that she was hindered in this goal by Wheat and her other lawyers, all the while enjoying generous treatment by Buchan and the other insurance company attorneys. By asking Sallie about these inconvenient epistles during her direct examination, her attorneys no doubt hoped that she could explain them away, or at least diminish their impact, and this effort may have succeeded to some degree. She explained the reference to "B_____" doing the right thing as a plea for help in getting Levi Baldwin to pay her the balance due on some notes he had signed in favor of John Hillmon. She could not remember what she might have meant about Messrs. Riggs and Borgalthaus. She said that the persons making inquiries about her in Lawrence were a "Mr. Ellison" and Colonel Walker.[32]

On cross-examination she repeated her account of the reasons that she signed the releases even though she knew her husband was dead. The insurance lawyers had made representations that John Brown would testify that Hillmon was still alive, she said, and they conveyed threats by the "rich corporations" that they would "throw a cloud over [her]" in court and "wear [her] out."[33]

Like an inkblot, these strangely shaped patterns of testimony can yield various apperceptions. One might see in them the understandable confusion of a naive girl confronted with machinations of a sort she has little experience with; or perhaps the marks of a dishonest woman who has succeeded rather brilliantly at turning a series of challenging predicaments at least somewhat to her advantage. Or one might rather perceive any number of less definitive portraits, in which Sallie displays an admixture of confusion and cleverness, sometimes taken advantage of and sometimes exacting her retribution. The reporter for the Topeka newspaper, obviously an admirer, carried away the following impression: "During a long and rigid cross-examination . . . Mrs. Hillmon answered all questions put to her without once displaying one particle of temper, preserving the calm demeanor and ever ready smile for which she is noted, under the most trying circumstances."[34]

For me and my ongoing effort to understand who this woman Sallie Hillmon might be, the letters she sent to Buchan provoke a different sort of disquiet as well. How could the person I had imagined, the woman capable of elegant speech despite her slight education and pedestrian profession, write a sentence as ugly as "I will be on the Wednesday's Train without something Offle happens"?

It was then the defendants' turn, for the third time, to present the evidence they hoped would persuade the jurors that the dead man was not John Hillmon. Their first witnesses emphasized the event in which (they swore) John Hillmon had, for purposes of his life insurance application forms, reported that he was five feet eleven inches tall, but later returned to confess that he was only five nine. One of these witnesses, Major Theo. Wiseman, gave testimony concerning this and several other matters that was vaguer and less emphatic than in the earlier trials. On this day he would say only that "according to [his] best recollection" the body was not Hillmon's, and merely that "there was something irregular" about one of Hillmon's front teeth. It is possible that this slight retreat of his enthusiasm for the companies' cause is explained in the very last portion of his cross-examination, in which he complains that the companies have paid him only part of what they owe him for his services, and that he has had to sue for the remainder.[35]

Many more defense witnesses then testified to John Hillmon's bad tooth or teeth, a scar on his hand, or a scar on his head. Several of these same witnesses testified to having seen the body and concluding it was not John Hillmon's. But the cross-examinations of these witnesses enjoyed some success. Many wavered on whether the tooth was damaged or missing, and they disagreed on whether it was on the right or left side of the face, and the upper or lower jaw; some said more than one tooth was bad. One (a sister of John Hillmon's) was sure about a bad tooth but knew of no scar on his hand. Nearly every witness who testified to observing Hillmon's bad tooth was shown to be unaware or uncertain about the condition of various friends' and acquaintances' teeth. Still, the vagaries of memory and perception must be accorded some role in these contradictions.[36]

Other testimony, however, was so clear and certain that it does not seem likely it could represent poor memory. A story told by W.W. Nichols, for example, might be either truthful or mendacious, but not mistaken: he repeated his testimony from the first trial that in 1875 he had been camped near Hillmon on a buffalo hunt in Texas when a firearms accident "almost severed the thumb" from Hillmon's hand, leaving an ugly scar that was still noticeable when he saw Hillmon again about a year later. He also repeated an accusation he had made in the second trial (but not the first): that Sallie Hillmon had asked him not to say anything about the scar on her husband's hand, and then accused him of being "bought by the insurance companies" when he would not agree.[37]

Nichols's testimony on the matter of the hand scar was consistent in all three trials, with small exceptions. On the tooth question, less so: he progressed from saying in the first trial that he had taken no note of anything unusual about Hillmon's teeth, to swearing in the second that Hillmon had a discolored tooth, to testifying on this third occasion that the tooth was "discolored . . . , probably gone." When he declined to estimate Hillmon's height, saying it would be "guess work," Sallie's lawyer suggested that his statements about the tooth were guesses as well, but Nichols replied, "No, I am certain it was discolored, or perhaps out."[38]

The testimony of W.W. Nichols exemplifies the difficulties of assessing, at a remove of more than a century, the credibility of the witnesses in the Hillmon matter. If we believe Nichols's account of the gun accident it is devastating to Sallie's claim, since there is no dispute that the corpse's hands were unmarked by such a serious scar as he describes. Her overture to him, if it happened (she always denied it), marks her as one who would lie and ask others to do so. Neither of these pieces of testimony lends itself plausibly to characterization as a possible case of faulty memory. Of course, that does not mean they are true: Nichols might simply be lying himself, and his claim that Sallie sought to suborn his false testimony might be a projected distortion of a genuine conspiracy between Nichols and the insurance companies, in which they have agreed to reward him for the fabricated account of the hand scar. The variances in his testimony about the tooth come into play here, but they cannot really clinch the matter: they're simply too minor to confer confidence that he is a liar, rather than a witness with ordinary shortcomings of perception and memory.

One could go through a similar process of thought and analysis with many other witnesses. No doubt many were simply confused or forgetful. Unquestionably, some of them lied outright, but no witness's testimony consists solely of lies. Mary McCarthy is reported to have said of Lillian Hellman, "Every word she writes is a lie, including *and* and *the*." It's a funny aphorism, largely because it describes the impossible: even a compulsive liar tells the truth some of the time, if only in conjunctions and articles. But the best liars are judicious, weaving their falsehoods plausibly together with truth to camouflage them and allow them to benefit from association with their virtuous company. It's hard to sort them out from the truthful, and even harder to distinguish them from the mistaken. Not that these are exclusive categories: some of the Hillmon witnesses were likely confused, accurate, mendacious, and forgetful, at various points in their testimony. As the *Topeka Daily Capital's* reporter reminds us, "Twice has a jury of twelve men tried to straighten out the evidence, and finally given up."[39]

Mr. Buchan must then be heard from for the third time. On direct examination, he gave the familiar, rather self-serving account of his representation of John Brown (and simultaneously of the insurance companies, who had, he agreed, supplied him with the only pay he received or expected in the matter). The only new disclosure in his testimony was the revelation that Sallie had actually stayed as a guest in the Buchan home for two or three weeks, during the confused period after Sallie Hillmon signed the releases and Lysander Wheat refused to turn over the policies to Buchan. This unusual nugget of information arrests my attention. Buchan knew Sallie only from his contacts with her in the case. Was she so desperate for a place to stay that she would accept the hospitality of a near stranger, who was in addition a man who rather clearly did not have her interests at heart? Or was Buchan so slippery that he managed to persuade Sallie, as he had John Brown, that his goal was to protect her against her adversaries? Or was it rather Sallie who was so confident a criminal that she believed she could win the lawyer over, or acquire some hold over him, during this period of cohabitation? What must the conversations at the breakfast table have been like? No solution to the case will erase, for me, the mystery that clings to these days of communion between guest and host.[40]

Buchan's pose as benevolent protector of John Brown began to unravel, of course, on cross-examination: he must admit that he never mailed the letter Brown wrote to Sallie and entrusted to him, but instead gave it to J.W. Green; he must acknowledge that he removed the torn copy of John Brown's affidavit from his office stove and pieced it back together. He could not deny that on at least one occasion he led a law enforcement officer to Brown at a time when the officer was authorized to arrest his client. All of this would have been familiar to anyone who had attended the first trial, but it was new to these jurors. They reportedly paid very close attention.[41]

A flurry of other witnesses, mostly familiar, followed J.W. Buchan to the stand. A few new themes were introduced. Two jurors from the Lawrence inquest elaborated on their earlier testimony that Sallie had not, at the inquest, been able to say anything about her husband's appearance; they now recalled that when asked about his hair, she replied only that he had more than Mr. Green. (Photographs from later in his life show J.W. Green with a bald pate and a tonsure; apparently he was losing his hair even in 1879.) This comparison may have represented an honest effort on Sallie's part to describe her husband's hair; or perhaps Messrs. Good and Huffman were correct in interpreting it as a malicious witticism at Green's expense. In any event, they seem to have taken umbrage on his behalf.[42]

At this juncture in the trial, Sallie's lawyers began to display an unexpected virtuosity in the deployment of evidentiary objections. A.L. Selig, insurance agent, attempted to testify that Hillmon had made some sort of request about his height measurement; presumably Selig intended to relate, as he had in the earlier trials, that Hillmon had returned some time after he was first examined for the policies to confess that he had exaggerated how tall he was. But Sallie's lawyers objected: any such testimony from Selig would be hearsay, they argued. They were quite right to do so, and Judge Shiras sustained the hearsay objection to any testimony from Selig about what John Hillmon might have said.[43]

Was the greater benefit that the hearsay rule promised for Sallie's case beginning to dawn on her lawyers? No more than a few minutes later Lysander Wheat interrupted the proceedings to ask the judge to strike out earlier testimony by any witness or witnesses that John Brown was five feet nine inches in height, on the ground that these witnesses had no personal knowledge of Brown and therefore were only repeating what they had been told. This was, in essence, another hearsay objection, and Judge Shiras sustained it as well, ordering any such previous testimony stricken.[44]

"Stricken," in courtroom parlance, does not mean what it sounds like; the matter would remain on the written transcript, but the jury would be instructed to disregard it. In itself this was no great victory: there is considerable doubt about whether jurors can successfully comply with an instruction to forget something they have earlier learned, and Brown's height would not seem to be important anyway. But regardless of whether the Hillmon jurors would succeed in disregarding the earlier testimony, something more important is happening here. For we can see, between the lines of the newspaper account, Sallie's lawyers discovering that they are armed with a powerful weapon in the form of the hearsay rule. This tool has rested in their armament all along, but it has taken them nearly a decade to appreciate its possibilities. Even the newspaper reporter seems to attach some significance to the turn of events, for he notes, "Messrs. Riggs and Hutchings, who have labored ably and zealously for the plaintiff, gave way yesterday for Mr. Wheat who scored a good point while his co-laborers were resting by having a batch of testimony stricken out."[45]

The agent Selig contributed one more nugget of information when he agreed that John Hillmon had wanted to take a policy with the Travelers Insurance Company, because their premiums were cheaper, but discovered that their policy would require him to foreswear riding fast on horses and carrying a firearm while mounted. Hillmon explained that he was in the stock business, said the agent, and so declined to take out a policy with these restrictions. Sallie's lawyers do not seem to note, now or later, the point that I would have taken from this account: Hillmon could have taken the cheaper policy if his only intention had been to disappear according to the plot attributed to him by the insurance companies. For the journey out west was to be accomplished by wagon; Hillmon would not be mounted.[46]

Another new piece of evidence arrived in testimony from a Lawrence doctor named Phillips, who said that in 1879 Levi Baldwin had made the following remark to him: "Doc, wouldn't it be a good scheme to get your life insured for all you can and have some one represent you as dead and then skip out for Africa or some other d—n place?" Dr. Phillips testified that when he was noncommittal, Baldwin went on to opine that such a thing could be done "like a top." (Neither Hillmon, the witness agreed, was present for this conversation.)[47]

The insurance companies also offered three witnesses to testify that a mysterious man named "Colton," whom they had known in New Mexico, resembled photographs they had been shown of John Hillmon. Plainly the circumstance that nobody had seen Hillmon since the death at Crooked Creek had become, with the passage of time, more of an argument against the companies' theory, and they were eager to provide some convincing evidence that he had been seen alive in the interim. Whether these witnesses served that need, however, was for the jury to decide. (The disappearance of Frederick Adolph Walter posed a similar difficulty for the plaintiff's side, of course.)[48]

The chief innovation of this trial on the defense side, however, was the production of several witnesses who placed a young cigarmaker named Frederick Adolph Walters in Lawrence and Topeka during 1878 and 1879—that is, in more or less the right neighborhood to have met Hillmon in Wichita in late February 1879. Perhaps the presentation of this testimony was prompted by a criticism of the defense case offered three years earlier by one of the second-trial jurors. After that jury hung, the juror told a reporter that he and some others had found the Dearest Alvina letter somewhat suspicious because no witnesses had testified to seeing Walters near Wichita at or about the date of the letter.

Most of these new witnesses, however, said they had seen or known the cigarmaker in Lawrence, not Wichita. Lawrence is a long way from Wichita, and nobody reported seeing Walters in Wichita immediately before the Hillmon party set out from that city, so it is unclear whether any of this location evidence would really have satisfied skepticism about the authenticity of the letter. Moreover, it carried a danger for the defendants.

Three of these witnesses reported having worked with Frederick Adolph Walters at the farm of a man named Metsker, near Lawrence. Some said he seemed unwell at the time. One of the coworkers, a James Tuttle, had a particular memory of Walters showing him his collection of cigarmaking tools; he recalled their shared labor on the Metsker farm taking place in 1879, ending in October.

This admission fell somewhere beyond surprising, for if true it would mark Walters as having been alive some months after the death at Crooked Creek; but it seems to have escaped much notice in the moment. The only cross-examination by Sallie's lawyers consisted of a brief question about how the witness would know what cigarmaking tools looked like. Someone must have pointed out the mischief-making capacity of James Tuttle's story, however, for a day later the defense recalled him to the stand—this time to amend his earlier account and say it was in 1878, not 1879, when he and Walters had worked together for Metsker. It was a near escape from disaster for the companies, and although James Tuttle would never testify again, his venture into witnessing would prove a harbinger of revelations about the cigarmaker still far in the future.[49]

As before, the defense witnesses whose testimony carried the most pathos were family members of Frederick Adolph Walters. The deposition of Daniel, the family patriarch, was read into evidence; it concluded with the old man's declaration that after his son's departure from home in 1878, the family had received letters from him every week or two until the last one, in March 1879. Then, as expected, the defendants offered into evidence a letter "signed Adolph Walters" and addressed (according to the reporter) to "Melvina Casten, Fort Madison, Iowa."[50]

"Is there objection, Mr. Riggs?" Judge O.P. Shiras states the query mildly enough. Mr. Samuel Riggs rises uneasily from his seat next to Mrs. Hillmon to acknowledge the judge's inquiry. He knows that Shiras is a man of unimpeachable formality, and the customary question need not imply that the judge thinks any particular objection is called for. But Riggs thinks that on this occasion he detects in the jurist more genuine anticipation than mere courtesy. *Might* there be some objection he ought to lodge?

Samuel Riggs is not accustomed to making numerous objections to his opponents' evidence in the course of a trial. He has seen this style of advocacy, practiced chiefly by some of the younger lawyers, but regards it with some disdain. It is his belief that jurors ordinarily regard efforts to keep information from them as ungentlemanly, at best. But the conviction has been growing in him that this d——d letter is the key to the insurance companies' very ungentlemanly treatment of Mrs. Hillmon's claim, and he is beginning to entertain some doubts about its origins.

That Tuttle witness, for example—the one who claimed that he had worked with Frederick Adolph Walters in the fall of 1879. The next day the witness had backed off from it, but Tuttle had looked confused during his second appearance, and worried. What if he had been telling the truth the first time, but was persuaded by Green's bullying to revise his memory?

Why, if so, then the d——d letter was a fake! If Walters was still working in or around Lawrence that fall, he wouldn't have written that letter from Wichita six months before. And he wouldn't have disappeared as far as his friends and family were concerned—unless he was somehow persuaded to disappear. Until this moment Riggs has been privately dubious about his client's claim, but his convictions are growing more in her direction. Perhaps Brown has told the truth all along about the journey that ended in Crooked Creek; perhaps Walters never did travel with the Hillmon party. On the other hand, Riggs has seen the writing on the letter, and also the writing on other letters from the Walters fellow. As far as he can see, it is the same, and the penmanship teacher he has consulted is of the same opinion.

"Mr. Riggs?" O.P. Shiras is a patient man, but Riggs knows he will be not be permitted to dither all afternoon. Lysander Wheat, seated next to him at the plaintiff's table, is fingering the arm of Riggs's jacket to acquire his attention.

"A moment, if you would be so kind, Your Honor," says Riggs, before turning with annoyance to his cocounsel. "What *is* it, sir?" he whispers, so loudly that two of the jurors exchange amused glances.

At first he does not hear, or does not take in, the single word that Wheat says. But when the older man says it again Riggs begins to sense, at first dimly and then with growing clarity, the shape of a point he should have perceived seven years before, and he turns slowly and wonderingly back toward the bench to repeat the word.

"Mr. Riggs?" Shiras has come to the end of his patience.

"Hearsay," Samuel Riggs stammers. And then with more confidence, "Hearsay, Your Honor. The plaintiff objects to this document on the ground that it is hearsay."

The judge's response is immediate. He turns to the bailiff and asks him to remove the jury to the jury room. A whispered commotion issues from the defense table, where Green, Barker, and Gleed have until that moment been examining some papers without paying much heed to the colloquy between judge and plaintiff's counsel. As soon as the door has closed behind the last juror, Dean James W. Green is on his feet.

"I do beg your pardon, Your Honor, I was momentarily inattentive. Has my learned opponent made an *objection*? One so provocative that it requires the jury's removal?"

Shiras peers over his spectacles with what seems to be a certain indecorous pleasure. "Yes sir, Mr. Riggs has suggested that this document is hearsay, and I am inclined to agree with him. You do offer it to prove the truth of the matters represented therein, do you not?"

Green glances back at the seated Barker, then at Gleed. Neither face seems to offer any intelligent advice. "Sir," says Green, summoning his most convincing air of decanal authority, "this letter was received in evidence without objection or question in each of the former trials. We are prepared to show that it is inscribed in the handwriting of Mr. Walters. It is central to the defendants' case, and essential to the jury's full understanding of the matter. Nobody has ever questioned its admissibility. It is far too late to do so now."

Riggs begins to answer, but Shiras holds a hand up, palm forward, soliciting silence, and then speaks. "I do not think it is in any wise too late, Mr. Green. If such an objection had been made and overruled at one of the earlier proceedings I might take a different view of it, as one might regard such a ruling as the law of the case. But I believe this court must entertain Mr. Riggs's objection, now it is made for the first time, on the merits. I do not understand the objection to be directed at this exhibit's authenticity, so your handwriting comparisons would not seem to be germane. The objection is hearsay. Do you maintain that the exhibit is not hearsay? Or that it falls within the compass of an exception to the hearsay rule?"

"Your Honor," Green begins, then pauses. Riggs, still in the process of achieving in halting mental steps a comprehension of the complete shape of the situation, watches his adversary with dazed fascination. James W. Green has always commanded a full battalion of blarney soldiers, and the sight of him at a loss for words is unprecedented. Lysander Wheat's mind must harbor less confusion; he grins with undisguised triumph. "Your Honor," Green repeats, louder this time, "may we have a moment to confer?"

"Certainly, Mr. Green. Perhaps this would be a good time for us to adjourn for the day in any event." Shiras strikes the wooden surface before him decisively with his gavel. "Court will be in adjournment until nine thirty tomorrow morning, at which time it will entertain Mr. Green's response to Mr. Riggs's objection. The bailiff will see to the jurors' supper, and have them ready to rejoin the court no later than ten o'clock tomorrow."

"All rise," the bailiff bawls, and everyone in the courtroom stands in silence as the judge departs through the exit that leads to his chambers. Some, however, can scarcely contain their sentiments. The instant the judge's door closes, Sallie Hillmon turns to Samuel Riggs.

"What happened? The jury may not see that letter?"

It is Wheat who answers. "The judge has not ruled yet, Mrs. Hillmon. But I believe the tide has turned our way." He turns his eyes with satisfaction toward the defense table, where the consternated Green is directing orders at Barker and Gleed in a hoarse undertone.

"Why don't you go find your cousin and allow him to discover some supper for you?" suggests Riggs to his client. "I must pursue a bit of study before Judge Shiras reconvenes us."

The courtroom is quiet the next morning, sunlight slanting through the dusty windows, when the bailiff calls the court to order and O.P. Shiras enters from his chambers behind the bench. The jurors are absent, and nine-thirty is early for most of the spectators to have arrived. The court's reporter is already settled below the judge's perch, his expression professionally blank as he stands for the judge's entrance. Green stands near the lawyer's podium, clasping and unclasping his large hands. Barker has not yet arrived, but when the bailiff bids the room to be seated, Charles Gleed lowers himself into a chair a few feet from Green. Gleed has inserted his right index finger between the pages of a leather-bound volume, as though to mark his place. He looks eagerly toward Green, who ignores the younger man in favor of the occasional inspection of a scribbled page that rests on the podium.

To starboard of the podium, Sallie Hillmon's lawyers Samuel Riggs, Lysander Wheat, and John Hutchings sit stiffly in a precise row. They have studied deep into the February night, and none of them has slept for more than two hours. Their disciplined posture, however, belies their emotions. Lawyerly joy has made them buoyant, and their uniform demeanor is a consequence of efforts to conceal a shared elation rather than of any unusual commitment to rigorous courtroom etiquette. They have persuaded their client to remain in the vestibule; even though they must acknowledge that she has become ever more conversant with the ways of the courtroom during the years of their acquaintance, they fear her behavior this morning will be insufficiently guarded.

Judge Shiras grasps his gavel, taps the bench lightly, and says, "Court will resume trial of the matter of Hillmon v. Mutual Life Insurance et alia. Mr. Green, have you something for us?"

"We have, Your Honor. Mr. Gleed and I have briefed this matter and are of the opinion that the exhibit objected to by Mr. Riggs is admissible as a document created in the regular course of business."

Samuel Riggs starts to rise, for he has foreseen this argument and has a reply to it, but Wheat tugs his elbow and thus persuades him to keep his counsel and his chair for a moment longer. O.P. Shiras examines his gavel, then peers owlishly through his glasses at James Green. "No sir," he says mildly. "It will not do. This was no business document, and it maligns the nature of the sentiments expressed therein so to describe it. The objection is sustained."

Green nods, as though unconcerned. In the course of the night before he has resigned himself to this outcome; moreover, he has a secondary plan. "We ask that the court note our exception to its ruling." A perfunctory ritual.

"Noted," responds the judge. "Shall I instruct the bailiff to bring in the jury, gentlemen?"

Riggs does rise then, and says, "Your Honor, I trust your ruling extends as well to any effort by Mrs. Rieffenach to describe the contents of the letter she claims to have received from her brother?"

Shiras looks puzzled, and Riggs remembers that he would not have heard this name before. "Your Honor, this lady is the sister of Mr. F.A. Walters," he explains. "In earlier trials, she testified to her receipt of a letter very similar to the one the court has just excluded, although she could not furnish it, saying it had been lost."

Shiras looks toward Green. "The witness will say that this unobtainable letter from her brother also reports having made the acquaintance of a man named Hillmon?"

"She will, sir," replies Green, this time with some agitation in his voice. He is now doubly dependent on the sister's testimony, and had counted on Riggs to fail to notice that it was subject to the same objection as the Kasten letter. "Mrs. Rieffenach's testimony corroborates in every respect the contents of the letter to Miss Kasten, which is why . . ."

"Then this testimony too must be excluded, Mr. Green," interrupts the judge, writing rapid notes on his tablet. "Even if the loss of the letter might excuse its production, the testimony is subject to precisely the same hearsay objection. A man no more writes business correspondence to his sister than to his sweetheart. Both objections are sustained. The court will note your exceptions." Ignoring both Green's exasperated muttering and Gleed's efforts, book in hand, to insinuate himself at the podium and make himself heard, the judge bangs the gavel and addresses the bailiff. "Please assemble the jury, and have them take their seats."[51]

The exclusion of both the Kasten letter and the testimony of Elizabeth Rieffenach about the family's letter from Frederick Adolph must have dismayed the defense considerably, but this ruling by no means led to the collapse of the defendants' case. Perhaps daunted but not stymied, the defense attorneys proceeded to present a lengthy parade of witnesses (both live and by deposition); it was the newspaper's opinion, however, that these witnesses did not add much to the jurors' store of information. This portion of the trial apparently produced a certain fatigue in those required to attend to it. The *Topeka Daily Capital* reported on March 16:

> The jury, the attorneys and the attaches of the court who have listened to the evidence or taken part for twelve days in the Hillmon case, begin to show signs of weariness. It was of absorbing interest so long as different witnesses were being constantly brought on, and each day was pregnant with new and startling features, but the reading of exhaustive depositions corroborating evidence already in has a tendency to cause the imprisoned twelve good men and others to glance longingly out of doors these bright sun-shiny days and sigh for liberty. The thoughts of the rural peers are plowing, sowing oats of potato and garden patch, and the further exemplification of the operations and appearance of vaccine sores on a fifteen-day cadaver, or whether or not Hillmon or Walters hair was dark brown very dark brown or just medium brown is lost for want of close discrimination. When, therefore, at 3:30 yesterday afternoon the defense announced that they would rest their case, there was evidence of general pleasure and satisfaction.[52]

The Hillmon lawyers were allowed to present evidence in rebuttal, and briefly did so. Then the arduous trial was suddenly over, all but the summations.

As in the prior trials, the closing arguments of counsel occupied several hours. John Hutchings opened the arguments for his client, and spoke for two and one half hours. The *Daily Capital* records that "[i]n the course of the argument Mr. Hutchings adduced many strong and apparently incontrovertible reasons for the correctness of his conclusions." The Topeka *Daily Commonwealth* opined more neutrally that Hutchings had offered "a thorough and exhaustive review of the plaintiff's case," and characterized the arguments on both sides as "entertaining and instructive because able."[53]

Hutchings was followed by J.W. Green for the defense. The Dean laid emphasis on the peculiarity of Hillmon's choice to seek out an insurance salesman, and particularly of his decision to purchase such a large amount of insurance. His passions fully engaged, James W. Green closed with a plea for the jurors to heed the promise they made when selected as jurors to try the case on the facts without regard to sentiment. These high-minded arguments were mingled, however, with a subtle appeal to sentimentality:

> We appreciate the fact that the plaintiff in this case is a woman and that the defendant is a corporation. We know that the hearts of men go out in sympathy to women. You have sworn to try this case as if it was between individuals, and while you may sympathize with this plaintiff, you must remember that there are other parties who also deserve your sympathy. You should sympathize with the aged father of Walters, who for nine long years has mourned his son as dead—with his sisters and brothers, who are waiting for a verdict from your hands that will justify them in taking up the body buried at Lawrence and burying him beside his mother in the cemetery at Fort Madison.[54]

On this note the court adjourned for the day, but scarcely had the judge's gavel called it back to order the next morning before Mr. Samuel Riggs took his turn pleading Sallie Hillmon's case to the jurors. His métier was righteous anger—against the agents who attempted to trick

Sallie Hillmon after the death was reported, against W.J. Buchan and his exploitation of John Brown's fears of prosecution, and particularly against the witnesses from New Mexico, whom he characterized as "saloon-keepers." The jury's duty, he argued, was not only to do Sallie Hillmon justice, but to "vindicate her husband."[55]

George Barker followed for the defense, but he seems to have been somewhat unwell. He began by saying that he "was not in condition to speak long or to present the case as he would like to," but then he seemed to recover somewhat. In its substance Barker's summation did not break new ground, but his style produced a more homespun oration than Green's. He characterized the case as a "tempest in a teapot" and averred that Samuel Riggs "don't mean half what he says." Mr. Barker enlarged on many matters that struck him as suspicious: the lack of warmth in John Brown's letter informing Sallie of her husband's death; the circumstance that John Hillmon's journal, which he carried with him on his travels, contained no reference to insurance; the absence of any testimony from Levi Baldwin's brother Alva, who according to the testimony was present when the Medicine Lodge grave was opened. He refuted the plaintiff's claim that the Lawrence inquest was a sham controlled by the insurance companies by proposing that "[t]here were no disreputable persons at the inquest but myself." He defended his cocounsel Green against attacks on his behavior with sarcasm: "His sins are so many he ought to have some one to help pack them." W.J. Buchan he described as a man "whom the people have trusted twelve years; who sat in the legislature longer than any one man," and here Barker waxed somewhat indignant himself: "Should the reputation of years be brushed away and Buchan be branded as a rascal on the testimony of this man Brown?" The plaintiff's only hope, he suggested, lay in the fact that there was a woman on one side and an insurance company on the other.[56]

Lysander B. Wheat addressed the jury last among the attorneys, and his summation, according to the reporter, was "in some respects the most notable of those delivered." The journalist's hand must have been tired from the day of ceaseless transcription, however, for he wrote very little about the features that made Wheat's address so notable, observing only that "with the aid of a vivid imagination and a keen insight as to human character and human nature and actions, [he] was enabled to present some vivid word pictures illustrative of the points he desired to make, which enlisted the closest attention of the jury and spectators."[57]

One matter went unmentioned in the closing arguments: the love letter. As it had been excluded from evidence, it could not be mentioned in summation. The name Frederick Adolph Walters was spoken by every lawyer in his argument, but no word about the letter bearing his name and addressed to Miss Alvina Kasten had reached the jurors' ears.

The twelve men spent their evening at home, anticipating the next morning's instructions from Judge Shiras. Sallie Hillmon Smith would have awaited the next day as well, her spirits possibly buoyed by an extrajudicial event that had occurred in the courtroom at the beginning of the afternoon session: she had been handed a "beautiful bouquet of cut flowers" with a card attached saying "From Topeka ladies."[58]

The judge's summing-up, accomplished during roughly an hour and a quarter on the morning of March 22, 1888, was reportedly "regarded by the attorneys on both sides as able, clear, and impartial." It considered the possible interpretations of John Brown's act of signing the affidavit, as well as the various meanings attributable to Sallie Hillmon's act of signing the releases. It touched on most of the disputed issues: teeth, scars, height, identification, photographs. It advised the jury concerning what matters they might take into account in assessing the credibility of various witnesses. But O.P. Shiras concluded by admonishing the jurors that all these matters were subordinate to the single question that they must decide: "whose body was it that on the evening of March 18, 1879, lay dead by the camp fire on Crooked Creek?" (The date was off by a day, but surely the jurors knew what he meant.)[59]

Thus instructed, the jurors retired to their deliberations. These occupied less than four hours; by 2:10 p.m. they informed the deputy who had them in charge that they had reached a verdict. Once brought into the courtroom by Judge Shiras, they disclosed through their foreman that their verdict was in favor of Sallie Hillmon. With accumulated interest, the total award was $37,650.[60]

The jurors, apparently a convivial group, had another communication for the judge as well. They conveyed in writing that they wished to "give expression of our appreciation of the uniform kindness and courtesy extended to the jury by the Hon. O.P. Shiras," and further to compliment the "eminent judicial fairness and ability" of the visiting judge from Iowa. This communication was signed by each member of the jury: Samuel Kozier of Shawnee County, G.W. Coffin of Morris County, Enoch Chase of Shawnee County, Furman Baker of Shawnee County, A.S. Davidson of Dickinson County, Riley A. Elkins of Clay County, J.P. Rood of Montgomery County, Jacob Moon of Lyons County, J.W. Farnsworth of Shawnee County, H.S. Miller of Morris County, J. S. Bonton of Greenwood County, and J.S. Earnest of Shawnee County.[61]

In such sturdy hands had Sallie Hillmon's cause rested, and in them found vindication. But this happy outcome (happy for her in any event) was only a way station; soon her fortunes would rest with men of very different lives and experiences than those of these Kansans, or even of Judge O.P. Shiras. By 5:30 on the afternoon of the verdict, the defendants had filed a motion for a new trial, the usual preliminary to an appeal.[62]

Back in Iowa, Judge Shiras summoned the attorneys to his home courtroom in June 1888 to present their arguments on the motion for new trial. The grounds put forward by the defendants were misconduct by the plaintiff, misconduct by the jury, the claim that the verdict was contrary to the evidence and the law, and "newly discovered evidence material to the defendants, which it could not by reasonable diligence have discovered upon the trial of this action." Judge Shiras denied the defendants' motion, whereupon the insurance companies immediately announced that they would appeal the case to the United States Supreme Court.[63]

What was the newly discovered evidence the defendants claimed to have found? The records do not disclose it, but it may have been related to a startling report that surfaced about a year after their motion for new trial was denied. In May 1889, while the companies' appeal was pending before the Supreme Court, the *Chicago Tribune* reported that a witness had claimed that John Hillmon was alive and in custody. The source of this information was said to be Detective J.H. Franklin of the "Santa Fe secret service," who maintained that until recently Hillmon had been living in the mountains of Old Mexico. Franklin asserted that Hillmon had been captured during a trip across the Arizona border, and was cooling his heels in the jail at Tombstone.[64]

Sallie Hillmon Smith, when asked for her reaction to this news, seemed unsurprised and unconcerned.

> I expect some of the insurance companies were getting ready
> to pay me and this story was gotten up by the others to stop
> them. This is not the first time they have claimed to have found
> Mr. Hillman. It was a trick of the insurance companies or their
> lawyers that they always resorted to about the time my case
> was ready for trial. I think one of the lawyers is the author of
> this romance. This will not be the first time the lawyers for the
> defendants have sent out false reports. They once went so far as to
> try to damage my reputation through the press. I am resting easy,
> however, and am not concerned in the gossip.[65]

From the beginning, the *Tribune* seemed to credit Sallie's account more than it did the report that Hillmon was alive. Indeed, it maintained that an agent of the New York Life Insurance Company had stated to their reporter "that his company would pay her attorney $16,500 this week, they having tired of the litigation."[66]

The Kansas papers, after at first reporting breathlessly that Hillmon had been found and arrested, turned the story around within a few days. Two days after its local rival reported that "John W. Hillman, whose supposed remains were found at Crooked Creek, in Barber County, shot through the head, has just been arrested near Tombstone, A.T., where he had been working in a mine," the *Atchison Daily Champion* inserted into its gossip column an item explaining that "Messrs Gleed and Green, two of the attorneys for the insurance companies in the Hillmon case, do not put a great deal of confidence in the reported arrest of Hillmon, in Arizona. The man who arrested the supposed Hillmon is said to be a detective by the name of Miller, who has been hunting Hillmon for years, and has become something of a crank on the subject." The *Lawrence Daily Journal* clarified further: "It is positively denied at the offices of the insurance company's interested that John W. Hillman . . . had been found. It is said the companies have no trace of him whatever and it is a mystery where the story of his discovery started."[67]

The *Chicago Tribune*'s prediction that the New York Life Insurance Company would settle with Sallie did not come to pass. None of the defendants settled her claim before the companies' appeal reached the United States Supreme Court.

Detective J.H. Franklin was not heard from again on the subject of John Hillmon, at least not in the national press. But he would not be the last operative to represent, before the Hillmon saga ended, that he could produce its hero (or villain) alive.

5

THE SUPREME COURT HEARS A CASE OF "GRAVEYARD INSURANCE"

1892

Four years were to pass before the Supreme Court rendered its decision on the companies' appeal. During this interval, Kansas occupied the center of remarkable political events that both reflected and created the tides of sentiment on which Sallie Hillmon's lawsuit rode. The People's Party, the organized wing of the populist movement, roared to success in Sallie's home state in the 1890s. In 1890, the year of its organization, the People's Party won control of 96 of 125 seats in the lower house of the Kansas Legislature, and captured five of Kansas's seven congressional seats. The populist candidate for United States Senate, William Peffer, defeated longtime senator John Ingalls.[1]

Midwestern populism grew out of the grievances of settlers whose dreams had been demolished by cruel weather, high railroad prices for the transport of their goods, poor wages for their labor, and a collapse in the value of their farms and homesteads. Populists tended to blame these injustices (apart from the weather) on the greed of capitalists, especially the banks, commodities merchants, and railroads. The party's platform included free coinage of silver (or at least a significant expansion of the money supply), nationalization of the railroads, farm subsidies, and direct election of U.S. Senators.[2]

The movement attracted both fierce loyalty and scathing ridicule. A sympathetic journalist called the People's Party "a great impressionistic picture, full of violent daubs and colors, framed in depression, gloom, financial distress, hot winds, droughts, hard times, grasshoppers, and tragedy." Charles Gleed (whose clients, it will be remembered, included the Santa Fe Railroad as well as Sallie Hillmon's antagonists), described it as "a large winding of respectable and decent though inarticulate and incoherent discontent on a small nucleus of political deviltry compounded of vicious stupidity and unscrupulous cunning." A political cartoon of the era in the satirical magazine *Puck* portrayed matters with even less ambivalence: titled "The Grangers' Dream of Cheap Money," it depicted Peffer employing a giant bellows to blow a river of greenbacks out of the doors of a windmill labeled "U.S. Treasury," while a gaggle of grinning rustics cart the cash away in wagons. According to this dystopian view of populism, the movement's success could lead only to anarchy and hyperinflation. John Ingalls, smarting from his defeat by Peffer, would have the harshest view. He wrote to a friend that the populists were "an enemy whose strength is unknown, a secret organization based on discontent, bound by oath, led by malevolent and vindictive conspirators."[3]

In the humid marsh where Washington, DC, had been built, a long way from the parched plains of Kansas and the suffering of its less fortunate residents, Horace Gray, Associate Justice of the United States Supreme Court, would in 1892 hire a new assistant or "law secretary." (Today we call such employees law clerks.) Gray, a man of impeccable Boston Brahmin pedigree, had joined the Supreme Court in 1882 after serving first as a Harvard Law School professor and then as Chief Justice of the Massachusetts Supreme Judicial Court, the youngest in its history. He was the first United States Supreme Court Justice to employ a law secretary; it was a custom he had inaugurated while on the bench in Massachusetts, when he found that enormous increases in the state court's docket had rendered the work of the judges impossible without assistance. For his first few years on the U.S. Supreme Court Justice Gray had paid his assistant's salary out of his own pocket, as the Court's funding did not include an appropriation for this purpose, but in 1886

Congress had authorized funds to enable each Justice to hire one law secretary, at an annual salary of $1,600 per year.[4]

Gray relied heavily on his law secretaries, and chose them carefully. Many went on to lead lives of great professional distinction. His first law clerk in Massachusetts had been Louis Brandeis, who would later follow his former employer to service on the United States Supreme Court. Shortly after Gray moved to the United States Supreme Court his law secretary was Samuel Williston, later to become a distinguished scholar of the law of contracts. And not long before the Hillmon case was scheduled for argument, Horace Gray offered the post of law secretary to the son of Professor James Bradley Thayer of the Harvard Law School, another distinguished Bostonian of his generation. The father was an esteemed scholar of the law of evidence who had been Gray's academic colleague. The son, Ezra Ripley Thayer, was widely regarded as a prodigy and a young man of extraordinary promise. It is doubtful that Sallie Hillmon Smith had heard of Thayer, or for that matter of Justice Gray, but the views and predilections of these prominent men would call the next turn in her winding journey as she sought to collect John Hillmon's life insurance proceeds.[5]

WASHINGTON, DC | 1892

Ezra enjoys the walk from his boardinghouse to the Capitol that morning, as he does on most days. The weather is not always fine; the steaming soggy summers wilt his collar and offend his New England sense of what weather ought to be. But he looks forward to greeting the tradespeople sweeping the sidewalks in front of their shops, and takes pleasure in watching the progress of the swaying delivery wagons loaded with foodstuffs and beer and laundered linens for the restaurants, or with gravel and marble to fuel the never-ending construction activity at this end of the great Mall. He stops most days at the Eastern Market to linger for a few moments in the lively bazaar, and to purchase a roll or small loaf of bread for his luncheon.

His circumstances require he practice a certain austerity, for the present, but this does not trouble Ezra. He knows that his post as Justice Horace Gray's law secretary is a necessary apprenticeship, the overture to a life of accomplishment and honor. And in truth the job is more satisfying than he had expected, for Justice Gray entrusts him with a surprising amount of independence. The Justice often signs, without altering a comma, the opinions and orders that Ezra puts forward for his approval. At first the young man had found this nonchalance of his employer's alarming, but in the last months he has come to expect that in many matters his suggestions will become Justice Gray's conclusions. It is more responsibility than he had anticipated, but the job is rendered thus more interesting, and Ezra Thayer knows that he is up to the task. He graduated at the top of his class at the Harvard Law School, but that is not all: law runs in his family's blood. His mother is descended from William Bradford, Governor of the Massachusetts Bay Colony, and his father serves as a professor at the Law School.

Indeed, Ezra engages in frequent correspondence with his father. James Bradley Thayer's advice has frequently found its way into the drafts written by his son, and from there into the opinions of Mr. Justice Horace Gray. Ezra knows he can trust his father's discretion; the famous professor would never boast of these subterranean contributions to the law, for he has no need of recognition or esteem from such a source. He derives more than enough of these from his teaching and his scholarship on the law of evidence.

On this day Ezra enters the Capitol Building by his usual route, climbing up the great stairs of the eastern entrance into the Rotunda, then descending again to the basement and the law library that serves both the Court and the Members of Congress. There is always talk that eventually the Court will be housed in a separate building, and Ezra thinks it will be a fine day when this comes to pass. Although the courtroom upstairs is stately enough, having once been the Senate Chamber, it is used only for the argument of cases. Apart from the courtroom, the only real estate the Justices command in the Capitol is a poky conference room and their Robing Room; in the absence of dining facilities they are compelled to eat their dinners in the latter. Many of them, finding these quarters ungracious, work at their homes when not hearing arguments or participating in conferences.

The secretaries enjoy even less accommodation, but Ezra has discovered a quiet corner of the basement law library that he finds suitable for reading briefs and writing his drafts. It is not yet nine o'clock when he hangs up his coat and unpacks a thick bundle of paper from his briefcase onto his usual desk. The blue sheet that wraps the bundle carries the inscription *Mutual Life Insurance Company of New York et al., Appellants v. Sallie Hillmon, Appellee.* At the sight of it he smiles, for the case amuses him. It trails a lengthy and somewhat bizarre history behind it, having to do with a cowboy of some description and his purported wife and their attempt to cheat some life insurance companies out of the proceeds of several policies. Murder seems to come into the picture as well. There is some $25,000 at stake altogether, a small fortune and a preposterous amount of insurance for such a person to carry. Ezra's father makes less than a quarter of that amount every year. Justice Gray had emerged from the Justices' conference ten days ago and handed the file to Ezra with a grimace of distaste; apparently the opinion had been assigned to him. "Brown calls it a case of graveyard insurance," the Justice had pronounced. "That seems about right. Find a way to reverse it, Mr. Thayer." Ezra was not familiar with the term and sought enlightenment from Justice Henry B. Brown's law secretary, who advised him that "graveyard insurance" was employed in the lawless reaches of the frontier to describe a scheme of life insurance fraud entailing the substitution of one body for another.

Within a day of receiving the Hillmon file, Ezra had produced an opinion sufficient to justify the reversal of the jury's verdict for the cowboy's wife. In its paragraphs he demonstrated that the trial judge had erred in not allowing the three life insurance companies, whose cases had been consolidated for trial quite against their wishes, the same number of peremptory challenges to the jury panel that they would have been allocated in separate trials; this error would require remand and retrial. The Court's customs discouraged the decision of unnecessary issues, so Ezra had deemed it uncalled for to discuss the companies' other eighty-odd assignments of error. But his Justice, after a cursory reading of the draft, had thrust the papers back to him.

"It won't do," Horace Gray had said gruffly. "We could give the companies two hundred challenges apiece out there in Kansas, and the fools left in the jury box would just make the same mistake again. They're mostly populists and sodbusters, and they despise the insurance companies almost as much as they hate the railroads. The only way to make sure that murdering hoodwink and his wife don't profit from their crimes is to get the dead fellow's letter in front of the jurors the next time. Find a way to do that, Mr. Thayer."

Ezra had been taken aback at first, but on reflection he saw Justice Gray's point. In theory the Court was there only to decide questions of law, in an impartial and learned fashion. Matters of fact were not their concern, and outcomes were to be disregarded. In theory. But a man of the Justice's stature could not be expected to allow himself to become an accomplice to fraud. Nor murder, of course.

Justice Gray's mention of a letter was puzzling, and Ezra had returned to the file to discover its referent. Eventually he located an assignment of error nearly at the end of the insurance companies' submissions. The trial judge had erred, the companies argued, in excluding from evidence a certain letter from a man named Walters to his betrothed, a lady named Kasten. The text of the excluded letter was reproduced in this document, and immediately Ezra saw Justice Gray's point. The letter had its comical aspect, but certainly it did seem to prove that the dead body belonged not to the over-insured cowboy, but rather to this Walters fellow. Moreover, a sister of Walters would have testified that she received a letter (later apparently mislaid) containing similar information, but the trial judge had not permitted her to tell the jury about it.

The difficulty was that the letters (the one that was produced as well as the lost one) were hearsay. There was no way to get around that, in Ezra's opinion. The companies didn't even attempt to argue otherwise; they maintained that they were business records, which if so would except them from the operation of the hearsay rule. But Ezra knew that even Justice Gray, eager as he was to put his imprimatur on the admissibility of this evidence, would never agree that a cigarmaker's half-literate mash note was a business record, nor would the other Justices.

Ezra had written to his father that very evening, describing his predicament and inquiring whether the country's most distinguished scholar of the law of evidence could perceive some exception to the hearsay rule that would justify the admission of the letter. J.B.T. had not disappointed him.

Ezra procures foolscap and pen from the briefcase, then studies the letter that his landlady had handed him that morning. His father's handwriting is precise and easily read: "One solution might be simply to declare that statements describing one's *intention* form an exception to the hearsay rule. I believe there is a New Jersey decision so holding. It is perhaps not the most convincing doctrine in general, but on its premise, your cigar-maker's letter might be admitted." Ezra places the letter carefully face-down on the desk and retrieves his rejected original opinion draft, which he rereads. It concludes, "The denial of the right to challenge, secured to the defendants by the statute, entitled them to a new trial."

No need to eliminate any of what he has already written, Ezra decides. The opinion may simply continue from there. He shakes his pen gently and begins to write: "There is, however, one question of evidence so important, so fully argued at bar, and so likely to arise upon another trial, that it is proper to express an opinion on it. The question is of the admissibility of the letters written by Walters on the first days of March, 1879, which were offered in evidence by the defendants, and excluded by the court."

The moments flow into hours, and the forenoon has expired by the time Ezra relinquishes his pen and rises to stretch his back for a moment. He surveys his work with satisfaction, with particular attention to the last paragraph:

> Upon principle and authority, therefore, we are of the opinion
> that the two letters were competent evidence of the intention of
> Walters at the time of writing them, which was a material fact
> bearing on the question in controversy; and that for the exclusion
> of these letters, as well as for the undue restriction of the defen-
> dants' challenges, the verdicts must be set aside, and a new trial
> had.

Ezra retrieves his coat. He will look for Horace Gray in the Court's quarters above, and if (as Ezra suspects) the Justice is not to be found there, perhaps Ezra will walk over to his house and show him this new version. A brief stroll in the sunshine would not go amiss.

Ezra believes Justice Gray will be pleased with his second effort; the use it makes of the previous authorities (apart from the one New Jersey case) is a bit extravagant, but the language Ezra has employed disguises this feature without making any outright misstatements. In any event, it was the Justice himself who instructed him to find a way to rule the letter admissible, and Ezra is convinced that J.B.T.'s way is more plausible than any other that could be constructed out of the available legal materials. Ezra will write to his father this evening to tell him whether his suggestion has carried the day. Despite its unprepossessing subject matter and his original setback, Ezra has found the drafting of the opinion in *Mutual Life Insurance Company et al v. Sallie Hillmon* a very agreeable assignment.[6]

At least, I imagine that it must have happened more or less like that. What is known for certain is this: Justice Horace Gray served on the Court for ten years after the Hillmon decision, until July 1902, when illness forced him to resign; he died a few weeks later. He is not remembered as one of the Supreme Court's most brilliant thinkers; indeed he is, as one scholar notes, "almost forgotten." Even one of his greatest admirers acknowledges that Gray "added few new concepts to the law. . . . He was not given to philosophy, nor to higher law, nor to natural law concepts, nor to speculation." He was instead a pragmatic man, who believed in "keeping law well-adjusted to the changing needs of society as judges saw those needs."[7]

Justice Gray's opinion in *Hillmon* cites a number of previous Supreme Court decisions, as well as those of other courts, as authority for the existence of a hearsay exception for statements of intention. But not one of these cases, with a single exception, supplies a precedent for what the Court holds in the Hillmon case. The one exception, a New Jersey case of dubious logic, had held a few years earlier that the son and wife of a murdered businessman could testify to the victim's predeparture explanation of where he planned to go and with whom, despite the hearsay nature of this evidence. The New Jersey justice who wrote the opinion in that case explained, "In the ordinary course of things, it was the usual information that a man about leaving home would communicate, for the convenience of his family, the information of his friends, or the regulation of his business. At the time it was given such declarations could, in the nature of things, mean no harm to anyone; he who uttered them was bent on no expedition of mischief or wrong, and the attitude of affairs at the time entirely explodes the idea that such utterances were intended to serve any purpose but that for which they were obviously designed." In other words, there was no possibility that a respectable businessman had lied (to his wife!) about where he was going, or with whom.[8]

The United States Supreme Court was under no obligation to respect this unconvincing New Jersey precedent, as it came from a lower court. And it *is* unconvincing: the proposition that a fellow could have no possible motive for misrepresenting (to his wife, among others) where he intended to go and with whom defies common experience. (It is mortally wounded, for example, by a twenty-first-century example: the Governor of a southern state confessed that he had flown to Argentina to visit his mistress after telling his family and associates that he was going to "hike the Appalachian Trail.") But a judge who believed in "keeping the law well-adjusted to the changing needs of society as judges saw those needs" might see the matter through a different commonsense lens: if a plausible-seeming rule would keep a criminal from enjoying the proceeds of his crime, it might be thought a good one, worthy of invention.[9]

At the end of his service to Justice Horace Gray in 1893, Ezra Ripley Thayer returned to Boston and enjoyed for nearly two decades a distinguished career in the private practice of law, turning down two opportunities to join the faculty of the Harvard Law School. He did acquiesce, however, when after the death of James Barr Ames in 1910 he was approached to become the Law School's third Dean. He served as Dean for five years, leaving behind a legacy of affection for his person and admiration for his work. He not only managed the institution's public and private enterprises but taught as well, chiefly the course in evidence. Dean Thayer published a small body of scholarship during his years at Harvard, including essays on aspects of the law of evidence and procedure, but he never mentioned the Hillmon case by name in his published writings.[10]

Ezra Thayer's many successes did not shield him, however, from whatever demon drove him in September 1915 to take his own life by walking into a basin of the Charles River. The magazine *The Nation* reported that he had "committed suicide while temporarily insane," but his devoted and stricken colleagues at the Harvard Law School blamed stress and overwork.

Ten years after Thayer's death, another evidence scholar by the name of John MacArthur Maguire published in the *Harvard Law Review* an article titled "The Hillmon Case: Thirty-Three Years After." In his essay Maguire, who was at the time in only his second year on the Harvard Law faculty, says he has acquired from the teaching notes of Dean Ezra Ripley Thayer some information about how the Court's opinion in the Hillmon case came to be written as it was.

According to Maguire, Thayer's "rough working notes" contained the following passage:

> That the doctrine of the Hillmon case is a new one no one knows better than I, as I remember how the case came to be written. In point of fact the case was miserably argued, counsel putting it on no ground except course of business. The court voted to sustain the exceptions on general principles (N.B. Brown's comment as to "graveyard insurance") and Judge Gray was in dense darkness about the matter except as I fed him with matter obtained from J.B.T. as he was writing the opinion. . . . [O]ne must remain in some doubt how generally and how fully it is to be accepted, but it seems that it has come to stay, and furthermore that it is sound and wise. . . . [S]ome broad and simple rule like this is really necessary.[11]

I cannot verify Maguire's claim about the contents of these notes, but I cannot conceive of a reason why he would invent it. I think one must credit Thayer's account of the origins of the rule in the Hillmon case, which makes admissible any out-of-court statement in which the declarant announces his intentions: it was a rule in no way compelled or justified by the precedents that the opinion cites, but instead "a new one," invented for the occasion. The occasion, that is, of ensuring that a cowboy and his wife did not succeed in their scheme of murder and insurance fraud.[12]

And the rule did indeed "come to stay": the work of the two Thayers is still with us. In the Federal Rules of Evidence, it takes the form of Rule 803(3), which makes admissible, over a hearsay objection, an out-of-court statement "of the declarant's then existing state of mind ... such as intent, plan, motive, design." The Advisory Committee to the Supreme Court that recommended the enactment of this rule in 1975 made clear in its notes where its recommendation originated: "The rule of *Mutual Life Ins. Co. v. Hillman* ... allowing evidence of intention as tending to prove the doing of the act intended, is, of course, left undisturbed."[13]

† † †

In 1893, however, Horace Gray was still sitting on the Court, James Bradley Thayer still teaching at the Harvard Law School, and Ezra Ripley Thayer just beginning his brilliant career in private practice. Sallie Hillmon and her lawyers, and the three insurance companies and theirs, were preparing for one more trial of Sallie's claims against the insurance companies. It was understood by all these actors that the jury in this fourth trial would have opportunity to read what Frederick Adolph Walters had written in a letter to his sweetheart back home in Iowa.

The marriage certificate of John Hillmon and Sallie Quinn Hillmon. Credit: Archives of the Kansas State Historical Society. Courtesy Shirley Brier and Jerry Ferrin.

1. WILSON SCHOOL.
2. MADISON BELL HOME.
3. WHERE CHILDREN WERE FOUND.
4. OLD FRIDAY'S LOG CABIN.
5. TOM SPARK'S SHOOTING.
6. ELM MILLS.
7. HILLMAN SHOOTING.
8. PADDOCK LOG CABIN.
9. FERGERSON CLAIM.
10. FERGERSON GRAVE YARD.
11. AMBER POST OFFICE.
12. RAINBOW LAKE.
13. ARROWHEAD LAKE.
14. 99-SPRINGS LAKE.

A hand-drawn map showing the location of the Barbour County, Kansas, campground where John Hillmon or another met his death. Credit: Map drawn by George Miller. Courtesy Kim Fowles and Jerry Ferrin.

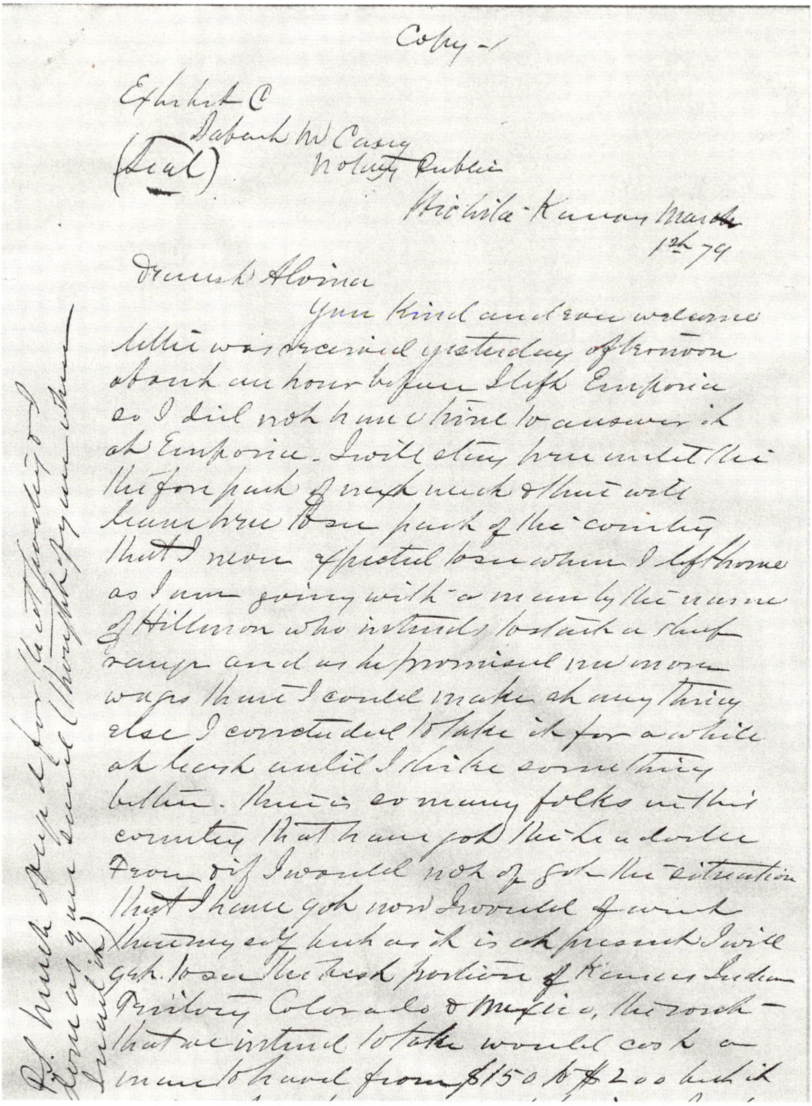

Copy ~

Exhibit C

(Seal) Sarah W Casey
Notary Public
Wichita Kansas March 1st 79

Dearest Alvina
Your kind and ever welcome letter was received yesterday afternoon about an hour before I left Emporia so I did not have a time to answer it at Emporia. I will stay here until the the fore part of next week & that will leave here to see part of the country that I never expected to see when I left home as I am going with a man by the name of Hillmon who intends to start a sheep range and as he promised me in one ways that I could make as any thing else I concluded to take it for a while at least until I strike something better. There is so many folks in this country that have got the head a dollar from off I would not of got the situation that I have got now I would of wish I myself luck as it is at present. I will get to see the best portion of Kansas Indian Territory Colorado & Mexico, the road that we intend to take would cost a man to travel from $150 to $200 but it

A handwritten copy (the original could not be found) of the famous love letter that was the centerpiece of the Hillmon case in the Supreme Court. Courtesy National Archives and Records Administration.

A photograph of James Woods Green, attorney for the insurance companies in all the Hillmon trials and founding Dean of the University of Kansas Law School. Credit: From *A Souvenir History of Lawrence, 1898*, courtesy Watkins Community Museum of History, Lawrence, Kansas.

One of the few images extant of Sallie Hillmon Smith, drawn as she was in 1895. Credit: Artist unknown, *Topeka Daily Capital*, March 10, 1895.

After the death of his brother John, who had represented Sallie in the second and third Hillmon trials, Charles F. Hutchings joined her trial team for the fourth through sixth trials. Credit: Artist unknown, *Topeka Daily Capital*, March 10, 1895

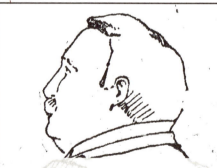

Edward S. Isham, a distinguished Chicago attorney and law partner to Abraham Lincoln's son Robert, represented the insurance companies in the fifth and sixth trials. Credit: Artist unknown, *Topeka Daily Capital*, March 10, 1895.

Judge Alfred D. Thomas, visiting from North Dakota, presided over the fourth and longest trial of the Hillmon case. Credit: Artist unknown, *Topeka Daily Capital*, March 10, 1895.

Circuit Court Room: the three Hillmon trials held in Topeka took place in this courtroom.
Credit: Jo Sheridan, *Topeka Daily Capital*, March 10, 1895.

Mob at the Kansas Statehouse, Topeka, February 5, 1893 (image number 24839).
Credit: Photographer W.F. Farrow, courtesy Kansas State Historical Society.

Mary Elizabeth Lease (image number 690). Credit: Photographer Deane, courtesy Kansas State Historical Society.

A photograph of John Hillmon's great-nephew Leray Hillmon, in May 2006. Credit: Photographer Rachel Griego.

Three of the largest bones found among the remains at Oak Hill Cemetery, including the shoulder bone from which DNA was sought to be extracted. Credit: Photographer Rachel Griego.

6

JOHN HILLMON IS REPORTED TO BE ALIVE AS THE ARDUOUS FOURTH TRIAL PROCEEDS

1893–1895

Although the Hillmon case enjoyed an audience from its inception, it gained even more widespread fame after it had been decided by the Supreme Court in 1892 and sent back for retrial. One Kansas journalist with a taste for classical allusion characterized the first retrial, in 1895, as a "final Titanic contest." The prediction of finality proved optimistic, but the other adjective may have been more apt. Even the national press began to employ similar encomia in describing the case: the *Los Angeles Times* referred to the case as "famous," while the *Chicago Daily Tribune* described it as "celebrated." The *New York Times* was more reserved in 1892, describing the lawsuit only as "somewhat celebrated," but by the time of the last trial in 1899 it had become, in the judgment of that newspaper, "the most noted in the West and, of its kind, in the United States, if not in the world."[1]

TOPEKA, KANSAS | JANUARY 1895

"I am sorry that you must contend with this business again, Mrs., ah, Smith," says Lysander Wheat, hoping she has not noticed his near mistake. He still finds it difficult not to think of her as Hillmon. The lawyer and his client proceed down the street toward the federal courthouse in Topeka; it is a route familiar to both of them, although somewhat altered by construction and demolition during the seven years that have passed since last they walked it together. Wheat keeps to the outside of the sidewalk, to protect the lady from the possibility of splashes thrown by passing hacks. Melting snow has left the street boggy and pocked with occasional puddles; the boots of those who step on the softer patches release the dense aroma of earth. It is an uncommonly warm day for January, and Wheat hopes this clemency may augur more good fortune to come.

The milky winter light reveals changes in the two walking companions as well, perhaps more marked in the man than in the woman. His hair is still abundant, but filaments of the steely shade that once characterized the whole are now outnumbered by their paler brothers; his bristle mustache is neatly trimmed, but one or two white whiskers poke out of his sunken cheeks where the razor missed them that morning in the inadequate light of his hotel bathroom. Sallie has grown just a bit plainer and stouter, and Wheat has detected that her eyes are milder by a small measure, less given to flashes of anger or amusement. The giddy woman who nine years ago swept into his office with a new husband appears to have settled into ordinary middle age. The lawyer, in his seventh decade, feels his own years in the slight stiffness of Sallie's gait as she steps over a puddle of dirty water.

"It is no matter, Mr. Wheat." Sallie says. "I no longer expect to profit from this case. I only want to see that you are paid for your many years of work."

The lawyer nods, for he knows that very little of the expectation, such as it is, still belongs to his client. It has been assigned to him, his colleagues, and some other investors, in dribs and drabs over the years, to finance the fees and expenses. Indeed, Sallie's motives for persisting in this litigation are somewhat mysterious to Lysander Wheat, but as the owner of a portion of her claims he is grateful for her perseverance, and wishes to acknowledge this. They walk half a block before he speaks again. "It is good of you to take matters in this spirit," he hazards. "We must not allow these insurance companies to bilk Kansas citizens. In this we are united, I believe."

"Oh, yes," says Sallie, but she is examining the contents of a shop window and does not turn to face him.

The lawyer takes her arm to assist her in stepping down off the tilted wooden sidewalk onto the crowded street they must cross. A figure on a bicycle approaches from the right with alarming speed, weaving in and out among the sedate pedestrians and spattering mud about. Wheat detains Sallie's step until the infernal whirligig machine has glided past.

"I will never understand why the Justices of the Supreme Court found it necessary to invent a new rule for the benefit of that damned letter," he says. "Perhaps they were right about the peremptory challenges, I do not protest that so much. But the hearsay rule was invented for a purpose, and their decision runs counter to any reason or sense." He coughs a bit after this speech, belatedly remembering that *damned* is not a term one should use in the presence of a lady.

But Sallie does not seem to notice. "They are determined that I should lose my case," she says. "They have seen the letter that the cigar-maker wrote, or that someone wrote at any rate, and having seen it they are sure that Mr. Hillmon killed the young man. Do not forget, Mr. Wheat, that those Justices are men of means and power who have never known want. They imagine that hardship reduces people to animals, so they will never believe that a poor man like John Hillmon would provide so well for his wife in the event he should die. That is all there is to it. If we should win again this time, they will again find some way to take it away from me, I am convinced of that. But I shall not give up, and some day I shall shame the companies into paying me what they owe."

The momentary blaze of her eyes alarms Wheat even as it reminds him pleasingly of the young woman he once knew. That is, if he knew her at all. He has never been certain, in his own mind, about the identity of the body that has been the subject of so much controversy. He is a lawyer: he has no need to convince himself one way or the other, he has only to persuade a jury. Nor is he certain whether his client is a liar or an innocent, although if required to say he would guess that she is neither the one nor the other altogether. It is no matter, for on this question as well it is best for him to remain, in the privacy of his thoughts, agnostic. He fears, however, that Sallie's speech suggests she may have got the populist fever, and hopes that if this is the case it does not become apparent to the jurors they will soon meet. It might please some, but it will surely antagonize others.

Wheat summons a tired smile as he opens the door to the court-house and gestures that Sallie should pass through ahead of him. The courthouse vestibule invites him inside with the cool familiar smell of stone, and with his first breath of it the weariness departs Lysander Wheat's aging body and he welcomes the accustomed quickening of his heart. He follows his client within and prepares to say his part of the rituals he has known for nearly forty years.

A clutch of newspapermen spots the pair and surges forward as one organism, but the lawyer waves them away. "Nothing yet, fellows," he says amiably. There seem to be more of them than ever, each one burning with the ambition to discover some "scoop." Green plays them like an orchestra, but that is not Lysander Wheat's way. He detests them, but it will not do to alienate them.

"Bastards," says Sallie under her breath, and Wheat looks at her in dismay. He would not have guessed she knew the word.[2]

Sallie Hillmon's persistence still mystifies me. Delay, expense, and ruin were inescapable hazards for nineteenth-century litigants, especially when they took on powerful capitalist organizations. What could have kept her going for a quarter century, especially after she was compelled to assign nearly all her interest in the lawsuit to her attorneys just to finance the litigation? Perhaps it was outraged indignation at the accusations of criminality against her deceased spouse (and on some occasions, against her as well).

But the behavior of her antagonists was perhaps even more mysterious: why would supposedly rational business actors like the officers of the three insurance companies remain so stubborn in their opposition to her suit? Surely the expenses of the litigation had early on outrun the cost of settlement. Curious about these questions, I asked one of my research assistants to discover whether any of the three insurance companies had preserved an archive of their documents related to the Hillmon case. Jon undertook a campaign of e-mail inquiries, and eventually a communications officer of the MassMutual Financial Group responded to him. MassMutual, formerly the Massachusetts Mutual Insurance Company, had merged with the Connecticut Mutual Life Insurance Company in the 1990s; Connecticut Mutual had been the last of the insurance companies to settle with Sallie.

The communications officer at MassMutual informed Jon that the company did possess materials related to the Hillmon litigation. Their materials, however, were not available for our inspection. Jon brought me this message with an air of defeat, but I wasn't ready to surrender yet. There were no lawful means for forcing the company to allow me access to their documents, but there was always persuasion.[3]

At about the same time, I received a phone call from a Tennessee lawyer named Donald Paine. Paine teaches evidence at the University of Tennessee while maintaining his law practice, and he told me that he had always been curious about the Hillmon case. He had himself tried to learn more about it a decade or so earlier, and having recently read about my efforts to exhume the body, he wanted to know more so he could share information with his students.

I told Don about our efforts, including those directed at obtaining permission to exhume the body buried at the Oak Hill Cemetery. In return, he furnished me with copies of correspondence he had carried on with the Connecticut Mutual Life Insurance Company, before it merged with MassMutual. When I examined these letters, I was encouraged: in July 1995, a librarian at Connecticut Mutual had written to Don, saying that the case transcripts in their archive were too fragile to be photocopied, but inviting him to travel to Hartford, where the company "would be happy to make all of the records available to you." The librarian reported that the records were "fairly well-organized" but that nobody there had examined them for quite some time. In addition to the trial transcripts, she advised, they had newspaper clippings, company correspondence, photographs of the body, and a tooth mold. Don had never made it to Hartford, so he had never seen the tooth mold. I hoped I'd have a chance to hold it; surely it must be the "plaster cast" displayed by a witness during the second trial and claimed to have been sculpted by the corpse's mouth. But it would probably not tell me anything I did not know, as there was no dispute about the excellence of the dead man's teeth. I was more interested in that company correspondence.[4]

I would have to bypass the MassMutual communications officer, that much was clear. I could not blame her, but plainly her job was to impede the flow of certain sorts of information. She was kind enough to inform me that a young lawyer in their legal division would be awaiting any further correspondence from me, and I wrote to him immediately.

When the Hillmon case came on for its fourth trial, Judge Cassius Foster, who had presided over the first trial, still sat on the bench of the federal trial court in Kansas. It was a solitary post. David Brewer, who had presided as a traveling circuit judge over the second Hillmon trial, had moved on to the United States Supreme Court; Judge O.P. Shiras from the third trial was back home in Iowa, presiding over his own docket (and possibly smarting over the rebuke the Supreme Court had addressed to his ruling on the matter of the Kasten letter). Foster must have been too busy with his regular caseload to take on the "Titanic contest," for a jurist from North Dakota, Judge Alfred D. Thomas, was pressed into service as a visiting judge. Judge Thomas summoned the parties and their attorneys—"a wonderful array of legal talent" said the *Topeka Daily Capital*—to his borrowed courtroom in Topeka on January 9, 1895, and announced that he expected the court's business to be conducted at a brisk pace. The jury was selected by the end of the day, apparently by a process that allowed the companies the enlarged number of peremptory challenges the Supreme Court had directed, although this aspect went unremarked in the newspaper.[5]

The jury was composed, as had been the first three Hillmon case juries, of twelve white men. Women did not achieve the right to sit on Kansas juries until 1912. Black men were not excluded de jure in 1895, but were nearly always eliminated "for cause" or by peremptory challenge when summoned. Kansas women were not permitted to vote or hold public office in 1895 either, except in municipal elections, this last a curiously limited right that resulted from the passage in 1887 of statewide legislation advanced by women's suffrage advocates. This victory, however modest, placed Kansas at the forefront of the campaign for women's suffrage, and it had immediate effects as well: the first municipal elections in which Kansas women could vote resulted in the election of the first woman mayor in the United States, Susanna Salter of Argonia.[6]

Still, in some parts of Kansas the belief persisted that women were too quickly forsaking home and hearth for public life. In 1889, the *Wichita Eagle* published a report that Benjamin Harrison was gaining on John Brown in popularity as a name for baby boys, along with the comment, "If the women of Kansas keep registering and voting it won't be long before there are no boy babies in Kansas to name. However, John Brown is a good name for boy babies in states where the differences in sex is recognized."[7]

At the other end of the gender equality opinion spectrum, famed Kansas women's activist Mary Elizabeth Lease disparaged municipal suffrage as a "pitiful crumb." Mrs. Lease, of Wichita, was an attorney, admitted to the Kansas Bar in 1885 after having taught herself law while raising four children and taking in other folks' laundry on a Texas farm. (Her name was often misreported as Mary Ellen, which allowed her numerous detractors to refer to her as "Mary Yellin.") An advocate for temperance, women's suffrage, and the working class, she was known as a charismatic, if not always coherent, speaker. She inspired the Emporia newspaper editor William Allen White, who was to put it mildly not an admirer, to report that she "could recite the multiplication table and set a crowd hooting and hurrahing at her will." Lease aligned herself with the populist cause in the late 1880s, and claimed credit for the successes of the Kansas People's Party in 1890. Her most famous speech, given at Kansas City in March 1891, was titled "Wall Street Owns the Country." In it she shouted that "[t]he West and South are bound and prostrate before the manufacturing East. Money rules, and our Vice-President is a London banker. Our laws are the output of a system which clothes rascals in robes and honesty in rags."[8]

Lease moved in 1896 to New York, where she later divorced her husband and worked for many years as a newspaper journalist, editor, and lecturer. She remained a passionate partisan for a series of causes until her death at age eighty.[9]

Despite the agitations of Mrs. Lease (or perhaps in part because of them), populist proposals that would have granted women the right to vote failed in Kansas in 1891 and again in 1894. Jury service for women enjoyed no greater success in the 1890s, and in 1895 when Sallie's case went to trial for the fourth time, it was still more than a decade away. The Hillmon case never would be submitted to a jury that included a woman. But those who believed that women ought to be protected from the sordid realities exposed in a courtroom would have found little reason to celebrate, for women accounted for a large proportion of the Hillmon trials' numerous spectators.[10]

Sallie was present during the jury selection process, her remarried status as "Mrs. Smith" noted by the reporter for the *Topeka Daily Capital*. Did she reflect on the composition of her jury, and wish that her sex were represented? Or was she content to rest her case on its universal strengths, such as they were, and perhaps to hope that a chivalrous impulse would flicker in the jury room?[11]

The Hillmon case of 1895, like the river that one cannot step in twice, could not be the same phenomenon it had been before. Nearly seven years had passed since any of the witnesses had been called on to state anything under oath about the Hillmon matter, which may account for the inconsistencies and lapses of memory that marked some of the testimony. On the day the fourth trial began, most of the important events in the case had taken place fifteen or more years in the past. Sallie, no longer a pitiful impoverished widow, had remarried. Some of the original witnesses were no longer available. John Brown would not appear; his brother Reuben testified that he had settled in Fayetteville, Arkansas, and was "prospering" in the lumber business. Arthur Judson was stipulated to be "dead or nonresident," a way of laying the foundation for the receipt of a transcript of his earlier testimony. (Dead seems more likely, for Mrs. Judson would testify at the trial, and divorce was uncommon in those times.) Colonel Samuel Walker was deceased, mourned as a hero of the Civil War rather than remembered for his role in the Hillmon matter. Fredrick Adolph Walters's mother was no longer alive. The photographer William Lamon, who took the corpse photos and swore that they could not have been of the man he knew as John Hillmon, had died in Mexico and so could testify only through his deposition.[12]

There had been changes to the roster of attorneys as well. One of Sallie's original attorneys, John Hutchings, had died; his brother Charles would take his place at the plaintiff's table. Defense attorney Charles Gleed's interests had drifted back to journalism, and in the following year he would purchase the *Kansas City Journal*. His brainy brother Willis had joined the faculty of the University of Kansas, serving in both the Classics and Law Departments. The Gleeds appear at intervals in accounts of the later trials, but they seem to have ceded most of their work on the insurance companies' trial team to their law partner Eugene Ware. (Ware was also known by his pen name "Ironquill," and is still Kansas's most famous native poet.)[13]

But the distinct environment of this fourth trial would not depend merely on changes in the cast of characters: many events had taken place in the world outside the courtroom during the interregnum. In particular, dramatic political developments in the preceding few years had altered and affected the Hillmon case and those who would decide it.

The lively quarrels that had birthed the People's Party did not die down during the first half of the 1890s. Populism's first spectacular victories in 1890 had laid on it the mantle of political power and produced passionate leaders, colorful spokespersons, and the inevitable internecine quarrels. But for a decade at least, the movement was powerful enough to transcend these differences, and to become not only a political party but a way of living and thinking for its adherents.

Even detractors of the movement could not shelter themselves altogether from the populist winds that blew through their streets. The speculation-driven expansion of the economy during the 1880s had slowed, then collapsed, and this general reversal combined with the overbuilding of railroads and overproduction of silver had prompted an economic crisis later known as the Panic of 1893. That year's cascade of unhappy events included the bankruptcies of numerous large business interests, bank failures, a credit crunch, and a precipitous drop in the value of silver. Manufacturing centers were stricken, but farm states like Kansas were affected greatly as well because the value of crops plunged. Many Kansas banks failed that year, including thirteen reported in a single week of July. As the drought persisted and unemployment soared, large numbers of homeowners and farmers walked away from their mortgages and the homesteads that secured them. The life insurance business was good in Kansas, however. In 1894, insurance companies collected more than $1.5 million in life insurance premiums in the state, and paid out losses of $548,736.79. The figures for 1895 were nearly as favorable for the industry.[14]

Populism insisted that the landscape of haunted houses, deserted farms, and ruined dreams could be explained by the excesses of capitalism and the investing class that had profited from them. At its most attractive the movement embodied what a recent historian has called the "humane preference" in the affairs of men and women, but it also gave a home to some less appealing attitudes. Some populists committed themselves to the struggle for women's suffrage, but others derided the women's campaign as a diversion or worse. Few of them, however attuned to the economic suffering of the fellow white citizens, noticed the African American Kansans who lived in segregated communities crushed by poverty. The governmental and private cruelties inflicted on Native Americans were largely a matter of indifference or ignorance to populism, and its devotion to elevating the status of the laboring man often led it into nativism and hostility to immigrants. Nevertheless, populism's focused critique of the injustices of untrammeled capitalism resonated profoundly during the Gilded Age, especially on the Kansas prairie.[15]

We cannot know for sure what the politics of the twelve jurors in the fourth Hillmon case may have been, but if they truly reflected their communities, it is certain they carried political disagreements into the jury room. Residents of Topeka or its neighboring areas, they could not have been unaware of the remarkable events at the nearby Capitol that had roiled the state in 1893. Newly elected populist governor Lorenzo Lewelling had given a stirring inaugural address in January of that year, promising that "those in distress who cry from the darkness shall not be heard in vain." Kansas had also voted to send to Congress the colorful populist farmer and attorney from Medicine Lodge, Jeremiah "Sockless Jerry" Simpson. But the aftermath of several contested elections for state representative had left the precise composition of the lower house of the state legislature in dispute: both the populists and the Republicans claimed to have a majority, and when the Legislature convened both set out to organize the chamber. Governor Lewelling formally recognized the populist legislature, but the Republicans did not concede his power to decide the matter, and a bizarre standoff ensued.

For the duration of one night the contending factions occupied Representative Hall jointly, each of the two would-be Speakers sleeping at the podium for fear of losing an advantage. Then for a while the disputants observed an uneasy truce in which the Republicans assembled in the hall in the morning and the populists in the afternoon. After about a month, one afternoon the populists remained in the chamber overnight and locked their opponents out; when the Republicans arrived in the morning they found the door fastened securely.[16]

Unwilling to be ousted in this rude manner, the Republicans broke the door to the hall, using a sledgehammer the populists would later claim carried the label of the Atchison, Topeka, and Santa Fe Railroad; they entered under the protection of private armed guards. The populists retreated, but threatened to ask the Governor to call out the state militia. Governor Lewelling issued an order that the Republicans quit the chamber, but they remained defiantly inside, although it is reported they grew very cold because the janitor, unsurprisingly a man of populist sympathies, turned off the heat. Lewelling summoned the militia and they surrounded the Statehouse, but their commander, a Republican colonel, refused the governor's direct order to clear the hall. These events clearly engaged the public: photographs taken during the standoff show hundreds of Kansas citizens standing uneasily about the Capitol grounds, wrapped and hatted against the chill.[17]

Eventually Lewelling agreed that the Kansas Supreme Court could settle the matter. The "Populist War" was ended in late February 1894 by the decision of that court, whose three members voted 2–1 along straight party lines to seat the Republican legislature. The court's divided decision, accompanied by a passionate dissent from the minority populist justice, did little to assuage the rancor.[18]

These events, so recent in memory, could not have been far from the minds of the jurors chosen to consider the claims of a working-class woman against three eastern corporations. But the politics of populism affected the Hillmon matter in other ways as well. Below the gubernatorial and legislative levels, numerous lesser officials in Kansas during the 1890s entertained populist sympathies. On several occasions the acts of one such officeholder outraged the insurance companies involved in the Hillmon litigation.

In 1893 Kansas Superintendent of Insurance S.H. Snider began a campaign to ban the removal of insurance lawsuits to federal court. It had long been the custom of out-of-state insurance companies to invoke the federal law that allowed them to transfer into the Kansas federal court any suit that a Kansan might file against them in the courts of the state. Snider had been elected as a Republican, but he was said by some to be "very radical on insurance matters," and the removals irked him. They were being practiced, he claimed, "for the purpose of expensive and vexatious delays, which make a compromise preferable to the policy holder, so forcing him into a partial relinquishment of his just and equitable rights."

Snider's new rule required any out-of-state insurance company applying for a license to transact business in Kansas to agree in advance not to remove to federal court any lawsuit filed against it in state court. Any company that declined to agree to this stipulation would be denied a license, and companies that held a license would lose it if they should seek a removal. The Hillmon case had not been removed, because Sallie's attorneys had filed it in federal court in the first instance (although they may have done so because they knew that it would have been pointless to file in state court, since removal would have swiftly followed). But when Snider announced a new policy in May 1893, he invoked the supposed injustices perpetrated by the insurance companies against Sallie Hillmon as one of the reasons it was needed.[19]

Told by several insurance agents that the companies they represented would withdraw from the state if he persisted in the policy, the Superintendent replied that in such an event the companies that remained and complied with the new policy would enjoy more business, and others would come as well when they saw this opportunity. Snider added in a more placatory voice that he believed many of the foot-dragging and dishonest practices he opposed were pursued without the knowledge of the companies' officers ensconced in their headquarters elsewhere; instead, he surmised, they were carried out by overzealous local representatives and counsel. He meant by issuing this order, he said, to call the attention of the responsible corporate officials to the injustices being carried out in their companies' names.[20]

The Superintendent got the attention of these officials, although the result was not altogether what he had hoped. The link that Snider had implied between the Hillmon defendants' behavior toward Sallie and his regulatory crackdown apparently stung, for the next few days featured an unusual amount of activity in the corporate offices of the New York insurance industry, coupled with some explosive claims about the true whereabouts of John Wesley Hillmon. The companies' strategy resembled one they had employed during the Lawrence inquest so many years before; they enlisted the press in an effort to persuade the public that their actions had not been unfair. They hoped that the newspapers would again aid them in persuading the public that their resistance to paying Sallie's Hillmon claims was principled, and founded on a single circumstance: John Hillmon was still alive.

It may be remembered that during the Lawrence inquest this strategy had consisted of suggesting to the local newspapers, chiefly the *Lawrence Standard*, various alternate identities for the corpse: the missing brother of Mrs. Lowell, the "young man of Indiana," a "man by the name of Willey," and Frank "Arkansaw" Nichols. None of these suggestions had panned out, of course (the companies first heard the name Frederick Adolph Walters many months later). But by 1893 the Hillmon case was notorious, national regulatory issues were at stake, and the companies' tactics had changed in two ways. They went further now, and claimed daringly that John Hillmon had been found alive. And on this occasion they bypassed small local publications to persuade some of the most venerable and important newspapers in the country to retail their story.

Whatever truth there may have been to Snider's suspicion that some of the companies' earlier schemes had been concocted in Kansas without the knowledge of the home office, there could be no doubt that the 1893 campaign to prove that John Hillmon was alive emanated from the highest levels of company management. On May 8, 1893, the *New York Times* published a lengthy story about the efforts of Superintendent Snider to punish insurance companies that mistreated their Kansas customers. The very next day, May 9, a page 1 headline announced "JOHN W. HILLMON NOT DEAD." The author of this second story reported breathlessly that he had "learned that the insurance companies had run down the 'corpse' in the great Hillmon case, and that they would produce the 'corpse' alive and well at the forthcoming new trial, which has just been ordered, fifteen years after the claim was first put in."[21]

The reporter's source was rather plainly Charlton T. Lewis, attorney for the Mutual Life Insurance Company of New York, and it is doubtful that any great investigative skill was required to winkle this disclosure out of him. Lewis is quoted thus: "We have at last found Hillmon alive and well, and know exactly where we can lay hands on him. After a search extending over fifteen years he has been finally traced to the Pacific coast, and he has made a clean breast of the whole affair."[22]

There follows an account of the entire Hillmon case that reads as though it is a closing argument delivered by Mr. Green; concerning each and every detail, it is the company's version that is stated, sometimes with such disregard of the evidence that even Green might have blushed. The canard that Sallie Hillmon could not describe her husband at the inquest is repeated, and the proposition put forward that after the inquest John Brown "ran away to Texas." It is claimed that the corpse's face had been burned beyond recognition, and that the amount of insurance at stake is $40,000.[23]

It is the last brief paragraph of the *Times* article that suggests why the insurance companies may have chosen to announce that they had found Hillmon at that precise moment. Charlton Lewis explains, "If Mr. Snider's ultimatum is based on the Hillmon contest you can see how little weight it is entitled to in view of our discovery."[24]

The next day, the *Chicago Daily Tribune* takes up the dramatic story of Hillmon's reappearance, reporting that the discovery that he is alive has "caused a sensation in life insurance circles." The Chicago version quotes William G. Davis, General Solicitor of the Mutual Life Insurance Company:

> We have Hillman under such surveillance that he cannot escape. He was located in the far Southwest and since then we have had his every movement watched. We have also taken to the place where he is a number of men who were intimately acquainted with him previous to his disappearance, and in that way established his identity beyond a doubt. He does not know yet that we have run him down, but he cannot elude us now, and when the next trial of the case comes up in Topeka in November we will produce him.[25]

Toward the end of his story, the journalist repeats a detail from the *Times'* earlier account, saying that the "principal in the swindle . . . consented readily enough to make a clean breast of the affair." By this reporter's account, Hillmon has laid the entire crime at the feet of Brown, and the reporter predicts that "all the conspirators will be brought up on criminal charges."[26]

Back in New York, the *Times* story published on the tenth a report that "[i]t is believed in insurance circles that the story of the finding of Hillmon will cause the discontinuance of the suit." The remainder of the article is devoted to reporting the views of several New York City insurance company executives about the recent regulatory activities of Superintendent Snider of Kansas. On the whole the insurance men are "not disposed to worry." One claims not to have given the matter a second thought; another says it is of so little importance he has not given it even a *single* thought. A third, less insouciant, opines that Snider's order is unconstitutional, and a fourth predicts that if the order is to stand, "large and substantial companies" will henceforth cease to do business in Kansas and Kansans will be thus deprived of their services. These men are, however, unanimous in opining that "the disclosure of the finding of John W. Hillmon would prove a boomerang for Mr. Snider."[27]

On May 24, the *Times* carried a front page story headlined "wanderings of a murderer." The story gives a highly circumstantial account of Hillmon's life since his disappearance in 1879, claiming that its source is the sheriff of Cochise County, Arizona. The details of Hillmon's career, it is asserted, have been given to the sheriff by an unnamed man who has contrived to become Hillmon's "chum," with the purpose of keeping him under surveillance and sending occasional reports back to the sheriff.[28]

These reports contain details both homely and lurid. Hillmon is said to be "dirty and slouchy," a "desperate character." His wanderings during the previous decade and a half have included a period of "taking up" with an Apache "squaw," a marriage to a Mexican woman, the fathering of a female child, and work as a cowboy, a miner, a sheepherder, and a prospector. Hillmon, having adopted the name "Coyote Bill," is said to have attempted to correspond with Sallie, only to receive a reply instructing him to stay out of sight and not to write again. He is claimed to have been rendered "desperate" by the news that she has remarried, and to have threatened vaguely to return to Kansas and expose the crime so that she and his other confederates would be compelled to "become the vagabonds that he himself had become." This Hillmon is reported to have confessed, apparently to his double agent "chum," that he committed a murder in Barbour County, Kansas. (Never mind that earlier reports said he had put the murder off onto John Brown.) The sheriff claims to have Hillmon in such a place that he could "never lose sight of him" and represents that "we hold ourselves in readiness to produce him at any time, though he is now on Mexican soil."[29]

Yet for all its welter of dusty Old West detail, the *Times'* story does not once address the question of why John Hillmon remains at liberty. The next day's edition, however, suggests a possible explanation: in it General Solicitor William G. Davis of Mutual Life (here called "Davies") is quoted as saying that the fugitive Hillmon's freedom might rest on Sallie Hillmon's willingness to surrender her claims. When asked whether he intends to "cause Hillmon's arrest" soon, he replies, "That I cannot say. . . . If Hillmon's widow attempts to push the case to trial again we shall certainly cause his arrest . . . [but] we do not care to waste any more money unless these people have not had enough of the law."

Davis goes on to predict that (in addition to this inducement) Sallie will be motivated to forfeit her right to a fourth trial by the Supreme Court's decision, which by Davis's estimation has "practically destroyed" her case. He seems not to remember that Sallie's lawyers had been able to wrestle his company's attorneys to a draw twice, in 1882 and 1885, even when the defense was aided by the evidence of Walters's letter to Alvina Kasten. Nor does he appear to realize that his use of the phrase "Hillmon's widow" is somewhat incompatible with his claims.[30]

Skepticism was expressed in a few quarters. In January 1894 the *Lawrence Daily Journal* observed that "[t]he late Mr. Hillmon has submitted to another interview, and has again accused himself of perpetrating a great fraud on the insurance companies. Mr. Hillmon will overwork that Banquo's ghost act if someone does not sit on him."[31]

Nothing more seemed to come of Hillmon's reported survival until eighteen months later, in December 1894; on the fourth of that month James W. Green persuaded Governor Lewelling, during his last weeks of office, to sign an arrest warrant for Hillmon. But no arrest was made pursuant to the warrant. Sallie's persistence was apparently unaffected by the claims that John Hillmon would be produced alive, for the fourth trial of the Hillmon case trial began as scheduled in January 1895.

Neither General Counsel Davis, nor the Sheriff of Cochise County, Arizona, nor James W. Green, nor anyone else produced John Wesley Hillmon at this trial, although various witnesses would claim to have seen him in Colorado in 1879 and in Arizona in 1889. Perhaps the claims about Hillmon's whereabouts had become a bit of an embarrassment to the

Hillmon defendants, for just as the trial began the insurance companies would insist to the reporter for the *Topeka Daily Capital* that they were "not hunting Hillmon, but that newspaper reports concerning Hillmon are gotten up by people who, on their own account, in view of the $2,500 reward offered, have thought it worth while to look into the case."[32]

Kansas Insurance Superintendent Snider left office in 1894, but the project of reforming the insurance business would appeal to later Superintendents as well, and would continue in fits and starts throughout the 1890s. Toward the century's end it would touch the Hillmon matter again before its energy was spent.

The fourth Hillmon jury was thus chosen at a moment of maximum political passion and division. Opening statements were concluded by early afternoon of the second day of trial, whereupon Sallie Hillmon's lawyers were directed to begin the presentation of their evidence. It became immediately plain that the insurance companies' lawyers had decided to give no quarter in this renewed contest. When asked to stipulate to the obvious propositions that their agents in Lawrence had authority to issue life insurance policies on their behalf, and that the policy papers were authentic, they declined. Sallie Hillmon Smith was thus compelled to take the stand and establish these matters. She made quite an impression on the *Topeka Daily Capital*'s reporter:

> Mrs. Hillmon is a wonderfully good witness on her own behalf and very positive in all her statements. Womanlike, she becomes somewhat excited under rapid "cross-firing," but never loses her head.[33]

This somewhat sexist praise should not necessarily be taken as a sign of the newspaper's sympathy for Sallie Hillmon Smith's case. To the contrary, the account of the Hillmon case's history provided by the *Topeka Daily Capital* reads suspiciously like a summary of all of the insurance company's talking points.[34]

Of the newspaper's political sympathies writ larger there can be no doubt. The Kansas State Historical Society has preserved a large celebratory cloth banner, produced after the 1894 elections ousted the populist governor Lorenzo Lewelling. Decorated with a large rooster, the banner reads "kansas redeemed, populism dead." At the bottom, in smaller lettering, appears the legend "*Compliments of the Daily Capital*."[35]

* * *

The early days of the fourth trial carried a few small moments of drama, but not much that was unexpected. Once they established the issuance of the insurance policies and their terms, Sallie's lawyers excused her from the stand. They would recall her later for more thorough testimony, but for now they were bent on addressing the matter of what they claimed to be the insurance companies' chicanery; their next subject would be the role that W.J. Buchan had played in John Brown's various accounts of the death at Crooked Creek. Rather than calling the Senator himself as a witness, the Hillmon trial team showed what the reporter called "a disposition to take the war into the enemy's camp" by summoning J.W. Green to take the oath. (The present-day prohibition against a lawyer's being a witness during a trial in which he represents a client was not well developed in those days.)[36]

After Green's five hours on the stand, even the *Topeka Daily Capital's* reporter was compelled to conclude that the former County Attorney had been representing the insurance companies "as early as the coroner's inquest," although Green himself would not quite admit it, pleading a lack of memory about when he acquired the companies as clients. George Barker, summoned some days later, would acknowledge without qualification that he had been in the pay of the insurance companies at the time of the inquest. As for Buchan and where his professional loyalties lay, there was evidence that "all papers that came into the hands of Buchan, sooner or later found their way into the hands of the attorneys for the defendants."[37]

After this excursion into the Buchan question, the plaintiff's lawyers seemed content to rest their case on the testimony of witnesses who had been heard from before, chiefly those who had seen the body and said it belonged to John Hillmon. The only eyewitness to the death, John Brown, did not forsake his prosperous lumber business in Arkansas to return and testify again; instead, the deposition he gave before the first trial was offered in evidence. Many other depositions from the earlier trials were read, a process the reporter, and no doubt the jurors, found tedious. Levi Baldwin testified, in no very novel manner; he denied firmly that he was to receive $10,000 of the life insurance proceeds. Mrs. Judson testified that the insurance men had tried to persuade Sallie not to have the corpse brought back to Lawrence, in order to prevent the body's identification. This was a curious claim, for in the earlier trials her testimony was that the men had attempted to discourage Sallie from *seeing* the body, and other witnesses had said the body was brought to Lawrence at the insurance companies' insistence. The passage of time had cast a haze over the memory of more than one witness, perhaps.[38]

Arthur Judson's earlier testimony (in which he recounted the height-measuring incident) was read. There having been testimony in earlier trials that the corpse had a mole on its back, a witness named Covey testified that John Hillmon had such a mole. This proposition, although potentially helpful to the Hillmon side, was somewhat impeached when Covey admitted that despite testifying in the Hillmon matter on two other occasions, he had never before mentioned this mole, but rather had (as the reporter rather sarcastically noted) "kept the fact locked in his bosom for fifteen years."[39]

Then it was time for Sallie Hillmon Smith's main appearance. Much of her testimony reprised the account of events she had given at the inquest and the various earlier trials, but there was also some new information of such a nature that its absence from her earlier testimony was at least surprising, perhaps even suspicious. She testified, for example, that she and John Hillmon had become engaged shortly after they first met in 1872, when she was fifteen years old. This claim was apparently intended to deflect the suspicion that her sudden marriage to a man she known for years was not a genuine union, but a convenience designed to enable their scheme of fraud. Possibly the long engagement was real, but she had not mentioned it before in three previous trials.[40]

Sallie's most startlingly novel claim pertained to when she learned the outcome of the Lawrence coroner's inquest. The issue arose during her cross-examination. Her lawyers objected to the question on the dubious ground that it would "open the sluice gates" to other similar questions. In the course of the arguments on this objection, it became clear that the insurance lawyers wanted to ask her when she had learned of the inquest jury's decision for a particular purpose: they hoped to lay the ground for an argument that it was this verdict, and not any persuasions of Mr. Buchan, that had convinced Sallie that her claims had no value and thus induced her to sign the releases. A lengthy argument ensued before Judge Thomas finally ruled that she must answer.[41]

No doubt Sallie had been in the courtroom during these colloquies; probably she understood, by the time the judge finally overruled her lawyers' objections, exactly why the defendants wanted her answer: they hoped to show that she had learned of the coroner's verdict, which was issued in April 1879, before she signed the releases in September. Thus prepared, she replied that she did not know in September what the verdict had been the previous April, and had no memory of reading any newspaper accounts about the inquest. Asked again by her own lawyers, she repeated that she never heard of the 1879 coroner's jury decision "until recently."[42]

The *Topeka Daily Capital's* fawning reporter would say Sallie "endured the ordeal of an extremely severe cross-examination carried on by an attorney well skilled in the art, with remarkable fortitude and clear-headedness." But I am less inclined to admire her performance on this occasion. In the course of sixteen years and three lawsuits she had never once learned what verdict the Lawrence inquest had produced? I don't believe her. Not for a second. Nor do I think a lapse of memory can account for this preposterous claim. The pro-Sallie forces that have dominated my imagination for so long are fallen into disarray; I cannot avoid believing that Sallie Hillmon Smith lied, under oath.[43]

If she lied about this matter, what else had she lied about?

Despite his announcement on the first day of this trial that he planned to proceed apace, the trial reportage reveals Judge Alfred Thomas to be an extremely unhurried jurist. His style found favor with the *Topeka Daily Capital's* reporter, who opined on one occasion that the previous day the judge "had several hard nuts to crack . . . and cracked them so carefully that the elucidation of the complex problems is probably more thorough than at any previous trial of the case."[44]

Judge Thomas's rulings often appeared only after days of indecision, and when finally announced were often tentative. Concerning one objection early in the trial he ruled, with characteristic courtesy and equivocation, that the objection would be "overruled for the time being, although assuring counsel for defendants that they would not be precluded from a further insistence upon it." On another occasion, at the time Sallie's attorneys rested their case in chief, the parties invested some intellect and ire in the argument of a somewhat intricate motion, resulting in the judge's pronouncement that "it was his desire to try the case upon its merits, and that in so far as he could prevent it, no technicality should interfere with this object." Since the arguments on both sides were technical, it is unclear which attorneys this observation would have pleased more. But no matter, for the nut-cracking judge went on to state that "[b]oth sides will be heard again upon the pending motions and objections."[45]

Well into the trial, the *Topeka Daily Capital*'s journalist maintained its admiration for the stately pace kept by the North Dakota jurist. Judge Thomas, he reported, "with exemplary caution seems determined to take no hasty steps, nor render suddenly formed opinions upon questions of importance which may ultimately become fatally detrimental to either party." He concluded, implausibly, that "every decision thus far rendered is unanimously applauded by council [*sic*] for both parties as being the result of deepest thought and profoundest consideration."[46]

The attorneys also came in for a generous measure of journalistic flattery, especially as pertained to their ability to raise and argue objections. They represented "the highest order of legal talent which has collaborated in the trial of any case in this city," and "[n]o doubt could arise as to their plenary knowledge of every technicality recognized in the vast store of jurisprudence." One could almost suspect the reporter of irony.[47]

The plaintiff's case had consumed about two weeks of the court's and jury's time; the defendants' would take three times as long. This ordeal could be attributed in part to the defendants' oversized witness list, but Judge Thomas's dithering also played a role. At one point the defendants desired to introduce the deposition testimony of the banker Crew, who had deposed that Levi Baldwin, not long before the death at Crooked Creek, had told Crew that he (Baldwin) would shortly come into some money. Sallie's lawyers objected that the testimony was hearsay, which it certainly was. The defendants argued that the statement was admissible against Sallie, just like any statement she herself might have made, on the ground that Levi was in a conspiracy with her when he made the statement. Judge Thomas heard argument on this matter for two hours before "he decided to rule on this matter at another time." Here, as at other moments, Thomas's agonies were unnecessary: generations of judges had recognized that an alleged conspirator's boasting about his anticipated wealth to one outside the conspiracy cannot satisfy the coconspirator exception to the hearsay rule. Levi's remark, if he made it, was not uttered in furtherance of the alleged conspiracy; this observation should have handily disqualified Crew's testimony about what Levi Baldwin had said, without the need for two hours of argument and further vacillation.[48]

Many days later the Crew deposition was finally read to the jury, but the part about Baldwin's prediction that he would soon come into money was not allowed. It must have taken some courage for Thomas to enforce the hearsay rule against the defendants after observing the solicitude of the Supreme Court toward another item of hearsay the companies had sponsored. But courage is not a substitute for speed, and there were to be many other such delays. Under Judge Thomas's leaden gavel, the fourth trial of the Hillmon case would last far longer than did any of the other five.[49]

Much of the defendants' lengthy presentation was repetitive of evidence that the first three trials had seen, with the familiar emphasis on height, teeth, and scars. But there were of course some new wrinkles. For the first time, the defendants produced John Hillmon's discharge papers from the Union Army; his height was there listed as five feet eight inches, but he was eighteen years old at the time. Of more complexity was an aspect of John Hillmon's life insurance applications. The circumstances that John Hillmon had recorded or reported his height as five feet eleven inches on those forms had been a source of difficulty for the companies in all the trials. It had been the insurance companies' consistent claim that Hillmon was only about five nine, and numerous witnesses had so testified.[50]

It will be recalled that in earlier trials Dr. G.G. Miller, examining physician for Mutual of New York, had attempted to explain this discrepancy with an unconvincing story about Hillmon having at first given his height as five eleven and the physician having failed to take a confirming measurement. Miller had claimed that Hillmon later returned to report that he had made a mistake, and confessed to the shorter height, a feature Miller said he had then verified for himself. The doctor had not corrected the application, however, but only made a record of the second visit and shorter height measurement in a different place, a "ledger book" he maintained. In the third trial, Dr. J.H. Stewart had given a similar account to explain the entry of five eleven on the applications for which he had examined the man: the earlier "mistake" and Hillmon's unexpected appearance to correct his misstatement.

In the fourth trial, however, Dr. Stewart had a new, or perhaps just additional, explanation for the inconvenient entry on the application that he had verified for the Connecticut Mutual Life Insurance Company. It had, he accused, been altered by someone! He swore that he had written five feet nine inches in the application, and that the alteration from nine to eleven had been made during the ensuing years. He had first noticed this forgery, he said, a mere two evenings before taking the stand on this occasion, when during preparation for his testimony Mr. Green had shown him the exhibit. The newspaper reports that "considerable interest was excited by this information brought out by defendant's counsel and numerous magnifying glasses were produced to examine the alleged forgery."[51]

The reporting of this skirmish leaves several questions unanswered. Had the second application that Stewart had taken (on behalf of the New York Life Insurance Company) also been altered by forgery? If so, why was there no mention of it? If not, why did it also say John Hillmon was five eleven? Had Dr. Stewart himself altered the height figures on the applications after John Hillmon made his second visit to confess his shortness? If he had not, wouldn't that by itself account for the entry five eleven, without the need to claim there had been a later alteration of the document? If he had, wouldn't the examination of the document with magnifying glasses inevitably detect evidence of alteration—Stewart's *own* alteration of the original entry? And if the exhibit was in the custody of attorney Green, how could one suspect someone in Sallie's camp of making an alteration? It wouldn't make any sense for someone on the *defendants'* side to make it look as though Hillmon was taller, would it? I didn't know whether to be more exasperated at the physician Stewart for his apparently nonsensical claims, or at Sallie's attorneys for failing to ask these obvious questions on cross-examination, or at the *Topeka Daily Capital's* reporter, whose obsequious admiration for each and every participant in the proceedings is exceeded only by his stunning lack of curiosity.

Among the defendants' height and tooth witnesses, E.A. Bittel stood out for the apparent precision of his memory. Bittel was the son of the proprietor of the Globe Hotel in Wichita, where Brown and Hillmon had stayed briefly during the winter of 1878–79; Bittel reported that they were "looking for an outfit, expecting to go farther west." When contacted by James Green in 1894 and asked about his acquaintance with Hillmon, Bittel had replied by letter that he would "know him now among a thousand, have always thought the circumstances attending their stay in Wichita ought to convince any intelligent jury that it was a put up job to get the insurance money." Bittel remembered that the two travelers had at first set out west from Wichita in late 1878, but that they had returned before long, their mission unaccomplished. Hillmon, said Bittel, had gone back to Lawrence, but then returned to Wichita by February 10, 1879. This could not have been right, for Dr. Miller reported vaccinating Hillmon in Lawrence on February 20; but nobody challenged Bittel's account. He said further that Hillmon and Brown frequently measured their own height and that of others, and that he had participated in this activity as well. Brown, he said, was five seven and a fraction, and Hillmon five nine and a fraction.[52]

Repeated measurement of one's own height seems like a paltry form of amusement for three fairly young men on their own in a lively frontier town like Wichita, but I have another reason to be skeptical of Bittel's account. Nobody called it to Bittel's attention, but Brown had testified in his 1881–82 deposition that he himself was five nine and a half, and Hillmon about an inch and a half taller. Brown had been required to sit for that deposition for many days over a period of two months, so I doubted that he would have lied about his own height; the insurance lawyers would surely have required him to stand and be measured if they had any reason to disbelieve his claim. As to Hillmon's being an inch and a half taller, that assertion was not susceptible to verification by measurement once Hillmon was gone. But as it happens, by luck I did acquire a piece of evidence on the question of Brown's and Hillmon's relative heights.

The letter I eventually received from the legal department of the Mass-Mutual Financial Group was polite but final. Until that time we had communicated via e-mail about my hope that I could access the company's archive of material related to the Hillmon case, but the attorney in charge of the matter must have believed that the formality of hard copy would discourage me from further pleading. "Dear Professor Wesson," the letter advised me, "Please be aware that in accordance with existing MassMutual policy governing confidential and/or attorney–client privileged materials, we are unable to honor your request. We hope that our efforts and responses to your other requests for information related to the Hillmon case have been helpful to you and we wish you the best of luck in your endeavors."

This outcome disappointed me, of course, but I could not be surprised. Nor could I quite believe that the decision to bar me from their archive rested on no motive but solicitude for the attorney–client privilege. If there were privileged materials in the archive, MassMutual, successor to the Connecticut Mutual Life Insurance Company, *was* the client, and could waive the privilege. Apparently Connecticut Mutual had been willing to do so a decade earlier when attorney Donald Paine had wished to see the materials. There was something, or possibly many things, hiding in their archival files that they did not want me to see.

MassMutual had, however, been good enough to provide me with some information before cutting off communication. They had furnished a typed inventory of the newspaper articles of which they had copies; I had already obtained nearly all of them, but the list was a useful confirmation that I had found most of the press accounts that mattered. And they had agreed to provide me with copies of three photographs that I had seen in the *American Heritage* article about the Hillmon case that I had read while still in law school. The tiny captions on the published photographs had said they were supplied courtesy of the Connecticut Mutual Life Insurance Company, so I was fairly certain MassMutual had them, and they did. They had charged me $150 to send three digital images, but it was worth it. It would have been worth it even if I had received only one photograph in return: the one below, which arrived with the label "Brown__Hillmon__retouched." (The retouching must have affected the color only, as otherwise it seems identical to the one published in 1968.)

One cannot judge the absolute height of the men from the picture, of course, but it is possible to get a fairly good idea of their relative heights. It's not just the heads, it's the shoulders. Hillmon looks to be the taller man by, in my estimation, about an inch and half.

Photographer unknown. Courtesy MassMutual.

The tintype of Brown and Hillmon together had never been received in evidence at any of the six Hillmon trials. Sallie Hillmon said that she had turned the tintype over to Green and had never received it back, and Green admitted that she had produced it at the inquest. Sallie's lawyers Samuel Riggs and Charles Hutchings complained that it had been concealed by the insurance company's lawyers, because of what it would show about the relative heights of the two men. James W. Green (although he admitted that he had once possessed, and then mislaid, the Sharps rifle) denied fiercely and indignantly that he or anyone on the defendants' side had possession of this photograph. "Take that tintype they claim we have lost," he fulminated at the last trial, "I only wish we had it." And yet here it was, digitally at least, furnished to me courtesy of the successor to Mr. Green's client, the Connecticut Mutual Life Insurance Company. They had had it all along.[53]

As the overlong trial dragged on through the Kansas winter, the attorneys' tempers began to wear thin. The reporter had written during the first week of the defendants' case that the proceedings were "characterized at times by brilliant sallies of wit from the counsel on both sides, who frequently indulge in considerable personality, which in the main is taken in very good part." But by the middle of February, this amused tolerance had eroded; a quarrel erupted in the courtroom in which Lysander Wheat "used some very harsh language to Attorney Hubbell of the defense, and the two were about to come to blows, when Attorney Smith jumped between the belligerents and prevented a personal conflict."[54]

The plaintiff's side, growing more aggressive, was able by employing clever cross-examination to make some points even during the defense presentation. Dr. Richard Morris, the coroner who had presided over the Lawrence inquest, admitted that "he had received his pay for conducting the inquest from the insurance companies and that he believed that the jurors and witnesses received their remuneration from the same source." He further agreed that James W. Green had prepared an arrest warrant for John Brown at the end of the inquest, and that he, as coroner, had issued it. He had heard thereafter that Green and Buchan had consulted with Brown, but he said he was never advised that Brown had been arrested. He had not authorized Green or anyone else to promise immunity to Brown, he said.[55]

But many of the defense witnesses had nothing but harmful evidence to contribute, from Sallie's perspective. One witness, a Mrs. Maggie Nixon, testified to an event she claimed had occurred during the first trial of the case. At the Continental Hotel in Leavenworth, she said, Sallie had come into a room where various witnesses were assembled; each of them was expected to testify that John Hillmon had a bad or missing tooth. By Mrs. Nixon's account, Sallie interrogated the persons in the room about their intentions, then said, "If this is going to be your evidence, you, his sister, you, his brother-in-law, and you, his friend, I might as well withdraw my case and give him up to the authorities." The *Topeka Daily Capital*'s reporter relates that Sallie, during this lady's testimony, "showed great agitation and made an attempt to dash at the witness, but was restrained by her counsel."[56]

Sallie's violent reaction to this testimony is curious, for there seems to be nothing greatly original about Mrs. Nixon's claims. The suggestion that Sallie had at times evinced an intention to give up her case in the face of overwhelming adverse evidence was as old as the affair of the John Brown affidavit, and she had been accused in previous trials of asking witnesses not to testify to matters that would harm her claim (although she had always denied it). Perhaps the lengthy trial had begun to fray her nerves as it had her attorneys'. In any event, she was compelled to listen to several more witnesses give nearly identical accounts of her statements that night at the Continental Hotel.

My own spirits grow ragged from time to time, including at moments during the exhumation. When the press conference in Lawrence is over, and we have spoken for a brief time to those who linger afterward, I suggest to Leray and Sandra that we proceed to the cemetery and see how the disinterment efforts are progressing. But when we arrive back at the cemetery we can see that the grave is deserted; even the journalists and photographers who had chosen to stay at the site during the press conference seem to have decamped, taking their ladder. I want to show the gravesite to the Hillmons, so we walk to its edge. An irregular sheet of plywood, muddy and splintered around the edges, covers the excavation; the surrounding clumps of torn ground present several obvious hazards to our footing. It is one of the most dismaying sights I have seen in some time.

"This is it?" asks Leray.

"Hold on a minute," I say, and call Ben's cell phone to ask where everyone is.

"We had to get out of there," he tells me hoarsely.

"Why?"

"The stuff in the grave got really bad. Remember that smoke that was coming off the water? There was something in it. One of the students just about passed out, and I started coughing and couldn't stop, and then Dennis sat up out of the mud at one point and said he couldn't see."

"Couldn't *see*?"

"Yeah, but you know Dennis. He kept saying it was no problem. I guess he was pretty much working by feel by then anyway. But Paul and I hauled him out of there, and Paul drove him back here. He could see again by the time we got here, but none of us wants to go back into that pit. It's like a horror movie, you know? *Friday the 13th*?"

"Today's the sixteenth."

"Whatever. Maybe more like *Indiana Jones and the Poisonous Grave*. Anyway, a bad movie you wouldn't want to be in."

"There's a board over the grave now," I say.

"Yeah. Mitch put it there as a temporary cover so nobody would fall in. Plus so no more of that gas would ooze out. That woman from the city reminded us we're supposed to put the remains back by Sunday afternoon. We took out something like forty-eight bones before we had to stop, plus some teeth. Oh yeah, and a shirt button. Dennis bit it and says it's glass. He says we'll spend all day in the lab over at KU tomorrow with the bones."

"He *bit* it? He could tell it was glass by biting it"

"I guess it's some anthropologist thing, he didn't think twice about it. He had mud all over his face and probably in his mouth anyway."

"But I've got Sandra and Leray here, and I wanted to show them the grave," I say pointlessly.

Ben is ready with the right question, in scientific if not in social terms. "Did Leray spit in the cup for you yet?"

"I don't even *have* the cup. I think Dennis has it. They never seem to have these problems on *CSI*."

"So, we'll take the Hillmons out to dinner, and sooner or later he'll spit in some cup or other. Come get me when it's time. I'm going to take a shower."

"Are *you* all right?" But Ben has hung up.

I turn to Leray and Sandra and explain what has happened.

"Of course, we understand," says Sandra. "I hope nobody has been hurt." Leray and Sandra are persons of impeccable manners. But they cast disappointed eyes toward the unsightly grave: they have driven a long way to see nothing more than a splintery wooden slab.

"We might have a souvenir for you," I offer by way of apology. I have in mind a glass shirt button (so certified by the teeth of a genuine anthropologist) that has been in the ground for more than a century.

The next phase of the defendants' case consisted of various depositions or transcripts of Fort Madison witnesses, and the burden of all this evidence was the same: the witness had known the young Walters and could describe him, consistently as nearly six feet tall and with a "Roman nose," an expression the witnesses used with curious uniformity. They saw in the photographs of the emaciated corpse an unmistakable likeness of their acquaintance (in the case of a witness identified as William Schoot, a "splendid likeness," a description that does not do much to flatter the young man's appearance while alive).[57]

The reporter notes that the disputes between counsel have become "more and more bitter" and hypothesizes that the monotony of the trial is to blame:

> This [acrimony] could not be counted strange, however, since the tediousness of the prolonged trial to those personally conducting it is unappreciated by the spectator or even the witnesses, and it would be an anomaly in human relations if men of brains who

are so thoroughly anesthetized on this problem, should always maintain their equanimity.[58]

Most trials probably suffer from the defect of tedium, if it is one, for many of the choices made by those who create the drama—the lawyers, chiefly—are dictated by the insistent demands of the law of evidence and procedure, rather than by the premises of art. There is a conventional wisdom that the courtroom provides great theater, but this is true only when art has been allowed to compress, reorganize, and misrepresent the proceedings. I feel compelled to avoid any serious artistic distortion of the genuine history of the trials, yet tormented by the worry that this fidelity will produce the same tedium that the reporter notes. Moreover, I have applied myself with conscientious care to the task of understanding the narrative and ferreting out the truth, but I seem no closer to any confident conclusions than I was at the start.

The defendants offered the Alvina Kasten letter, always the bête noire of the plaintiff's case, at the end of the reading of Kasten's deposition. Despite the Supreme Court's rather unmistakable direction that the letter should be received in evidence, Sallie's lawyers objected gamely that the letter should be excluded in the absence of proof corroborating that Walters had been in Wichita at the time the letter was dated. Thomas, decisive for once (and surely correct), overruled the objection, and the letter was read to the jury.[59]

Reading the letter myself for surely the hundredth time, I am struck by the variety of Frederick Adolph Walters's mode of addressing Alvina Kasten: he refers to her as "my (old woman) sweet little girl," and also addresses her as "pet," "love," and "honey." He's quite the rough poet, the author of this letter, and has a sense of humor, too, joking about swindling the post office out of three cents by enclosing two sheets in the envelope. Alvina Kasten must have been quite smitten with her cigarmaker beau. I wonder what she was doing, in 1895, while this letter was being read to the fourth jury. For years I had imagined her as an American Miss Havisham, cherishing a disintegrated bouquet of flowers and a bundle of letters tied up with a lavender ribbon, but recently a genealogist helping me with my research has reported that Alvina had married another Fort Madison resident in the mid-1880s; moreover, her husband, C.W. Schott, was one of the witnesses who identified the photographs as those of his friend Frederick Adolph Walters during the third trial. The discovery that Alvina has been, by the time of this fourth trial, married for more than a decade to one of the other witnesses for the defense gives me pause and, irrationally, somewhat reanimates my sympathy for Sallie.[60]

This revelation prompts other reflections. Fort Madison, Iowa, was quite a small town in the 1880s. The defendants produced literally dozens of witnesses from that city to testify that the corpse photographs depicted their friend Frederick Adolph Walters (called "Adolph" by his friends, one of them said). Most of these witnesses were linked to Walters and his family by a web of small-town networks: they were neighbors, childhood acquaintances, schoolmates. Some were fellow cigarmakers. Secret societies like the Masons and Odd Fellows also played a significant role. What kind of social solidarity might have been at work to produce this unanimous outpouring of certainty about the identity of a damaged corpse, seen only in a photograph? What degree of courage or recklessness would have been required for a Fort Madison resident to say that the photograph did not so much resemble Adolph after all?[61]

F.A. Walters's siblings next took the stand, first the brother C.R. Walters, and next his sister Fannie. C.R. did not deviate from his testimony in the earlier trials that he had received a letter from Frederick Adolph at his home in Missouri during the winter of 1879, describing an intention to "drive cattle for a man named Hillmon." Shown a letter that he had written shortly after his brother's disappearance saying that Fredrick Adolph had a gold tooth, he claimed that he could not remember writing it. Fannie spoke of the different letter that the family at home in Fort Madison had received from F.A., posted at Wichita, Kansas, and also mentioning the man named Hillmon. But Fannie's chief utility to the defendants seems to have been what the reporter claimed was a "striking resemblance which her features bear to those of the dead man as photographed." One hopes, for Fannie's sake, that this resemblance depended more on the reporter's imagination than on any actual likeness. Both siblings said that the corpse photographs resembled their brother. Over what seems to have been a strenuously argued hearsay objection, Judge Thomas allowed Fannie to say that her mother, when first shown the photographs of the corpse, exclaimed, "That's my boy."[62]

Dean James W. Green reads the day's trial reportage in the Topeka newspaper that night at his hotel, but his mind is half-distracted. It is the thought of Edward Isham that interferes with his enjoyment of the evening. Green had objected in the first instance to bringing him into the case, but he had been overruled by some Wall Street fool in a bespoke suit, who had explained that the defendants wanted someone "to look after the law points as the trial goes on." Is not he, James W. Green, the Dean of the state's law school? Cannot he look after the law? His irritation is aggravated by the suspicion that the companies are paying Isham at a higher rate than he himself has negotiated. And just as he had expected, the Dean has come to find the Chicago lawyer's bulky presence and unhelpful objections quite tiresome. Isham was not in the case at the beginning as Green was, and he should in all decency defer to those whose knowledge of the matter is both more particular and more nuanced than his. But he will persist in putting forward his views in the courtroom without first conferring. Green is certain their clients expect *him* to act as lead counsel, even if this has never been made explicit, and he has spent some time rehearsing the terms in which he will communicate this truth to Isham; but he has not yet found the right moment.

In faith, all of the insurance companies' lawyers are growing weary and frustrated. Green had expected to be back in his classroom weeks ago, and he knows that Gleed and Ware, as well as Barker, are losing business while they are required to attend court and supply Judge Thomas's appetite for intricate and lengthy argumentation. Green's own initial admiration for the Dakota jurist's meticulous jurisprudence has long since been replaced by impatience at his willingness to treat seriously any objection, however trifling.

Green had wished, for example, to introduce into evidence the deposition of John Brown, but only as evidence of his collusion and conspiracy with Sallie Hillmon. This last condition was not a trivial matter for Green and his colleagues: the jury must be made to understand that Brown's deposition was not testimony they endorsed, for of course it is their position that by the time he gave his deposition, John Brown had been corrupted by Sallie Hillmon and her lawyers, and had unpacked a large suitcase of lies in service of her fraudulent claims. Yet the deposition itself was the clearest token of his corruption, and the jury must be made to see it as such. The proper method for ensuring that the jury understood the difference between John Brown as reliable witness and John Brown as coconspirator is a familiar one: Judge Thomas must instruct the jurors in these matters. Green had even formulated an appropriate instruction, one that explained that the deposition was offered into evidence "as one of the acts done by him (Brown) in furtherance of the conspiracy to defraud the defendant insurance companies . . . and for that purpose only, and in no respect as evidence of any matters and things therein stated." Green had even arranged for Gleed (the older brother Charles, whose dramatic instincts are better than those of the retiring Willis) to read the deposition to the jury, and the courtroom reading had begun and gone on for some time.

And yet when, a couple of hours into the reading, the matter of the instruction was broached, the insufferable Riggs must caterwaul and object, and say that a deposition cannot be introduced for one purpose and not for another. And Judge Thomas must pull his beard and purse his lips as though these arguments are to be taken seriously, and indeed he does take them seriously, and sustains the plaintiff's objection, saying that if the deposition is to be read it must be without the instruction and qualification Green has so carefully prepared for him. And Green must then decline to have the deposition read any further at all, for it might otherwise be mistaken for an account that his clients commend to the jury as a trustworthy one, which of course they do not. He must, indeed, ask that the portions already read be stricken from the record and withdrawn from the jury's consideration, a retreat that cannot be accomplished altogether with dignity.

Then his efforts to introduce into evidence the promissory notes Hillmon and Brown had signed in Texas a year before the Crooked Creek fraud are met with no success, the judge taking Mr. Riggs's view that they are irrelevant. In all this the famous Mr. Edward Isham is of no assistance either, but can be seen sitting grandly at counsel table, as erect as his girth will permit, looking for all the world as though his imposing presence is worth the large fees the defendants are paying him. And finally, when court adjourns, Green must contend with the preparation of W.J. Buchan for his testimony, a task to which he does not look forward.

Thoroughly irritated by these reflections, Dean James Green folds up his newspaper and leans back into the chair with a sigh. It is far too long since he has seen his students. Fine fellows! They always greet him with respect, indeed on some happy occasions with downright huzzahs, and they would be sure to share his low opinion of Chicago lawyers if he should explain the reasons to them. Which some day, perhaps, he may do.[63]

† † †

Senator W.J. Buchan was on the stand for a very short time before Sallie's lawyers objected to his repeating anything at all that Brown may have told him, on the ground of attorney–client privilege. This argument made fine use of Buchan's consistent claim that he was Brown's attorney at the time of any conversations had between the two, but Green and his cocounsel were ready with a rejoinder: Brown, they contended, had waived the privilege by testifying in the first trial of the case and speaking unhesitatingly about all his transactions with Buchan.[64]

It could have surprised nobody at this point that Judge Thomas required a great deal of time to consider this objection. The argument over it consumed nearly two entire days of courtroom time. The judge then took the matter under advisement, and ordered that the court be in adjournment until the following week, at which time "he would be willing to hear more argument."[65]

While the question of Buchan's competency to testify was thus subject to judicial cogitation, the defendants did succeed in placing before the jury one of their favorite pieces of evidence: John Brown's affidavit, the one in which he told the story of the lonely traveler "Joe Berkley or Burgis," whom Hillmon persuaded to join their party, hid from view under the blankets, inoculated with smallpox virus from his own vaccination site, and shot to death at Crooked Creek. Arguments about this piece of evidence, and the reading of it, occupied nearly an entire day.[66]

But at the very end of this day, according to the newspaper account, appeared a witness named D.E. Sheldon, "sworn in as an expert witness in the identification of handwriting." To the seasoned reader this seems more interesting than anything that had happened in the fourth trial to date, but it appears that "the papers concerning which he testified were not admitted . . . and the witness was dismissed."[67]

The Sheldon episode must have added to the general store of frustration experienced by the fourth trial's jurors, who at this stage seem to have spent days listening to arguments about evidence (or perhaps, even worse, being required to leave the courtroom during these quarrels and cool their heels in a jury room), all the while hearing very little actual evidence. Even worse for their sense of useful participation must have been listening to a couple of hours of the John Brown deposition, only to be later instructed that it had been withdrawn and they were to disregard it. And the question of whether Mr. W.J. Buchan was to be allowed to testify further still rested under Judge Thomas's solemn consideration. Would this trial ever again contain any actual evidence?

Happily, it would. The jury returned the morning after Mr. Sheldon's dismissal to some witnesses who took the case in a far more interesting direction. While awaiting Thomas's ruling on the Buchan question, the defendants took the opportunity to call in turn four men, each of whom swore under oath that he had seen John W. Hillmon quite alive in the months after the death at Crooked Creek. One claimed that he had spotted the elusive Hillmon in Leadville, Colorado, in 1879; the others said they had seen him in the jail in Tombstone, Arizona, ten years later. The Tombstone witnesses said that Hillmon had been taken from the jail in handcuffs and under heavy guard.[68]

Unexplained in any of this testimony is how the notorious criminal Hillmon, the subject of a large reward, could have been taken from the Tombstone jail, helpless and shackled, in May 1889, and yet be unavailable for production at this trial. Presumably the companies' position was that the prisoner had somehow escaped, but no evidence of this miraculous event was put forward.

After the Hillmon sighting witnesses testified, Judge Thomas recovered from a bout of scholarly agonizing long enough to rule that John Brown had waived his attorney–client privilege, and consequently that W.J. Buchan could resume testimony about their conversations. Buchan gave the by-now familiar account of his retention by John Brown's father to assist the son in getting out of trouble for his role in the Hillmon matter; as before, his pious narrative was rather successfully impeached on cross-examination when he had to admit that he had never been paid for these services by anyone named Brown, but only by the insurance companies. Concerning those releases signed by Sallie, the *Topeka Daily Capital's* reporter noted that "there appears quite a discrepancy" between Buchan's explanation and Sallie's. At the end of the Senator's evidence, the defense rested.[69]

I imagine that nearly everyone felt by then that the end of the trial was a consummation devoutly to be wished. The spectators may have retained some enthusiasm for the drama, for they were not compelled to attend and could come and go as they wished, but the jurors almost surely felt trapped in some purgatory, and there was still rebuttal evidence to be gotten through.

Before the bench the attorneys' truculence was growing ever more unmistakable. A *Topeka Daily Capital* article that appeared just as the defense rested reported of the lawyers that "an almost ungovernable spirit of belligerence is lying dangerously near the surface." Sallie's attorneys had interposed objections with fierce diligence and some success (often delayed while the judge pondered) during the defense case. The indolence or gentlemanliness that had lulled them into the failure to even raise a hearsay objection to the Kasten letter for the first two trials seems to have been replaced by a militant vigilance, encouraged by Judge Thomas's willingness to take every objection seriously. Their transformation is understandable, considering the chicanery of which Messrs. Wheat, Riggs, and company justly suspected the insurance companies' lawyers by this point, but it may not have served them altogether well in the end. For eventually (although not in this trial), their success in making and advocating for various objections, often on hearsay grounds, would prove their undoing.[70]

Whatever suspicion and hostility may have simmered in front of the bar, however, these do not seem to have affected the gaiety of the spectators. The *Topeka Daily Capital's* summary describes public interest in the Hillmon trial as "intense," especially among the ladies, who are claimed to enjoy this "judicial romance a la Conan Doyle . . . almost to the point of infatuation." And no wonder, in the reporter's estimation, for according to him the Hillmon case is "the greatest mystery of its kind ever designed by artistic man or allowed to happen by a careless omnipotence." In consequence of the frequent attendance by various ladies, he observes, on some afternoons the courtroom "has more resembled a delightful social function than an austere auxiliary to the United States department of justice."[71]

The rebuttal testimony was blessedly brief, and objections do not seem to have occupied too much of the court's time. Rebuttal consisted chiefly of Levi Baldwin denying any participation in a conspiracy, and contradicting several of the defense witnesses as to transactions they claimed to have had with him. Sallie was on the stand for longer, also to disclaim various pieces of conduct or conversation attributed to her by witnesses for the defense. Sallie's lawyers revisited the curious matter of the alteration of the height figure on John Hillmon's application for insurance. They called both James W. Green and their own Samuel Riggs to the stand; each man denied making or procuring the alteration or having any knowledge of who had done so. The defendants took advantage of Riggs's presence on the stand to inquire of him who would own any judgment in favor of Sallie Hillmon. He confessed not only that he and his fellow attorneys owned shares of the proceeds, but that "many of the witnesses were also financially interested." He could not say how much of the judgment, if any were to be obtained, Sallie Hillmon Smith would own.[72]

The attorneys' final arguments in the fourth trial consumed three days. At first plaintiffs and defense lawyers alternated their presentations, so Hutchings opened, followed by Ware, then Riggs, then Green. But George Barker spoke after his cocounsel Green, and Lysander Wheat addressed the jury last.

Each of these men spoke for several hours, but the reporter's account of these arguments is quite brief in all cases but Green's. Every summation save Green's is described in two or at most three paragraphs, but the report of the Dean's closing argument occupies nearly four pages of newsprint, and appears to be a verbatim rendition of his remarks. I can imagine only one explanation for this asymmetry: Green must have furnished the reporter a copy of his speech, and the reporter must have faithfully reported each word of it.

And what a speech it is! James W. Green storms into his argument with a full head of fury. The target of most of this ire is not Sallie

Hillmon, but her lawyers. He begins by assailing the opposing attorneys in fairly conventional language, for example dismissing the questions they have raised about his role in the Lawrence inquest as "only another of their rash and extravagant statements." But as he warms to the task his rhetoric becomes more scarifying, especially his retort to what he says are their claims that they have represented Sallie out of "charity."

> What is the truth, gentlemen? We have seen these charitable attorneys, before they have taken up this poor sorrowing widow's claim, who is grieving for her husband, insisting they shall have 40% of the insurance, $10,000, gentlemen, before they had executed a stroke of the pen. Think of that. That is what they call charity. We now find them having 50% of the insurance, and all disbursements, which leaves Mrs. Hillmon, if she ever recovers, little or nothing. It is questionable, gentlemen, whether she will ever receive a cent. And the men who will take this money will be these attorneys, these charitable attorneys, these men who are willing to walk over the bodies of the innocent dead and to scurrilously vilify the reputation of the living that they may steal from the coffers of these defendant companies, and thereby line their own pockets.[73]

Lest one get the impression from these words that Sallie Hillmon is the victim of her attorneys' sharp practices, however, Green goes on to make clear who the genuinely injured party is.

> And these are the men who come into this court and call every witness but one a liar and perjurer; and who come into this court and vilify me and my friend Barker. Who are they, that they should do this? Who am I that I should be thus accused? I, gentlemen, have lived in Kansas for fifty long years; have been honored by the confidence of my fellow countrymen; held important offices; have been looked up to in my community and am without reproach from my fellow man. And, gentlemen, I have gone through three trials of this case, and God knows that I have done nothing to be ashamed of in it. My conscience is clear. And yet these three attorneys come here and vilify me that they may

secure this money for themselves. Gentlemen, go to Lawrence where I live; ask my fellow townsmen about "Jim Green"; hear what they have to say, and then hurl these slanders back at these, my false accusers.[74]

Sallie is no victim in the universe Green summons up, but he reserves his bitterest censure for her lawyers, the men who have defamed him so despicably. The very last words of his closing are not about Sallie, nor John Hillmon, nor Frederick Adolph Walters and his family, nor any other witness, but about Mr. Samuel Riggs:

> Referring to the statement made by Mr. Riggs in his invocation for pity on behalf of a poor struggling widow in her fight against these "soulless corporations," I venture the assertion that while these corporations may be soulless they will soar into heaven while the pusillanimous soul of this man will sink into oblivion and roast in hell.[75]

This furious speech must have been in several respects a hard act to follow, and it appears that the next morning George Barker did not even attempt such flights of apocalyptic emotion. The reporter's brief account suggests that Barker laid emphasis on two hardy perennials of the defense case: the Kasten letter and John Brown's affidavit. Barker calculated that forty-six witnesses had testified that the body was not Hillmon's, while only six had said that it was, and concluded that "while Brown was Hillmon's tool, Walters was his victim."[76]

The reporter opined that Lysander Wheat's address, the last of the closings, was "one of the most powerful as well as the most interesting of the series," especially at the moments when Wheat displayed great familiarity with the testimony and exhibits. He argued his client's cause "most earnestly," and was altogether a "convincing speaker [with] a graceful delivery, [and] an effective orator."[77]

The next morning, Judge Thomas's instructions occupied the hours from ten until nearly noon. The jurors then retired to their deliberations. It was nine-thirty that evening when the jurors reported to the judge that they could not agree; Thomas sent them home for the night, instructing them to return on the next day. They did, that morning and the morning after as well, until four days had elapsed and still they could not achieve unanimity, and the judge finally agreed that the jury could be discharged.[78]

Later reporting described the ebb and flow of the jury's deliberations. The first balloting among the jurors had produced a division of seven to five in favor of Sallie Hillmon Smith; but it appeared that for most of the four days, eleven members of the jury were prepared to find in her favor. The holdout, Mr. Joseph Young, claimed that the other jurors had all made up their minds within twenty minutes of their retirement, but that one and then another would pretend to vote his way for time in order to feign sympathy as a way to persuade him to join the majority. If this had been their goal, they failed miserably in it, for Joseph Young never budged, and after the jury was discharged he had nothing kind to say about his fellow jurors. The others, he said, had "called him names that he would not apply to a dog and . . . when he told them so they said they would not let a dog of theirs associate with him." He further represented that "he was never abused in his life as he was last Friday night and although he was not personally injured, he was more frightened than he was at any time during his service in the civil war."[79]

Even the remaining eleven jurors were disgruntled by their experience. They all signed a "certificate" reciting that each of the eleven had voted to award the verdict to the plaintiff, and in addition they adopted a resolution "against the unanimous jury system."[80]

The *Topeka Daily Capital* reporter's pen ran purple ink to the end. "The belief that a thing to be everlasting must be eternal is exploded," he wrote, "as this trial undoubtedly had a beginning but the possible end cannot be discerned."[81]

⊲ 7 ⊳

THE FIFTH TRIAL PROGRESSES BRISKLY BUT ENDS INCONCLUSIVELY, AND NEW YORK LIFE CAPITULATES

1896–1899

It had not been easy to acquire permission to exhume the remains buried at the Oak Hill Cemetery. Once Dennis told me that exhumation might allow us to identify the man in the grave recorded as John Hillman's, I contacted the Lawrence City Attorney's Office, for the grave rested in that city's municipal graveyard. After months of back-and-forth, their answer was no. No, we could not exhume; no, it would not be helpful for me to travel to Lawrence to discuss the matter; no, there were not any conditions or contingencies we could satisfy to change their minds.

By then I knew I could never conclude that my mystery had been thoroughly investigated without exhumation. Popular culture has exposed most Americans to copious information about the forensic sciences, and when I tried to explain my research project people inevitably asked me, "Why don't you just check the DNA?" I knew that no matter what other evidence I found on the Hillmon mystery, if I didn't do all I could to gain access to the remains, for the rest of my life I'd be explaining why I hadn't.

It appeared that the law of exhumation, at least exhumation sought by a nonrelative of the deceased, was very unclear. The only way to proceed in the face of the City's adamant refusal was to obtain a court order, but what court was going to issue an exhumation order over the objection of the cemetery owner, when the judge could not be sure what the law governing such a situation might be?

I needed a lawyer. Someone with a license to practice in Kansas, generous enough to contribute some time to this peculiar venture, smart enough to figure out what needed to be done, and powerful enough to make it happen. I cast my mind back over my inventory of acquaintances from years of belonging to the legal profession, and it came to me exactly who I needed: Thornhill.

I had met Mark Thornhill in the early 1980s, when I worked as a federal prosecutor in Denver and Mark had been sent to Colorado from the Justice Department's Tax Division to assist in the prosecution of tax protestors. These were an interesting and exasperating lot, folks who believed (or claimed to believe) that they were not required to pay federal income tax because, well, they had a variety of reasons. Because United States currency was not actually backed by silver or gold, and hence the citizen had really earned zero income because any income they may have received was not in real dollars; because being required to declare the amount of one's income violated the privilege against self-incrimination; or, more audaciously, because the income tax was unconstitutional. This last argument was particularly poignant, I thought. Tax protestors were a decidedly populist bunch, if one could characterize their politics in nineteenth-century terms; the ones we saw were usually self-employed in professions like carpentry or farming, and didn't make much money to begin with. They must have hated the aristocracy of wealth with at least as much passion as had Sockless Jerry Simpson or Mary Elizabeth Lease. But they were credulous, and believed the propositions they'd heard put forth by slick self-help "legal consultants" who sold them videotapes and poorly printed tracts. In consequence they'd put their faith into an argument that was last employed by wealthy capitalists to win a Supreme Court victory in 1895. They had less success in the 1980s, of course, Congress having pretty much rendered this argument hopeless by passing the Sixteenth Amendment in 1913.

One thing about tax protestors was that they were true believers; they never pleaded guilty. They wanted a chance to explain their earnest theories to a jury, and insisted on a trial. The Justice Department had finally been required to deploy around the country some specialists in the patient explanation of these matters to often-baffled jurors.

Colorado had more than its share of tax protestors, and some of these prosecutions had been assigned to me, and so it was that one day Mark Thornhill showed up in the shabby office that I occupied in the United States Attorneys' Office in Denver and said he was ready to help me try some cases. We did try one or two together, eventually. The defendants either represented themselves, or were represented by a highly eccentric local attorney, impervious to embarrassment, who specialized in such trials. They presented a certain challenge to Thornhill's formidable skills, in the way a clumsy, unpredictable tennis player can present a challenge to a gifted one, but he navigated our way through the difficulties with brio. We agreed that most of the protestors were more victims than criminals, and that it was the Pied Pipers advising them who deserved to be convicted; but the guys with the expensive haircuts always seemed to evade arrest.

Not long after his return to Washington, Thornhill left the Justice Department to go to work for a Kansas City law firm called Spencer, Fane, Britt, and Browne. He duly sent me a pair of business cards. One was of the traditional attorney's variety on creamy cardstock, containing his name and his new firm's in a typeface that somehow contrived to look both austere and prosperous. The second was similar, but contained only his name and, in gilt letters below, "Counsel to the Establishment." It was ironic, but not inaccurate. He might have been somewhat abashed about it, but Thornhill had arrived.

I did not hear from him often, but knew that he had stayed with the firm and risen to become a senior partner in the litigation department. Could I ask such an important (and no doubt expensive) litigator for free legal services, in such a dubious venture? It took me weeks to nerve myself up to send him the e-mail, but in the end I did, because once I thought of him I knew that nobody else would do.

Thornhill, his associate Mackenzie Wilfong, and his firm came through for us in March 2006, when a Kansas judge signed an order allowing us to exhume the remains from the grave. There were restrictions: we could keep only a small portion for forensic analysis, and must return the rest to the grave not more than forty-eight hours after their removal.

† † †

A mere twelve months passed between the inconclusive end of the fourth Hillmon trial in March 1895, and the convening of the fifth. Kansas history produced an unspectacular but colorful year in the interval. In September 1895, the *Emporia Daily Gazette* reported that two agents of the Santa Fe Railroad "claim to know the whereabouts of John W. Hillmon and have offered to produce him for a consideration. They refuse to talk about the matter or to give any intimation as to where Hillmon now is, but it is understood that they have made a proposition to the insurance companies for $10,000. . . . The attorneys here for the companies say they do not want Hillmon—it is unnecessary to produce him in order to win the suit for insurance now pending in the federal courts."[1]

In November, the *New York Times* added to its ongoing coverage of the insurance industry with a story deploring the prevalence of life insurance fraud and the difficulty that insurance companies experienced obtaining a fair trial when they were forced into the litigation of a false claim. The immediate cause was a case in Beaufort, North Carolina, in which it was said that a life insurance company had unearthed a conspiracy to defraud by the multiple substitutions of one body for another. So clumsy were these crimes said to be that "invalids had been personated by robust men, and moribund octogenarians by residents in the prime of life," but even so a jury had just acquitted two of the conspirators. "Such evidence of sympathy with scoundrels of this kind," wrote the *Times* reporter, "recalls the long litigation in the Hillmon case, in Kansas, and other similar controversies."[2]

Eugene "Ironquill" Ware, well-known poet and defense lawyer in the Hillmon case, said in a speech that wars were "the schooling of the nations," and that they produced more good than ill. "I hope we will have another soon," he said. "We need it; there is an occasion this very day for war, and we ought to open it." Mary Elizabeth Lease took up bicycling; in May she threatened to call on the editor of the *Wichita Eagle*, whom she claimed to be "anti–new woman," in a fancy bloomer suit. An inquiry into troubled financial matters at Kansas University concluded that "the regents were ruled by the chancellor, faculty salaries were too high, and the school was attempting to compete with Harvard and Yale when the financial condition of the school did not justify it." The Bank of Topeka foreclosed on the *Topeka Daily Capital* for unpaid debts, and took over operation of the paper, naming a new editor.[3]

It once again became necessary to impose on a judge from a nearby jurisdiction to preside over a Hillmon trial: in March 1896, Judge John A. Williams of the United States District Court for the Eastern District of Arkansas arrived in Topeka to take charge of his borrowed courtroom and lend his leadership to the fifth adjudication of Sallie's lawsuit. A Civil War veteran and lifelong Republican activist, Williams had been appointed to the federal bench by President Benjamin Harrison in 1890. His snowy white hair and beard, coupled with a short stature and heavy physique, were said to create a "striking appearance," and contribute to "a magnificent illustration of a sound mind in a sound body." Judge Williams commanded a strong and penetrating voice, and demanded that others project their words as well, saying at frequent intervals, "What's that? Speak up so we can hear you!!" Like his immediate predecessor, he announced at once his intention to move matters along, and to tolerate no dillydallying by the lawyers. But unlike Judge Alfred Thomas, Judge Williams carried out these intentions. The fifth trial was convened on March 10, 1896; by April 3 it was over.[4]

The 1895 contest had nearly exhausted public interest in the Hillmon case; coming so close on the heels of that histrionic but inconclusive match, the brief and austere fifth trial struggled to attract an audience. The trial reportage published in the (by then bankrupt, sold, and reorganized) *Topeka Daily Capital* displays a certain sobriety, as though these chastened proceedings no longer call for the ornate prose of the chronicler who had supplied the reports of the previous trial. The journalist assigned to the courtroom even solicits sympathy for his predicament. "Unfortunates, who by virtue of their official position, who are compelled to maintain at least a desultory association with all cases on trial in the federal court are preparing for the strain of another siege of the famous Hillmon case," he grumps. He expects to have little company in the courtroom, for "interest, waning through a period of sixteen years and four months, has now almost reached a minimum," and the trial "will be greeted with pleasure by no one except the legal fraternity."[5]

Jury selection proceeded quickly. Prospects who held opinions about the Hillmon case acquired from reading or hearing about the prior trials were excused if they stated that "evidence would be necessary to change them." But individuals who held policies in the defendant companies were not challenged, for they all promised that this circumstance would not affect their deliberations. After less than a day of examining prospective jurors, the court empanelled twelve white men. Their number included four farmers or retired farmers, three merchants or retired merchants, an agent for a cheese factory, a "lumberman," a real estate agent, a schoolteacher, and a carpenter. They were said to be "an intelligent class of men," ranging in age from thirty-five to seventy.[6]

In this fifth outing, the plaintiff's lawyers' pursued the opening strategy of calling a number of witnesses who had known John Hillmon in life, then examining them very briefly to elicit their agreement that the body they saw looked like the man they had known. Their faith seemed to be in numbers rather than in details. Perhaps Wheat and company had been embarrassed when George Barker, summing up after the fourth trial, had compared the number of their identification witnesses to his: six to forty-six, by his count. Most of these fifth-trial witnesses described Hillmon as nearly six feet tall. The defendants' cross-examination strategy was to compel each witness to say that his estimate of Hillmon's height was "only a guess."[7]

Then a number of depositions given by male citizens of Medicine Lodge were read into evidence. They all said that the body they saw belonged to the man they knew as John Hillmon. These witnesses' identifications of the dead man found near their city carried particular weight, because these Medicine Lodgers had made Hillmon's acquaintance during his and Brown's earlier stay in their city, in late 1878. If Hillmon and Brown had really substituted another body for Hillmon's, it seemed unlikely they would have chosen a location so close to a town where resided a number of men who had enjoyed a recent opportunity to observe at close range what Hillmon looked like. Nor could Hillmon and Brown have presented Walters as Hillmon during this first visit, for if Hillmon and Brown ever encountered F.A. Walters at all, it would have been many weeks later.[8]

Judge Williams had maintained a breakneck pace all the first week of trial, compared to what the lawyers had experienced in the previous trials. In consequence of this enforced diligence, the attorneys were, by report, "more than ready to take a rest" when Judge Williams mercifully declared a weekend recess at noon on Friday, March 14. All those who labored at the Hillmon case, or nearly all, gratefully repaired to their homes for the weekend.[9]

Sallie Hillmon Smith pokes her needle irritably at the expanse of muslin imprisoned within the circle of her embroidery hoop. The light is dim here in the sitting room of her boardinghouse and she wishes she could take her leisure elsewhere in Topeka, perhaps at a tea shop, or even at the home of one of the ladies who have attended her trial from time to time. Several had sought her acquaintance during her sojourn in this city the preceding year, a few by sending her little scented notes but most by attempting some conversation when they encountered her outside the courtroom. Mr. Wheat, however, had prohibited any response to these overtures last year, and he has sternly cautioned her against any social interactions with the citizens of Topeka during this trial as well. It is impossible to know whom you can trust, he had said. And she knows it is true, and it is one of the reasons she is so bone-weary of this lawsuit and the years it has claimed from the life she thought she would lead. Despite her stout assurances to Wheat and the others, she has contemplated in her private thoughts whether there might not be a way for her simply to turn away from this cursed life of courtrooms and lawyers.

Lysander Wheat would have vastly preferred that she return this weekend to her home in Leavenworth for some rest, as her testimony is anticipated next week, but Sallie had protested that the house would be empty, and the travel tiring; she preferred to remain in Topeka to conserve her energies. And it is true that her husband, who travels for a barber supply firm, is on a two-week circuit of the southern part of the state and the Indian Territory. James Smith had joked before his departure last weekend that the need for barber supplies to refurbish the faces of the men in that part of the country was very great.

Moreover, as she had reminded Lysander Wheat, she has no other relatives near her in Leavenworth, now that her cousin Levi has lost his ranch in Tonganoxie and gone off to New Mexico. This is true as well, but the loneliness of Sallie's house is not her real reason for desiring to remain in Wichita this weekend.

She says an unladylike word as the needle pierces the flesh of her thumb, and drops the hoop and needle in exasperation. Perhaps it is as well that she has not gone to a tea shop to pursue her embroidery. She rises to survey the shelves of the sitting room, and is pleased to see packets of Mr. Dickens's work tied up in ribbons. These she removes, but they are *Great Expectations*, which she has already read, and *Bleak House*, which sounds too grim to be the right tonic for her mood this gray afternoon, so she replaces them without untying the ribbons. On the shelf below sits a newer volume, all bound, its light covers still clean and many of its pages yet uncut. Pulling it from the shelf, Sallie widens her eyes in surprise: it is *The Problem of Civilization Solved*, by the very writer whom she plans to hear speak tonight! Someone has evidently begun reading the book, but has not gotten very far. She pulls the small scissors she employs for cutting thread from her sewing kit, and repairs to the divan with the book in one hand and these in the other. They will serve to cut the pages quite well.

Several hours later Sallie finds herself in rather an awkward situation, one she is certain Mr. Wheat would not approve of. She had hoped to go unnoticed this evening, but here at Constitution Hall she is surrounded by ladies who seem to know her. At least many of them nod, and some smile at her in an inviting way. She finds her way to a seat and looks down at her lap, wishing at first she had brought her needlework, but the ladies of this crowd do not seem to be carrying needlework, and indeed are on the whole standing about talking boldly among themselves, taking no care whatsoever to keep their voices soft or their expressions becoming. There are a few men in attendance, but they seem to cluster with one another and rather keep to themselves, somewhat like ladies at the courthouse or the theater.

Eager to meet the eyes of others, Sallie pulls a paper from her reticule. It is her boardinghouse account statement, which she pretends to read with interest. This pretense is difficult to maintain, for it is fully a quarter of an hour before the gas lamps in the great hall are dimmed and then brightened again. All the ladies and the small contingent of gentlemen make their ways to chairs, and after a great scraping and squirming and settling an expectant silence prevails. There is a podium at the front, and to it strides a small woman in a black two-piece suit. The fronts of her boots are clearly visible beneath the hem of it, which is scandalously short.

She has a loud, harsh voice for such a small woman, and with it she says, "Ladies and gentlemen, there is no need for me to describe for you the lady whose presence honors us tonight. But I will repeat what one of our southern brothers wrote about her after she visited his part of the country: 'She is a plumb sight. . . . She could set a stump in the shade and keep the cows out of a 100 acre corn field without a gun. She's got a nose like an ant-eater, a voice like a cat-fight, and a face that is rank poison to the naked eye!'"

Sallie nearly trembles as she takes in these mortifying words. How could these people invite Mrs. Lease to speak to them and then repeat such calumnious phrases? But everyone around her is now laughing merrily, and even in a few cases shouting and clapping, and Sallie realizes that these women take the terrible insults as a kind of praise.

"Ladies and gentlemen," cries the woman, "Mrs. Mary Elizabeth Lease!"

A very tall woman strides up to the podium and waves, and the crowd greets her appearance with all manner of cheers and stomping and waving back for very many minutes, and Sallie finds herself joining in, even though she has never before permitted herself to yield self-control to this sort of unruly joy. She stands and claps until her palms sting, and a rhythmic four-syllable chant arises from the crowd that Sallie cannot at first make out, but she soon realizes it is "less corn, more hell, less corn, more hell," and even though the meaning of this phrase is by no means clear to Sallie the rhythm of it is irresistible and she joins in, shouting "less corn, more hell" until after a few minutes it dies out and there is finally a general bustle of reseating.

Mary Elizabeth Lease then begins to speak, striding about the front of the room as she does. Her long skirt is of a conventional cut and length, but there is nothing conventional about the manner in which she swirls it about each time she turns to walk in a new direction. Strongly marked features define her narrow face, and her dark hair is loosely captured by a knot on top of her head. She is not, perhaps, a beautiful woman, but she owns a voice so sweet it could be made of golden honey, and Sallie is from time to time tempted to surrender to the melodious sound of it, without worrying overmuch about the words. But on the whole Sallie resists this seductive impulse, for it is the words she has come to hear.

Mrs. Lease's words are of temperance, and women's suffrage, and monopolies, and the slavery of wage labor, and the perfidy of the railroads, and the lies told by politicians. She speaks of farmers raising their corn and wheat with the sweat of their brows, only to be told they have overproduced and there is no price for their crops. She acknowledges with a smile that some have accused her of telling Kansas farmers to raise less corn and more hell, and although she declares that in fact she did not invent this proposal, she wishes she had, for it is right good advice, she says. She gives a harrowing account of little shop girls in New York forced to sell their virtue for bread because their wages are so niggardly. She uses no notes or papers of any kind, and she maintains her seamless speech for fully three quarters of an hour before she ends it by employing a phrase that will ring in Sallie's memory for the rest of her life: "The people are at bay; let the bloodhounds of money who dogged us thus far beware!"

The roar of applause shakes the walls of Constitution Hall for many minutes, and the chant of "less corn, more hell" arises again. Sallie discovers that her eyes have overflowed onto her cheeks and chin. It is clear to her that Mrs. Lease has given this same speech, or most of it, many times before. Indeed, Sallie is sure she read some of it in the book this afternoon. But that is no matter; Sallie is trembling again, this time with excitement. It is not so much that she is persuaded of everything the lady has said. Much of it, about tariffs and bimetallism and monopolies, is beyond her understanding. But she knows she has been in the presence of something she has not seen before, and perhaps will not ever again.

She loses sight of Mrs. Lease during the lengthy pandemonium, and when it finally dies out Sallie has recovered her composure and prepares to leave. But as she edges toward the front door with lowered head, worrying about the drizzle and the solitary walk back to her boardinghouse, she discovers that a receiving line has formed in the vestibule, and a great number of women wait to shake the hand of Mrs. Lease. Sallie does not intend to join it, fearful of being recognized and unsure of what she might say if she were required to speak to the formidable woman. But she is swept into a spot in the queue somehow, and once she has advanced a few places from the end, she finds she is reluctant to abandon it. She concentrates on steadying her hands as the line moves slowly forward and the minutes pass. The lady immediately ahead of her, once she attains Mrs. Lease's attention, launches into lengthy and ecstatic praise of Mrs. Lease's speech, and although Mrs. Lease nods and smiles, she turns her head twice while the other lady is speaking to look at Sallie with dark, puzzled eyes.

When the previous lady has finally taken her leave, and Sallie's hand has been grasped by that of Mary Elizabeth Lease, the taller woman speaks first.

"I know you, I believe."

Sallie finds that this mistake puts her curiously at ease. "I do not believe so, ma'am, although I would like to know you. Everyone in this room would, I think. I am Sallie Smith."

"Mary Elizabeth Lease," she replies, as though Sallie might not be aware of her name. "But have we not met?"

"I am certain I would remember if we had," says Sallie, "for I would have asked you for legal advice. You are a lawyer, are you not? But not I think educated at this state's law school?"

Mrs. Lease laughs. "I did not study with Mr. Green, if that is what you mean to ask. I am rather of his sister-in-law's view about that gentleman. No, I have my law license but no degree; I took my legal education by reading books propped over my washboard. There is not a page of my law library but boasts a water stain."

Sallie smiles at this image, and surprises herself by saying "I wish I had met you earlier, for I have a legal case and I would have liked for you to be my lawyer."

"Oh, I'm afraid that would not have been possible in any event. I have closed my legal practice, for my husband and I are moving to New York next month."

At this Sallie murmurs a farewell and starts to move on, for the lady behind is beginning to make certain small exasperated movements as if to inform her that she has taken enough of Mrs. Lease's time. But as Sallie begins to withdraw her hand, Mary Elizabeth Lease suddenly grasps it all the more tightly and narrows her eyes. "I know who you are! I saw you in the courtroom here last year. You are Sallie Hillmon!"

Sallie hesitates, but then merely says, "Yes." The lady behind has stopped her fidgeting and watches in fascination, and a small whisper runs down the line of women beyond her and indeed all about the vestibule: "Sallie Hillmon!"

Mary Elizabeth Lease puts her hands out and then, to Sallie's great mortification, takes her shoulders and turns her about to face the room in general, and says in that golden voice, "Ladies and gentlemen! Please join me in recognizing Sallie Hillmon, a very brave woman who has made it the purpose of her life to show Wall Street that it cannot trample the rights of ordinary citizens!"

And the rest Sallie does not altogether remember, except applause and huzzahs and many ladies who then wish to shake her own hand, which Mrs. Lease does not seem to mind in the least, and a gentleman who summons a hack and pays the driver to take Sallie back to her boardinghouse, where she must worry that this will all come to the attention of Mr. Wheat and that he will be very cross. But this is not so much on her mind, as later she lies alone in the dark, as are Mrs. Lease's parting words.

Before allowing the hack driver to lead her out the side door to his carriage, she had turned to say good-bye to Mrs. Lease. As the tall woman embraced her with murmured farewells, Sallie found the courage to say haltingly that she admired her book. And that lady had pouted her lips and made a "pooh" sound, as though it were altogether nothing to mention, and had then said, before turning back to the gentleman with whom she was conversing, "It is you, my dear, who should write a book!"[10]

† † †

On March 16, 1896, Sallie Hillmon Smith took the oath and returned to the witness stand to speak about her husband, John Hillmon; it was the sixth tribunal (counting the Lawrence inquest) before which she had testified. The Topeka reporter estimated that by the time she was excused on this occasion, she had spent eight entire days of her life on the witness stand. Mr. Barker, it was claimed, "asked something like 1000 questions just to test her memory." Sallie was "a little confused over some of the dates," the reporter noted, "but in the main she passed through the ordeal remarkably well. Sometimes she cried and some-times she laughed, but only occasionally did she lose her temper."[11]

She testified again to having measured her husband's height ("five feet eleven and one-half inches"). She complained that she had not authorized her husband's body to be sent to the undertaker's, and said that the insurance agents had attempted to discourage her from see-ing the corpse when it did arrive. She described the moment when she placed her signature on the releases that W.J. Buchan had prepared for her. "His hand," she said, "was on mine." (Later called to the stand by the defendants, Buchan would deny any contact with Sallie's hands, although he would reluctantly admit that he "may have" asked her to sign the releases.)[12]

Sallie's attire did not escape comment, perhaps in part because she presented herself in two different outfits during the long day. In the morning she wore a brown dress, but during the afternoon she appeared in "black, with her face covered with a veil at times."[13]

After her testimony, Sallie's lawyers rested without offering either John Brown's deposition or his affidavit. They had chosen at this trial to base their case on other evidence, avoiding reliance on the only eyewitness to the death, who had given two such violently different accounts of what he saw. Edward Isham argued at length that Sallie's side should be *required* to present Brown's earlier sworn statements in evidence, but Judge Williams disagreed.

This decision must have been a serious disappointment to Isham and his cocounsel. His side could employ John Brown's deposition if it wished, for depositions of an absent witness conducted with both par-ties represented are admissible as an exception to the hearsay rule. But Brown's deposition told the plaintiff's version of the death and would not serve the companies' purposes. Brown's affidavit, on the other hand, told the story as the defendants wished, but it was not given under those formal circumstances and so would be susceptible to a hearsay objec-tion. If Isham could have compelled Sallie's side to put on the affidavit, of course, that would have served the companies' purposes splendidly; and if she had offered his deposition the affidavit would have become admissible at least to impeach the deposition's account, because it told a radically different story. But according to Williams's ruling Sallie was not required to produce either, and her lawyers had chosen not to; the defendants' hands were tied.

For their part, the companies presented very little evidence that varied from what the previous trials had seen. Disputes about hearsay continued to require the judge's rulings. Judge Williams permitted Theodore Wiseman, by then sixty years old (and, the reporter believed, "somewhat deaf"), to give testimony that Judge Thomas had ruled inadmissible hearsay in the fourth trial. It seems that Levi Baldwin had brought his brother Alva with him to Medicine Lodge, and Wiseman said that when the body was brought up from its grave, and a cloth that covered its face removed, Alva Baldwin had exclaimed, "Hell! That ain't Hillmon!" There had been similar testimony in the first and third trials, no hearsay objection having been made on those occasions. (This was hearsay, no doubt, but Williams must have thought it satisfied the hearsay exception for "excited utterances.") Wiseman also revealed that he had been compelled to sue the insurance companies for $2,500 in fees and expenses they owed him for his labors in disproving Sallie Hillmon's claims.[14]

Mayor of Lawrence and erstwhile insurance agent A.L. Selig, facing a reelection campaign, repeated his claim that when Sallie Smith called on him after the death had been reported, she said that she could not describe her husband because she did not know him well. Charles Hutchings conveyed his incredulity toward this testimony by insisting that Selig "[t]urn around and face the jury and say that." The Mayor did so.[15]

The three postmortem doctors, Stewart, Morse, and Mottram, appeared again, all giving very consistent accounts of their findings, especially their certainty that the vaccination mark on the corpse was too new to be from the procedure that Stewart had inflicted on John Hillmon nearly a month before the death at Crooked Creek. Of the physicians Dr. Mottram was the most cantankerous, as evidenced by the reporter's rendition of his cross-examination testimony:

> "You say most emphatically that was not Hillmon?"
> "Yes, sir."
> "Did you ever talk to Hillmon?"
> "I might and I might not."

"You were never introduced to him?"

"I might and I might not have been."

"You never saw him with his hat off?"

"I don't know."[16]

All the lawyers excited the admiration of the reporter; he was especially taken with their excellent memories for the evidence and their command of the exhibits. "Mr. Riggs," he says, "had Hillmon literature in every pocket, and he never has to think twice about what pocket any document is in. Mr. Wheat has locks of hair, teeth and that sort of things scattered all over his person." Of J.W. Green it is said that he has brought with him a "large valise" full of exhibits, any one of which he can produce at short notice. Edward Isham, however, seems to have little truck with exhibits; instead he "keeps his mind on all the law points and that's enough for any man."[17]

Amid much familiar evidence, some innovation arrived in the form of witnesses to Hillmon's reputed presence in various places after the death at Crooked Creek. John Mathias, who impressed the reporter as "an old soldier who is just recovering from the effects of a railroad wreck," was sworn in after being helped to the stand. Mathias had testified in the previous trial that he knew John Hillmon from the Texas buffalo hunting years of 1876 and 1877, and that he had recognized Hillmon in the Tombstone jail in 1889. He now testified to the same propositions, except as to the year: on this occasion he said it had been 1879 when he saw Hillmon in Tombstone. Perhaps the train wreck had affected his memory. When asked a second time when he had seen Hillmon in the jail, he said 1881. His redirect examination was brief and poignant:

"When you last saw this man in Tombstone, what did he say?"

"Good-bye, Jack."[18]

As the defendants came to the end of their notified witness list one afternoon, they announced that they had a new witness of great significance, one not endorsed on their witness list because he had just come to light. His name, they said, was Patrick Heely; he was en route and would reach Topeka by 10:30 the next morning.[19]

Heely embodied that useful element of courtroom dramas, the surprise witness. The case had not seen one for some time, except for the most insignificant. Sallie's lawyers protested the defendants' tardy noti-fication of their intention to present the latecomer's evidence, and it is said the attorneys on both sides "became bitter in their statements," making this "one of the most exciting days of the trial." In the end Judge Williams decided to allow Mr. Heely's testimony. The judge adjourned court in mid-afternoon, saying he would call it back to order when the witness had arrived.[20]

When Patrick Heely stepped off the train the next morning he was whisked into the courtroom directly from the train station, and exam-ined by George Barker. A current resident of St. Louis, Heely said that he had lived in Wichita during the winter of 1879, and had there known Frederick Adolph Walters. Walters, indeed, had worked for him, Heely claimed, for he was in the business of "handling railroad excursion tick-ets" and Walters had served as his assistant in selling them. This activity had taken place for about two months prior to March 1 of that year, he said, and had stopped just about the time Walters introduced Heely to two men named Hillmon and Brown. A short time later Walters told Heely that he was leaving town with Hillmon and Brown to head for Barbour County to start a cattle ranch. About a week after that, Heely said, he heard from an acquaintance of his in Medicine Lodge that "a man had been killed."[21]

On cross-examination Heely said that he had seen Walters at least once a day, sometimes two or three times, during the period when they worked together. Walters had been in Wichita continuously during this time, he said. His descriptions of Hillmon and Walters were compatible with the defendants' claims: Walters was about five feet ten inches tall, with "nice-looking teeth." Hillmon's height was about five eight or five nine.[22]

The proposition that Patrick Heely was a recently discovered wit-ness sustained some damage when he testified on cross-examination that he had told Major Theodore Wiseman what he knew seventeen years earlier. He also said he had known Eugene Ware for years. With that, Heely was excused from the witness stand. (Sallie's lawyers would later point out that Walters's sister had testified that her brother's let-ters had arrived from other cities during the time Heely claimed that the cigarmaker was continuously in Wichita.) A brief flurry of rebuttal testimony produced nothing new, and the presentation of evidence was declared to be at an end.[23]

The brevity of the trial was the subject of some astonished comment. The attorneys, it was said, "are free to admit that they had never believed it possible. But it was possible, and has been accomplished."[24]

Despite its brevity, the fifth trial did contain one episode to intrigue the conspiracy-minded: the matter of the trunk. A few days into the fifth trial, this trunk was delivered into the custody of the clerk of the court. Described by the reporter as John Hillmon's property, present with him at Crooked Creek, the container apparently had never been returned to Sallie, but had instead rested in the custody of James W. Green for all the ensuing years. Samuel Riggs complained of this matter in his opening statement. Green took umbrage at the suggestion that he had sequestered the trunk from the plaintiff or her attorneys, and arranged for the trunk to be brought into the courtroom, whereupon he represented to Judge Williams that it had been present at all the previous trials and that the plaintiff's lawyers could have opened it or employed it for any purpose at their convenience. Indeed, he invited them to do so on the spot. Samuel Riggs protested that there was no assurance that its contents of the box now were the same as they were before it spent so many years in the company of Mr. Green. Green retorted that the trunk had been neither loaded nor unloaded in the interim. Judge Williams directed the clerk to take custody of the trunk, and there is no indication that either party ever made any use of it or its contents in the later course of the trial. Of course, each may have discovered that it contained nothing more interesting than ill-smelling old clothes, but it would be an unimaginative spectator whose thoughts did not turn from time to time to the contents of the trunk.[25]

The lawyers took turns, as before, addressing the jurors in summation. On each side the gloves of deference had been removed, together with any inclination toward giving the benefit of the doubt. Each side described the strategy of the other in the plainest terms: it was to lie, to induce witnesses to lie, and to present this perjured evidence as though it were true.

Although all six lawyers participated in the summation, only the arguments of Charles Hutchings, James Green, and Edward Isham are recorded in any detail. Sallie's lawyer Charles Hutchings opened the volley of charges and countercharges by invoking a scriptural narrative. Comparing his poor gifts to opposing counsel's, he proposed that they were of "vastly superior ability, forensic power, reputation, and influence." He was, of course, David to their Goliath, armed only with "the smooth pebble he took from the brook."[26]

With this pebble (or possibly with the other weapon he claimed to possess, the "keen-edged sword of truth") Hutchings launched his attack, making clear that no combination of lost memory, differing perception, or various narrative styles could account for the gulf that divided the plaintiff's case from the defendants'. Someone, more than a single someone, was lying to defeat the truth. The insurance companies, while seeking to depict John Hillmon as "the most cunning of rogues," had produced one witness after another who had told the most unequivocal of lies. Hutchings singled out for particular notice Mrs. George Nichols and William Hillmon, the defense witnesses who said they were the sister and brother of Hillmon, and who had testified to certain of his characteristics (chiefly bad teeth) incompatible with the features of the corpse. Mrs. Nichols had also reported the scene in which she claimed Sallie had said she would give up her claims and turn her husband over to the authorities. Of this familial disunity, Hutchings said, "Is it not your observations, gentlemen, that blood is thicker than water? Do brothers and sisters, without some most potent influence, voluntarily go from distant states to dishonor and disgrace each other, and especially to blacken and defame the memory of one who is dead? . . . It is contrary to human nature. . . . The trail of the serpent is over them all."[27] Hutchings went on to address some of the other difficulties in the defendants' case, but it was his invocation of the serpent that would later be thrown back at him, clothed in righteous anger, by Edward Isham.[28]

J.W. Green's summation was highly focused on the evidence, not filled with injured dignity as it had been in the fourth trial. But he did seek to arouse some of the jury's anger by suggesting that efforts to impeach the members of the coroner's jury were aimed at "men of the highest standing." Propounded to a jury that contained both farmers and merchants, an emphasis on the social standing of the defendant's witnesses may have carried risks for them. But Isham, when it was his turn to speak, returned to this theme.[29]

The great lawyer of Chicago claimed that he would have preferred to leave the speaking to his cocounsel, but that "it has been a matter of some insistence by them that I should call your attention to certain lines of thought in this connection, and I have yielded to them in that particular." Whether this was true (or whether it was instead the clients who insisted that their prize racehorse should show his talents at this point), Isham proceeded to narrate a rather convincing version of the events of the case, in which Levi Baldwin, about to lose his ranch to financial hardship, and his employee John Hillmon originated the entire scheme of insurance fraud. Levi unwisely explored this scheme aloud with various acquaintances during the summer of 1878, and attempted to stave off a creditor with the claim that he soon would be coming into money. Sallie Hillmon had no real relationship with her husband in Isham's account, but was rather conscripted to marry him in order to create a puppet beneficiary for the insurance proceeds, which Levi Baldwin would in fact collect. And she was still a puppet, Isham suggested, for "the only thing which has kept this litigation alive is the persistence not of the plaintiff, but of the counsel to whom she has transferred perhaps the larger interest in this thing." While "talking to you and pleading to you for this poor woman who cannot get her rights," he said, they are "pleading more for themselves than for her."[30]

His most dramatic moments came when he reminded the jury of Charles Hutchings' mention of the serpent. He spoke of various witnesses in sentimental terms: Dr. Mottram as a "venerable old gentleman," the inquest jurors as "reputable and influential gentlemen of Lawrence," and others as "multitudes of men and women, good, honest, trustworthy people, scattered among the homes of Kansas." Were these worthies to be branded by the mark of the beast who destroyed the Garden of Eden?[31]

Hutchings's accusations, Isham proposed, were "founded on his suspicion that in the community and state where he lives the mere power of the money of such corporations could go among those citizens and bring in what it wanted by such an influence as that." He asked the jurors whether they believed this about "their people." "I tell you," he said, "that the serpent of his vision was the serpent of his own bosom; it is a serpent that has crept back again into the place from which it came, and it has made its unhallowed nest there among the ashes of self-respect and respect for his fellow men, and confidence in all the obligations of morals and duty and in the stability of moral character among his fellow citizens." Isham concludes this part of his speech by predicting, "If counsel can find no better reply than that, I do not believe he can prevail with men who respect themselves and their fellow men."[32]

Coming from a lawyer for parties who had confessedly paid the coroner, the witnesses, and all the jurors at the coroner's inquest into the Hillmon case, this might have been a bit rich. But maybe not; perhaps it really was effective. Certainly, with its flattery of the common man and its suggestion that the opposition had contempt for their honor, it was a speech firmly situated in a great tradition of Kansas (or for that matter American) political discourse.

Later on that year Kansans would elect a number of populists to state office, but the nation would choose William McKinley, the Republican, over Williams Jennings Bryan for President, and Kansas would be represented by two Republicans in the United States Senate. These tensions point to the difficulty that Kansans were experiencing by mid-decade making up their minds whether the trouble with Kansas was the unchecked depredations of the investing class, or the circumstance that this class seemed less and less interested in investing in their state. In Hutchings's David-and-Goliath reference and his conjuring up of the image of the serpent, as well as in Edward Isham's insistence that the real serpent lay in the breast of those who would suggest that their state was available to be corrupted by money and influence, we can hear these themes played out in the Hillmon contest. By now the case's notoriety had as much to do with its theatrical realization of these abstractions as it did with the proceeds of John Hillmon's life insurance policies.

† † †

The summations concluded a few minutes before six on the evening of March 31, and then Judge Williams delivered his instructions, which took twenty minutes or less. The brevity of his charge to the jury matched the simplicity of his vision: the case was one of identity, no more or less. If on the whole the jurors were persuaded that the dead body found at Crooked Creek was John Hillmon's, they should return a verdict for Sallie. If they were persuaded that it belonged to Frederick Adolph Walters or any other person, or if they should be poised on the knife-edge of doubt, their verdict must be for the defendants.[33]

Judge Williams sent the jurors to the jury room rather than excusing them for the evening. The judge apparently intended to maintain his enforcement of extended hours during the jury deliberations. The jurors retired for one evening and then a second without reporting a verdict.[34]

Judge Williams, eager to return to Arkansas where he had a matter scheduled, summoned the jury in at ten o'clock on the third morning and inquired after their progress. The news was not good: the foreman reported that they had "exhausted all of their resources," and yet failed to agree. When asked what might assist them in coming to agreement, the foreman suggested that the instructions be read to them again. Judge Williams agreed, but before embarking on that process he admonished them with some asperity concerning their obligations as jurors:

> I want to say to you, gentlemen, that a mistrial, a hung jury, is a bane, an annoyance, everything I may say to be avoided, in the administration of justice. There have been mistrials, too many of them, in this case before. It is getting to be celebrated for that reason. Some jury has got to decide this case: it is a jury case, one entirely for a jury, and I do not see why twelve men of your intelligence, evidence fairness, and integrity, can not dispose of it. True, there is a conflict in the testimony, but there always will be. As I said to you, some jury has got to decide it, and it is in the interest of justice that it be decided now, and that there be no further delay about it. You have taken a solemn oath to decide the case in accordance with the law and the evidence, not only to be governed by the evidence and the law, but to endeavor honestly to decide the case in accordance with the law and the evidence.
>
> That obligation is also undertaken and it is no light matter. You are not empaneled for mere form, but you are empaneled to listen to the evidence and the law as given by the court, and to decide the case. That is what is expected of you. I do not

expect any juror to surrender an honest and earnest conviction, but I expect the jurors to talk together, to go over the testimony, to go over it kindly, without taking sides as partisans, but to endeavor to honestly and earnestly arrive at a verdict. . . . It seems to the court that there are some tangible things in the case from which you can ascertain the right, and decide the case under the instructions given to you by the court. Not only is the expense incurred by both sides immense, but it begins to look now as though justice cannot be administered in the courts as far as this case is concerned.[35]

Then the judge reread all of his earlier instructions, and sent the jury to continue their deliberations. He told them that he would be available to receive their verdict until midnight, but that thereafter they would have to report to Judge Foster, as he was compelled to prepare for his return to Arkansas.[36]

But neither his rereading of the instructions, nor his further admonitions, nor his implicit threat to keep the jury at work until midnight had the desired effect. At four-thirty, the attorneys conferred and agreed that there was little likelihood this jury would ever arrive at a verdict, and they so informed the judge. With the parties' joint stipulation that a mistrial could properly be declared, Judge Williams discharged the jurors and sent them home, shortly thereafter setting out for his own.[37]

The *Topeka Daily Capital*'s reporter claimed that he had learned from "perfectly reliable sources" that the jury had stood seven to five in favor of the companies. Indeed, he claimed, they had all agreed to a system for counting and weighting the testimony of the witnesses, with a commitment on the part of each that he would then vote according to the result. (Reportedly each witness was scored from 0 if deemed worthless to 5 if judged perfectly believable.) But by this account, when the calculations produced a finding in favor of the companies, one juror who had favored the plaintiff refused to acquiesce in returning a verdict for the defendants. This juror, however, Mr. C.J. Peck of Council Grove, later told others that the jury was evenly divided, a claim the remaining jurors would neither confirm nor deny. However their discussions and votes had gone, plainly the jury had been significantly at odds.[38]

Sallie's attorneys could not conceal their dismay from the press. Lysander Wheat, having at first said that he would have no comment on the matter, was asked whether the case would be tried again. "Don't you know enough to stop asking questions when a man tells you he has nothing to say?" he replied. Samuel Riggs displayed even more testiness, accusing the reporter of being in league with the companies, and saying the newspapers had worked against his client from the start. It was enough, he opined, to make a man into an anarchist.[39]

For their part, the insurance company lawyers claimed that the outcome vindicated the holdout juror from the last trial, Mr. J.C. Young. He had, they complained, been subjected to all manner of false and damaging reports circulated by Hillmon supporters. Nor were the jurors in better temper. Those who would speak for the record complained of their accommodations, and "all said they had a great plenty of the Hillmon case."[40]

The insurance companies approached Sallie's lawyers with a curious proposition: suppose the parties agreed to retry the case in front of the five federal judges who had to date presided over the case, and abide by the majority decision of that panel? It is not known how Sallie's side responded, but it seems unlikely the judges would have gone along with such an unconventional procedure. Nothing came of this proposal, in any event, and eventually the case was set down for its sixth jury trial.[41]

About a year later, the first cracks began to appear in the solidarity of the three Hillmon defendants. This disunity was prompted at first not by any direct actions by Sallie's attorneys, but by an ambitious regulator. In 1897, following dramatic victories of the People's Party in the statewide elections of 1896, Webb McNall had been appointed the Kansas Superintendent of Insurance. The selling of life insurance in Kansas was, if not exactly a license to print money, at least a very lucrative proposition; in 1896, life insurance companies statewide had taken in nearly $1.5 million in premiums, and paid out only $414,000 in losses. (Property and miscellaneous insurance were also highly profitable, but the premium-to-loss ratio was most favorable for life insurance.) An avowed populist, McNall was determined that the insurance industry would not take advantage of Kansas policyholders, and he concerned himself especially with the practices of out-of-state companies.[42]

As early as 1894 Sallie's lawyers had filed a complaint with the Superintendent of Insurance at the time, W.S. Snider, over the conduct of the defendant companies. Snider had ordered the companies to pay Sallie the policy proceeds, but when they did not comply he had taken no action to enforce his demand. Neither of the two ensuing Superintendents, both Republican, had pursued the matter, but shortly after taking office Webb McNall revisited the complaint and concluded that the three Hillmon defendants had unjustifiably refused to pay Sallie Hillmon the proceeds of her husband's policies. He further embraced the even more controversial view that it was his right and obligation as Superintendent to discipline the companies for this misbehavior. In March 1897 the licenses of all three companies came up for renewal, and McNall refused to issue new ones, saying the defendants could not do business in the state until they settled the Hillmon matter.[43]

Jacob L. Greene, President of the Connecticut Mutual Life Insurance Company, shot off an angry letter to McNall, asking how he could be so sure that the companies were wronging Sallie Hillmon when no final decision of a competent tribunal such as a court had ever contained this conclusion. (No doubt the insurance executive discounted the 1888 jury verdict in Sallie's favor because it had been overturned by the Supreme Court.) In response, on March 31, 1897, the Superintendent by letter invited Mr. Greene's company to submit its own evidence to him on the question. McNall said he would be especially interested in any vouchers or receipts the company had kept showing what they had paid to various witnesses in the course of five trials, and what they had paid to any individual in connection with the Lawrence coroner's inquest. "Also," wrote McNall, "the amount of money expended in giving banquets, banqueting jurors after the jury had failed to agree, standing eleven for the plaintiff and one for the defendants. . . . Also give the names of any parties who were middlemen, if any, in paying out the various sums of money that have been paid from time to time." If this request were to be complied with, the Superintendent advised, then "we may ask for additional information along other lines." This reaction was not what Connecticut Mutual had been looking for.[44]

Events related to Webb McNall's aggressive exercise of what he took to be his regulatory powers became known retrospectively as the "Kansas Insurance War" of 1897. Despite these dispiriting and various assaults, all three Hillmon defendants managed to march in formation long enough to ask Judge Cassius Foster, still chief judge of the Kansas federal courts, to hold McNall in contempt of court in the still-pending Hillmon case, arguing that his interventions had shown a willingness to subvert the legitimate processes of the court. But perhaps McNall's uncompromising stance had temporarily diminished Connecticut Mutual's and New York Life's appetite for pursuing other countermeasures. About a week after the contempt motion was filed, the Mutual Life Insurance Company of New York, acting alone, initiated a separate suit against McNall. The lawsuit sought $20,000 in damages for the interference with their business that Mutual Life claimed the Superintendent's actions had caused.[45]

Judge Foster, although he opined that Superintendent McNall's acts were illegal, denied the motion for contempt on the ground that he could not summarily punish an act that had not taken place in the presence of the court. But Mutual Life's damage action against McNall was docketed and seemed to be headed, eventually, for trial.[46]

Other Kansas political figures weighed in on the insurance war. Former Superintendent D.W. Wilder, who had held that office from 1887 to 1891, denounced McNall's actions in emphatic terms:

> It has long been understood that the lawyers own the policies; that Mrs. Hillmon has not a penny's interest in them. The murder was committed in 1879. Why then is the case still in court? Because the defendants are rich corporations. Had this been a controversy between citizens it would have been settled long ago. Once all the jurymen except one voted for the defendants. The ordinary jury decides against rich corporations or fails to agree. The case has become political. It is brought into campaign speeches. Public opinion is against corporations and for Hillmon. It is a distinction to have been a Hillmon juryman. The superintendent of insurance is playing to the grandstand. "Around this murderer I draw the awful circle of the state."

Former Superintendent Wilder offered these remarks from his office in Chicago, where he was editor of the *Insurance Magazine of Chicago*. He was, perhaps, not the most dispassionate of observers.[47]

Nor for that matter could one regard Governor John Leedy, a member of the People's Party, as a neutral commentator. Defending McNall late in the summer of the latter's campaign against the companies, the Governor said that it was his desire to "make the Supreme Court declare the Commissioner's order good."[48]

Several of the state's newspapers criticized Webb McNall for his zeal. The *Leavenworth Times* characterized him in its headline as "an arrogant official."[49] The *Atchison Daily Globe* accused him of blackmail and opined that he deserved to be removed from office. It appears, however, that McNall's pro-consumer stance found favor with many Kansans. One historian believes that McNall enjoyed "widespread bipartisan support from state and local officials, the press, and the public generally." A resident of the town of Mankato may have spoken for many when he wrote the following letter to the Superintendent:

> The people here in Mankato, from the town handyman to our doctors, are one in expressing their anger at those big life insurance companies who are giving that Mrs. Hillman so much trouble. . . . I think times are getting better but we all remember a few years back when money was scarce and a schoolteacher here died and left three children without a living parent. Her children finally had to settle for $100 on a $1000 policy. The whole town was mad. . . . We complained to the company and later to your department but got no assistance. We in Mankato think it is high time that those arrogant companies obey our laws. We know you're for the people.[50]

Whatever their reservations about mounting a direct challenge to a popular official, by the fall of 1897 the three Hillmon defendants had apparently concluded that they could not lie down in the face of Webb McNall's attacks. Together they approached Judge John Williams of Little Rock, who had presided in the fifth trial of the case, with a request that he issue an injunction against the Superintendent's efforts to bar them from doing business in the state. Judge Foster had refused them similar relief earlier in the summer, but this time they were not disappointed.

Apparently Judge Williams believed that he still occupied the position of presiding judge in the Hillmon matter, and thus enjoyed jurisdiction to consider the defendants' petition for relief. Moreover, upon reflection he agreed with the companies' view of the impropriety of McNall's actions. On September 27, 1897, he issued the injunction they had requested.[51]

Thus matters in the Hillmon case remained throughout the fall of 1897, so far as the public was concerned. McNall had suffered a rebuke, but it did not seem to daunt him, for he continued to speak as though he had the power to exclude companies whose conduct offended his sense of justice, and meantime sought an order from the Kansas Supreme Court affirming his power to regulate the insurance companies as he saw fit. The complicated situation seemed to portend a possible conflict between state and federal court rulings, but McNall did not appear worried about the prospect. Perhaps he calculated that if the Hillmon case were to embark on a retrial, Williams, whose only connection to the case was having presided over the fifth trial, would lose jurisdiction to enjoin him from doing as he pleased. And the case was set to be tried for the sixth time in early 1898.

This possibility may have occurred to the companies as well, for despite Judge Williams's injunction, it was reported in early 1898 that Connecticut Mutual would not fight McNall's order that they cease doing business in the state, and had withdrawn voluntarily. Moreover, on January 12 of that year, the Superintendent obtained a judgment from the Kansas Supreme Court confirming his decision that Mutual of New York would be ousted from the state until he approved of their reinstatement; this reinforcement was understood to nullify the effect of Judge Williams's earlier injunction, and Mutual of New York also withdrew from the state.[52]

As for New York Life, furious negotiations apparently took place behind the scenes. In January 1898 a startling announcement appeared in the *New York Times*: the New York Life Insurance Company had reached a settlement with Sallie Hillmon. The terms of this agreement were not officially announced, but the *Times* said that "one report" maintained that Mrs. Hillmon had received the full amount of her claim: $10,000, plus accumulated interest of $11,000 more.[53]

The public reaction no doubt varied from place to place, and person to person, but many were unhappy. The *Atchison Daily Globe* labeled the settlement "one of the greatest outrages ever perpetrated," and insisted that there had never been "the slightest doubt that the Hillmon claims were fraudulent." Further, it reported, all the money would go to Mrs. Hillmon's lawyers, and none to her. (This latter seems to have been the common understanding, but one newspaper quoted Sallie's husband, James, as saying that the settlement fund would be divided fifty-fifty between Sallie and her lawyers.) Other news outlets were merely sardonic; the *Wichita Eagle* said, "Perhaps no insurance company has ever wanted to sob its shoestrings loose as much as the New York Life did when it socked $10,000 into the extended paw of Mrs. Hillmon."[54]

The belief was general that the New York Life Insurance Company had been intimidated into the settlement by the aggressions of Superintendent McNall. The Atchison paper described the settlement as a "great victory for Web McNall," and regarded this victory as one more disgrace to be laid at the feet of the administration of Governor Leedy. The Governor, it claimed, "kn[e]w that Mrs. Hillmon had no interest in these claims, and that they were dishonest," but had nevertheless encouraged the Superintendent to persecute the companies until they yielded.[55]

Nor had the anti-Hillmon news outlets any sympathy for New York Life in its decision to break ranks with the other two defendants. "It looks as if the New York Life played both of these companies false in settling with McNall," reported the Atchison paper, "and hopes to steal their business."[56]

It did appear that New York Life had by its collapse blindsided at least one of the attorneys who had theretofore represented its interests. When told of the settlement, J.W. Green told a reporter for the *Lawrence Daily Journal* that he "it was the first news to him" and that he would be "very much surprised" if there had been such an agreement. He said he had been told only a few days before that New York Life would "fight the case to the bitter end."[57]

New York Life may have been sobbing its shoestrings loose, but with the sixth trial impending Sallie Hillmon Smith was definitely feeling unwell. An affidavit signed by her physician S.B. Langworthy recites that in early January 1898 she took seriously ill with "La Grippe," the name then used for influenza, and was still weak and anemic in February. A letter from her attorney Charles Hutchings dated February 4 said that he had been to visit his client at her home in Leavenworth, and that she was too ill to transact any business at all. The trial had been scheduled to begin on February 15, but with the receipt of these documents, the court granted a continuance until May. The *Atchison Daily Globe* reported the postponement, offering its characteristically acid opinion of the reason for Sallie's claim of illness: "Mrs. Hillmon has gone through five trials, and her colossal nerve is failing her."[58]

The prospect of a May trial date was then abandoned when Mr. Hutchings, in a heart-wrenching affidavit, pleaded the grave illness of his daughter, who was afflicted by paralysis and whose life was in danger. The case was then set for September 1898, but as that date approached another motion for continuance was granted. The last trial of the Hillmon case would not be held until late in 1899.[59]

As soon as the settlement with New York Life was announced in January, Webb McNall permitted that company to resume business in the state without further burden. It was widely predicted that the Mutual Life Insurance Company of New York and the Connecticut Mutual Life Insurance Company would follow suit and compromise as well. (Only the rebarbative *Atchison Daily Globe* insisted that the two remaining defendants would "fight until Hell freezes over, and then fight on the ice.") In May 1898, shortly after Charles Hutching pleaded for a second postponement of the trial to allow him to care for his sick daughter, the Mutual Life Insurance Company of New York moved to withdraw the suit for damages it had filed against Webb McNall a year earlier; this motion had all the appearance of a precursor to some settlement with Sallie Hillmon Smith.[60]

But no agreement between Sallie Smith and either company materialized; the move toward settlement somehow stalled. Whatever discussions may have ensued, they are not memorialized in any public records.

In March 1899, the new Republican Governor, William E. Stanley, removed Webb McNall from office; within ten days, his successor had reinstated Mutual of New York's license to do business in the state. When the Hillmon case was called for its sixth trial in October 1899, James W. Green and his associates were down to two clients. These two, however, were now relieved of any worries about overzealous regulation by the state of Kansas, and still resolutely committed to the defense of their position that they owed Sallie Hillmon nothing.[61]

† † †

Saturday morning finds me in a lab at the University of Kansas Anthropology Department, trying to observe but also stay out of the way while Dennis and Paul inventory, analyze, describe, and photograph the remains they took out of the grave, and Ernesto and his film crew record the proceedings. Dennis seems none the worse for his toxic adventure at the gravesite, but I know that Ben is still feeling the effects of whatever gas seeped out of the murk there; he had coughed quite a bit in the night.

Dennis hypothesizes that the miasmic vapor had contained many years' accumulation of herbicide. "Think about what a cemetery looks like," he suggests. "All perfect green grass as far as the eye can see. You don't have that kind of a surface without using a lot of poisons to keep the weeds out."

"I just hope it didn't do you any lasting harm," I say. "I hear you weren't too cooperative about getting out of the hole."

Dennis shrugs. "I just wanted to see if there were any more bones in there. But if there were, it was just going to be more fragments. We've got what we need, unless the water has destroyed all the protein in these bones."

By the time Mitch Young temporarily re-covered the hole yesterday, Dennis and his assistants had pulled forty-seven bone fragments, five teeth, eight fragments of nail (coffin, not finger), and one small shirt button (glass) from the murky water of the grave. They have washed these items now, and they inspect them minutely. The bones and teeth have been classified by scientific name, and organized by body region for photography. The button and coffin nails are, Dennis tells me, "cultural artifacts," and their presence too must be documented.

It is obvious that Dennis's original desire to identify the remains by facial reconstruction or by measurements of various bone structures will be disappointed, for the remains are far too fragmented for those old-fashioned techniques. But we have hope for the classic twenty-first-century forensic technique: DNA matching. We don't have any of John Hillmon's (or for that matter Frederick Adolph Walters's) DNA, of course; we haven't been lucky enough to find a toothbrush or lock of hair belonging to either man. But thanks to amazing good luck, we do have a sample of Leray Hillmon's DNA. And we know that Leray's Y chromosome is identical to that of his great-uncle John Wesley Hillmon.

Late yesterday, after cleaning up from the exhumation, Ben and I dined with Leray and Sandra Hillmon. Sandra is quieter than Leray; she sat calmly against the banquette last evening, listening to our husbands talk about the trucking business and the price of diesel. It is only the e-mail that she sent me a month or so again that has saved us from leaving Lawrence a very dejected crew, now that it is clear that no useful investigation of the fragmented remains will be possible except for DNA analysis. I tried at one moment, in an aside, to explain my gratitude to her, but she shook her head as though to say it was nothing.

Having failed to ask Leray for it earlier in the day, I had intended to invite him to give us his DNA sample in the course of dinner. But in the moment, surrounded by red leather upholstery and enormous bottles of olive oil, I began to think that soliciting a guy to spit into a plastic cup while at a semi-fancy restaurant betrayed a certain lack of manners. Leray had laughed when I confessed my reluctance, and agreed to show up at the lab the next day for this purpose. He arrived this morning before I did, so I missed the crucial moment of spit, but his sample is secure in the lidded cup that Dennis brought along for the purpose. We will carry this specimen back to Boulder, along with some bone tissue from the grave, and ask our colleagues in the Molecular Biology Department to extract DNA from the saliva and the bone, and to determine whether the Y chromosomes are a match. If so, the remains belong to John Hillmon; if not, they don't.

I sidle back to the table where Dennis and Paul are still working together to classify every single bone. To me they all look alike, but to those who know bones, apparently each one speaks volumes. We will be here for the rest of the day.

SUNDAY, MAY 21, 2006 | OAK HILL CEMETERY | LAWRENCE, KANSAS
We assemble before ten o'clock in the quiet, sunny cemetery. Dennis has wrapped one shoulder bone fragment carefully, and stowed it in the glove compartment of his car. The time we are allowed to keep the other remains from the grave will soon expire, and we want to offer the bones our thanks.

I believe we ought to say a few words, so I thank the man whose death has brought us all here, whoever he might be, for what he has permitted us and taught us, and for what we hope to learn from him in the near future. And then Dennis speaks, and says that there are two tragedies: to be forgotten, and to be misremembered. "It's wrong," he says, "to be remembered as a scoundrel if you weren't, or a victim if you weren't. We hope to ensure that you will be remembered for who you were." Dennis nods toward Mitch to indicate that was all he has to say.

Sorrow for the man dead for these 125 years takes me by surprise. My hands are too dirty for wiping my eyes and I have no handkerchief, so the tears slide down unhindered. Ben, the only one among us who has remembered to wear boots, climbs back into the muddy trench and gently tips the fragments of John Hillmon, or Frederick Adolph Walters, or some other wayfarer, into the gray water, and then he and Dennis and Paul each toss a handful of earth into the pit. We all stand back and Mitch goes to work again with the backhoe. The ground is restored to its contours with shocking speed. Within ten minutes, a cemetery worker is leveling the last uneven hills with a rake, and then he finishes and walks away and it is done.

◁ 8 ▷

THE HILLMON CASE
IS TRIED FOR THE LAST TIME

1899

The sixth and last trial of the case of *Hillmon v. Mutual Life Insurance Company et al.* was called to order on October 8, 1899, at Leavenworth, under the gavel of Judge William Cather Hook. President McKinley had appointed Hook to the federal judgeship held by Judge Cassius Foster following Foster's retirement the previous January from a quarter century on the federal bench. Until his appointment, William Hook had maintained a private practice of law in Leavenworth. He would be the first Kansan to preside over a Hillmon trial since David Brewer, fourteen years and four trials earlier.

A new lawyer had joined Sallie's team: John Atwood of Lawrence, a former law partner of Judge Hook. The sixth trial thus opened with a bang, as controversy immediately arose (or was stirred up) over charges of impropriety directed at the two former partners. The contretemps would become the opening skirmish in a bitter contest between two newspapers, the *Leavenworth Times* and the *Leavenworth Evening Standard*, each eager to persuade its readers what view to take of the Hillmon case.

It was the *Times* that opened the hostilities. The newspaper had published a seriously partisan article about the Hillmon case and its history on Sunday, October 15, the day before the court was to begin jury selection for the sixth trial. We have seen that no newspaper of the time thought it necessary to separate news articles from expressions of editorial opinion, but even taking into account this generally freewheeling journalistic culture it is a bit startling to encounter some of the vitriol displayed by the *Times*. "The five trials have only strengthened the belief that there was fraud perpetrated and a scheme concocted to beat the insurance companies," the paper wrote, and "Each succeeding trial has confirmed the belief of the companies that the entire case was a fraudulent conspiracy, attempted to be consummated by means of murder and they would clearly have been remiss in duty if they had not resisted and continued to resist the claim, not only in the interest of other policy holders, but in the interest of the public at large."[1]

The *Evening Standard*'s preview article, published a week earlier, had been less biased than darkly humorous. It explained that "[t]wo federal judges who tried the case have passed to the great beyond, some say because they were tired to death of hearing the case, and several attorneys of each side killed themselves in the efforts to win and end the case." (The part about the attorneys was exaggerated, but it was true that Judges Foster and Thomas were dead by this time.) The article's chief focus was the mystery of John Hillmon's trunk, which the lawyers were said to regard as a "hoodoo," and to be universally reluctant to open. "It is supposed," the *Standard*'s reporter noted, "that both sides are suspicious of its contents and may be influenced by superstition in not having the contents examined." On the whole, however, the reporter found this explanation of the lawyers' reluctance unconvincing, for "gruesome as the cerements of a man would appear who has been dead so many years, lawyers are not prone to be overcome by gruesome spectacles unless the sight is liable to damage their side of the case."[2]

Jury selection commenced on the day after the *Times*' scathing article had appeared. Judge Hook had ruled that Sallie would enjoy six peremptory challenges to prospective jurors, and each of the two remaining defendants would be permitted to exercise three. The Supreme Court's 1892 ruling, as this judge saw it, guaranteed that each defendant would enjoy three peremptories, but said nothing about how many Sallie could employ. In his opinion, the correct number was six. The defense lawyers protested, but Hook was firm.

The lawyers then undertook the process called voir dire, the questioning of prospective jurors to see whether any might be excused "for cause," as well as to gain information useful in exercising one's peremptory challenges. John Atwood, the new member of Sallie Hillmon Smith's legal team, inquired of the jurors during the voir dire process whether any had read the *Times'* article of the day before. A failure by Sallie's lawyers to make this inquiry would have constituted something close to professional negligence, for exposure to the article would have provided grounds to remove for cause any prospective juror who said he had read it, believed it, and was unlikely to be dissuaded from its premise that the plaintiff's case rested on fraud. But this aspect of the matter carried no weight with the *Times'* reporter, who opined at the end of the day that "the court should have promptly ruled such questions out of order, and any attempt to try newspapers in the United States court, instead of trying the legitimate claim of Mrs. Hillmon, is not only impertinent but dishonest."[3]

The *Times* had a theory concerning why the newly appointed judge had permitted this impertinent line of voir dire: he was allied with the plaintiff's lawyers. The evidence of this association, according to its report, was complex and chain-like, but it amounted to a damning intimacy between the judge and Sallie's counsel, especially Atwood. The *Times'* imputation of impropriety took in its rival newspaper as well: "In years past the law firm of Atwood and Hook always tried their cases in the *Standard*, a paper which they controlled through their influence with [its publisher] Neely."[4]

It is perhaps safe to discount the accusation of trying one's cases in the newspapers when it appears in a newspaper that has the day before jury selection published a notably one-sided article about the lawsuit those jurors chosen will try. The real source of the *Times'* hostility is revealed in its opinion that "it is rather cheeky of Mr. Atwood at this late day to engage as counsel for Mrs. Hillmon." Wheat, Hutchings, and Riggs seem to have pulled off a bit of a coup by hiring the new judge's former partner as cocounsel, and the company's partisans seem to have resented this bold maneuver. Or wished they had thought of it first, for it will be recalled that the defendants had once hired and paid the Lawrence coroner, the Assistant County Attorney, and all the inquest jurors, not to mention John Brown's lawyer. When it came to seeking advantages through the strategic employment of influential persons, Sallie's team had a lot of catching up to do.[5]

The *Evening Standard* took no notice of the complaints of its competitor. On the day of jury selection its reporting was concise, but also unquestionably slanted, although in a subtler way than that of the *Times*. The *Standard's* reporter recounted the history of the case briefly, noting that when Sallie had requested the proceeds the companies "commenced a fight to keep her from getting the insurance money." The defendants, it was said, "by means of detectives found Hillmon alive and well several times, but as often it would turn out that it was not Hillmon." In closing it reported that "Mrs. Hillmon was in the court room this afternoon neatly and modestly attired in black."[6]

The jury was chosen in a day and a half; as always it consisted of twelve men. Not necessarily all white men on this occasion, however: one of the jurors, Prior Dickey of Oak Mills, Leavenworth County, was reported to be "a colored man." Another juror was P.G. Lowe, a former State Senator from Leavenworth.[7]

Opening statements commenced after the noon break on the second day. John Atwood's two-hour presentation for Sallie emphasized the questions presented by John Brown's two accounts of the death at Crooked Creek, and characterized W.J. Buchan as a "double-barreled lawyer" who had "sold out to the insurance companies for $700." As for Sallie and the releases she had signed, she was a "silly, green, unsophisticated country girl, who knew little or nothing of the world of lawyers."[8]

J.W. Green, speaking next, peered into the anticipated evidence and naturally predicted that the jurors would take away a very different impression than that suggested by Atwood. He foretold, among other things, that the jurors would learn that Levi Baldwin's brother had said, when the body was dug up from its first grave in Medicine Lodge, "Hell, that's not Hillmon!"[9]

Green also took the opportunity to do a bit of unsworn testifying himself, explaining his own role in the events thus:

> On the day the body arrived I was coming down from University hill and I heard of it. They said a large number of people had viewed the body and said it was not Hillmon. I was county

attorney and hearing this concluded there ought to be an investigation. I then suggested to the coroner that an investigation of the matter be made. I had not been employed by the company nor as the opposite side says, by Mr. Barker.

Green emphasized that his clients had no burden to prove that the body was not Hillmon's; the burden of proof rested with the plaintiff. Nevertheless, he told the jurors about the cigarmaker Frederick Adolph Walters, and insisted that "the man who was buried at Lawrence was Walters." He promised that "as one method of proving that [the corpse] was not Hillmon we shall show you gentlemen that it was Frederick Adolph Walters and none other."[10]

The sixth trial proceeded crisply under Judge Hook's leadership, and every day seemed to yield some new nugget of information, sometimes puzzling, sometimes explanatory, and once or twice astonishing. On the first day of testimony, a small novelty appeared. Dr. Patterson, the dentist who had been called by the defense in previous trials to testify to having made a tooth mold from the cadaver's mouth, was instead summoned as a witness for Sallie, and asked if he had seen a photograph "of the body." Apparently he understood this question to inquire whether he had ever seen a photograph of the living man whose body had been the source of the tooth mold he had made, and he answered that he had: he had seen a "tintype of Hillmon and Brown." I scrutinized the blurry newspaper report with great interest at this point, for I thought this Patterson must have been shown the same photograph that the guardians of the MassMutual archive had sent me; it was the only photo of Hillmon and Brown together I had ever seen.[11]

But no matter. Whatever photograph Dr. Patterson had seen, he had been told that one of the men pictured was John Hillmon, and he believed that it was this man whose corpse he had been asked to examine on the occasion when he made the tooth mold. Since nothing is so satisfying in a courtroom drama as a complete reversal, the use of this former defense witness to score an important point for the plaintiff was greatly engaging.

Mr. Edward Isham, however, was having none of this; he objected altogether to Patterson's testimony. First he argued that for Patterson, who had never known Hillmon in life, to say that it was Hillmon in the photograph must be hearsay; someone must have told Patterson so. In this, I have to admit that Isham had a point. But it is in a way too good a point, for if it were taken seriously no witness could ever testify that another person was John Hillmon or anyone else: we never know anyone's name (including our own) except by having been told it. All courtroom identifications of anyone by name would have to be banned on Isham's theory, and they are not. The hearsay rule yields to practical necessity here, although scholars of the law of evidence do not often remark on this somewhat embarrassing circumstance.[12]

But Isham had another objection as well to Dr. Patterson's testimony. Since Patterson had not known the living Hillmon, he argued, the doctor's identification of the corpse must be based only on his acquaintance with a photograph of the living man. Such testimony, Isham argued, rested on too flimsy a basis to be reliable—it was "beyond the range of human probability and all facts." The *Times'* reporter is plainly impressed by the august lawyer's speech, for he writes that his "objections were delivered with force and feeling."[13]

Yet an irony attends Isham's objection, and it grows out of the nature of some of his own clients' evidence. In the companies' own frequently stated judgment, some of their most compelling and persuasive witnesses were the family members and friends who had identified the corpse as F.A. Walters. But not one of these witnesses had ever been in the presence of the *corpse*; they had seen only photographs of it. Isham's position must be, then, that a witness's identification of a corpse as that of a particular man is competent if the witness knew the living man but saw only a photograph of the corpse; but if the witness knew the corpse and saw a photograph of the living man, his identification is unreliable and cannot be admitted. Why the corpse/photograph comparison should be useful in one direction but not the other, Mr. Isham does not explain.

The newspaper account does not make altogether clear how Isham's objection fared with Judge Hook, but Dr. Patterson was permitted to say, in the jury's hearing, that he had seen the photograph of two men, that he understood that one of them was Hillmon, and that in his judgment the taller figure "was the picture of the cadaver I worked upon." The judge granted a motion to "strike" the testimony (meaning, as always, that the jury would be instructed to disregard it). The ruling reportedly rested on hearsay grounds, but the hearsay rule would not disallow Patterson from saying that in his opinion the taller of the men in the photograph had become the corpse that he examined, and it is not clear whether that portion of the testimony was allowed to stand. In any event, it scarcely mattered practically; nobody believes that jurors can comply with an order to disregard what they have just heard.[14]

In my own opinion, nobody who had seen the other photographs of John Hillmon could fail to recognize him in the tintype of the two men standing together. He is the man on the right, the taller of the two. Whatever the jury was instructed, I doubted they would neglect to grasp the point of Dr. Patterson's surprising revelation: he believed the corpse he had worked on to be that of John Hillmon.

The next day the defense experienced another witness defection with the appearance of Dr. Phillips of Lawrence. Phillips had testified in the third trial that Levi Baldwin had made a jocular remark to him about what a good scheme it would be to defraud a life insurance company by insuring one's life and then decamping for "Africa or some other damn place." But he, too, appeared as a plaintiff's witness this time, testifying that he had once met Hillmon and that the man was a little taller than he was himself. Phillips was five feet ten inches tall.[15]

Apparently Phillips was also asked, on cross-examination by the defense, about any remarks that Levi Baldwin might have made to him, but he was not permitted to repeat them after Sallie's lawyers lodged a hearsay objection. The companies argued that Baldwin's remarks to Phillips ought to be admitted under the coconspirator exception to the hearsay rule, but Judge Hook did not agree: he observed that they did not seem to have been made in furtherance of the conspiracy, and in any event the companies had never claimed that Sallie Hillmon, the party against whom these statements were offered, was part of any conspiracy at the time they were made. The jury, accordingly, never heard Dr. Phillips's testimony on this point, but for purposes of a possible appeal it was made part of the record. If permitted, Phillips would have testified that Baldwin had asked him whether it would not be a "good scheme to get an insurance on one's life in a large sum, and then go south and get the body of a greaser and palm it off as your own body."[16]

Sallie's lawyers did not inquire further about this alleged statement of Levi Baldwin to Phillips, since the judge had ruled it inadmissible. It is noteworthy that Phillips's recitation of this conversation during the earlier trials had included a reference to hiding in Africa, and in this one to "getting a greaser" (a pejorative name for a Mexican). Each statement contained a characteristically nineteenth-century invocation of the exotic and dangerous, but in one case it was Africa and in another Mexico. The judge's ruling ensured that no exploration would be had of this colorful inconsistency, although Phillips's excluded testimony would yet have a role to play in the Hillmon saga.

The defense team successfully deployed the name-as-hearsay objection again that day, against the attempted statement of a Medicine Lodge witness. The witness, a man named Stanford (no objection was lodged to his stating his own name), wished to say that he had met Hillmon and Brown in his store the December before the fatal expedition, that he had seen the body brought back from Crooked Creek, and that it was the man he knew as Hillmon. George Barker raised the hearsay objection, and the judge instructed the jury that the portion of the statement in which the witness said the dead man was Hillmon would be stricken, but that the witness could say whether the body brought back from the campsite was of the man he had met in his store "the December before in company with Brown." This curious instruction seems to allow the hearsay evidence of Brown's name, but not Hillmon's. In any event, no doubt what was left of the witness's information after this caution had been delivered served Sallie's purposes well enough. But the *Times* reporter, ever the admirer of the defense case, either missed this aspect of the matter or chose to overlook it, for he reports that "the defendants have won the majority of the points for which they have contested so far." By way of illustration, he says that "a considerable amount of evidence that had been submitted at former trials, particularly the testimony of Stanford of Medicine Lodge, was stricken from the records."[17]

Apart from these witnesses and the reading of some depositions, this day in court brought forth only more speculation about the mysterious trunk. The *Times* relates that the trunk, reposing in the clerk's office, has become a "source of amusement by both sides," but one unidentified attorney's reported comment suggests apprehension more than amusement: he said the trunk was like a torpedo, for nobody wished to examine its contents.[18]

The next day's reporting in the *Times* begins with the observation that the opposing attorneys are getting along well with one another, as a "quiet and good nature prevails." But this goodwill was not to endure, for the ensuing proceedings brought the deposition of John Brown, which was read aloud to the jury during Sallie's case. Its length would make the day's proceedings tedious, and familiar quarrels arose over the uses to which Brown's deposition (which told Sallie's side of the tale) and his earlier affidavit (which told the companies') could be put, and what jury instructions should be formulated about them. In one curious transaction, the court told the jury to disregard, at least temporarily, a colloquy recorded in the deposition in which Brown was asked whether he had told Buchan (in the affidavit, the question implies) that Hillmon had killed a man at Crooked Creek. Judge Hook took the view that the jury could not properly consider this portion of the deposition until the affidavit was brought to court. George Barker knew he could produce the affidavit, for it was the one W.J. Buchan had rescued from the fire, but he did not have it in hand, and the judge's ruling left him indignant. "When are these papers to be produced?" he asked. "I did not think we were expected to leave court and get the papers or I would have done so. It would work a hardship on the defendants to produce that statement now, as I did not understand at the time the offer was made that we were expected to take it up at once."[19]

Judge Hook was unmoved. "I cannot see how the counsel's position has been altered in the remotest degree," he said. The upshot of this ruling was that the portions of John Brown's deposition that discussed the affidavit he had given to Buchan could not be read to the jury until the defendants' case.[20]

The *Times* reporter, fond of foreshadowing testimony to come, reports at this juncture that Levi Baldwin's brother Alva (whom he misnames "Allmon Baldwin") has been located and will testify. His evidence, the reporter predicts, "may be considered a point of advantage for the defendants in the case." The article reminds its readers that Green had stated in his opening that this Baldwin brother would affirm that he had said, when shown the body, "Why hell, that is not Hillmon." Accordingly, the reporter expects that the appearance of this Baldwin, who has never before testified, "will undoubtedly produce a sensation."[21]

And if this suspense were not sufficient, three days later the *Times'* scribe again forecasts the appearance of a previously unheard-from witness whose testimony will aid the defense. The life of Frederick Adolph Walters will be "minutely followed," he predicts, and "not a link will be left missing" in the defense's proof that the dead body was that of the cigarmaker. "A feature of the testimony which will be offered," he writes, "is that Walters was in Leavenworth in the year 1878 and that while here worked for the tobacco house of Simmons and Staiger." The witness who will provide this information is apparently to be Arthur Simmons, a proprietor of the tobacco business.[22]

This is the first mention of any witness who employed Walters in his chosen trade, so his appearance is an interesting prospect, but when I first read this prediction I could not see that if Mr. Simmons testified as described he would advance the defense case to any discernable degree. Even if he were to place the cigarmaker in Leavenworth late in the year 1878, that would be three months, according to the defense, before he made the acquaintance of Hillmon and Brown in Wichita, a town nearly two hundred miles distant.

The defense witnesses from earlier trials who placed Walters working at a farm near Wichita in the fall of 1878 were much more useful. But then I remembered that one of them, Tuttle, had gotten confused while on the stand during the third trial, and had at first testified that he knew Walters at the farm in October 1879. He had to be recalled later to correct his statement and place these events in 1878, a year less devastating to the defense (for a credible sighting of Walters alive in the fall of 1879 would have undermined their theory completely). Unsurprisingly, Tuttle had not appeared again. Maybe this Simmons was to be a kind of substitute for him, I decided. In any event, it seemed clear that these defense-favoring predictions about Arthur Simmons emanated from the companies' camp, to be helpfully repeated by the *Times*.

The day after these reports, the *Times'* reliability as a prophet of events to come sustained some damage when Alva Baldwin was called not by the defense, but by the plaintiff. He had traveled from his home in Ohio, despite suffering from lameness that required him to walk with both a crutch and a cane. He agreed that he had traveled with his brother Levi to Medicine Lodge, and witnessed the removal of the body from the hasty grave in which it had there been placed. He had known John Hillmon in

Lawrence, although briefly. He swore that he had not said, at the gravesite or anywhere else, that the body was not Hillmon's. His brother Levi had said that it was, and Major Theodore Wiseman had claimed it was not. He himself, Alva testified, was certain that he recognized the body as the man he knew as Hillman, but he had said nothing either way.[23]

The defense tried to discredit Alva Baldwin by suggesting that it was curious he had not been called to testify at the Lawrence inquest, but Judge Hook did not permit much inquiry along those lines, as the witness could not know why persons were or were not summoned to that tribunal. Barker also sought to impeach Alva Baldwin by suggesting that he had told a man named Emery that the body could not be Hillmon's, but Baldwin stoutly denied it. Baldwin did offer, however, that he had talked to one Spangler, a man who had come to Ohio to question him a few years earlier; he said he had told Spangler the same things to which he had just testified, and the man had written down his statement. Charles Hutchings demanded that the defense produce this statement, but Barker claimed that they knew nothing about it.[24]

Sallie appeared next, a seasoned witness by this time. Her direct evidence addressed mostly the circumstances under which she had signed releases of her claims for Mr. Buchan; on cross-examination she denied, again, that she had ever requested any witness not to testify to some inconvenient fact. (Later, during the rebuttal case, she would give her own account of the meeting between her and the Hillmon relatives who told her they were going to testify that John had suffered from bad teeth. By her account, she had said to them, "You have forgotten what your brother looked like or you are in the employ of the insurance companies and you are no friends of mine.")[25]

On redirect questioning, Sallie said that her husband had no scar on his hand. He did, however, have a mole on his back. Barker was not about to let this last go by unchallenged, and requested recross-examination. She had been present at every trial, had she not? She had heard Walters's brother testify that the cigarmaker had a mole on his back, had she not? But had she ever before testified that her husband had such a mole?[26]

Yes, she said, every time the question was asked. "Here it was stated by the lawyers for the defense," reports the *Times*, "that the records would show that the question had never been answered by the witness before, but it was found by them that it had been asked at the last trial."[27]

Things were not going so well for the defense. Sallie's lawyers finished off their case by reading from the deposition of Dr. Fuller, who stated that the postmortem examination had discovered a mole on the back of the corpse.

† † †

Judge William Hook leans back uncertainly into the chair behind his desk. It is not a comfortable one—it had belonged to Judge Foster, and Hook has had no opportunity to replace it, nor any other of the furnishings of these dusty chambers. The judge rearranges his legs to relieve the cramps that have begun to trouble him during this trial. He is not accustomed to so much sitting, and has been surprised at the end of every day by the aches and fatigue that catch up with him once he has gaveled his court to a close. Judging had looked like easy work when Hook stood on the other side of the bench; but he has discovered that every day brings new difficulties, and that often enough one has no idea of the right thing to do. One must, however, project an air of confidence and certainty at all times.

William Hook presses his forearms against the armrests of his chair and sits erect; he will maintain the same posture here as he would in the courtroom, for he is not alone. One of the jurors stands before him, awkwardly shifting from one foot to the other. Judge Hook is not at all sure what he ought to say to the man, nor how he should proceed in the face of what the juror has just told him.

"You are right to have brought this information to me," says the judge. "I commend you for it. Now you must leave it to me." That came out rather well, he thinks.

"Ought I say anything to the others?" says the other man. "Maybe the same thing happened to them."

"No," says Hook after a pause. "No, I will manage this, sir. Say nothing, if I may so impose on you. Neither now nor later. Do not say who it was that spoke to you, nor what was said. Especially the former."

"Whatever you wish, Your Honor." Hook studies the man closely as he says these words, and then nods, satisfied.

He then turns to the bailiff, who has been standing in the shadow at the far end of the chambers, his hands clasped behind his back. "Show this gentleman back to the jury room to join the others, Mr. Fenton. And please tell them that court will remain in recess for another half hour. Then advise the attorneys of the same. You need not say why."

Once the two men have closed the creaking door behind them, the judge steeples his fingers and closes his eyes. His reflections last no longer than five minutes. The safest thing would be to declare a mistrial, but William Hook will be damned if the acts of some crook will prevent him from bringing the Hillmon matter to an end once and for all. The judge has little doubt which party is responsible for this outrage, and he guesses that the juror has no doubt at all, but on this matter both will maintain their silence. He must rely on the discretion of the man, but he has looked into his eyes and believes he can do so.

PARTIAL TRANSCRIPT OF SIXTH TRIAL OF
HILLMON V. MUTUAL LIFE INSURANCE COMPANY
(KANSAS STATE HISTORICAL SOCIETY)

BY THE COURT: I desire to say this: There is a juror here whose conduct is very commendable, and whom I honor for it, has stated to me that a communication was made to him, which he interpreted as preliminary to an offer to bribe. He stated to me the language that was used to him, and it looks very much to me as it did to him, bus inasmuch as there might be some mistake, I think it best not to mention the name of the party who made the communication, or the name of the juror to whom it was made; but I desire to say this, that if there is any further effort made in that direction, I will have that man's name presented to the United States grand jury for indictment.

Mr. Barker here offered to speak.
BY THE COURT: It is no lawyer connected with this case. I do not mean to say that the effort came from either side of this case, and no counsel is called upon, it is not necessary in the mind of the Court for any counsel to say anything one way or the other about it. There is no reflection cast upon anyone directly connected

with this case, so far as I know, but I desire to say to the person that that must stop; it must proceed no further. If I can prevent it, this case will not be tried with anything of that sort in it.

The hour of 12 M. having arrived, the Court arose in recess until 2 P.M.[28]

Of the many mysteries surrounding the Hillmon case, none is deeper nor more troubling than the question of who attempted to bribe one of the jurors in the sixth trial. When Judge Hook recalled the court into session after the noon recess on that day, the defendant's lawyers asked the court to excuse the jury so the events of the morning could be discussed further. Once the jury had been removed, attorneys Isham and Barker were adamant in their objections to allowing the matter to rest where the court's earlier remarks had left it. Barker insisted that the jurors would naturally conclude from the information given them that the insurance companies were responsible for the attempt. He argued that "the imputation would go out; the impression would go out; it would make an impression upon the jury that if anybody had done that, it was the defendants in this case, because the defendants have the money." This impression would be grossly unfair, Barker complained: "We are over here, so far as that is concerned, in Leavenworth county where the plaintiff lives; where her counsel, two of them, live."[29]

Judge Hook replied mildly that inasmuch as this was so, the jury would have as much reason to suspect the plaintiff's side as the defendants', and that as far as he could see his remarks did not operate to the prejudice of either party more than the other. He went on to say that the overture that the juror had reported was an invitation for the juror to go to a certain place, coupled with a representation that "there would be something in it for him." Hook further disclosed that the person named by the juror had been in the courtroom at the time the court had issued its warning about the result of any further attempts. He had considered letting the matter go, the judge said, but had concluded that this tolerance was beneath the dignity of the court. He reminded the lawyers that he had told the jurors that no counsel or party to the case was implicated in the attempt. What more could he have done? "[A]m I to discharge this jury," he asked, "and lose all the time, all the care, and all the energy that counsel and litigants have devoted to it up to the present time?"[30]

For Edward Isham, the answer to the judge's rhetorical question was clear: yes. He and his cocounsel were not mollified by the judge's defense of his handling of the matter. Isham rose to take Barker's place at the podium. The jury must be discharged and a mistrial declared, he maintained. Elaborating on a theme introduced by Barker, he complained that his clients had been assailed at every turn with the suggestion that they enjoyed unlimited wealth and could procure what they wished with it.

> Your Honor is perfectly aware that from the beginning to the end, in the long history of this case, there has been a parade that is familiar to the people of Kansas from one end to the other, of the poverty and weakness of this plaintiff, and of the moneyed power—that is the phrase dwelt on here in this forum continually—of the defendants. We cannot bring a witness from a distance; we cannot take a single step that involves a little expense, but it is immediately dwelt upon and has been here to an extent before the Court, to an extent that I think ought to have been stopped, and ought not to be permitted, as evidence of the money power, and of the corruption of their witnesses and all that sort of thing, with nothing on the face of the earth to found it upon except the fact that we have been able to bring witnesses from a distance, or we have been able to do this, that or the other, to throw light upon the identity of this body at Lawrence.[31]

Under these trying circumstances, Isham contended, his clients could not possibly obtain a fair trial from a jury that had been informed of a bribery attempt; the jurors would surely conclude that his clients must be to blame, since "this poor woman has nothing to buy jurors with." The Chicago lawyer was also indignant about the judge's willingness to allow the perpetrator, his identity known to the judge but not to the lawyers, to escape punishment for his crime. "[T]his man, whoever he may be, should be hauled right up now. I haven't the slightest idea who he is, but he and his relations and whoever is behind him, all should be brought right up, and the matter explored to the bottom now."[32]

It does not appear that Sallie's lawyers spoke at all during this passionate discussion; apparently they were content with Judge Hook's handling of the matter. The *Leavenworth Times*, never admiring of the plaintiff's case, found their silence suspicious. "It was noticeable," that paper recorded, "that the plaintiffs made no motion and offered no remarks on the matter of the attempt to bribe the jury." The *Standard* merely reported that "[t]o say this was a bombshell expresses it mildly. Within a few minutes the news spread about the hotels and business houses and it was not long until it was the chief topic, everybody wondering who at this stage of the proceedings would be bold enough to approach a juror in such a way."[33]

Judge Hook swiftly denied the defendants' motion for mistrial. The trial would continue, he ruled; the jury would not be discharged. Concerning the suggestion that the perpetrator ought to be summoned and further punished, he said he would consider it. He does not appear to have pursued the matter, however.[34]

The defense lawyers' insistence that the would-be briber ought to be brought in and interrogated suggests that they do not believe he will reveal any connection to them. But might their clients have arranged for this intervention without the attorneys' knowledge? It does not seem impossible. Certain tactics past, for example some of the claims that John Hillmon had been found alive, seem to have been the brainchildren of company officials acting without the participation of the lawyers, who were later required to distance themselves from the results.

On the other hand, the plaintiff's lawyers' relative lack of interest in the identity and motives of the perpetrator begs for an explanation. At the moment the juror was approached, Sallie's case seemed to be going better than the defendants'; she had just finished her testimony, and both Alva Baldwin and Dr. Patterson had provided useful evidence for her case that no previous juror had heard. It seems an odd moment for her side to attempt the dangerous act of bribery. Perhaps someone representing the plaintiff's lawyers' had made this overture, never intending to follow up on it but hoping it would tend to cast suspicion on the defendants? This premise would explain Sallie's attorneys' apparent indifference to identifying the miscreant, but it is not the only possible explanation. Perhaps they were simply unsurprised that their opponents would resort to such a tactic.

There is one other possible piece of evidence about the bribery puzzle, albeit one that no court would ever consider, as the rules of evidence would bar it. Not all the rules of evidence have to do with hearsay; some create other sorts of prohibitions and limitations, and one intricate web of rules concerns itself with the admissibility of character evidence. The applications of these rules can generate debate, but there is no uncertainty about one general principle: it is forbidden in an American court of law to offer proof of the prior (or later) bad acts of a person, merely to support the argument that on some occasion in question he probably acted in the same bad way. In other words, if there were evidence that one of the lawyers had resorted to bribery in some other situation, it would not be admissible as any proof that he had done so in the Hillmon case.

But we are not in court here, and this rule against the use of character evidence, whatever its virtues, runs counter to common sense if employed outside the courtroom—for we all make judgments every day about whether someone has probably done something by consulting our beliefs about that person's character, which in turn we have formed from what we know or believe about what she has done in the past. Such judgments may be wrong, may even be dangerous, but they are irresistible, and for a reason: often the best gauge of how someone will act on a particular occasion is how he acts or has acted on other occasions.

In the spirit of this commonsensical premise about character evidence, then, but in defiance of what I know to be the law's rules, I will offer this information: Charles Gleed was on another occasion accused of involvement in bribery, or at least the appearance of it. In 1887 the Kansas Legislature had passed a law appropriating money to compensate victims of Quantrill's 1863 Raid on Lawrence. There was widespread dissatisfaction about the amount and method of compensation, and several sources complained that (in the words of one) "a Topeka lobbyist serving as a member of the University of Kansas Board of Regents" (this could only have been Gleed) had taken

$50,000 raised by the claimants to purchase votes in the Legislature, and was now refusing either to pay the bribes or return the money. Gleed did not deny that he had lobbied for the legislation, but disputed that he had offered any bribe or represented that he would. He excoriated his accusers by deeming it a pity that they had not been "gathered in by Mr. Quantrill." And indeed, clients disgruntled because their lawyer has taken money to carry out an illegal act for them but had then failed to perform it, are not altogether the most sympathetic, nor credible, of victims. According to Gleed's biographer, a number of citizens and newspapers believed the accusation, but it was never proved against him.[35]

Even if it had been, of course, it would not demonstrate to any degree of certainty that he had a role in the Hillmon bribery affair. Unlike the authors of the rules of evidence, however, I do not deem it altogether inadmissible. Yet even with the knowledge of Charles Gleed's past taken into account, I know that to this mystery a confident solution is impossible. No matter what Dennis and his scientific colleagues may be able to tell me about the bone he took from the grave in Oak Hill Cemetery, it will not reveal who approached the juror, or why.

In late June, I receive an e-mail from Dr. Ken Krauter, who is supervising the DNA extraction effort being performed by his coworker Helen Marshall.

> I returned from a seminar this afternoon and found the attached picture on my desk from Helen.
>
> It shows a photograph of DNA derived from your Kansas friend (you remember him, the one who prefers to rest in underground rivers?) after it has been "amplified" using the Polymerase Chain Reaction (that is a method that allows tiny amounts of DNA—the sort we get from live people too—to be detected and analyzed). In this picture there are 17 rows that are sorta glowing at the top and streaking down the page. These are replicate samples and all have significant amounts of DNA. While it is still possible this is an artifact (for example we do not yet know if it is

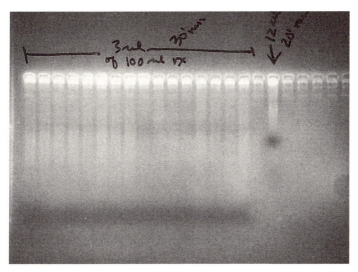

DNA extraction of bone sample. Courtesy Ken Krauter.

human—it could be DNA from microbes that were living in the bone for example) that is not likely. Next week we will run some analyses of this material and will know for sure if it is human. We also have plenty of DNA from the saliva samples so if this DNA is the real McCoy, we should have a preliminary answer about who is more closely related by the end of next week or early the following week.

Also, if it turns out to be impure, we have only used a tiny fraction of the fragments you gave (I think the bone, not the tooth, right Helen?). So there are many avenues to explore to clean it up more prior to extraction.

Very exciting (he said in his usual understated manner. . . .).

Ken

My untrained eyes cannot make much of the picture attached, which looks like a piano roll, but even so it *is* exciting. The bone has DNA in it! But Ken's next e-mail, about a month later, is less encouraging:

Well, we are beginning to become pessimistic. We have now tried about 5 different approaches and have tested for DNA in many different ways. As near as we can tell, there is no human DNA in that material. We are still trying a couple more things but I am losing hope. I think living in a contaminated bog for 100 years has either destroyed or rendered unusable any DNA. In parallel we have extracted good DNA from newer bones found out in a yard so we don't think our methods are wrong (we are using the methods we have found in the literature for old bones). Only in the Kansas sample do we seem to have the problem. Give us another week or so to try our last efforts. We are ordering some special Y-specific markers that use a different method of detection than the chip-based method we have used so far—which is supposed to be the most sensitive.

But I am concerned. Sorry there is not better news yet. If you want to come by we can give you a little seminar about the methods and results we have tried. I would actually like to do this so you at least understand the problem. It is not molecular rocket science though, to realize that storing an organic molecule in a swamp is not ideal! It is a bit like looking for a blood spot on the wall of the Titanic. There is DNA in it, but not human—probably fungal and bacterial—organisms that can eat DNA.

And although Ken and Helen continue loyally to work on the bone, trying various techniques, they are never able to extract any human DNA. All the work to achieve permission to exhume the remains, the digging, the mud, the exposure of Dennis, Ben, and the other diggers to the miasmic gases—for nothing, except a portrait of the DNA of some fungus! I try not to descend into a hopeless sadness about this outcome, and to reconcile myself to the reality that I will never know with any certainty who is buried in the grave recorded as John Hillmon's. And if I cannot be sure who is in the grave, then I will never know Sallie Hillmon, since I cannot be sure whether she lied or told the truth. This prospect disturbs me even more: I can never repose any confidence in the approximate accuracy of the personality I have constructed in my mind. I feel as though I have lost a friendship, a strange friendship to be sure, but a real one.

† † †

Judge Hook insisted that the trial proceed with no further distractions generated by the bribery incident. The plaintiff having rested after Sallie's testimony, the judge called on the defense to proceed. But before calling any witnesses, the defense presented a pleading called a demurrer: a motion to dismiss the case altogether on the ground that the plaintiff had failed to prove her case as a matter of law. The basis of this unusual claim was Sallie's lawyers' neglect to put forward any evidence that the two defendant life insurance companies were citizens of a state other than Kansas. The court's jurisdiction rested on "diversity of citizenship" between the defendants and Sallie, and this relationship had not before been a matter of controversy: Sallie was plainly a Kansas citizen, and Green and his cocounsel had never disputed that their clients were out-of-state corporations. Indeed they did not deny it now; they simply declined to admit it. In an ordinary case the defendants would have stipulated to such an uncontested matter, but the spirit of generosity in such matters had been eroded by time. In the absence of such a stipulation Sallie's lawyers bore the burden of proving this jurisdictional fact, and apparently they had not done so. The defense was within its rights to insist that they do so, or suffer the dismissal of Sallie's case.[36]

Judge Hook noted the plaintiff's failure, but did permit her lawyers to reopen the presentation of their case long enough to supply proof of diversity of citizenship. Sallie's Kansas citizenship was easily established by a few moments of her own testimony, but to prove the defendants' citizenship without their cooperation, her lawyers were compelled to send emissaries on a dramatic overnight mission. These aides traveled to the state capital and (with the special permission of the Assistant Commissioner of Insurance) opened a vault in the Office of Insurance Regulation. There they located and borrowed the originals of the Kansas charters of the Connecticut Mutual and New York Mutual companies, in which the companies' New York and Connecticut citizenship was recited. These documents were then transported to Lawrence on a 5:00 a.m. train, and arrived in court in time to be received in evidence as complete and perfect proof of the diversity of citizenship between the parties to the Hillmon case.[37]

This curious difficulty having been resolved, the defendants called Major Theodore Wiseman as their first witness. He repeated the testimony he had given so many times before about the exclamation Alva

Baldwin had made when the grave at Medicine Lodge was opened: "Hell, that ain't Hillmon." On the question of whether these damning words had been uttered, Wiseman's and Baldwin's testimony stood in equipoise, and the jury would have to decide whom to believe.[38]

Before Wiseman could be cross-examined, Eugene Ware asked that old soldier be allowed to depart and continue his testimony on some other day; the lawyer said that the witness was not well. Judge Hook granted this leave, and Wiseman did not return for two days. In the meantime, the jury heard the familiar account of Dr. Stewart, as well as some novel testimony from a Mrs. Annette Corkadel. Mrs. Corkadel had been a childhood acquaintance of John Hillmon in Ohio, and indeed confessed after some coaxing that she had been engaged to him "before he went to the war." (Hillmon enlisted in the Union Army at the age of sixteen, so this would have been quite a juvenile romance.) Mrs. Corkadel remembered that her swain had a black tooth even then. Another witness said that once in 1864 a dentist had come to Valley Falls to work on some of the citizens' teeth, including John Hillmon's, in which the dentist had placed a filling. These revelations were followed by the inevitable Mrs. George Nichols, sister to John Hillmon. She "could not be shaken," according to the *Times*, from the claim that her brother had suffered from bad teeth; she also retold the tale that Sallie Hillmon had expressed an intention to dismiss her case and turn her husband over to the authorities once she heard Mrs. Nichols insist on this circumstance.[39]

But then Major Wiseman returned to the stand to be cross-examined, and during this testimony, the old soldier said something quite remarkable: so remarkable that it is difficult to account for the very small impression it apparently made on the reporter and in the courtroom. Wiseman agreed that about a week after he started to look for him in Topeka, he located "Frank Nichols," the man whose friends had initially reported him to have gone missing after telling them that he was going with "a man named Hillmon." This was perhaps not altogether startling, as the Nichols report had been circulating during the very early days of the Lawrence inquest.[40]

But then Wiseman admitted that he had also, a month or so after finding Nichols, located Burgess, quite alive. *Joe* Burgess. The man who, as Wiseman's questioner described him, "was also suspected of having been the man shipped back." Yes, agreed Wiseman, he had found that

Joe Burgess. In other words, the individual that John Brown swore, in the affidavit prepared by W.J. Buchan, to have been exactly the man that Hillmon had murdered at Crooked Creek. The man who, according to the defense argument in every one of the five preceding trials, was really Frederick Adolph Walters.[41]

How could this bombshell—Joe Burgess alive after the death at Crooked Creek!—have gone so unremarked? Of course, the *Times* reporter has by now revealed himself as an unmistakable shill for the defense, but the trial is also being covered by the *Lawrence Evening Standard*, which seems sympathetic to Sallie. How could its coverage fail to take note that this witness, an agent of the defense for two decades, has just blown an enormous hole in the consistent and vociferous claim of the companies that Frederick Adolph Walters was Joe Burgess was the dead body at Crooked Creek? But the only information that newspaper offers is that the testimony of Major Theo. Wiseman was used "to show that the body was not that of Hillmon."[42]

Perhaps, I surmise, Sallie's lawyers have made quiet note of Wiseman's testimony, and plan to remind the jury of it to maximum effect during their closing summations. Often this is the wisest choice: if your opponent inadvertently furnishes you a weapon, accept it offhandedly, as if you do not quite know what use it might be, and perhaps he will forget you have it.

The defense forged ahead, without much in the way of evidence that had not been heard before. Many persons said that John Hillmon had bad teeth, as always without much consensus about which tooth or teeth were bad, when these dental defects had first appeared, and whether they had been repaired. Various witnesses said that the body they saw was not their acquaintance John W. Hillmon. W.J. Buchan defended his handling of the legal affairs of his client John Brown. In satisfaction of Judge Hook's ruling about the need for the original document, the Senator also produced Brown's affidavit, torn into a number of pieces (and presumably somewhat scorched from the stove, although this is not mentioned). On another subject, he explained that he had not intended any threat to his client by bringing along the deputy sheriff Ward when he went to visit John Brown at his brother Reuben's home; he had done so only because Ward had a "good team" of horses and was willing to transport him.[43]

As they had in the other contests, signs appeared that the cumulation of exhausting trial days was eroding the attorneys' goodwill. On one occasion John Atwood began an objection by saying "At this stage of the game—," whereupon George Barker interrupted by saying he objected to counsel referring to the proceedings as a game. Atwood apologized. But the days were no shorter, and no more agreeable, thereafter.[44]

By November 4 the defendants, according to their admirer on the staff of the *Leavenworth Times*, were "on the track of Walters and propose to trace every move he made from the time he left home until he was murdered on Crooked Creek near Medicine Lodge on March 17, 1879 and his body shipped to Lawrence as that of Hillmon." But first they called the Lawrence coroner's juror E.B. Good, and asked him how Sallie had behaved at the inquest where he had served on the jury. Atwood objected in dramatic terms, invoking a recent miscarriage of justice: "Dreyfus was found guilty because the court said that he looked guilty. Are we going to allow such methods to come into this trial?" The President of France had pardoned Alfred Dreyfus about two months earlier; the reference would have been particularly pointed. But Hook allowed Good to answer.[45]

"She laughed and made light of the trial," he said. "She did not appear as a woman who had lost her husband."[46]

I find myself resentful on Sallie's behalf. Even the *Lawrence Standard*, no friend to Sallie in the days of the Lawrence inquest, had reported at the time that "her grief, because of his death, has all the appearance of being genuine and heart-felt." And if she were a cold and cunning coconspirator of the sort Mr. Good's description suggests, wouldn't her capacity for deception extend to the impersonation of a grieving widow? Or was it their theory that Sallie was both venal and stupid?[47]

More predictable defense witnesses shuffled through the courtroom: the agent Griffith, Hillmon's brother-in-law W.W. Nichols and his sister, more observers of Hillmon's bad tooth or teeth, the Lawrence coroner Morris. But some of the defense witnesses were new. Two half-brothers from Wichita took the oath to describe their experiences with Brown and Hillmon just before the latter pair embarked for Medicine Lodge in early 1879. The brothers, who were in the gardening business, said that Hillmon and Brown had stayed with them at their place for about a week before leaving around March 1. One brother, Michael Mesh, testified that for amusement the men had compared their heights and weights. Hillmon, said this brother, was five feet nine inches tall. The other brother, Benjamin Hilda, had not witnessed this measuring activity, but he had something even more sinister to report: John Brown had tried to persuade him to leave gardening behind and to travel west with himself and Hillmon to help with a stock farm. Brown had promised there would be plenty of money in it, according to Hilda. The gardener had declined to join this venture, but said that Brown kept after him about it. Not long after, he said, he heard that a man had been killed at their campsite. Mr. Hilda was convinced he had experienced a near escape from untimely death.[48]

The traffic of witnesses to and from the stand was interrupted briefly by a quarrel over the admissibility of the deposition of James Crew. Crew's testimony—to the effect that Levi Baldwin had told him, in an effort to delay foreclosure on Baldwin's property, that he would soon repay his debt with some of the Hillmon insurance money—had been received in the earlier trials, but kept away from the jury in the fourth trial on hearsay grounds. The defendants claimed that it was admissible under the hearsay exception for statements made by one coconspirator and offered against another. Judge Hook found the question difficult, and temporized in uncharacteristic fashion: he allowed arguments on the point to consume nearly a day, and then told the lawyers that he would consider the matter further overnight, and in the morning "hear their arguments in regard to the objections further."[49]

The Crew statement seems small enough in comparison to the profusion of other evidence on both sides, but it would prove to be an outsize contributor to the history of the case. Judge Hook eventually ruled it inadmissible: as he saw it, there was no proof that Sallie was a member of any conspiracy, even if there had been one at work at the time Baldwin made his statement to Crew. Indeed, even in the defendants' account of the matter, Sallie joined the conspiracy only when she saw the body, realized that it was not her husband's, and chose to go along with the deception. Levi's statement to Crew, if he made it, came before that time. The coconspirator exception to the hearsay rule would require proof of Sallie's participation in the plot at the time the statement was made, and also some reason to believe that the statement was made to further the goals of the conspirators. Judge Hook doubted that either requirement had been satisfied. The coconspirator exception, he ruled, could not aid the defendants in overcoming the hearsay objection, and the jury would not hear the deposition of Mr. Crew.[50]

The next few days were, as we would say in the twenty-first century, all Fort Madison, all the time. Many of the witnesses from that city were heard from only by deposition, and no doubt the reading of these transcripts became monotonous, as it always had. But Alvina Kasten's deposition, I would suppose, held some interest despite the absence of its deponent. The famous letter, attached to the deposition, was offered for reading as well. Sallie's lawyers gamely objected, but of course if there was one exhibit whose admission was guaranteed in advance, it was this letter. If the Hillmon case had been a film, Alfred Hitchcock would have called Alvina Kasten's letter the McGuffin of the story—an object without which it could not have been told.[51]

Apparently the original letter was produced. "It was much mutilated," says the *Times*, "but still can be read." I am indignant. Why then is the original not in the archive, instead of a handwritten copy apparently produced by the hand of James W. Green? "There is no doubt as to the genuineness of the letter," says the *Times*. "There can be none as to the truthfulness of its contents, being as they were the confession of a lover to his sweetheart."[52]

I try to think if ever in the history of mankind a lover has told a lie to his sweetheart. Perhaps I am jaded, but I believe this may have happened from time to time. I am becoming partisan here in the last stretch of this sixth trial. I have had a bellyful of the *Leavenworth Times* and of Mr. James W. Green and his cocounsel, and am at risk of deciding that Sallie was truthful merely because they are such bad liars. But I know logic cannot support this conclusion.

Never in six trials have Sallie's lawyers suggested that this letter is not genuine. I think it is because they have seen other letters in Walters's handwriting and been advised they are in the same hand. But "genuineness," like its synonym "authenticity," can mean more than one thing. We commonly speak as though an item, of evidence or in the everyday world, is either genuine or not. But as I am wont to remind my students, some items may be genuine in certain of their aspects, and not in others; it all depends on what is claimed for them. What is claimed to be a copy of the program for *Our American Cousin* autographed by Abraham Lincoln just before his assassination may turn out, upon inspection, to be a genuine copy of that program for that production, but one that carries a forged signature.

Is it possible that the Alvina Kasten letter is genuine in some ways, and not in others?

When I get back to the newspaper account of the trial, the Walters relatives are entering the courtroom for their testimony. The family was represented on this occasion by the brother Charles R. Walters of Missouri, and the sisters Elizabeth Rieffenach and Fannie Walters. Charles testified to having received a letter from his brother saying that he had hired himself out to a man named Hillmon. Charles confessed that he had made some untrue statements in his correspondence with H.R. Clark, the Sheriff of Douglas County; he said it was because he had come to believe that Clark was "a detective in the interests of Mrs. Hillmon" and he did not propose to give the sheriff "any advantage." These circumstances, he said, accounted for the misleading statements. (The *Times* does not record what these "misleading" statements may have been, but in earlier trials it was shown that one of his letters to the Sheriff had said that his brother's teeth had fillings.)[53]

Elizabeth Rieffenach's testimony was markedly similar. She, too, had had such a letter from Frederick Adolph, mentioning a man named Hillmon, and she, too, had never been able to produce this letter. But she was able to produce a sheaf of other letters from her brother, written from such places as Council Bluffs, Kansas City, Aladdin, Paola, and Lawrence. These were unremarkable documents, although it is hard not to notice one circumstance: in one of the earliest letters, written shortly after his departure from home, he asks his sister to tell "A.D.K.," presumably Miss Kasten, how to address her letters to him at the general post office. But in his last letter to his sister in February 1879 (i.e., the last before the allegedly missing one) he does not mention Alvina. Instead he writes this postscript: "Compliments to Annie Baker & the rest of the good looking girls."[54]

Green's efforts to elicit what the witness's mother had said when shown the photograph of the corpse were thwarted when Hook sustained an objection, saying that under the circumstances any mother who believed her son was dead would naturally have a dramatic reaction to a photograph of a corpse. Hook similarly sustained an objection to any evidence of the inscription on a stone the family had placed in its cemetery lot in Fort Madison. Green insisted that it be placed in the record for purpose of appeal, and it was: "SACRED TO THE MEMORY OF FREDERICK ADOLPH WALTERS, WHOSE BODY LIES BUR-IED AT LAWRENCE, KANSAS."[55]

The next day Fannie Walters testified that she bore a strong resemblance to her brother Frederick Adolph. At that point Sallie's attorneys rose to object, for they knew from experience what intentions Green harbored regarding this witness. Judge Hook listened to argument for an hour before permitting Green to carry them out. The jury was furnished with the photographs of the corpse; then Fannie Walters stood and first faced the jury, then turned to show them her profile. "The resemblance between the features of the cadaver and the living witness," wrote the *Times* reporter, "were so startling that it almost caused exclamations from those who looked at both." Not satisfied with this effect, Green requested that the witness display her teeth to the jury. She showed the twelve men "a set of fine, large, white, regular molars, resembling very much the wax mold which was made by Dr. Patterson, the dentist, from the mouth of the body at Lawrence." And with this evidence of admirable dental endowment, the defense rested.[56]

No sign had so far been seen of Arthur Simmons, the man who would, it had been claimed, place young Walters at work in his Leavenworth cigar factory in the year 1878.

Judge Hook invited the plaintiff's attorneys to put on any rebuttal evidence they might have. The additional evidence offered by Sallie's side seemed piffling at first, as rebuttal evidence often is. A man named Phillips testified that Major Wiseman had told him during the inquest that the insurance companies would rather have Brown driven away than arrested, and attempted to hire him to harass Brown until he left town. The witness said that he had refused this commission. He admitted on cross-examination that Sallie Hillmon had at one time lived in his home, and thereafter court was gaveled into recess for the day.[57]

This trial seems to be drawing to a sleepy close, but its inventory of surprises has not been entirely exhausted.

† † †

A stir circulates through the courtroom as Charles Hutchings stands and says the name Arthur Simmons. But the commotion is a small one; most in attendance are unfamiliar with the name, and for the others it prompts only a vague sensation of recognition. No need for the bailiff to fetch the witness; apparently he is standing just outside the court-room doors, for he enters immediately. Lysander Wheat permits him-self a small glance at James W. Green; his old adversary looks tired, but not confused. Wheat believes that he knows what is to come.

After their conference late last night, Wheat and Hutchings had agreed that the latter would conduct this examination. Wheat was senior and could have insisted that it was his prerogative. But it was Hutchings who had noticed that the witness trumpeted by the defense's favorite journalist had not appeared, and wondered why. It was Hutch-ings who had found the man at his home in the course of the evening, had shown him certain photographs, had persuaded him to allow an examination of his books, and had prevailed on him to be in court this afternoon. He has earned the right to present this witness's evidence.

They have not told Sallie. The hour was late last evening when they finally became confident of their accomplishment, and this morning she appeared at the courthouse only minutes before Judge Hook called the court to order. The time since has been occupied with their efforts to debunk the defendants' claims about the vaccination scab, for Mr. Simmons had required some time during the morning to arrange for his unanticipated absence from the cigar factory. But now he is here.

Mr. Arthur Simmons is a prosperous-looking man of about fifty, dressed in the city style. He looks only at the judge as the oath is admin-istered, and nods at the end.

"You must say it aloud," says Judge Hook.

"I am sorry, Your Honor. I do." Simmons has a deep confident voice.

Sallie looks questioningly at Mr. Wheat, who smiles and pats her hand as Hutchings arranges his papers, of which there are not many, on the podium, and turns toward the witness.

THE LEAVENWORTH TIMES, NOVEMBER 14, 1899

In the Hillmon trial yesterday Arthur Simmons caused a sensation by testimony in which he swore that Frederick Adolph Walters worked three weeks for him in the months of April and May, 1879, or nearly two months after he was believed to have been murdered near Medicine Lodge, his body substituted for that of John W. Hillmon and shipped back to Lawrence where it was buried.

This is the first time Simmons ever testified. He was summoned by the plaintiff and his evidence although new is rebuttal.

The evidence of Simmons was given yesterday afternoon. He testified to having remembered Walters very well, produced his day book for the year of 1879 on which was inscribed the name of F. Walters, the days he worked and the number of cigars manufactured by him. He said that he had never connected the man Walters with the one in the Hillmon case and probably never would have had not Attorney Hutchins for the plaintiff called on him and shown him some pictures of Walters. The moment he saw the pictures he declared the man was remembered and he found his name on his books. He said the characteristics by which he remembered Walters was his talkativeness while at work. Walters, he said, was accustomed of talking of the towns he had visited and bragging of the number of love affairs he had had.

This evidence of Simmons appears somewhat slim in the face of the facts the evidence hitherto given has brought out. It looks improbable that Walters could have been in Leavenworth at the time Simmons says he worked here. That was but two months after the tragedy in Medicine Lodge, which occurred on March 17, 1879. The news of that affair had been aired through the newspapers, had been talked about in public and privately and it had been openly and publicly charged that a fraud had been attempted against the insurance companies by the murder of a man named Walters and the substitution of his body for that of Hillmon.[58]

Ah, but this last is not right. Nobody had mentioned the name Walters in connection with the Hillmon case for many months after the death; it had been January 1880 when Wiseman and Tillinghast had shown the corpse photographs to the Walters family, and first spoken with Miss Alvina Kasten.

Of course, the defense lawyers could not allow the Simmons testimony to go undisputed. Barker's cross-examination focused at first on the written records that Simmons had bought with him into court.

"A name has been erased and the name of Walters written above it," Barker suggested.

"Yes."

"What name was erased?"

"The name Anderson was erased and the other was written above it."[59]

Apparently content to leave this suspicious circumstance temporarily unexplicated (for one of the first rules of cross-examination is not to let the witness explain), Barker moved on to another question: how could Simmons be so sure that his employee had been Frederick Adolph Walters? After all, more than twenty years had passed. Barker hoped to get Simmons to admit that he could not remember a single other man whose name was recorded alongside Walters's, but this effort was not very successful, for Simmons did remember one of them. Still, Barker persisted: surely Simmons had had too many employees to be remembering individuals after so long?

"How many have you had altogether from that time until now?" Barker demanded.

"I could not say," replied Simmons.

"Can't you answer?"

"Not exactly. They changed often," Simmons said.

"Do they travel around?" Barker asked. "Are they like lawyers?"

"Yes."

"What do you mean by that?"

"Well, they like to travel around, like lawyers," said the witness, picking up on Barker's suggestion.

"What do you mean by that?" Barker challenged. "Are you joking on the witness stand?"

"No, sir," said Arthur Simmons. He must have been befuddled by this treatment—hadn't his antagonist suggested himself that lawyers travel around? And now, for agreeing, Simmons was accused of joking in disrespect of the court? Nevertheless Simmons seems to have retained his politeness even during this rather harsh interrogation. He agreed that Mr. Hutchings had recently shown him a photograph of Walters, leading him to recognize it as his former employee. Walters worked for him for about three weeks, he explained after looking at his records; his name appeared in the book twice during these three weeks.[60]

Barker next took what must have been a calculated risk: he invited Simmons to explain the erasure.

"I was accustomed," the factory owner testified, "to keep account of the work which the men did by taking care of the cigars which they made and keeping an account for each man. I went around among the men to do this and took the cigars from their tables. When I came to the week ending April 16, 1879, a man by the name of Anderson quit with 900 cigars. As Walters took his place I simply erased Anderson's name and wrote Walters' above it in order to keep the column even. On May 4 Walters has to his credit 1,200 cigars; on May 31, 900."[61]

Here Sallie's lawyers offered the account book into evidence, but the defendants objected, and their objection was sustained. The newspaper does not say what the objection was; the book was hearsay, but ought to have qualified as a business record. Unlike the Dearest Alvina letter, it was made in the regular course of an ongoing business operation. In any event, the book itself never became part of the record, and so I could not find it in the lawsuit's archives. All we know about it is contained in Arthur Simmons's description.

On redirect the plaintiff's lawyers brought out two useful points. Apparently Hutchings had not merely shown the witness a photograph of Walters and asked whether he knew the man; the lawyer had mingled the young Iowan's picture with several others, and Simmons had been able to pick it out. But an even more telling exchange returned to the question of how Simmons could remember this one short-term employee among all the others who had worked for him.

"What was there peculiar about that man that made you recognize him?" asked Hutchings.

"He was a man who was all the time talking to the men about him and telling of his many travels. He had been in a large number of towns in different places and he also talked a great deal of his love scrapes and how he had gotten out of them."[62]

Love scrapes! Oh my, poor Alvina. Had the cigarmaker left Fort Madison to escape from the particular "scrape" that she represented? I remember her reluctance, in her deposition, to say that she and Frederick Adolph were engaged; had he told her to keep it to herself because in his heart he did not intend to marry her? I cannot help thinking of the postscript in the letter Walters wrote to his sister just before his final disappearance, a letter that made no mention of Alvina Kasten: "Compliments to Annie Baker & the rest of the good-looking girls."

With this flourish, and brief rebuttal testimony from Sallie, her lawyers rested their case. The next morning, however, they would ask Judge Hook for leave to reopen it; they told the judge that in the course of the evening they had located a witness by the name of T.S. Cookson who would corroborate the evidence of Mr. Arthur Simmons. "It was claimed," reports the *Times*, "that Cookson worked for Simmons at the time he claimed Walters was in his employ and remembered Walters." But Hook would not grant leave; the evidence was closed. He announced that he would allow the attorneys eighteen hours to prepare their summations; but first he would entertain their objections to the instructions he proposed to give to the jury.[63]

What had happened to Frederick Adolph Walters? If Simmons was telling the truth, why did Walters allow the insurance companies, the agents who were looking for John Hillmon over nearly the entire American West from Mexico to Colorado, and (most shocking of all) his family back in Iowa, to believe that he had died at Crooked Creek? Surely, a desire to escape a betrothal that had become a burden, even if we attributed this wish to him, would not account for such a dramatic choice. The mystery of the cigarmaker's motives lurked in the shadowy recesses of my thoughts as I read about the final hours of the sixth trial of *Hillmon v. Mutual Life Insurance Company et al.*

The attorneys spent most of a day with Judge Hook outside the presence of the jury arguing about the proper jury instructions. The two sides could scarcely have been further apart on these matters. The defense objected to all but three of the instructions requested by the plaintiff, and the plaintiff objected to all but one of the defendants' proposals. Judge Hook listened attentively, but then ruled decisively on most of the objections.[64]

Some of the arguments were quickly dispatched. Hook refused the plaintiff's suggestion that he tell the jury that a person's absence for a period of longer than seven years is prima facie evidence of his death; he also declined their request that he tell the jury to disregard any testimony by Dr. Stewart if they found that his act of removing the vaccination wound had been carried out without Sallie Hillmon's consent and to her detriment.[65]

There were two matters of dispute that Hook would require further time to consider, and which would presently prove consequential. One was the plaintiff's request for an instruction that "if the dead body is proved to be the body of Hillmon it is immaterial whether there was a conspiracy or not." Barker and Isham objected. Their clients' position was that even if John Hillmon really had died at Crooked Creek, the defendants should prevail if the jury were convinced that his purpose there had been to defraud the insurance companies. Green and his colleagues had never stopped insisting that John Hillmon had walked away from Crooked Creek, but perhaps the testimony of Arthur Simmons had started them thinking about alternative arguments. What should the jury do if they believed that John Hillmon had conspired to defraud the defendants, but then had somehow ended up dead at Crooked Creek anyway, through accident or betrayal? (This factual possibility may seem bizarre, but it may be recalled that the Medicine Lodge journalist T.A. McNeal proposed it in his memoir *When Kansas Was Young.*) Isham compared the situation to that of an insured ship destroyed while carrying an illegal cargo of slaves; in such a case, he maintained, the insurer could set up the illegality of the ship's activities as a defense to the insurance claim. Accordingly, he argued, the defendants should prevail if John Hillmon intended to defraud them, even if he actually had died at Crooked Creek. Hook took the question under advisement.[66]

The second troublesome instruction was proposed by Sallie's lawyers and concerned Brown's affidavit. The hearsay nature of this document had been troubling to several of the presiding judges. There was no question that since Brown's deposition had been read and the original affidavit produced, the jury was entitled to learn the contents of the affidavit, and they had. All agreed that an out-of-court statement may be received in evidence if it contradicts the witness's in-court testimony or

his deposition; this is the unchallengeable practice of showing impeachment by prior inconsistent statement.

But what should the jury be told about how such a statement should
be considered? The traditional view of such impeaching statements
was that they were no proof of the propositions they recited; they were
admissible only to show the unreliability of the witness, to persuade the
jury not to believe the in-court testimony or the deposition. Wheat,
Hutchings, and Atwood had accordingly asked Judge Hook to instruct
the jury as follows: "Brown's statement does not show that Hillmon
killed anyone or was a party to the conspiracy."

Barker objected, seeming to invoke the coconspiracy exception to the
hearsay rule. Brown's affidavit, he said, was "in aid of the conspiracy,"
and accordingly could constitute evidence that its account was true. It
was a curious and dubious claim, for it proposed that the affidavit W. J.
Buchan, in service of the defendants, composed for his clients and persuaded Brown to sign was actually an act done by Brown in furtherance
of a conspiracy among Brown, John Hillmon, and Sallie. Only if this
were to be believed would Brown's affidavit achieve the status of actual
proof, instead of mere impeachment, and only then would the instruction Sallie's lawyers requested become clearly improper. Yet despite the
unpersuasive nature of the defendants' argument, Hook apparently
took this question under advisement as well.[67]

He would have a bit of time to reflect, for the delivery of instructions
would follow the attorneys' arguments in summation to the jury. These
were to begin the next morning, and they would occupy the better part
of three days; each side was permitted nine hours, to be divided among
the attorneys as they wished. As was the custom of the day, the lawyers
for the two sides alternated presentations: a plaintiff's lawyer would
be followed by a defendants', and so on until all had spoken. Taken
together, the closing arguments in this last trial of the case touched on
nearly all the themes that had resonated through the Hillmon mystery
for the two decades since its origins.

LEAVENWORTH TIMES, NOVEMBER 16, 1899
. . . The argument in the Hillmon case began yesterday morning.
Attorney Hutchings for the plaintiff was the first lawyer to address
the jury and his pleadings continued until nearly 5 o'clock last

night. He talked four and one-half hours, using exactly one-half of the time allowed the plaintiff in which to present her case to the jury. His address covered every point which has been brought out in the trial. He went much into detail, reading abstracts from the evidence of the witnesses who had testified in the trial.

A great part of Attorney Hutchins' speech was directed toward the sentimental side of the case, and he appealed time and again to the jury to take into consideration the fact that it was one poor, lone woman fighting for her rights against great, heartless, unfeeling and powerful companies, notwithstanding the fact that her interest in the policies has been assigned to her lawyers. Attorney Hutchins evidently forgot this fact.

† † †

Apart from the aspects of his presentation rather sarcastically noted by the *Times*, Hutchings proposed a few other salient points. He offered at one moment a suggestion unheard in the previous trials: that when W.J. Buchan gave Sallie Hillmon railroad passes during the autumn of 1879, his intentions were not merely to keep her away from her attorneys. Hutchings told the jurors that Buchan's purposes were far more sinister: "He then secured a pass for her to Colorado, where he sent her without money, far from home and friends, among human wolves, where she would go the way of fallen women, down to hell and destruction."[68]

When he addressed the matter of the Kasten letter, Hutchings made no effort to contest its authenticity. (I continue to surmise that he had seen those letters produced by Elizabeth Rieffenach, and satisfied himself that the handwriting on the Kasten letter was the same.) In common with every one of Sallie's attorneys from the beginning, the lawyer implicitly conceded the letter's provenance, attempting to disparage only its significance. He argued that the young cigarmaker was notable for how infrequently he went to the places where he said he was planning to go. "For instance," said Hutchings, "he wrote home he was going to Nebraska, but he did not go. Why not then, gentlemen of the jury, believe that he did not leave Wichita with Hillmon?"[69]

*   *   *

When his turn arrived, the defendants' lawyer Eugene "Ironquill" Ware showed the qualities that must have given rise to his nom de plume. "The side of the insurance companies in this case has no sentiment," he told the jurors. "We have no lady in the case and can arouse no sentiment from such a source." Later, his cocounsel Edward Isham would return to the idea that the plaintiff's case had resorted to sentimental and unmanly methods by attempting to generate sympathy for Sallie Hillmon.

Ware evinced a willingness, however, to see the contest resolved on the grounds of the *character* of the plaintiff and her witnesses, versus that of the defendants and theirs. Moreover he struck a note (one that would find its echo in the later addresses of his cocounsel) concerning where to find evidence of character: it could be discerned in certain external circumstances. For example, he contrasted the defense witness Theodore Wiseman to the Hillmon witness John Eldridge. "Major Wiseman was a major holding his commission from President Lincoln, while Eldridge was a saloonkeeper in the Indian Territory. I leave with you to decide the weight of the testimony of each."[70]

James W. Green's summation attracted as much favorable opinion from the *Times* as Hutchings's had unfavorable. Green's address was, according to their reporter, "a masterly statement of the case in its true light" that "left a powerful impress upon the jury as well as every spectator in the room." In particular, the Dean's dismantling of the proposition that Arthur Simmons's testimony should be believed was "so sweeping, so complete and so overwhelming that it left Simmons' evidence a story of the wildest improbability, a coincidence of names so common as to be unworthy of notice, and Simmons' recognition of the photograph after twenty years 'as much a matter of chance as the guessing of the right card in a game of three card monte.'"[71]

Green's most prominent theme, however, was (as the reporter put it) "the character of Hillmon, every point of which he brought out in a manner that left no doubt of his crime, notwithstanding the subtle means he employed to cover every foot track of his dark career." And indeed Green spoke at length about what he called character, that of John Hillmon and of others. But his real subject was class, and his argument was that the Hillmon side depended on the jury's willingness to believe, or find in favor of, persons whose conditions in life rendered them unworthy. Green suggested, for example, that "even if Hillmon had taken [the insurance] out for the benefit of his wife it would more than provide for her wants, for she did not require $25,000 to supply them. These facts must be considered." As for Hillmon himself, he "was not able to go to a cheap hotel and stay over night. At Wichita he stayed in a one roomed cottage with Hilda and his brother, sleeping on the floor. At other times they camped out. The weather was bitter cold then too."[72]

The defendants' witnesses, however, suffered from neither poverty nor lack of social standing; indeed, calling their testimony into question bordered on insolence. "We have any number of witnesses who knew Hillmon intimately, who will swear he was not 5 feet 11 inches tall," said Green, "so that, gentlemen, we have a lot of perjured rascals high in social and other circles, who have willfully and maliciously misstated Hillmon's height or else he was not that tall."[73]

Green appeared to be aware of his frequent return to this theme might be taken for a certain snobbery, for he confessed as much in his description of the Hillmon ménage: "I would allude to the house which Hillmon took his young wife to, but I would be accused of sneering at poverty. Think of the place Hillmon took her, a man who was able to carry $25,000 insurance. One room, a cook stove in it. I do not say it was not commendable and better than to rent a large house and beat his landlord out of the rent. I only point out what a man earning that insurance could afford to do."[74]

Of course, each of the barbs Green aimed at the condition of John and Sallie Hillmon could be defended by some justification other than an effort to equate their poverty with criminality and character defects. The rude household arrangements, the camping out: Green might say these were mentioned only to show the incongruity of such a man taking out so much insurance. He could claim they were meant to show that John Hillmon did not "earn" (Green's unusual word) the insurance proceeds, and that Sallie Hillmon did not need them in order to maintain a life of comfort, for she had enjoyed no such life beforehand. But the theme of circumstances as markers of character is unmistakable: once again before ending, Green referred to *his* clients' witnesses as persons "of the highest character."[75]

*   *   *

When Edward Isham took to the podium, these notes were struck again at even greater volume. Referring to Sallie's attorneys, Isham claimed, "They show they do not believe in manhood, honesty and integrity, but roll truth under foot and substitute a vile suspicion for facts." Isham described Hillmon's career before his purchase of the life insurance in scornful language. Making no mention of Hillmon's service to the Union Army, he described him thus: "After coming to this country we find him roaming around as a cattle herder and buffalo hunter for a number of years." Isham maintained that Hillmon had ended up at Baldwin's place "insolvent" after cheating a man who had sold him cattle and wagons in Texas, and had contracted a "sudden" marriage to Sallie.[76]

In Edward Isham's rendering of John Brown, the equation of character and class is finally made explicit. "He was always wandering from place to place, from Colorado to Texas and back," said Isham, "eternally restless, except for the short time he was with Hillmon. His life was spent in the company of irresponsible, reckless men. Not that it is a reproach that he lived among mining camps and rough characters, for there are no nobler hearts and stronger, sturdier manhood found than in these places, but there are a rougher class of men found in these places and it shows the character of the man. It is not such a life as the quiet home life where a man grows up in a better school and is free from evil influences. And this was the life of Brown."[77]

Yet in the case of one actor in the Hillmon drama according to Green and Isham, itinerancy and poverty did not equate to dishonesty: Frederick Adolph Walters was a perfect gentle knight, a man of his word, and a faithful lover. It was accordingly the task of James Green to distinguish him from the boastful philandering F.A. Walters who was plying his trade as a cigarmaker for Mr. Simmons at Leavenworth two months after the death at Crooked Creek. "Why, gentlemen," Green offered, "F. Walters whom Simmons knew was as far from the F.A. Walters of Fort Madison as the sun is from the moon." If the real F.A. Walters had been alive in May 1879, would he have stopped writing home to his family and fiancée? Of course not, Green assured the jurors. "I tell you it was foreign to the character of Walters. Why has he not written since? Because he did as he said he would. He went with Hillmon, the man who enticed him with good wages."[78]

Green and Isham wove other strands into their speeches as well, notably the need for insurance companies to guard militantly against fraud. Green reminded the jury of the Winner–McNutt case and emphasized the features that attempt at fraud shared with the Hillmon matter: "Winner . . . enticed a poor painter to Wichita and there tried to burn the body out of recognition, but he couldn't. These things are unnatural but they happen."[79]

Isham pursued this thought with a related one, meant perhaps to humanize the defendants and possibly in addition to hint at an interest in eradicating insurance fraud that the jurors might share with them. Many citizens, he said, were "policyholders and stockholders and interested in the mutual insurance companies which therefore, were not corporations." Perhaps Isham went too far, for this last point seems to have excited the conscience of one juror, the former Senator P.G. Lowe. He stood during Isham's speech and interrupted him, "I understood the judge to say that the fact that a juror held a policy would disqualify him from serving."[80]

Judge Hook evidently thought that the reference was to him. "I did not say so," he told Lowe. But the juror evidently meant "Judge" Isham.

The Chicago lawyer was quick to disclaim the implication. "If I have said so I merely used the matter as an illustration," he protested.

But Senator P.G. Lowe was not satisfied, and seemed to think he might be called on to disqualify himself from the jury. "I took your meaning for what you said," he insisted, "and as I hold a policy in the Connecticut Mutual, thought it my duty to mention the fact."

Both Isham and Ware hastened to assure the court and Senator Lowe that they meant no suggestion that his ownership of a policy in one of the companies constituted any kind of conflict of interest. "[H]e is exactly the kind of a man we want on the jury," said Isham. And there the matter of the insured juror ended; Sallie's lawyers seem to have made no contribution to this uncomfortable moment in the trial.[81]

It was Isham who introduced into his summation the claim that the companies had not one, but two distinct defenses to Sallie's claims. The Chicago lawyer must have intended this suggestion as a hedge against the possibility that the jurors would believe the testimony of Arthur Simmons, and accordingly conclude that the dead man at the campsite was not Walters but Hillmon. "It is one of the primary issues in the case whether that body was Hillmon's, and another is whether fraud in using that contract was not practiced," he informed the jurors. This theory of the case represented a return to a proposition that Isham had urged when debating the jury instructions before Judge Hook. He had then argued that the defendants should prevail even if the jury should find that John Hillmon died at Crooked Creek, if the jury also found that Hillmon had intended to perpetrate a fraud and those intentions had brought him to the place of his death. Isham seemed to presume that he had won that argument, for he told the jury "[t]hat this is one of the forms of fraud which insurance companies are subjected to and often is a matter of record. They are peculiarly exposed to fraud of this kind. So often is this true that there is a special provision in the policies that where there is fraud found to exist, it makes the policies void. Of course such a state of affairs presents a case that must be met by the plaintiff."[82]

Although Isham sought to persuade the jurors of this novel way of looking at the case, he was working at cross-purposes to his cocounsel. For in his last words to the jury, J.W. Green bound himself and his clients inexorably to the premise of F.A. Walters's death at Crooked Creek.

> We show it was not Hillmon by uncontrovertible evidence and we go farther and show that it was Walters and identify the body as that of F.A. Walters, the man who disappeared from his home and friends, whom they recognized from the photographs of the cadaver, and who lies buried at Lawrence.[83]

Whatever advocacy talent each man may have possessed, Isham and Green were not much of a team. In any event, Isham's suggestion that his client might prevail even if the jury believed John Hillmon had died at Crooked Creek met no favor with Judge Hook, and found no place in his instructions he would soon give the jurors.

For the final closing remarks of Sallie's attorney John Atwood, the *Times'* reporter had nothing but scorn. "His address," according to the *Times*, "was bombastic and characteristic to the last degree." His methods included an "appeal to the jury upon prejudice and feeling," as well as the employment of various passages from Shakespeare, which he delivered while "in the role of an impersonator exploit[ing] his talents."[84]

The one substantive description of Atwood's address in the *Times* concerned the lawyer's explanation for the Walters letter. Borrowing a ploy from Green's portrayal of the two F. Walterses, Atwood suggested that there were two John Hillmons about in Kansas, and that it was the *other* John Hillmon who had offered employment to the young Frederick Adolph Walters. This unconvincing suggestion was coupled with the point that the Kasten letter had mentioned a "sheep ranch," while Hillmon was a cattleman. But never did John Atwood suggest that the letter was written by anyone but the young cigarmaker from Iowa.[85]

I had been a fairly contented consumer of these accounts of the sixth trial until about this point, but my own vexation level with all the lawyers is rising again as I read these arguments. Not one of the lawyers—not the companies' and even more inexplicably not Sallie's—has said a word in closing about the stunning piece of testimony offered by Major Theodore Wiseman, who said (without being specific about the date) that not long after the events that birthed the Hillmon controversy he had found Joe Burgess, *the same Joe Burgess who was mentioned in the affidavit signed by John Brown*, alive. This disclosure had to mean that the affidavit, which said that the traveler Hillmon had picked up and had killed at Crooked Creek was named "Joe Berkley or Burgis," was false. Which in turn had to mean at the very least that Brown's account of the affidavit—that Buchan had composed it and coerced him into signing it—must be the true one. (It's my surmise that Buchan had learned that a young man named Joe Burgess was missing, and had felt safe in putting this lost soul's name in the affidavit he prepared for Brown to sign. He did not anticipate that the young man might turn up again.) And of course, Wiseman's testimony put the lie to Green's continued insistence, even during his closing argument, that Joe Burgess and Frederick Adolph Walters were the same (dead) man. The former was not dead at all, at least not on March 18, 1879. Moreover, Green surely knew this was the case, for Wiseman had been his own chief investigator on the Hillmon matter.

The only effort the defendants had ever made, so far as appears, to avoid the apparent significance of Wiseman's confession was essayed by George Barker, at a time the jury was not present to hear it. When arguing about the instructions that should concern the Brown affidavit, Barker had proposed to Judge Hook that Brown had skillfully worded the affidavit in such a way that it was all true (and so could still be relied on) except for the name of the victim ("Berkley or Burgess"), which Brown had falsified as a kind of poison pill that could later be used to disavow the entire statement.[86]

This argument, although perhaps a bit intricate and somewhat at odds with what was known about John Brown's level of sophistication, might have had some force, for Buchan had on many occasions claimed that he composed the affidavit from information supplied to him by Brown. But it was never made to the jury, for it was never needed, Sallie's lawyers either did not hear what Theodore Wiseman had said about Joe Burgess's survival after the Crooked Creek shooting, or did not appreciate its significance, and they never called the jury's attention to it. On Sallie's behalf, I am infuriated by this malpractice.

I realize that I have by now entirely lost any historical objectivity and become a complete Sallie Quinn Hillmon Smith partisan. Whatever her own shortcomings may have been, my sympathies are all with her.

William Hook's instructions to the jury disappointed the defendants (or at least their counsel Edward Isham) in one respect. The judge noted that the defendants had never in their pleadings suggested that they intended to defend the case by invoking the "fraud" clause of the policies; their consistent and solitary position had been, until nearly the end of the trial, that John Hillmon had not died at Crooked Creek. Hook took the view that it was too late for the companies to introduce this new defense, and he told the jurors that the existence or nonexistence of a conspiracy was "not the controlling question in the case." He instructed them that if they believed the corpse brought to Lawrence was that of John Hillmon, it would be unnecessary for them to address the question of conspiracy. "The essential point in these cases," he explained, "is the identity of the corpse." He then sent the jurors to begin the consideration of their verdict.[87]

It was a Saturday morning, and the jurors worked into the afternoon. The judge had originally told them that if they failed to agree by midafternoon they would be allowed to disband and go to their homes for the Sunday holiday, to return to their deliberations on Monday. But evidently Hook reconsidered, for the twelve men remained together through the afternoon and were taken to supper at six in the evening. Some of them asked for a glass of beer with their meal, but the bailiff in charge of them refused, worried that one of the attorneys might take exception to the administration of alcohol to a jury still in deliberation. The jurors returned to the courtroom after their meal, and shortly after ten o'clock the judge recalled them to the courtroom to discharge them for the night. The jurors, however, told the judge they were close to a verdict, so he agreed that he would allow them to return to their work for one more hour. Fifteen minutes was all they required.[88]

LEAVENWORTH TIMES, NOVEMBER 19, 1899

The jury in the Hillmon case returned a verdict for the plaintiff, Mrs. Sallie E. Hillmon, now Mrs. Smith, in the sum of $33,102 last night after being out from 11:35 o'clock yesterday morning until 10:40 o'clock last night.

The verdict which was rendered was against the two insurance companies, the first being the Mutual Life of New York against which the verdict is $22,068, and the second the Connecticut Mutual Life Insurance Company against which is $11,304. These sums included the interest on the original policies for a little over twenty years. The original policy in the Mutual of New York was $15,000 and in the Connecticut Mutual $5,000.

The verdict for the plaintiff in the case was not unexpected but it came with some surprise last night, as it was generally believed the jury would not arrive at a verdict as soon as it did. All preparations had been made for keeping the jury over Sunday at the expense of the parties to the suit.

The verdict which was rendered last night is the second which has been given to the plaintiff in the six trials that the case has gone through. The jury was out just ten hours and fifty-five minutes and was about to be discharged for the night when it arrived at the conclusion.

The pro-Hillmon *Lawrence Evening Standard* had nothing but encomia for Sallie's lawyers. It reported that Lysander Wheat, although he had grown white-haired in the two decades of service of his client, seemed twenty years younger after the verdict was announced. Fred Hutchings had "proved himself again to be one of the greatest lawyers of his time." (One hopes that the extravagance of this praise somewhat compensated Charles Hutchings for having his first named misstated.) And John Atwood "added fresh laurels to his rapidly growing national reputation." But even defense counsel George Barker rated the title "Judge" in the *Standard*, and got credit for a sense of humor. Suggesting that the attorneys should join the jurors and allow the occasion to be commemorated with a photograph, Barker reportedly added, "If a little time could be granted I could go out and prepare myself so I could appear in mourning by putting on a little crape."[89]

As a matter of course the defendants immediately moved for a new trial, but Judge Hook denied the motion on the spot. Barker announced promptly that the companies were not discouraged by the verdict, and that the case would be "carried up" on appeal. "On just what grounds the case will be appealed has not been given out by the defendant companies," reported the faithful pro-defendant *Times*, "but they affirm there are a number of causes for a new trial which will be contained in the bill of exceptions to be presented to the court."[90]

It was not only the Leavenworth newspapers that informed their readers of the outcome of the trial, of course. The news about the verdict gained notice nationwide, but it had to compete for public attention with numerous articles concerning the impending "turn of the century." Still, even the *Chicago Daily Tribune* gave the Hillmon story prominent treatment, albeit in a story containing a few odd inventions (for example, it reported that "Mrs. Hillmon and her friends refused to take any notice" of the inquest at Lawrence).[91]

I suppose I cannot be surprised that the Chicago newspaper has gotten it somewhat wrong, again. It and the New York and Los Angeles papers have a lengthy record of misrepresentation when it comes to the

Hillmon case. Why, then, does my chest start to vibrate when I read the last paragraph of the story?

> The person most deeply interested in the case is Mrs. Sallie E. Smith, formerly Mrs. Hillmon. She remained single for many years after the excitement over the reported death of her first husband—Hillmon—before she married a traveling man named Smith eight years ago. She resides in Leavenworth. Mrs. Smith proved herself a match for the ablest lawyers of the insurance companies. *She possesses considerable literary ability and has written several novels.*[92]

Those italics are, of course, mine. There is no particular reason that I ought to give credence to this proposition. It resides in a paragraph that contains at least one significant misstatement: Sallie had married James Smith in 1886, thirteen years before the appearance of this story. Still, I find I fervently want to believe that Sallie had become a writer, and to read those novels.

Later I find this information echoed in a Kansas newspaper published four years later: "Mrs. Hillmon-Smith is a bright woman and she possesses considerable literary ability. She has written several novels." The similarity of the language suggests that this is not an independent report, but rather a repetition of the earlier item. Still, that doesn't mean that it isn't true. Or that it is, for that matter. Sallie never fails to surprise and perplex me, and my hunger for the solution to the puzzle grows ever greater.[93]

⊲ 9 ⊳

THE CENTURY TURNS, AND THE HILLMON CASE IS CONCLUDED

1900–1903

The new century, although ushered in with a bout of harsh winter weather, seemed to mark the country's progress toward easier, less hazardous, more comfortable lives for Americans. Science and technology produced wonders, like Henry Ford's invention, which flew over the icy streets of Detroit in the new century's first February. A railroad train was reported to reach a speed of over one hundred miles an hour (on a downhill grade, it is true). Electricity transformed cities like New York, where it ignited incandescent lamps and powered trolleys. Rural residents would have to wait for the electric lines to reach them, in some places for decades, but whale oil and kerosene were gradually becoming unnecessary to the enjoyment of light and comfort.[1]

Some scientists were less interested in technology than in the human mind; they believed that the exploration of this most challenging scientific frontier of all would yield insights into the meaning of life. And perhaps of death as well, for some psychologists undertook to investigate such phenomena as the receipt of messages from the ostensibly dead, through the "medium" of ordinary living persons. Nor was it only marginal figures in the new profession who interested themselves in the uncanny and occult. William James, one of the founders of American psychology, was drawn to the study of apparently supernatural phenomena, including mediums. Together with several other distinguished figures (including his publisher Henry Holt), he founded a venture called the American Society for Psychical Research.[2]

Much of the work of the Society and others like it consisted of discovering and revealing fraud. Many mediums were obvious fakes, entertainers in essence; a few appeared to have genuine and inexplicable gifts, although some of these were not above resorting to tricks to supplement the unpredictable appearances of the spirits. But William James and his associates studied one medium, a quiet New England housewife named Leonora Piper, for decades, and never caught her cheating.[3]

On the whole it seemed that Americans, at least in their public pronouncements, manifested pride in the accomplishments of their young country during the previous hundred years. Concerning whether the next hundred would call for celebration, however, some doubt crept in. Would the twentieth century be one of peace, prosperity, and progress? Or did the seeds of war, want, and destruction lie waiting to grow and spread? The California journalist John Ingalls wondered in print whether a writer at the end of the new century could rejoice that "the encroachments of capital have been restrained and that labor has its just reward; that the rich are no longer afflicted with satiety nor the poor with discontent; that we have wealth without ostentation, liberty without license, taxation without oppression, the broadest education, and the least corruption of manners." On the whole, he thought not.[4]

It did not take long for the two insurance companies remaining in the Hillmon case to identify the errors they alleged to have tainted the sixth trial. Within weeks after their loss in Judge Hook's courtroom, the Mutual Life Insurance Company of New York and the Connecticut Mutual Life Insurance Company filed their appellate papers in the Circuit Court of Appeals for the Eighth Circuit. This court was one of eleven Congress had created in the Judiciary Act of 1891 to serve as appellate tribunals empowered to hear and decide appeals from federal trial courts. No longer would cases on appeal travel directly from the judgment of a trial court to the Supreme Court; in most cases, now including Sallie's, the Court of Appeals must first consider the matter.

The defendants' arguments to the Court of Appeals had a distinctly Isham-esque cast to them, and for good reason: the Chicago lawyer was the chief author of the appellate brief. Judge Hook had made several errors, the brief claimed. He had:

- erroneously refused to instruct the jurors in the "dual defenses" theory (put forward at trial by Isham), that the defendants were entitled to prevail even if John Hillmon had been killed, if he had intended fraud when he purchased the policies
- erroneously kept away from the jury certain testimony about things Levi Baldwin had said that would have been provided by witnesses Phillips ("[W]ouldn't it be a good idea to get some life insurance money by getting the body of a 'greaser'?"); Blythe (inquiring for the names of good insurance agents on behalf of a "friend"); Crew (saying he had borrowed money from a bank to pay Hillmon's insurance premium); and Carr (saying that he and Hillmon had a "scheme under brogue")
- erroneously disallowed evidence that Hillmon had in 1878 removed from the state of Texas certain mortgaged property and thus defrauded the mortgage holder
- erroneously instructed the jury that Brown's affidavit was not affirmative evidence and should be considered only as impeachment of Brown's credibility
- erroneously refused to instruct the jury that the affidavit "might be considered as evidence of the facts stated therein" and given "like effect as the deposition"
- erroneously allowed Sallie Hillmon to enjoy six peremptory challenges, as many as the two defendants had together been allowed.[5]

The attorneys argued their case before the Court of Appeals on April 2, 1900. Perhaps the officers of the Mutual Life Insurance Company of New York believed that the oral arguments had not gone well for their clients. Whether for that reason or some other, Mutual Life must have thought it detected handwriting on the wall: in August 1900, before the Court of Appeals had issued a decision, it settled Sallie's claims against it for $22,000. Connecticut Mutual was now alone in the litigation. Sallie was, too, but of course she always had been.[6]

The Court of Appeals issued its opinion a year later, on April 3, 1901. None of the defendants' assignments of error had found a very respectful reception. Concerning each, a majority of the three-judge court found either that Judge Hook had not been wrong at all, or that the defendants had failed to make proper objection or submission at trial and hence could not raise the allegation of error for the first time on appeal. The third judge, Walter Henry Sanborn, dissented concerning Judge Hook's treatment of the Brown affidavit. In Judge Sanborn's view, Hook should have told the jury that the affidavit could be viewed as evidence of the truth of the facts it narrated, and not just as impeachment. Since Sallie's side had placed the affidavit in evidence, he argued, they could not thereafter disclaim the truth of the document they had put before the jury.[7]

But his was not the prevailing view, and the Connecticut Mutual Life Insurance Company was faced with another loss. It found itself, in early April 1901, compelled to consider whether it wished to continue the fight against Sallie Hillmon. It could ask the Supreme Court to hear its further appeal by requesting that the Court issue a writ of certiorari (that is, an order agreeing to consider the companies' arguments), but the result could by no means be counted as certain. The Court could decline to consider the case for any reason it wished, and even if it did agree to hear it, there was no guarantee that the companies would be as successful in their second appearance before the Court as they had been in their first. Moreover, it appeared that Sallie's lawyers had secured a writ of execution against some property that the company owned in Leavenworth County, a document that would have enabled them to claim the property to satisfy Sallie's judgment against Connecticut Mutual. A foreclosure under this writ could be staved off if further review were sought in the courts, but even so the writ would cloud the title to the property and diminish its value as collateral in the event the company required credit.[8]

The Connecticut Mutual Life Insurance Company was undeterred by these obstacles, apparently committed to resisting Sallie Hillmon Smith's claims no matter what the cost. On May 14 it filed a Petition for Writ of Certiorari with the United States Supreme Court.

*   *   *

On June 28, 1901, another sighting of the living John Hillmon was reported. On this occasion the news appeared in the *Los Angeles Times* by way of an "exclusive dispatch" from Topeka, under the headline "FAMOUS INSURANCE CASE TURNS THIS WAY."

"This time," wrote the reporter, "he is said to be in jail in Los Angeles, and relatives who live in Jefferson county, Kan., have gone there to see him. If they identify him, the insurance companies which claim that he defrauded them, will bring him back to Kansas." The dispatch went on to say that a "detective from Los Angeles" has just departed Kansas with several Hillmon relatives, to bring them to identify this incarcerated soul.[9]

There was more wrong with this account than its dodgy punctuation, however, and the *Times* was forced to renounce it so swiftly that the retraction actually appeared on the same page as the original story. The headline of the second story was "not known here":

> There is no man named John W. Hillmon confined in either the County Jail or the City Jail, and neither the Sheriff nor the detectives know anything about the case mentioned in the foregoing dispatch from Topeka. As to the alleged Los Angeles detective mentioned in the dispatch, the members of the regular detective force know nothing. It is possible that one of the numerous so-called private detectives has been working on the case. If they have found any clew to Hillmon's whereabouts they have guarded their secret closely from the regularly-appointed officers.[10]

This is the last newspaper report I have found claiming that John Hillmon was alive.

On November 15, 1902, the Supreme Court heard argument in Connecticut Mutual's appeal from the judgment of the Court of Appeals affirming Sallie's victory in the sixth trial. As always, the Justices took the case under advisement. After their conference, the opinion was assigned to Justice Henry Brown.[11]

Sallie and her lawyers had no way to know which Justice had been assigned the task of writing the opinion, but if they had known they would have been discouraged. The assignment of an opinion necessarily went to a Justice who appeared to be in the majority. And according to Ezra Ripley Thayer, it was Justice Henry Brown who had suggested, when the Hillmon case had been on the Court's docket ten years earlier, that the dispute was one about "graveyard insurance." That is, about fraud. Of course, whether the insurance companies had been the targets of fraud was not at all the question before Court, or should not have been. The question was whether any of the assignments of error had merit. In theory, that was the question.

On January 2, 1903, the Supreme Court decided the Hillmon case for the second time. And for the second time, its decision favored the insurance companies. Judge Hook had erred, the majority Justices held, in failing to tell the jurors that the John Brown affidavit could be treated as evidence of the truth of the matters it recited, not merely as impeachment of Brown's deposition testimony. And the trial judge had further strayed from the correct path when he ruled inadmissible the testimony of the witnesses Phillips, Blythe, Crew, and Carr. The Court's opinion acknowledged that there was no evidence, nor indeed even any claim, that Sallie was a party to any conspiracy at the time Levi Baldwin made the statements to which these witnesses would have testified. Nevertheless, the Court said, her cousin's out-of-court statements ought to have been admitted against Sallie "upon the theory that any fraudulent conduct on the part of the insured in procuring the policy, or in procuring the dead body of another to impersonate himself, was binding on her."[12]

On this occasion the Court's decision was not unanimous. Justices Edward D. White and David J. Brewer dissented, although they wrote no opinion explaining their disagreement. David Brewer had presided over the second trial of the Hillmon case; he would have enjoyed a perspective on the case that the others could not have shared. His dissenting opinion, had he written one, would have been worthy of some study.

Compared to the towering precedent it created in 1892, the Court's opinion on the occasion of its second consideration of the Hillmon matter is, at least as a source of law, little noted nor long remembered. It is noteworthy only because it set the stage for yet another round of the

Dickensian saga of the litigation, for by its mandate the case would have to be tried yet again.

Sallie and the Connecticut Mutual Life Insurance Company must not have gotten far in their preparations for a seventh trial, however. The settlement of their dispute was reported on the first day of July, 1903. Some newspaper reports state that Connecticut Mutual paid Sallie no money at all, but simply agreed to bear their own costs should she dismiss her suit, relieving her of the worry that she (or her surety) might become liable to reimburse some of them if she could not win another trial. According to other reports, Sallie's lawyer F.W. Hutchings (this may have been Charles's brother Fred, who was also an attorney) insisted that she had been paid several thousand dollars in addition. No doubt the archive now held by MassMutual would shed some light on the true state of affairs, but it remains as closed to me as ever.[13]

If there was a cash settlement, there is reason to believe that Sallie did not see a penny of it. Whoever it was that had sustained a fatal bullet wound at Crooked Creek, he had on that date been dead for more than twenty-four years. By now, the entire affair reeked of anticlimax.

I haven't seen Dennis much since the exhumation, except for a day we spent with Ernesto's crew shooting some interview footage for the documentary film. Even though I tell myself that an unsolved mystery is still worth writing about, the news from Ken Krauter that the bone is unlikely ever to tell us the identity of the dead man has deflated my spirits. I miss the days when we planned our project with so much anticipation, and now I need Dennis's enthusiasm to keep me motivated.

I know, however, that I will probably see him in October, because the University of Colorado President's Teaching Scholars will be having their annual fall retreat at the Stanley Hotel in Estes Park. Dennis and I had made a presentation of our preliminary work for the PTS group the previous fall, before the exhumation. I expect that everybody there will want to hear what we have discovered. The prospect of explaining that we have enjoyed no success at all leaves me unhappy. I am considering the invention of some excuse to stay away.

A week or so before the retreat, Dennis calls me.

"I solved the case," he says.

"What?"

"The Hillmon case? Funny old case about who a dead body belonged to? I thought you might've heard of it."

"You solved it? How??"

"You gotta come to Estes Park to find out."

My back and head ache as if from the flu as I drive onto the grounds of the Stanley Hotel that Saturday morning. I had struggled all night to grasp a few shards of sleep, but they mostly eluded me, and during the lengthy intervals between I worried about what Dennis could have meant about solving the case.

There is a lot to enjoy at the Stanley, which is the site of Stephen King's novel *The Shining*. The basement museum affords a chance to touch an authentic Stanley Steamer, the invention of the hotel's founder; a guided tour allows you to hear stories about the misbehavior of various ghosts, and learn whether your room is one of those they have been known to haunt; the hotel's broad front porch offers a dazzling view of the Rocky Mountains. I don't enjoy any of these experiences that morning; I sit through two sessions in the Stanley's ornate old meeting room, staring at Dennis's stony face, which tells me nothing.

Finally, just before lunch, it is time for the Hillmon session. I am asked to remind the group of the case, the mystery, the reasons for our interest, and to state the disappointing results of the exhumation. Enveloped in a fog of anxiety and dread, I speak for a while, without much enthusiasm. Dennis sits next to me, tapping expressionlessly at his laptop.

When I finish he asks for the lights to be turned off and the curtains that frame the enormous windows to be drawn. The ensuing darkness wraps us like a blanket, complete except for slender straws of brilliant sunlight that edge the heavy curtains. It must be that he then turns on the LED projector that is hitched to his laptop, for the large projection screen behind him that has until then been empty begins to glow; it casts some dim illumination out into the cavernous room.

"I explained to Mimi Wesson from the start," Dennis says, "that whatever the science told us, that would have to be what I went with. I knew what she wanted: she wanted the body to belong to John Hillmon, and not the cigarmaker. But there was always the chance that the evidence would take us somewhere else." He sounds serious. I cannot see his face in the dark.

He then explains how a method for solving the case had come to him after we learned that the bone would not yield any DNA. "I had always thought it would be pointless to try to compare the corpse photos to the pictures we had of Hillmon and Walters, because the studio portraits were full-face to the front, and the only really usable corpse picture was in profile. There was a face-on corpse picture but its proportions were compromised by the body being tilted backward at an angle that we could not know.

"But then one night I was lying in bed in my underwear, watching television." ("Too much information," somebody yells out in the dark, to general laughter, but he ignores this.) "I was flipping through channels with the remote control, and I looked at the damn thing in my hand, and suddenly I had it. I could turn it sideways, and all the buttons would still be in the same relative positions, but now in profile. I realized, looking at the TV remote, that I *could* use the profile picture. I could just rotate it into the plane we needed for a comparison, like this."

He clicks something and this picture appears on the screen:

Photoshop work by Dennis Van Gerven and Paul Sandberg.

Photoshop work by Dennis Van Gerven and Paul Sandberg.

There is a collective intake of breath. The corpse looks pretty hideous with the coin over its damaged eye.

"I used Adobe Photoshop," says Dennis, "to align the pictures next to each other. First the corpse and Walters, that's what you have here." [*See above.*]

Dismay squeezes my heart. They match!

"What I did," says Dennis, "was match the corpse and life photos at two standard anatomical points in order to control for differences in scale. The points, which are indicated by the parallel lines, are *gnathion*, or the lower margin of the chin, and *nasion*, a point at the top of the nasal bones between the eyes."

"You mean," someone interrupts, "these points match because you made them match?"

"Exactly," says Dennis. "We had to make sure that the two photographs were to the same scale. We haven't proved anything yet, this is just preparation."

Of course, I tell my racing pulse. It's not over.

"Then," he says, "we did the same for the corpse and Hillmon."

Another picture appears. [*See next page.*]

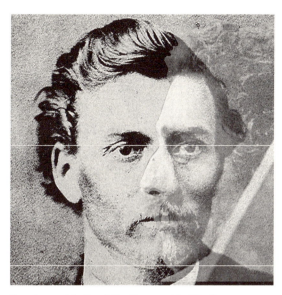

Photoshop work by Dennis Van Gerven and Paul Sandberg.

"Now," says Dennis, "if the photographs depict the same person, the other standard points of comparison ought to match as well."

"You didn't really draw the lines on the living guys exactly at the bottom of the chin," someone objects.

"Right," Dennis says. "Because we're looking to mark the bottom of the chin bone, not the place where the cartilage ends. They're not the same, unless a body is very emaciated, like the corpse here." And I think every one of us, in the dark, grasps his or her chin to confirm that this is true.

"So I took the cigarmaker first," he continues, "and looked to see what happened when I connected the other points of comparison. Here's what I got. Note that the other lines connecting the comparison points are not parallel." Click; the next image is revealed. [*See next page.*]

What am I looking at? My mind feels like a pile of slush. It is left to someone else to state what is obvious, I think, to nearly everyone but me.

"So. This guy, the cigarmaker, he's not the corpse."

"No," says Dennis. The syllable ricochets inside my head.

"What about the other guy, Hillmon?"

Photoshop work by Dennis Van Gerven and Paul Sandberg.

"Let's look," says Dennis, and he clicks again. "In this one, observe the lines that connect the comparison points." [*See next page.*]

I think there is silence for a few endless seconds. After that, I am not sure. I believe I am heard to take the name of the Lord in vain several times in loud succession, and then to emit loud whoops of the sort I very much disapprove of in general. Others are more articulate.

"So," someone asks, "these points all match. Does this prove the corpse is Hillmon's?"

"If you tell *me*," says Dennis, "that it had to be either Hillmon or Walters, then I can tell *you* it definitely wasn't Walters. So, do the logic. It has to be Hillmon."

The questioner persists. "But do we know for sure that it had to be one of those two men?"

Dennis kills the screen and for a moment the room is in darkness. "That's not my department," he says. "Ask Mimi."

"I, ah . . . " I begin. "Nobody, ah, ever suggested that the body belonged to anyone else. Or, that is, there were some other suggestions

Photoshop work by Dennis Van Gerven and Paul Sandberg.

at one point, but they were all shot down when the guy suggested turned up alive."

"So, it could be someone else?"

I look toward Dennis as the lights come back up. "The comparisons just show that the body could have been Hillmon," he says. "And could not have been Walters. We don't have an adequate database to allow us to say that Hillmon was the only guy with those facial proportions."

"Still," says someone, "awesome work!" And our friends break out in a round of raucous applause. I am thrilled, sure, but I need some time to think about what Dennis's discovery means. I am still thinking several days later.[14]

There is one immediate practical question: shall we arrange for the grave to be marked? We had promised the City of Lawrence, as part of our negotiation over the exhumation, that we would obtain and place a marker on the grave if we were able to determine which man was buried there. We now know that it was not Frederick Adolph Walters. Do we know enough to mark the grave as John Hillmon's?

I ask Dennis what he thinks.

"Seems like we have three choices," he says. "No gravestone at all, a stone that says something like 'Tomb of the Unknown,' or a stone marked John Hillmon."

"I just remembered something," I say. "Frederick Adolph's parents placed a marker in the cemetery at Fort Madison that said their son was buried in Oak Hill Cemetery in Lawrence, Kansas."

"I guess that was their opinion."

We are both silent for a moment, but I know Dennis well enough by now that I'm pretty sure he and I are thinking the same thing. "It's my opinion that the grave in Lawrence is that of John Hillmon," I venture. "I mean, the odds that it is are huge."

"Huge," Dennis agrees. "And the poor guy never got a gravestone anywhere else. That we know of."

So I telephone Mitch Young at the Oak Hill Cemetery, and ask him to order a plain monument from a stoneyard he knows of. I send him a drawing of how we want it to look.

Photographer Mimi Wesson

In March 2007, Dennis and I, and his wife, Claudia, and my student Andrea Viedt return to Lawrence with the film crew. Mitch has the stone ready, and has volunteered to place it for us himself. The Sunday morning we choose for the placement is suitably overcast and somber. We watch Mitch as he prepares the ground, mixes some concrete, and expertly maneuvers the heavy stone into place at the head of the plot we dug up the year before. A surprising amount of grass has already grown over the grave. After the stone is set, each of us places a sunflower on it. As I kneel to lay mine against the granite, I touch the cold hard surface briefly.

"Good-bye, John," I say.

This little ceremony is very satisfying, but I cannot pretend that we have demonstrated to any scientific certainty that the fragmented remains buried at Oak Hill were those of John Hillmon or of anyone else, excluding only Frederick Adolph Walters. Dennis has shown only that the corpse does not belong to the cigarmaker.

In any case, however, one great question remains: how does one explain that letter that Walters wrote to Alvina Kasten? Coincidence, I think, is not plausible. The insurance company lawyers had argued that the constellation of events as they proposed them could not be happenstance: that the young cigarmaker had written a letter from a place and at a time when we knew Hillmon and Walters were nearby, had mentioned "a man by the name of Hillmon," had spoken of traveling west to start a ranch, and had never been seen or heard of again; moreover, John Hillmon was reported dead about two weeks later. I find this argument very powerful. If you believe that the letter is authentic and truthful, you must believe that Walters died at Crooked Creek, or you must believe in a coincidence so unlikely as to mark you a crank.

But I have to conclude that the argument goes the other way as well. If the dead man was not Frederick Adolph Walters, and Dennis assures me he was not, then it is unlikely to the point of impossibility that the Dearest Alvina letter is both authentic and true. For to believe that, one would have to believe that the cigarmaker did have the encounter with Hillmon he describes in the letter, did agree to travel with him, but then somehow at that moment disappeared forever *without* becoming a murder victim at Crooked Creek, although someone else did take a bullet there. This constellation, too, represents an unacceptable accumulation of chance.

Forgery of the letter seems like an appealing explanation, but for reasons previously discussed I have become persuaded, despite the difficulty of making the necessary comparisons today, that the Dearest Alvina letter was written by Frederick Adolph Walters—that it was authentic at least to that degree. So how does one account for the letter, if the explanation of coincidence must be discarded as too unlikely? And why was Frederick Adolph Walters never found, if he did not die at Crooked Creek? I cannot know the true explanation, of course; here history's trail is too cold to allow for confident claims. But I am able to imagine a scenario that, if not proved by the available evidence, is not foreclosed by it either.

METSKER FARM, NEAR LAWRENCE, KANSAS | SPRING 1880

"I don't see what business it is of yours," says the young man peevishly. "I have no truck with lawyers. Don't tell me Alvina hired you, I know she wouldn't do that. She's not that sort a girl."

"I don't work for Miss Kasten," says the older man. "I think perhaps I could be of assistance to you."

The young man looks around the barn, where he has been engaged in some repairs. The two men have no company, for Buchan has chosen his moment deliberately. Something about the lawyer's presence sends fingers of unease to pluck at the other man's composure. "Let's go outside," he says.

There is a rickety wooden table in the shade of an oak tree. The men settle on either side for balance, the lawyer hitching up the knees of his pants to reveal white shins above his silk socks.

"Mr. Walters," he says, "my name is W.J. Buchan. Perhaps you know it? I am a State Senator as well as a lawyer."

The young man spits onto the ground, but this action seems to prompt a spasm of coughing. His eyes are tearing before he recovers himself. "I'm not from around these parts, and I never heard a you."

"You are from Iowa, in fact."

F.A. Walters looks up sharply. "How do you know me? Did my parents send you?"

"You are perhaps not aware that your family believes you to have come to some harm."

Walters shakes his head in annoyance and looks out across the adjacent field. "They expect me to write them a letter every week for the rest of my life. I got things to do, I don't have all that much time. And I'm not going back there, either. It's deadly there, mister. I need to stay moving or I'm not going to make it. You go back and tell them I'm just fine, and I love them but—"

"Oh, you mistake my meaning. It is not your family that has sent me. I am not in touch with them myself, I am afraid."

"Who sent you then? And how'd you find me anyhow?" The younger man is evidently becoming curious despite himself.

Buchan produces the smile that has served him well during his years in elected office. "We heard you were making cigars at Simmons and Staiger. You had left that place, but one of your friends told us that you liked to work for Mr. Metsker from time to time. Evidently you like to stay on the move, Mr. Walters."

"I do. It makes me twitchy to stay in one place too long."

The lawyer nods approvingly. "Have you read a book called *The Adventures of Tom Sawyer*, Mr. Walters?"

The cigarmaker does not have the appearance of a reader. "Heard of it," he says noncommittally.

"You remind me of that fellow, I suppose. Footloose, a bit. Wise beyond your years. Folks tend to underestimate you, I'll wager."

Walters nods, pleased by the description but still wary. "You didn't say what you want. I have to get back to work or I'll get fired, and I can't afford to lose this job."

The lawyer reaches deliberately into the back pocket of his pants and produces a calfskin wallet, from which he draws a twenty-dollar bill that he places on the table between them. "If you and I are able to understand each other, your worries about money will be in the past. But for now, would this make up for your losses if we were to confer during the remainder of the afternoon?"

The cigarmaker eyes the money uneasily, but then covers the bill with his hand when an errant breeze flutters it. "I'd need a little time to speak to my foreman."

Buchan nods. "It would be best if we were to talk elsewhere, in any event. Where do you board?"

"I sleep over the stables. It's not much of a place to visit." He is seized again by the coughing, and the lawyer waits until he has recovered before speaking.

"No, that would not be a good idea. I believe there is a vacant dwelling two fields over? The old Magruder place?" Buchan handled the foreclosure, so he knows that the house is overgrown and isolated.

"I know it. Falling down house."

"We'll meet there in an hour, shall we?" says Buchan.

"I'll be bringing me a gun, in case you got any ideas."

"By all means."

The young man tucks the currency into a pocket and walks back toward the barn. He is near the right height, notes the lawyer. It is somewhat at variance with his family's description of him that tobacco has stained his teeth. But this is a fate that awaits all who labor for long in his profession, and perhaps it is true that his teeth were still white when he left home. The cough that racks the young man from time to time is a bit alarming, but on reflection Buchan concludes that it doesn't matter. It is all the better, when you think about it.

The sun is crawling low by the time the two men finally come to terms.

"Suppose I get hurt or something out there in Colorado or wherever?"

"Your money will arrive no matter what, as long as you keep me informed where to send it. For as long as you live. You see, we will be indebted to you; if we should stop sending the money, you might make yourself known, might even come back to Kansas or to Iowa. You can be easy in your mind, knowing that you will have us in your power, in a manner of speaking."

F.A. Walters touches the gun at his hip. Not out of fear, observes the lawyer. It is more as though the cigarmaker is already coming to occupy the role he has agreed to assume. He fancies himself a bit of a desperado, it seems, as well as a ladies' man.

"And that's all I have to do? Just stay away, and use some other name?"

"That, and the letter. I am quite ready for us to proceed to that task, if you are. I have brought some supplies." Buchan gestures toward the writing board he has laid across the arms of a rotting chair. Paper and ink lie on its smooth surface.

"Now this is the part I don't really see, y'know. Why do I want to write to Alvina? I finally sort of tailed off the letters to her so she wouldn't be expecting another, I thought. She got the wrong idea about us, and I don't want to get her going all over again. That was more than a year ago! Can't I write to somebody else? Maybe my sister?"

The lawyer pulls a splintery bench closer to the young man and lowers his voice. "You must write to Alvina, Frederick. That is the bargain. And to your sister as well, sure, that's a good idea. But you must make Miss Kasten think that you intend to return to Fort Madison for her."

Walters twists away from the lawyer. "All right! But I don't know what to write."

"I'll tell you a few things. And for the rest, just make it as much as you can like the sort of letters you wrote her at first."

The young man picks up the pen, hunches over the writing board. "Okay. What's the date today?"

"March 1, 1879."

He looks up, irritated. "It is not. That's more than a year ago." His head still itches with confusion.

"That's the date you will write. And then *Wichita, Kansas*."

"But it's not . . . " He gives up, writes a line at the top of the paper. "I wrote the town first, before the date. That's the way I allus did. Then what?"

"Splendid. Now write something about receiving her last letter in Emporia."

"Emporia?"

The lawyer nods. "She has said that is where your last letter that she can recall was sent from. Do you think she is mistaken?"

"N—no. That might be right. I thought you said you weren't in touch with the folks in Fort Madison!"

"Never mind, lad. I have associates, you know. So write something like *thank you for that last letter, which I received in Emporia, just before I came here to this place*. Only in your own words, of course."

Silence is broken only by the scratching of the pen, the writer's coughing, and the buzz of insects. "Then what?"

"Now this next part is very important. You must say that you have met a man named Hillmon."

"Hillman."

"With an *o*. Hillmon with an *o*."

"All right. How did I come to meet this man named Hillmon and why would I be telling Alvina about him?"

"Because he has offered you very generous wages to travel out west with him, and you have decided to take him up on it."

"What am I supposed to do after we get out west?"

"He, ah, is looking for a place to start a ranch. You are to help him. But only for a while, then you will be seeing your Alvina again, with money in your pocket."

The cigarmaker grimaces as he considers this. "I'd be likelier to go out to Leadville for the gold than to work on some ranch for another man."

"That's good, lad. Say something about that, about why you'd go with this Hillmon fellow instead of going out to the mines."

"Why would I?"

"Because he promised you high wages!" The lawyer's patience is fraying.

More scratching, punctuated by a hushed oath as the pen leaves a large blot on the paper. "Okay, is it done?"

The lawyer looks over his shoulder, rubbing his chin. "Write some more of love, son. Make her believe that nothing will keep you away from your Alvina once you have filled your pockets out west."

Walters narrows his eyes in protest. "I might need more money to write that. It makes me sick, Mr. Buchan."

"There will be plenty of money when you finish your work, sir. Just write it near as you can to the way you wrote her after you first left home. Put in a bit of humor like she will recognize, or little things you can remember to refer to—things that only you and she would know."

As the pen moves, another thought seems to strike the writer, and he stops abruptly. "How are you going to make anyone believe this letter was sent a year ago? The postmark, Mr. Buchan! And then suppose someone asks Alvina when she got the letter? Then what?"

"Suppose you leave that to me, lad. Just finish writing. Ah, that's very good. Poetry, that's excellent! Did she really send you poetry?"

"Mr. Buchan, she completely got the wrong idea about me. She thought we was to get married when I come back, and maybe I let her think so one time. . . . What happened's nobody's business. Are lots of folks going to see this letter?"

"Yes sir. But by then you will be somewhere else. Will be *somebody* else. It might be well for you to grow a beard, son. Change your hair up some. I'll pay you for this letter tonight, but we can only send you the monthly sum so long as everybody thinks Frederick Adolph Walters is dead."

"You mean I'm more good to you dead than alive."

Buchan starts to wave this away, but it is undeniable. "That's true, I suppose," he acknowledges. "Another reason you don't want to be found. Are you finished there?"

"I think so."

"All right, then. Just the envelope, if you please, sir. And then a brief letter to your sister, and our business will be concluded for now."[15]

It could have happened that way. The longer I think about it, the more I believe it *must* have happened that way, more or less. And even if my imagination has got some of the details wrong, as it surely has, there is no explanation for the Dearest Alvina letter, beyond a truly preposterous coincidence, that does not require the statements in the letter to be untrue. From the implicit claim *I am writing this in Wichita, Kansas on March 1, 1879*, to the explicit statement that the cigarmaker has met a man named Hillmon and plans to travel west with him, to the representation that he wants to see Alvina again as badly as she wants to see him—these all were lies. A conclusion that leads to another, even more disillusioning point: that the United States Supreme Court invented in 1892 an important and enduring piece of law, but not a very good one, for the sake of allowing into evidence a document filled with falsehood.

The Justices, so eager to ensure that the next jury saw the Hillmon matter in its true light as a case of fraud, failed in that goal, for even with the letter in evidence no jury ever found in favor of the insurance companies. What the Court did accomplish in 1892 was instead to weaken the hearsay rule, a rule designed to advance the search for truth in the courtroom by requiring that witnesses must ordinarily give their accounts in court, subject to oath, observation, and cross-examination. They did so by creating an exception to the rule for a class of statements—statements about one's intentions—that are among the least trustworthy statements one can imagine. The exception to the hearsay rule for statements of intention would have been bad law even if it had been invented to allow into evidence a document that contained only the sober truth. But one must acknowledge the withering irony that the iconic piece of evidence for which the rule was invented itself dripped deceit from nearly every sentence.

How do we know that the Hillmon rule is a bad rule? Can we be certain it has produced bad decisions based on untrustworthy evidence? The demand for proof of this sort is nearly impossible to satisfy: consider the perpetual dispute over whether the American justice system has ever executed an innocent man. But, as in that debate, there are some worrisome cases.

Larry Adell, the sixteen-year-old son of a very wealthy Palm Springs man, was last seen for certain by a group of his high-school friends on June 1, 1974, as they all ate together in a restaurant one evening. Adell left the table where he sat with his friends, explaining that he was going out to the parking lot to get some marijuana from "Angelo." His friends understood this as a reference to Angelo Inciso, an older man known to all of them. Adell did not return to the restaurant, and his family never saw him again.

The Adell family received ten ransom notes, and there were two telephone calls. Four times there were attempts to deliver the ransom, but for various reasons these all failed, and Larry Adell did not return home. The letters and phone calls ceased after June 1974, and shortly thereafter FBI agents arrested Angelo Inciso and Hugh Pheaster, both of whom they had had under surveillance.

Inciso and Pheaster were indicted for twelve federal offenses, including conspiracy to kidnap and extortion using the mail. Adell had not been found at the time of the trial, although some time later a body found buried in the California desert was identified as his. The evidence at their trial left little doubt that Pheaster had been involved in Larry Adell's disappearance, although the defense argued that some of it (especially reported sightings some weeks later of Adell under no apparent restraint in a Las Vegas casino) suggested that he had been not an unwilling victim, but a participant in a scheme to obtain money from his wealthy family.

Concerning Angelo Inciso, however, there was much less evidence. Apart from some contacts with Hugh Pheaster that were susceptible to other explanations, the only convincing evidence of Inciso's involvement in Adell's disappearance was the statement that Adell had made to his friends as he left their company the night of his disappearance: that he was "going to meet Angelo."

After both men were convicted on all counts, they appealed. The Court of Appeals for the Ninth Circuit considered their various assignments of error, and disposed of all of them handily, except for one, which gave the appeals judges more pause. Angelo Inciso's lawyers pointed out that Larry Adell's statement that he was going to meet Angelo implicated not only his own intentions, but those of Angelo Inciso as well. The Hillmon case made plain that hearsay statements about the speaker's or writer's own intentions were admissible. But unavoidably, Inciso's lawyers argued, the jury would understand this evidence of Adell's explanation to his friends as being in addition some evidence that *Angelo Inciso* intended to meet *Larry Adell*. The Hillmon rule surely did not cover statements made by one person, Adell, about the intentions of another, Inciso. Moreover, the jury would certainly conclude that Adell and Inciso had spoken earlier and made this arrangement—which was a proposition about the *past*, not a statement of anyone's intentions. The Supreme Court had made plain in a case called *Shepard v. United States,* decided forty years after *Hillmon,* that statements about the past were not eligible for the Hillmon exception to the hearsay rule.[16]

The judges of the Court of Appeals acknowledged the correctness of this analysis, and agreed that the admission of Adell's statement about going to meet Angelo presented some "theoretical awkwardness." One of the judges even noted that the Hillmon decision had been the subject of "severe criticism." But, they explained, they were without authority to say that Adell's statements should have been kept from the jury. For in the Hillmon case itself, did not the Dearest Alvina letter also invite the jury to draw some conclusions about Hillmon's intentions, as well as Walters's? And did the letter not suggest, even mention explicitly, that the two men had at some point in the recent past reached an agreement? Since the Hillmon case, a Supreme Court precedent that could not be disregarded, had sanctioned precisely the same sort of evidence as the conviction of Angelo Inciso rested on, the judges of the Ninth Circuit Court of Appeals could not justify overturning the conviction.

Angelo Inciso was in his sixties when he was convicted. His sentence was to life in prison.[17]

I believe the Supreme Court stumbled profoundly in its first Hillmon decision, by creating a new rule of law to make possible the receipt into evidence of a document that was full of falsehood. Unless one believes in a series of coincidences staggering in their unlikelihood, this conclusion is compelled by Dennis's findings, quite apart from whatever I may have found in my own ventures into the history of the case. And that is reassuring, for by now my historical vision is clouded by indignation and desire.

The indignation flows from my conviction that the insurance companies and their many lieutenants cheated and lied in numerous ways during the battle over John Hillmon's life insurance policies. The desire, of course, is my aching wish to know Sallie for who she is. She's in my life now as vividly as my family and my colleagues, perhaps more so in the dark of certain nights. But I still don't know whether she is a victim or criminal, or some of each or neither. And as it would trouble you not to have this basic level of understanding about a person with whom you regularly share your bed, just so this uncertainty plagues me like a case of poison ivy.

Knowing that the insurance companies acted villainously does not help all that much, for Dennis's caution about his conclusions has reminded me that it is possible for all parties to the Hillmon litigation to have acted badly. Certainly the insurance companies lied and falsified evidence, at the very least the evidence that the dead man was Fredrick Adolph Walters. But possibly John Hillmon did lure another man, someone other than the cigarmaker from Iowa, to his death at Crooked Creek. And perhaps Sallie knew this to be true, knew it from the moment she viewed the body at Bailey and Smith's undertaking establishment in 1879 and saw that it was not John Hillmon's. Maybe she even had known all along what to expect, having been a party to the conspiracy from its inception. Or perhaps, just perhaps, she was unsure herself, especially after the years had fogged her memory, whether the body she had once looked on in the undertaker's parlor belonged to the man she had married such a short time before, or to a stranger.

I don't want to believe in any of these scenarios, but nothing I have found disproves them, and in truth I have encountered the occasional disquieting fact that might point in the direction of one or more. Even the circumstances that seem to point away from them—Sallie's remarriage, for example—can be reconciled with a theory of her complicity in murder and fraud. The evidence seems to run out here, just when I need it the most.

What did Sallie Hillmon know, and when did she know it? On this question, more than on any other mystery embedded in the Hillmon case, my curiosity is doomed to dissatisfaction. And yet it has come to form the center of my motivation to understand the case. Historical and scientific investigation have led me into a cul-de-sac, with no company but my imagination.

Sometimes I believe the likeliest thing to be this: that by the time it was all over, Sallie Hillmon Smith herself no longer knew the truth. Without claiming for a moment that the events that follow happened, I think it possible that they capture her predicament.

BOSTON, MASSACHUSETTS | SEPTEMBER 1903

"Are you certain you don't wish for me to accompany you, my dear?" James Smith has been quite half an hour at the window of their hotel room, peering down to the street below. Most of the traffic consists of carriages and pedestrians, but twice he has seen a motorcar pass by. He would very much admire to see one of the vehicles close up. One of those that drove beneath the window was surely an electric; but he thinks the other, which belched smoke and made a rumble that he could hear even through the glass, may have been an even more thrilling prospect: an Olds of the sort that combusts gasoline.

"I have already arranged through the desk to hire a hansom to take me to Beacon Hill," says Sallie, drawing on her gloves. "There is no need for you to come along, James. I shall ask the driver to wait, or to come back after perhaps. I shall be perfectly safe."

James is grateful to hear his wife's reply, for this will free him to stand beside the street and await the passage of other motorcars. And Sallie, on whom the evidence of her husband's new infatuation has not been lost, gives silent thanks for the invention of the automobile; she will be able to visit Mrs. Piper alone.

Sallie knows that the woman has been studied extensively by great men of science and found free of artifice or deception, but still, she is skeptical. She does not wish merely to be entertained by someone who has investigated her and deduced her identity and her intentions. She hopes to have given the medium no clues about who she is. She has even taken the precaution, when making an appointment for the sitting, of employing another name altogether. She is not often recognized by strangers; but James, who was a quiet man in his younger years, has grown rather tiresomely voluble with age, and is wont to explain to the most casual acquaintance who his wife is and why she is famous. His presence would be a complication, and she is happy that she need not manage it. She checks to see that the item wrapped in her handkerchief rests safely inside her bag, then kisses her husband lightly on the cheek and bids him enjoy the day.

Three hours later she sits in the drawing room of the Beacon Hill house, sipping hot tea from a cup of the finest bone china. The man who shares her teatime is bluff and hearty, not at all what she had expected, and the impression of vigor is enhanced by what must be his Australian accent. Sallie has never heard one before. It is charming, but does little to make up for her disappointment. There will be no communications from beyond today, nor any unmasking of fraud. The session has produced nothing. Mrs. Piper had simply rested her head on a pillow for quite a long time, uneventfully, then arisen to inquire whether the results had been satisfactory.

"I am sorry for this failure, Mrs. Clay," says her companion.

"Yes, thank you," she replies. Sallie had not expected to feel so let down, in truth, for it had not occurred to her that the experience would be so dispiriting. In a manner of speaking. Appreciation of her own unspoken and unintended witticism does nothing to cheer her. "Does this occur often, Dr. Hodgson?"

"Call me Mister, Mrs. Clay. Or simply Richard. I am not a doctor, of any sort. And yes, it seems sometimes that the spirits simply do not wish to appear. It is no use asking Mrs. Piper why, for she claims she remembers nothing about her trances, and she must ask me when she returns from them whether anything has happened."

The word *claims* does not escape Sallie's notice. "You sound as though you are not yourself convinced that Mrs. Piper has a gift."

Hodgson sets down his teacup, nearly spilling the contents as his powerful fingers struggle to maintain a grasp on the dainty handle. He is silent for a moment, then raises his eyes to Sallie's. "No, I am persuaded. Rather against my will, but I am. Still, I try to maintain a scientific attitude toward what I am seeing, for Mrs. Piper is still the object of study among me and my colleagues."

"Do you understand her gift, then?"

"No. Not at all. But I have seen, when the sittings are more successful, certain regularities in the way it performs."

"Is it possible that the object I handed to her was not . . . the right sort?"

"May I see it?" Hodgson unfolds the cloth she hands to him and examines the thin gold band within. "I assume this ring had some connection to the deceased?"

"Yes," she says. "He was wearing it on his little finger when we met, more than thirty years ago. And then later he gave it to me, as a wedding ring. I had to ask him for it, as I recall. He was not really a sentimental person." Hodgson's gaze flickers to her left hand, where a wider band surrounds her third finger. "It was a previous marriage," she adds in haste, her voice breaking past a curious thickness in her throat. No need to be secretive now, she has realized, for she will not see Mrs. Piper again. She will go home to Kansas and never again have a reason to come to Boston, and . . .

"Please do not distress yourself, Mrs. Clay," says Hodgson kindly. He hands her the handkerchief in which the ring had been wrapped, and she dabs her eyes efficiently.

"I am so sorry." She has not cried for John Hillmon in years.

"No need. This parlor has been the scene of many tears, as you may imagine." He hesitates, turning the ring over in his hands. "This seems to be the sort of object that often produces an appearance. It was well chosen."

"Then can you tell me why we had no success today?"

Hodgson shakes his tawny head and hands the ring back to her. "As I said, I can explain none of this. Nor can Mrs. Piper, although she will be happy to return your dollar, Mrs. Clay. But I believe some would say that the spirit with which you attempt to communicate does not wish to appear to you. Or—are you quite sure he is dead?"

The words linger in the silence of the spacious room, and Sallie looks out through the window to the thin sunshine. She does not reply to Hodgson.[18]

† † †

Nor does she speak to me. I must make a home for my uncertainty, as perhaps Sallie had to live with hers. The Hillmon case has taught me much, but that lesson—history's occasional resistance to our efforts to know it—may be the most difficult, and the most important.

ACKNOWLEDGMENTS

If I named everyone whose advice, encouragement, reflection, and labor went into this book, the list would go on nearly as long as the work itself. If you're not here but you contributed in one of those ways, I haven't forgotten you. You belong in the *karass*, whose membership list is indelibly recorded elsewhere.

I send special thanks and acknowledgments, however, to those below.

At the University of Colorado
    The Law School, particularly
        Dean David Getches, whom I miss very much
        Dean Phil Weiser
        Former Vice Dean Dayna Matthew
        Jane Thompson, Associate Director, Wise Law Library
        Andrea Viedt, research assistant extraordinaire
        Colleagues (present and former) Barbara Bintliff, Deborah Cantrell, Clare Huntington, Sarah Krakoff, Helen Norton, Pierre Schlag, and Charles Wilkinson
    Continuing Education, especially Wynn Martens
    Department of Molecular and Cellular Biology

Ken Krauter, DNA detective

Helen Marshall, painstaking lab magician

Department of Anthropology

Dennis Van Gerven, esteemed colleague, breathtaking teacher

Paul Sandberg, man with a limitless future

Film Studies program

Ernesto Acevedo-Muñoz, force of nature

Rachel Griego, still photography and artistic sensibility

Mike Lawrence, quiet man of endless competence

Lee Sarter, source of energy and reassurance

Department of History

Marjorie McIntosh, meticulous reader and editor

Susan Kent, source of courage and at least one great idea

At the City of Lawrence

Toni Ramirez Wheeler, City Attorney's Office

Mitch Young, Cemetery Superintendent

Lisa Patterson, Director of Communications

Frank (last name unknown), cemetery worker

At the University of Kansas

Professor David Frayer, generous host, inventive chef, excellent scientist, and fine talking head

Professor Jim Mielke, fine scientist and contagious enthusiast

At Spencer, Fane, Britt, and Browne of Kansas City, Missouri

Mark Thornhill, genius litigator

Mackenzie Murphy-Wilfong, mistress of attention to detail

Maria Donigan, backstage tolerance and encouragement

Elsewhere

M. Carlene St. John of Berkeley, California, tireless genealogist of great distinction

Andy Popper, Hiroshi Motomura, and Susan Appleton, virtual colleagues and fine readers

Dan and Kim Davis of Spokane, Washington

Leray and Sandra Hillmon of Montana
Ben Herr of Lyons, Colorado
Katie Tepley Jackson of Manhattan, Kansas
Jerry Ferrin, Kim Fowler, Shirley Brier, and Dee and Phyllis
Scherich of Barber County, Kansas
Kansas State Historical Society, Topeka, Kansas
National Archives and Records Administration, Kansas City,
Kansas

Research assistants
Kianna Ferguson
Molly Ferrer
Jon Grevillius
Sarah Hamilton
Brent Jordheim
Melissa Kerin
Alejandro Augustin Ortiz
Jessie Polini
Andrea Viedt
Hannah Wanebo

Manuscript preparation
Cynthia Carter
Beth Ann Lennon
Justine Pierce

At the Frances Goldin Literary Agency
Sam Stoloff, tireless and thoughtful advocate for this work

At NYU Press
Deborah Gershenowitz
Constance Grady
Despina Papazoglou Gimbel
Clara Platter
Alexia Traganas
Betsy Steve

NOTES

Some sources have been employed so often that it is convenient to refer to them by abbreviations. They include (beginning with the abbreviation employed hereinafter):

1888 Transcript: Transcript of Record, Supreme Court of the United States, October Term 1890, Nos. 858, 859, 860, 861, *Mut. Life Ins. Co of New York et al., Plaintiffs in Error v. Sallie E. Hillmon* (containing documents and testimony offered in evidence at the third trial in 1888).

1899 Transcript: Transcript of Record, Supreme Court of the United States, October Term 1902, No. 94, *The Connecticut Mutual Life Ins. Co., Petitioner v. Sallie E. Hillmon* (containing documents and testimony offered in evidence at the sixth trial in 1899). The transcript is paginated according to two different systems; the page numbers here given accord with the "Print" system as recorded in the Index to the Transcript of Record, not the higher stamped numbers apparent in the upper right-hand corner of some pages.

ancestry.com: Database online, Provo, Utah, http://www.ancestry.com/.

Wilder's *Annals of Kansas*, 1st ed.: Daniel W. Wilder, *The Annals of Kansas* (Geo. W. Martin, Kansas Publishing House ,1875) (reprinted by University of Michigan Library Scholarly Publishing Office). This volume covers the years 1542–1874, noting for nearly every day various items that were reported in the newspapers, journals, newsletters, and other written sources in the state on that date.

Wilder's *Annals of Kansas*, 2nd ed.: Daniel W. Wilder, *The Annals of Kansas, New Edition, 1541–1885* (T. Dwight Thacher, Kansas Publishing House, 1886). This volume reprints the contents of the previous edition with certain amendments, and adds material from the years 1875–85.

KSHS *Annals of Kansas: Annals of Kansas, 1886–1925*, vol. 1 (Kansas State Historical Society, publication date not given). This collectively authored volume covers the years 1886 to 1910. A second volume, not cited in this book, covers the years 1911 to 1925.

Clanton's *Populism*: Gene Clanton, *Populism: The Humane Preference in America, 1890–1900* (Boston: Twayne, 1991).

Davis's *Kansas*: Kenneth S. Davis, *Kansas: A Bicentennial History* (New York: Norton, 1976).

Harmon's "Gleed": Terry Harmon, "Charles Sumner Gleed: A Western Business Leader, 1856–1920" (PhD diss., University of Kansas, 1973) (on file with author).

KSHS: The archives of the Kansas State Historical Society, Topeka, Kansas.

Miner's *Kansas*: Craig Miner, *Kansas: The History of the Sunflower State, 1854–2000* (Lawrence: University Press of Kansas 2002).

NARA Archive: Documents and records in the keeping of the National Archives and Records Administration, Central Plains Division, in Kansas City, Missouri. Those documents pertaining to the Hillmon litigation that have been preserved are found at Records for the U.S. Circuit Court for the District of Kansas, 1st Div., Topeka, Range 21, boxes 220–28. The invaluable documents in this collection are neither indexed, chronological, nor complete.

NOTES TO THE PROLOGUE

1. *Mut. Life Ins. Co. of N.Y. v. Hillmon*, 145 U.S. 285 (1892).
2. The insurance companies' assignments of error may be found in 1888 Transcript, 90-101 (Petition in Error), 100 (claim of error pertaining to letter).
3. The letter is quoted *ibid.*, where the word is given as "ranch." But the handwritten version deposited with the case records at the NARA Archive is ambiguous to my eye. This handwritten version is not, however, the original letter, of which more will be said later in the text. "Letter from F.A. Walters to A. Kasten," NARA Archive, Box 221.
4. Alvina Kasten's testimony was given in a deposition in 1881; it was this deposition and not her live testimony that was received in evidence at the six trials. She never testified in person. "Deposition of Alvina Kasten, June 1881, Ft. Madison, IA," NARA Archive, Box 222.
5. Fed. R. Evid. 803(3).
6. Judge Shiras's ruling is described in the 1888 Transcript, 91–101 (Petition in Error). For a general description of the hearsay rule and its operation, see G. Michael Fenner, *The Hearsay Rule*, 2nd ed. (Chapel Hill: Carolina Academic Press, 2009).
7. The evidence about the Supreme Court's deliberations in the Hillmon case is described in chapter 5, *infra.*
8. Oliver Wendell Holmes Jr., "The Common Law," *The Common Law and Other Writings* (Birmingham: Legal Classics Library, 1982).
9. Concerning British law, see Paul Roberts and Adrian Zuckerman, *Criminal Evidence* (New York: Oxford University Press, 2004), 651–53. Concerning Australian, see *Walton v. R* (1989) 63 A.L.J.R. 226 (Austl.); and the thoughtful discussion of it in Colin Tapper, "Hillmon Rediscovered and Lord St. Leonards Resurrected," *Law Quarterly Review* 106 (1990): 441.

NOTES TO CHAPTER 1

1. Sallie and John Hillmon boarded with the Judsons during their brief marriage, and Sallie stayed with them at least through the 1880 census. Sallie is often described as a "waitress," and Arthur Judson testified in the first trial that she and her mother had worked in Lawrence in the dining room of a hotel called the *Globe*, which

her mother managed. On the morning the inquest began, Sallie visited Bailey and Smith's undertaking establishment on New Hampshire Street before attending the inquest. Sallie's thoughts, the jump rope chant, her attire, and the conversations she had with Mrs. Judson are invented.

2. John Hillmon was listed as a thirteen-year-old living in his father Benjamin Hillmon's household in Grasshopper Springs, Kansas, in the 1860 census. "1860 United States Federal Census: John Hillman," ancestry.com, accessed July 29, 2008, cited by M. Carlene St. John in Report to Author. Civil War records suggest that John Hillmon enlisted twice, first in 1862 at the age of fourteen, and again in 1864 with a Nebraska company. "American Civil War Soldiers: John W. Hillman," ancestry.com, accessed Jan. 5, 2010, cited by M. Carlene St. John in Report to Author.

3. For a good general account of conflicts between Indian peoples and settlers in western Kansas after the Civil War, see Miner's *Kansas*, 94–95, 106–21. For accounts of the 1879 hostilities, see John H. Monnet, *Tell Them We Are Going Home: The Odyssey of the Northern Cheyenne* (Norman: University of Oklahoma Press, 2001).

4. Sallie and John's marriage certificate, located by Shirley Brier at KSHS, shows his age as thirty, hers as twenty-seven. "John W. Hillmon and Sadie E. Quinn: Marriage License, Douglas County, Kansas," *Hillmon Case*, accessed Feb. 8, 2011, http://www.thehillmoncase.com/. But the certificate, apparently filled in by the Douglas County probate judge who issued it, probably recorded her age incorrectly. Records of the 1880 census, which show her still living as a boarder with the Judsons, give her age as twenty-three at that time. "1880 United States Federal Census: Sallie E. Hillman," ancestry.com, accessed July 29, 2008, cited by M. Carlene St. John in Report to Author. Sallie herself testified in April 1879 that she was twenty-three. "The Hillman Horror," *Lawrence Standard*, April 10, 1879, 1,

   Another likely error perpetuated by this certificate is the name "Sadie" for Sallie. There is no evidence that she ever referred to herself by that name, and all census records located give her name as Sarah or Sallie, or use her initials, S.E., ancestry.com, *passim*. The judge who issued the marriage certificate wrote in the bride's name. It was probably meant to be "Sallie," but the writing is hasty and imprecise; the double *l* could easily be misread as a *d*. When Rev. Henning signed the bottom half of the certificate after the marriage, he recorded the name as "Sadie" (suggesting that he relied on the upper portion of the document, and also perhaps that he did not know the bride very well). The brief newspaper item that reported the marriage called the bride "Miss Sadie E. Quinn"; it also misreported the date of the nuptials. "Marriage," *Lawrence Daily Tribune*, Oct. 5, 1878. *Hillmon Case*, accessed Feb. 8, 2011, www.thehillmoncase.com/marriage.html. She was often thereafter referred to in newspapers as "Sadie," usually when the context was one of skepticism about her claims.

5. Miner's *Kansas*, 24. A prominent man named Alfred Gray gave voice to these ideas in 1879, claiming that the view that land west of the hundredth meridian was too arid for cultivation resembled the myth that certain areas of the continent were suited for slavery, and deserved to be rejected with equal passion. Wilder's *Annals of Kansas*, 2nd ed., 849. They played a large role in the creation of the American Dust Bowl, as chronicled in Timothy Egan, *The Worst Hard Time: The Untold Story of Those Who Survived the Great American Dustbowl* (New York: Houghton Mifflin, 2005), 12, 38.

6. Concerning the importance of barbed wire, see Davis's *Kansas*, 123–24. Concerning the Medicine Lodge Treaty and its aftermath, see *ibid.*, 103; and Miner's *Kansas*, 112–21.

7. The details of Brown and Hillmon's previous acquaintance were described by Brown in his deposition, taken in 1881 and early 1882. "Brown Deposition," 1899 Transcript, 342–521. Attorney Samuel Riggs's argument for the wisdom of their wintertime expedition is recounted in "Conclusion of the Argument in the Hillman Case" *Leavenworth Times*, June 23, 1885, 4.

8. "Brown Deposition," 1899 Transcript, 342–521.

9. "George W. Paddock Deposition," 1899 Transcript, 322–38.

10. The Douglas County Coroner, Dr. Richard Morris, presided at the inquest, and James W. Green and his assistant represented the interests of the County, or so they claimed. E.B. Good, a grocer, served as one of the coroner's jurors, and Colonel Samuel Walker was present. John Brown testified substantially as described, although his exact language is my invention. Mr. R.J. Borgalthaus appeared, although whether on that occasion as a private citizen or by an agreement between him and Sallie or him and Levi Baldwin is ambiguous. Borgalthaus was, however, one of the attorneys who signed the complaints in Sallie's eventual lawsuits. The letter is verbatim correspondence that Brown sent to Sallie after the death at Crooked Creek. Sallie's thoughts and her conversations with others are invented.

11. Governor John St. John, a longtime advocate of prohibition, finally persuaded the voters of Kansas in November 1880 to approve a constitutional amendment banning liquor sales. The measure had been presented to the Legislature in January of the preceding year, three months before the Hillmon inquest. Sallie said nothing immediately upon seeing the corpse at the undertaker's that morning, but would later testify many times that she had recognized it immediately as her husband. The young law student and journalist Charles Gleed would later claim that he had been one of the first journalists to cover the inquest, although the stories in the Lawrence papers are unsigned, in the manner of the time. George Barker was a younger man than Green, and often described as corpulent or heavy. Sallie's presence at the "joint" with Levi and Borgalthaus, and all of her thoughts and conversations with others, are invented.

12. These details of Gleed's life are from his biography, Harmon's "Gleed."

13. See Charles S. Gleed, "*Hillman v. Insurance Co.,*" in Daniel W. Wilder, *Eighteenth Annual Report of the Kansas Superintendent of Insurance* 49–74 (1887), 50.

14. *Lawrence Standard*, March 27, 1879, 1; *Lawrence Standard*, April 10, 1879, 1.

15. *Lawrence Standard*, April 10, 1879, 2.

16. "The Hillman Trial," *Topeka Daily Capital*, Feb. 16, 1895, 6 (Morris's testimony); "Wiseman Testifies," *Topeka Daily Capital*, Jan. 31, 1895, 6 (Wiseman's testimony).

17. *Lawrence Standard*, April 17, 1879, 4.

18. Sallie and John Hillmon were wed in the Judson's parlor by a Rev. Henning. Apart from this event I have found no evidence of any sort concerning John Hillmon's religious beliefs, if he had any, nor of Sallie's. The body was buried in the Oak Hill Cemetery one evening during the course of the inquest, after a brief procession led by Sallie and some friends and relatives. Levi's predictions about what the insurance companies would claim regarding the vaccination were accurate. George Barker argued at the last trial that John Hillmon had left his wedding ring at home when he

left for the second time, in February 1879. But at the third trial Sallie described the ring as one he had worn "on the little finger of his left hand." She said he had worn it for years before their marriage but that it was too small for him, and that she had asked him for it. She had worn it, she said, at the previous trials. The newspaper quotations are verbatim. Sallie's and Levi's testimony at the inquest was substantially as described. Sallie's thoughts and conversations, apart from her testimony on the stand, are invented.

19. Glen Schwendemann, "Wyandotte and the First 'Exodusters' of 1879," *Kansas Historical Quarterly* 26, no. 3 (Autumn 1960): 233; J.G. Van Deusen, "The Exodus of 1879," *Journal of Negro History* 21 (April 1936): 111.

20. C.S. Gleed, "As Others See Us" (addresses delivered at annual banquets during the first ten years of the club's existence, 1982–1900), quoted in Harmon's *Gleed.*

21. The newspaper account is verbatim from "The Hillman Inquest," *Lawrence Daily Tribune*, April 7, 1879, 4. All the testimony from the inquest is substantially as it was reported in contemporaneous accounts. One newspaper reported that the jurors "snapped the gun around" during Brown's testimony. Sallie did produce two tintypes for the inquest, one of Hillmon alone and one of Hillmon and Brown together, as described. Sallie's thoughts and feelings, and her conversations except her testimony on the stand, are invented.

22. All accounts are from J.B. Lewis, MD, and C.C. Bombaugh, AM, MD, *Remarkable Stratagems and Conspiracies: An Authentic Record of Surprising Attempts to Defraud Life Insurance Companies* (New York: G.W. Carleton, 1878).

23. The grave was uncovered late in the inquest at the request of a Lawrence woman named Mrs. M.L. Lowell, who said her brother was missing and she feared the body might be his. When she saw the body, however, she could not identify it. Sallie's trip to the cemetery and her thoughts and feelings are invented, as well as her conversations.

24. The complaints filed in the Hillmon lawsuits (there were three suits at the beginning, later consolidated to one) are handwritten, and not all the pages are by the same hand. But at least some appear to be in Sallie Hillmon's writing, as it may be seen in her signature on many documents.

25. The disclosure that "Arkansaw" had been found alive, not long after it was suggested that the corpse was his, did not come until much later. In 1899 Major Theo. Wiseman would testify that he had located the living Frank Nichols in 1879. "Damaging Evidence by John Hillmon's Sister," *Leavenworth Times*, Nov. 1, 1899, 6.

NOTES TO CHAPTER 2

1. Most of the features of Buchan and Ward's encounter with Brown in September 1879 are taken from Brown's deposition testimony. A transcript of the entire deposition may be read in the record on appeal following the sixth (and last) trial. "Deposition of John H. Brown," 1899 Transcript, 342 *et seq*. The text of the affidavit may be found in the same record beginning on p. 460. The text of the "letter" to Sallie Hillmon may be found on p. 482. My inventions include Polly, Eliza, the lemonade, John Brown's sojourn in jail, and Reuben's role in getting him the job at Fulton's mill.

2. The discovery of Nichols alive in 1879 was described by company agent Major Wiseman in his testimony at the sixth trial. "Damaging Evidence by John Hillmon's Sister," *Leavenworth Times*, Nov. 1, 1899, 6.

3. The policy applications show that Sallie E. Hillmon was the named beneficiary of each policy. 1899 Transcript, 167 *et seq.*

4. The banker's account of these events is given in "And Still Another," *Topeka Daily Capital*, March 24, 1896; Daniel Walters's deposition account is described in "Trying to Shut Out Conspiracy Evidence," *Leavenworth Times*, Nov. 9, 1899, 4; and Major Wiseman's version recorded in "The Hillmon Case," *Topeka Daily Capital*, Feb. 1, 1895, 8.

5. "Defendants' Day," *Topeka Daily Capital*, Feb. 19, 1895, 4.

6. "How Tall Was He?" *Topeka Daily Capital*, March 18, 1896 (testimony of Theodore Wiseman); "Walters' Sister," *Topeka Daily Capital*, Feb. 24, 1895, 2 (testimony of Fanny Walters); "Wait for a Witness," *Topeka Daily Capital*, March 27, 1896 (testimony of Fanny Walters).

7. The current version of this exception in federal law is codified at Rule 803(2) in the Federal Rules of Evidence. A useful history of this exception may be found in John W. Strong, ed., *McCormick on Evidence*, 4th ed. (1992), 216.

8. Daniels's testimony to this effect was given in his deposition, and described in "Defendants' Day," *Topeka Daily Capital*, Feb. 19, 1895, 4. On the role of expectation in perception generally, see Elizabeth F. Loftus, James M. Doyle, and Jennifer E. Dysart, *Eyewitness Testimony: Civil and Criminal*, 4th ed. (LexisNexis, 2007), 36–37.

9. "Brother and Sister Swear It Was Walters," *Leavenworth Times*, Nov. 11, 1899: 6.

10. See *Simmons v. United States*, 390 U.S. 377 (1968).

11. Alvina Kasten's deposition was given at Fort Madison in June 1881 before Notary Public Sabert Casey. The deposition excerpts and the text of the letter are quoted verbatim as they are found in "Deposition of Alvina Kasten, June 1881, Ft. Madison, IA," NARA Archive, Box 222. Tillinghast's important role in eliciting Miss Kasten's story and preparing her to give her testimony are described in her deposition, although the details of the conversation given here are invented. I have no evidence that Kasten was promised that she would never have to testify before a judge— except for the circumstance that she never did appear in person at any of the six trials, although scores of other Fort Madison witnesses did so.

12. The magazine account I read was Brooks W. Maccracken, "The Case of the Anonymous Corpse," *American Heritage* 19, no. 50 (1968), available at http://www.americanheritage.com/content/case-anonymous-corpse?nid=52283.

13. "Deposition of Alvina Kasten," 1899 Transcript, 1693; "Letter from F. A. Walters to A. Kasten," NARA Archive, Box 221; Photographs of Walters and Hillmon (alive), NARA Archive, Box 223; W. H. Lamon's photographs of the corpse, NARA Archive, Box 221; "John Brown's Affidavit," 1899 Transcript, 462 (Brown's statement regarding the name of the young man he said Hillmon had killed).

14. "Deposition of John H. Brown," 1899 Transcript, 461.

15. The events surrounding Sallie's signing of the releases, and L.B. Wheat's subsequent refusal to turn over the policies themselves to W.J. Buchan, were the subject of consistent testimony by Brown, Sallie Hillmon, and Buchan himself in the several trials. The same is true of the events of the next day, when the affidavit was thrown into the stove, except that on one occasion Buchan claimed that it was he who had attempted to destroy the document. Brown and Sallie Hillmon always maintained that it was Brown who had thrust the document into the stove. Given his confessed later actions, which included rescuing the affidavit from the stove and turning it

over to the insurance lawyers, Buchan's account is not especially credible. The lawyer admitted that all his pay for working with John Brown came from the insurance companies. The thoughts and conversations here attributed to Buchan are invented.

16. Wilder's *Annals of Kansas*, 2nd ed., 847 (March 20, 1879: "McNeal and Iliff start the Medicine Lodge Cresset"). The quotation is from T.A. McNeal, *When Kansas Was Young* (Topeka: Capper Publications, 1922), 91–92.

17. McNeal, *When Kansas Was Young*.

18. *Ibid.*

19. Viviana A. Rotman Zelizer, *Morals and Markets: The Development of Life Insurance in the United States* (New York: Columbia University Press, 1979), 67.

20. *Ibid.*

21. "The Romance of Life Insurance," *Harper's New Monthly Magazine* 19 (Oct. 1859): 664–65, quoted *ibid.*, 69.

22. *Ibid.* at 77; 68–69 (the minister's quotation); *ibid.* at 68 (the quote from the *Insurance Gazette*); *ibid.* at 56–57 (material pertaining to the success of the "domestic hero" marketing motif).

23. The insurable interest doctrine is discussed *ibid.* at 71–72.

24. "Brown's Confession," *Topeka Daily Capital*, March 10, 1888, 4. Crew's testimony on this point was not always consistent. In the first trial the banker had testified that Baldwin was facing not foreclosure but *arrest* for nonpayment of the debt. Sallie's lawyers apparently did not note the discrepancy, if it was one. "More Mystery," *Leavenworth Times*, June 28, 1882, 1, 4.

NOTES TO CHAPTER 3

1. The newspaper account is verbatim. "The Hillmon Cases," *Leavenworth Times*, June 13, 1882, 4. The case of *Wood v. Crall*, a dispute of the sort described, was called just before the Hillmon case on the trial docket, and the verdict there was as described. E.B. Borgalthaus was the first witness called by Sallie's lawyers, and testified as described. "U.S. Circuit Court: Hillmon Cases Reached," *Leavenworth Times*, June 15, 1882, 1. The jurors were all men, and almost certainly all white. *Ibid.* Judge Foster did grant Sallie Hillmon's request to proceed without posting a bond, after she pleaded an inability to do so on account of poverty. *Ibid.* The Supreme Court decided, in the 1872 case of *Bradwell v. Illinois*, that any state could bar women from practicing law. The Court cited the great importance of women's roles as wives, mothers, and keepers of the hearth. *Bradwell v. Illinois*, 83 U.S. 130, 141–42 (1872). The remaining conversations and thoughts attributed to the various characters are invented.

2. "Beecher Bibles," *Kansapedia*, Kansas Historical Society, available at http://www.kshs.org/portraits/beecher_bibles.htm, quoting *New York Tribune*, Feb. 8, 1856, 6.

3. Correspondence between the author and Jerry Ferrin (on file with author); "Died: Harrison Jones," *Medicine Lodge Chief*, Sep. 9, 1887, available at http://www.rootsweb.ancestry.com/~ksbarber/jones_harrison.html; "Died: A Fatal Accident," *Medicine Lodge Herald*, Dec. 27, 1890, available at http://www.rootsweb.ancestry.com/~ksbarber/robinson_frank.html.

4. E-mail correspondence between author and Sandra Hillmon (on file with author).

5. All the witness testimony is substantially as it was given at trial, as reported in "The Hillmon Cases," *Leavenworth Times*, June 16, 1882, 1. Sallie's thoughts, memories, and decisions upon hearing Arthur Judson's testimony are invented.

6. "Strange Uses for Photographs," *Western Jurist* 8, no. 484 (Nov. 1879), 484, quoted at Thomas Thurston, *Hearsay of the Sun: Photography, Identity, and the Law of Evidence in Nineteenth-Century American Courts*, at text accompanying note 1 to chapter 1, available at http://chnm.gmu.edu/aq/photos/frames/essay01.htm.

7. The quotation from the Supreme Court may be found in *Luco v. United States*, 64 U.S. (23 How.) 515 (1859), quoted *ibid.* at text accompanying note 2 to chapter 1. The hearsay opponent was Albert Southworth, quoted *ibid.* at text accompanying note 8 to chapter 3. The article was "The Legal Relations of Photographs," *American Law Register* 17, no. 1 (Jan. 1869), quoted *ibid.* at text accompanying note 14 to chapter 1.

8. *Ruloff's Case*, 11 Abbott's Practice Reports (N.S.) 245 (1871), at 290–91, cited in "A Note on the Case of *Ruloff v. People*," *Albany Law Journal* 3, no. 186 (March 11, 1871), all cited *ibid.* at text accompanying note 3 to chapter 2; Federal Rules of Evidence 801, available at http://chnm.gmu.edu/aq/photos/texts/3alj186.htm.

9. Lamon's confession is recorded in "Was It Walters?" *Leavenworth Times*, June 29, 1882, 1. The quote concerning retouching is from Heinz K. Henisch and Bridget A. Henisch, *The Photographic Experience, 1839–1914: Images and Attitudes* (University Park: Pennsylvania State University Press, 1994), 92.

10. The first quotation is from an unidentified contributor in "The Legal Relations of Photographs," *American Law Register* 17, no. 7 (1869). The second was said by Marcus Aurelius Root, one of the earliest American photographers, as recorded in Alan Trachtenberg, *Reading American Photographs: Images as History, Mathew Brady to Walker Evans* (New York: Hill and Wang, 1990), 28.

11. The treatise was Wharton and Stilles, *Medical Jurisprudence*, quoted in George E. Harris, *A Treatise on the Law of Identification: A Separate Branch of the Law of Evidence* (Albany, 1892), wherein the newspaper quotation may also be found. All quoted in Thurston, *Hearsay of the Sun*, note 7 to chapter 2.

12. For the lawyers' arguments about Hillmon's temples, see "Strong Plea by J.W. Green," *Topeka Daily Capital*, March 17, 1895, 6. For the lawyers' arguments about Hillmon's eyebrows, see "Picked to Pieces," *Lawrence Evening Standard*, Nov. 16, 1899.

13. "Strong Plea by J.W. Green," *Topeka Daily Capital*, March 17, 1895, 6.

14. The witnesses, their names, and their testimony are all substantially as recorded in newspaper accounts of the trial. "The Hillmon Cases," *Leavenworth Times*, June 16, 1882, 1. Levi's thoughts are invented.

15. "A Long Story," *Leavenworth Times*, June 17, 1882, 1.

16. *Ibid.*

17. *Ibid.*

18. "Brown's Letter," *Leavenworth Times*, June 18, 1882, 5.

19. *Ibid.*

20. "How It Happened," *Leavenworth Times*, June 20, 1882, 1.

21. *Ibid.*

22. All of Sallie's testimony is substantially as recorded in contemporaneous newspaper accounts. *Ibid.* Her thoughts are invented.

23. "The Other Side," *Leavenworth Times*, June 21, 1882, 1.

24. *Ibid.*

25. "That Tooth," *Leavenworth Times*, June 22, 1882, 1.

26. *Ibid.*

27. *Ibid.*

28. *Ibid.*
29. *Ibid.*
30. *Ibid.*
31. *Ibid.*
32. *Ibid.*
33. *Ibid.*
34. *Ibid.*; and "Vaccine Virus," *Leavenworth Times*, June 23, 1882, 1 (the account of Mr. Buchan's examination spans both days' newspapers).
35. *Ibid.*
36. *Ibid.*
37. "Vaccine Virus," *Leavenworth Times*, June 23, 1879, 1.
38. *Ibid.*
39. *Ibid.*
40. *Ibid.*
41. *Ibid.* The reference to "B_____" is transcribed in "A Daisy Witness," *Topeka Daily Capital*, March 7, 1888, 5.
42. Andrew Delbanco, *The Death of Satan: How Americans Have Lost the Sense of Evil* (New York: Farrar, Straus and Giroux, 1995), 105–6; Alexis de Tocqueville, *Democracy in America*, trans. Henry Reeve, rev. Francis Bowen, ed. Phillips Bradley (New York: Knopf, 1949), 2:155, 243–44. "Lessons of Barnum's Life," *New York Times*, Dec. 16, 1854; all these sources are quoted in Scott A. Sandage, *Born Losers* (Cambridge: Harvard University Press, 2005), 13–14, 75, where Sandage's own words may also be found.
43. "Vaccine Virus," *Leavenworth Times*, June 23, 1882, 1.
44. *Ibid.*
45. *Ibid.*
46. *Ibid.*
47. "Hillmon's Hair," *Leavenworth Times*, June 24, 1882, 1.
48. *Ibid.*
49. "More Damage," *Leavenworth Times*, June 21, 1882, 4.
50. Concerning Justice Gray's appointment, see http://www.fjc.gov/public/home.nsf/hisj.
51. The resolution is described in "Was It Walters?" *Leavenworth Times*, June 29, 1882, 1. The temperance material is discussed in Davis's *Kansas*, 143. Remaining aspects of St. John's career are described in Miner's *Kansas*, 150–55.
52. Buchan's chairmanship of the Credentials Committee is reported in "The Chosen Ones," *Leavenworth Times*, June 30, 1882, 1. On the same page, an item from the *Topeka Commonwealth* describing Buchan as one of the "brainy politicians" is reprinted. *Ibid.*
53. Barker's appointment to the Central Committee is reported in "The State Ticket," *Leavenworth Times*, Aug. 11, 1882, 1; McNall's participation is described in "The Chosen Ones," *Leavenworth Times*, June 30, 1882, 1.
54. Brewer's nomination to the Kansas bench is recorded in "The State Ticket," *Leavenworth Times*, Aug. 11, 1882, 1. His later appointment and service are described at the website of the Federal Judicial Center, http://www.fjc.gov/public/home.nsf/hisj.
55. "Hillmon's Hair," *Leavenworth Times*, June 24, 1882, 1.
56. *Ibid.*
57. *Ibid.*

58. "Photograph Palaver," *Leavenworth Times*, June 27, 1882, 1.
59. *Ibid*.
60. *Ibid*.
61. "More Mystery," *Leavenworth Times*, June 28, 1882, 1.
62. *Ibid*.
63. *Ibid*. The text of the letter can be found in "Letter from F.A. Walters to A. Kasten," NARA Archive, Box 221.
64. *Ibid*.
65. "Was It Walters?" *Leavenworth Times*, June 29, 1882, 4.
66. "Coming to a Close," *Leavenworth Times*, June 30, 1882, 4.
67. "City News," *Leavenworth Times*, July 1, 1882, 4.
68. "Foster's Finding," *Leavenworth Times*, July 2, 1882, 5.
69. *Ibid*.
70. *Ibid*.
71. *Ibid*.
72. The scene is altogether invented. It is certain, however, that Gleed joined the defense team before the second trial and remained a member until the end, and that he often voiced sentiments about the importance of maintaining Kansas as a comfortable home for investment capital.
73. Kate Stephens, *Truths Back of the Uncle Jimmy Myth in a State University of the Middle West* (self-published, 1924) (copy available in Norlin Library of the University of Colorado).
74. This scene is altogether invented. There is no evidence of the discussions Sallie and her attorneys had about the question about settling her suit. Indeed, no evidence proves that they had any at all, but it would be surprising if they had not.

NOTES TO CHAPTER 4

1. The fortunes of the Gleed law firm are described in Harmon's "Gleed," 65. Judge (later Justice) Brewer's career is described at "Brewer, David Josiah," in *Judges of the United States Courts*, http://www.fjc.gov/history/home.nsf/page/judges.html.
2. "United States Court," *Leavenworth Times*, June 6, 1885, 4. The fact that four of the jurors were ex-members of the legislature is cited in "The Hillman Trial," *Leavenworth Times*, June 25, 1885, 4.
3. "U.S. Court," *Leavenworth Times*, June 7, 1885, 5; "U.S. Court," *Leavenworth Times*, June 9 1885, 4; "United States Courts," *Leavenworth Times*, June 16, 1885, 4.
4. "United States Courts," *Leavenworth Times*, June 16, 1885, 4.
5. All testimony recorded in *Leavenworth Times*, June 12–20, 1885. The accounts of the trial are usually to be found on the fourth page of a day's issue.
6. "The Hillman Case," *Leavenworth Times*, June 19, 1885, 1.
7. "The Hillman Case," *Leavenworth Times*, June 14, 1885, 4.
8. "United States Courts," *Leavenworth Times*, June 16, 1885, 4.
9. "The Hillman Case," *Leavenworth Times*, June 19, 1885, 1. The paper's report of the first jury's division is in "City News" *Leavenworth Times*, July 4, 1882, 4.
10. "The Hillman Case," *Leavenworth Times*, June 20, 1885, 4.
11. "United States Courts," *Leavenworth Times*, June 21, 1885, 5.
12. "Conclusion of the Argument in the Hillman Case," *Leavenworth Times*, June 23, 1885, 4.

13. "The Jury in the Hillman Case Charged by Judge Brewer," *Leavenworth Times*, June 24, 1885, 4.

14. *Ibid.*; "The Hillman Trial," *Leavenworth Times*, June 25, 1885, 4.

15. "The Hillman Trial," *Leavenworth Times*, June 25, 1885, 4.

16. *Ibid.*

17. *Ibid.*

18. Sallie Hillmon married James Smith, a traveling salesman of barber supplies, in 1886. Financing the expenses of the lawsuit posed a difficulty for Sallie and her attorneys from the beginning to the end. The remaining events, thoughts, and conversations are invented.

19. Davis's *Kansas*, 123.

20. The flyer is available at the Kansas State Historical Society's website, "The Last Chance for Desirable Cheap Homes in Kansas," *Kansas Memory*, http://www.kansas-memory.org/item/212270/page/1. The brochure is available at "Immigrants' Guide to the Most Fertile Lands of Kansas," *Kansas Memory*, http://www.kansasmemory.org/item/1445/page/1. Concerning the practices of loan agents, see Davis's *Kansas*, 123.

21. *Ibid.* at 122–25.

22. *Ibid.* at 126.

23. *Ibid.* at 126–27.

24. Harmon's "Gleed," 70–73.

25. *Ibid.* at 79.

26. *Ibid.*

27. "In the Courts," *Topeka Daily Capital*, Feb. 28, 1888, 8.

28. "A Jury Secured," *Topeka Daily Capital*, March 1, 1888, 4.

29. "The Hillmon Case," *Topeka Daily Capital*, March 2, 1888, 4; "The Hillmon Case," *Topeka Daily Capital*, March 4, 1888; and "What She Says," *Topeka Daily Capital*, March 6, 1888, 4.

30. "What She Says," *Topeka Daily Capital*, March 6, 1888, 4.

31. "A Daisy Witness," *Topeka Daily Capital*, March 7, 1888, 5.

32. *Ibid.*

33. *Ibid.*

34. *Ibid.*

35. *Ibid.*

36. "A Daisy Witness," *Topeka Daily Capital*, March 7, 1888, 5; "Tricks of Memory," *Topeka Daily Capital*, March 8, 1888, 4; "Readable Testimony," *Topeka Daily Capital*, March 9, 1888, 4.

37. "Readable Testimony," *Topeka Daily Capital*, March 9, 1888, 4.

38. *Ibid.*

39. *Ibid.*

40. Buchan's testimony is reported in "Brown's Confession," *Topeka Daily Capital*, March 10, 1888, 4.

41. *Ibid.*

42. *Ibid.*; "Expert Testimony," *Topeka Daily Capital*, March 11, 1888, 4; "About Walters," *Topeka Daily Capital*, March 13, 1888.

43. The objection sustained during Mr. Selig's testimony is reported in "A Daisy Witness," *Topeka Daily Capital*, March 7, 1888, 5.

44. *Ibid.*

45. *Ibid.*
46. *Ibid.*
47. "Expert Testimony," *Topeka Daily Capital*, March 11, 1888, 4.
48. "Was It Walters?" *Topeka Daily Capital*, March 14, 1888. These latter witnesses did not know Hillmon, of course, but based on the photographs they thought that he and "Colton" were the same man.
49. "About Walters," *Topeka Daily Capital*, March 13, 1888, 4; "Was It Walters?" *Topeka Daily Capital*, March 14, 1888, 4.
50. "Was It Walters?" *Topeka Daily Capital*, March 14, 1888, 4.
51. The objection to the Dearest Alvina letter on hearsay grounds was made toward the end of the afternoon on March 13, 1888. The jury was dismissed so the matter could be argued at length, and then set over for further argument the next morning. The defendants eventually maintained that it was a business record, but Judge Shiras was not persuaded, and on the morning of March 14 he ruled that the letter was inadmissible. *Ibid.* The remainder of the scenes, including the thoughts of the attorneys and the precise language employed by them and by the judge, is invented.
52. "Nearing the End," *Topeka Daily Capital*, March 16, 1888, 5.
53. "The Hillmon Case," *Topeka Daily Capital*, March 20, 1888, 8; "The Hillman Case," *Topeka Daily Commonwealth*, March 20, 1888.
54. "The Hillmon Case," *Topeka Daily Capital*, March 20, 1888, 8.
55. "Arguments Closed," *Topeka Daily Capital*, March 21, 1888, 5.
56. *Ibid.*
57. *Ibid.*
58. "The Hillman Case," *Topeka Daily Commonwealth*, March 21, 1888.
59. "A Verdict at Last," *Topeka Daily Capital*, March 22, 1888, 4.
60. *Ibid.*
61. *Ibid.*
62. *Ibid.*
63. "In the Courts," *Topeka Daily Capital*, March 23, 1888: 4, the grounds for the motion are set forth in "A Verdict at Last," *Topeka Daily Capital*, March 22, 1888, 4.
64. "Has W. P. Hillman Been Found Alive?" *Chicago Daily Tribune*, May 29, 1889, 2.
65. *Ibid.*
66. *Ibid.*
67. *Atchison Daily Globe*, May 28, 1889; *Atchison Daily Champion*, May 30, 1889, 2. "Hillman's Arrest Untrue," *Lawrence Daily Journal*, May 10, 1889, 1.

NOTES TO CHAPTER 5

1. Miner's *Kansas*, 174–75.
2. See generally Clanton's *Populism*.
3. The sympathetic journalist wrote in the *Kansas City Journal*, Oct. 30, 1910, found in populist party clippings, vol. 2, Kansas City Historical Society (mentioned in Miner's *Kansas*, 174). Gleed's words are found in Charles Gleed, *A Birds-Eye View of the Political Situation in Kansas, with Especial Reference to the People's Party* (Topeka: Republican State Headquarters, 1893), 5 (mentioned in Miner's *Kansas*, 179.) The cartoon is archived with the Kansas State Historical Society, http://www.kansasmemory.org/item/210559. The Ingalls quote is found in a letter, John Ingalls to P.I. Bonebrake,

Aug. 18, 1890, Ingalls Papers, Box 2, Kansas State Historical Society, quoted in Miner's *Kansas*, 177.

4. Details of Justice Gray's career may be found at the Federal Judicial Center's website, http://www.fjc.gov/public/home.nsf/hisj. Concerning the Justice's origination of the custom of using law clerks, see "Origins of the Supreme Judicial Court Law Clerk System" at http://sjclawclerks.socialaw.com/about-us/law-clerk-history/.

5. A partial list of Justice Gray's law secretaries may be found at "Origins of the Supreme Judicial Court Law Clerk System," ibid.

6. The descriptions of the Supreme Court's premises in the Capitol Building in 1892 are accurate. Many of the Justices did work from home at the time, on account of the inadequacy of their working space. The Supreme Court Historical Society, "History of the Court: Home of the Court," accessed Feb. 5, 2011, http://www.supremecourthistory.org/history-of-the-court/home-of-the-court/. A photograph of the basement library (formerly the Court's only premises) taken in 1900 may be seen at William B. Bushong, ann., *House Document No. 108–240, Glenn Brown's History of the United States Capitol* (Washington, DC: U.S. Government Printing Office, 1998), chap. 5, p. 194 (Plate 94). Details of Ezra Ripley Thayer's career and family, and that of his father, are factual. All quotations from Thayer's draft of the Hillmon opinion are verbatim from the Court's opinion as it eventually appeared. The sources of details about Thayer's correspondence with his father, and the latter's suggestion of how the Hillmon case might be resolved, are described in the following section. The source for the "graveyard insurance" statement made by Justice Brown may also be found there. Other events and aspects of this section, including Ezra Thayer's thoughts, are invented.

7. Robert M. Spector, "Legal Historian on the United States Supreme Court: Justice Horace Gray Jr. and the Historical Method," *American Journal of Legal History* 12, no. 3 (July 1968): 181–210.

8. *Hunter v. State*, 40 N.J.L. 495, 534–38 (N.J. 1878).

9. Chris Cillizza, "The Fix: Where in the World Is Mark Sanford? (The Appalachian Trail)," *Washington Post*, June 22, 2009.

10. For details of Thayer's career and accomplishments see *Ezra Ripley Thayer: An Estimate of His Work as Dean of the Harvard Law School* (Cambridge: Harvard Law School Association, 1916); and William H. Dunbar, "Ezra Ripley Thayer," *Harvard Law Review* 29, no. 1 (Nov. 1915): 1–12.

11. John Macarthur Maguire, "The Hillmon Case: Thirty-Three Years Later," *Harvard Law Review* 38, no. 6 (April 1925): 711–12.

12. The Harvard Law School Library does catalog two items described as the evidence course teaching notes of Ezra Ripley Thayer. The Library has advised me, however, that one of the items is missing and cannot be located. The other, which I was able to examine, contains no mention of the Hillmon case.

13. Fed. R. Evid. 803(3) (Advisory Committee's Note).

NOTES TO CHAPTER 6

1. "It Is Unparalleled," *Topeka Daily Capital*, Feb. 5, 1895, 4; "Flashes from the Wire," *Los Angeles Times*, April 4, 1896, 2; "A Famous Case," *Chicago Daily Tribune*, June 30, 1885, 3; "The Hillmon Insurance Case," *New York Times*, May 17, 1892, 1; "A Noted Insurance Case," *New York Times*, Oct. 16, 1899, 7.

2. The fourth trial convened in Topeka's federal courthouse in January 1895. The defendants offered evidence in the course of this trial that plaintiff's counsel had placed liens against the defendants to secure their accession to "a measure [of] Mrs. Hillmon's interest in the case." "Defendants' Day," *Topeka Daily Capital*, Feb. 19, 1895, 4. Samuel Riggs acknowledged the authenticity of the documents and their meaning. Many descriptions of Lysander Wheat during this time remark on the manner in which he has aged since the case began. Bicycles were indeed a novelty in Topeka at about this time. The remaining features of the scene, including Wheat's thoughts and his conversation with Sallie, are invented.

3. Jon Grevillius, e-mail messages to and from the author, Oct. 28, 2008, to Feb. 12, 2009.

4. Margaret Mair to Donald F. Paine, July 10, 1995, in the author's possession.

5. "Hillmon Case Jury," *Topeka Daily Capital*, Jan. 10, 1895, 3.

6. Miner's *Kansas*, 221 (women on juries), 164–68 (Salter).

7. KSHS *Annals of Kansas*, 75.

8. Miner's *Kansas*, 168 ("pitiful crumb"); Clanton's *Populism*, 42–45 (Lease's origins and career). The quote from White may be found *ibid.*, 42. Clanton reports the date of Lease's 1891 speech; the text may be found at Mary Elizabeth Lease, "Wall Street Owns the Country," *History Is a Weapon*, accessed Feb. 19, 2011, http://www.history-isaweapon.com/defcon1/marylease.html.

9. Lease's later life is recounted in Richard Stiller, *Queen of Populists: The Story of Mary Elizabeth Lease* (New York: T.Y. Crowell, 1970).

10. The two failures to enact female suffrage are described in Clanton's *Populism*, 89, 138.

11. "Hillmon Case Jury," *Topeka Daily Capital*, Jan. 10, 1895, 3.

12. "Brown on the Stand," *Topeka Daily Capital*, Jan. 12, 1895, 4 (John Brown); "Grinding Away," *Topeka Daily Capital*, Jan. 22, 1895, 4 (Arthur Judson); "Say It Was Not J.W. Hillmon," *Topeka Daily Capital*, Feb. 2, 1895, 5 (Samuel Walker); "Strong Plea by J.W. Green," *Topeka Daily Capital*, March 17, 1895, 6 (William Lamon). Marie Elizabeth Walters's death occurred in 1888, according her husband Daniel's obituary in the *Ft. Madison Weekly*, July 7, 1909, 7.

13. Charles Hutchings is mentioned as Sallie's lawyer in "Hillmon Case Jury," *Topeka Daily Capital*, Jan. 10, 1895, 3. John Hutchings's death in 1892 is reported at Perl W. Morgan, *A History of Wyandotte County Kansas and Its People* (Chicago: Lewis Publishing Company, 1911), accessed Feb. 19, 2011, http://skyways.lib.ks.us/genweb/archives/wyandott/history/1911/volume2/h/hutchifd.html. Charles Gleed's purchase of the *Journal* is documented in Harmon's "Gleed," 232. Ware's position in the Gleed law firm, and his fame as a poet, are described *ibid.*, 65.

14. Concerning the Panic of 1893, see David O. Whitten, "The Depression of 1893," *EH.net*, accessed Feb. 1, 2010, http://eh.net/encyclopedia/article/whitten.panic.1893. The bank failures are recounted in KSHS *Annals of Kansas*, 154. The figures on life insurance company profits are found *ibid.*, 188, 208.

15. Clanton's *Populism*, *passim*. Concerning the uneasy relationship between populism and women's issues such as suffrage, see *ibid.*, 137–39.

16. Lewelling's inaugural address is quoted in Miner's *Kansas*, 183. Concerning Simpson's election see *ibid.*, 182–83. Concerning the ensuing events in Topeka, see *ibid.*, 183–86; and Clanton's *Populism*, 107–11.

17. This account of the Populist War is drawn largely from Miner's *Kansas*, 182–84; and sources he cites. Lewelling's inaugural address is quoted *ibid.*, 183. Concerning

the ensuing events in Topeka, see also Clanton's *Populism*, 107–11. An image of the famous sledgehammer may be seen at "George L. Douglass' Sledgehammer," *Kansas Memory*, accessed Feb. 19, 2011, http://www.kansasmemory.org/item/24861. An image of the Governor's order that the Republicans vacate the chamber may be seen at "Executive Order No. 2, Governor Lorenzo Lewelling," *Kansas Memory*, accessed Feb. 19, 2011, http://www.kansasmemory.org/item/210830. Photographs by W.F. Farrow, KSHS, online at "Crowd at the Kansas Statehouse, Topeka, Kansas," *Kansas Memory*, accessed Feb. 19, 2011, http://www.kansasmemory.org/item/24895/page/1; and "Mob at the Kansas Statehouse, Topeka, Kansas," *Kansas Memory*, accessed Feb. 19, 2011, http://www.kansasmemory.org/item/24839/page/1.

18. Miner's *Kansas*, 182–84; and Clanton's *Populism*, 107–11. Lewelling's ecstatic inauguration may have marked a high point for populism in Kansas, for the decision by the Kansas Supreme Court was only the first of many setbacks. In 1894, Lewelling was defeated for reelection by his old opponent Edmund Morrill. Morrill's successor, John Leedy, elected in 1896, was nominally a populist, but not such a reformer as Lewelling; the Kansas populists were running out of steam at the state level. But their programs and agenda remained vital for much longer, and many of their aspirations were taken up by the Democratic and Progressive Parties of the later 1890s and twentieth century. Miner's *Kansas*, 187–88.

19. "Must Reform or Get Out," *New York Times*, May 8, 1893, 5.

20. *Ibid.*

21. "John W. Hillmon Not Dead," *New York Times*, May 9, 1893, 5.

22. *Ibid.*

23. *Ibid.*

24. *Ibid.*

25. "Is Hillman Alive?" *Chicago Daily Tribune*, May 10, 1893, 2.

26. *Ibid.*

27. "Hillmon's Insurance Fraud," *New York Times*, May 10, 1893, 5.

28. "Wanderings of a Murderer," *New York Times*, May 24, 1893, 1.

29. *Ibid.*

30. "Hillmon in Mexico," *New York Times*, May 25, 1893, 1.

31. "This Day in History," *Lawrence Daily Journal and Evening Tribune*, Jan. 5, 1894, 2.

32. The warrant and Green's affidavit can be found at "Misc. Hillman, John W.," KSHS. The quote is from *Topeka Daily Capital*, Jan. 11, 1895, 3.

33. *Ibid.*

34. *Ibid.*

35. An image of the banner may be seen at "Kansas Redeemed: Populism Dead," *Kansas Memory*, accessed Feb. 19, 2011, http://www.kansasmemory.org/item/209351.

36. "Brown on the Stand," *Topeka Daily Capital*, Jan. 12, 1895, 4.

37. Green's testimony is reported at "For Mrs. Hillmon," *Topeka Daily Capital*, Jan. 13, 1895, 2, as is that of Buchan. Barker's confession is reported at "The Hillmon Trial," *Topeka Daily Capital*, Jan. 26, 1895, 2.

38. "Brown on the Stand," *Topeka Daily Capital*, Jan. 12, 1895, 4; "Mrs. Hillmon's Case," *Topeka Daily Capital*, Jan. 19, 1895, 1; "Hillmon Testimony," *Topeka Daily Capital*, Jan. 20, 1895, 5.

39. "Hillmon Testimony," *Topeka Daily Capital*, Jan. 20, 1895, 5; "Grinding Away," *Topeka Daily Capital*, Jan. 22, 1895, 3.

40. Sallie's testimony about her lengthy engagement is reported at "Mrs. Hillmon's Tale," *Topeka Daily Capital*, Jan. 23, 1895, 8.

41. "Still Testifying," *Topeka Daily Capital*, Jan. 25, 1895, 4.

42. *Ibid.*

43. "On the Stand Again," *Topeka Daily Capital*, Jan. 24, 1895, 6.

44. "Still Testifying," *Topeka Daily Capital*, Jan. 25, 1895, 4.

45. Thomas's first comment is reported at "Mrs. Hillmon's Tale," *Topeka Daily Capital*, Jan. 23, 1895, 8; the second is at "Defense Is Begun," *Topeka Daily Capital*, Jan. 30, 1895, 4.

46. "The Hillmon Trial," *Topeka Daily Capital*, Feb. 8, 1895, 3.

47. "On the Stand Again," *Topeka Daily Capital*, Jan. 24, 1895, 6.

48. The judge's nondecision is reported at "The Hillmon Trial," *Topeka Daily Capital*, Feb. 10, 1895, 8. Concerning the rule on statements by coconspirators, see *United States v. Gooding*, 25 U.S. 460 (1827); and *Logan v. United States*, 144 U.S. 263 (1892).

49. The reading of the Crew's deposition is recorded at "Very Little Done," *Topeka Daily Capital*, Feb. 22, 1895, 3.

50. The discharge certificate is described in "The Hillmon Trial," *Topeka Daily Capital*, Feb. 16, 1895, 6.

51. "Stuart Testifies," *Topeka Daily Capital*, Feb. 13, 1895, 3.

52. "The Fortieth Day," *Topeka Daily Capital*, Feb. 14, 1895, 6.

53. Sallie gave her account of the tintype's disappearance in the third trial, as recorded at "A Daisy Witness," *Topeka Daily Capital*, March 7, 1888, 5. And indeed, its presence at the inquest is reported at "The Hillmon Inquest," *Lawrence Daily Tribune*, April 10, 1879, 4. Green eventually acknowledged receiving it from her, according to an account in "Advised His Brother to Swear to a Lie," *Leavenworth Times*, Oct. 24, 1899, 4. Riggs's complaint formed part of his summation on the third trial, reported in the *Topeka Daily Capital*, March 21, 1888, 5. Hutchings made the accusation again at the last trial—see "Mrs. Hillmon Would Not Get a Dollar of Money," *Leavenworth Times*, Nov. 16, 1899, 4—prompting Green's remarks, reported in "Simmons' Testimony a Footless Fancy," *Leavenworth Times*, Nov. 17, 1899, 4.

54. The first quotation is from "It Is Unparalleled," *Topeka Daily Capital*, Feb. 5, 1895, 4. The second and third are from "The Hillmon Trial," *Topeka Daily Capital*, Feb. 16, 1895, 6.

55. "The Hillmon Trial," *Topeka Daily Capital*, Feb. 16, 1895, 6.

56. "Defendants' Day," *Topeka Daily Capital*, Feb. 19, 1895, 4.

57. "Say It Was Walters," *Topeka Daily Capital*, Feb. 20, 1895, 3.

58. "They Knew Walters," *Topeka Daily Capital*, Feb. 21, 1895, 3.

59. *Ibid.*

60. "County Seat Contests," *Topeka Daily Commonwealth*, March 15, 1888, 8, reports the live testimony of "Mr. C.W. Schott" during the third trial, identifying the corpse photograph as Walters. Schott had been married to Alvina for more than four years on the occasion of that testimony, although this circumstance goes unmentioned. Randy Johnson, "Lee County Marriages, Schm thru Scu," *Lee County Iowa Genealogy*, accessed Feb. 19, 2011, http://iagenweb.org/lee/marriages/marr-s2.htm.

61. The witness who testified to the nickname was Charles Helsig, who said he had known Adolph "ever since he could remember." "Say It Was Walters," *Topeka Daily Capital*, Feb. 20, 1895, 3.

62. "Goes Right Along," *Topeka Daily Capital*, Feb. 23, 1895, 5 (testimony of C.R. Walters); "Walters' Sister," *Topeka Daily Capital*, Feb. 24, 1895, 2 (testimony of Fannie Walters).

63. Edward Isham was frequently described in the newspapers as a lawyer who had been brought in to do the heavy lifting pertaining to points of law. The descriptions of the arguments and rulings concerning the admissibility of the Brown deposition and the documents pertaining to the Texas cattle transaction are accurate. The thoughts of James W. Green are invented.

64. "Buchan Testifies," *Topeka Daily Capital*, Feb. 27, 1895, 3.

65. *Ibid.*; "Adjourned to Tuesday," *Topeka Daily Capital*, March 3, 1895, 3.

66. "Say They Have Seen Hillmon," *Topeka Daily Capital*, March 5, 1895, 4.

67. *Ibid.*

68. Charley Hay, who said he had known Hillmon slightly from the time when both lived in Lawrence, testified that he had seen Hillmon at a mine near Leadville, Colorado, in July 1879, and that one evening the two men had taken dinner together in the company of several others. John W. Mathias of Bisbee, Arizona, testified that he had hunted buffalo in Texas with Hillmon during a period of some months during 1875 to 1877, and then in May 1889 had seen Hillmon in the jail at Tombstone, Arizona, had conversed with him there, and had noted (although Hillmon tried to conceal it) a scar on his right hand. He had later seen Hillmon removed from the jail and placed in a stagecoach, handcuffed and under guard. G.S. Baker corroborated Mathias's story. He too had known Hillmon on the Texas buffalo range in 1875–76, but later Baker had moved to Arizona and become deputy sheriff at Tombstone. Like Mathias, he had seen John Hillmon in the jail there in 1889, had observed a scar on his right hand, and had seen him removed in handcuffs. Charles W. Hart of Tombstone swore that he also had known Hillmon from their days together on the buffalo range in Texas. He had seen Hillmon in the Tombstone jail in 1889, and believed that his old acquaintance was in custody for being "the notorious John W. Hillmon for whom the insurance companies had offered a large reward." All testimony reported *ibid.*

69. "The Hillmon Trial," *Topeka Daily Capital*, March 6, 1895.

70. "Hillmon Trial Nearly Done," *Topeka Daily Capital*, March 10, 1895, 11 ("an almost ungovernable spirit").

71. *Ibid.*

72. "The Hillmon Trial," *Topeka Daily Capital*, March 12, 1895, 6.

73. "Strong Plea by J.W. Green," *Topeka Daily Capital*, March 17, 1895, 6.

74. *Ibid.*

75. *Ibid.*

76. "Nearly at an End," *Topeka Daily Capital*, March 19, 1895, 6.

77. *Ibid.*

78. "Hillmon Case Gone to Jury," *Topeka Daily Capital*, March 20, 1895, 6; "Unable to Agree," *Topeka Daily Capital*, March 23, 1895, 8; "Eleven to One," *Topeka Daily Capital*, March 24, 1895, 6.

79. "Eleven to One," *Topeka Daily Capital*, March 24, 1895, 6.

80. *Ibid.*

81. *Ibid.*

NOTES TO CHAPTER 7

1. "Will Find Hillmon," *Emporia Daily Gazette*, Sep. 16, 1895, col. C.

2. "Life Insurance Crimes," *New York Times*, Nov. 11, 1895, 4.

3. Ironquill's quote is memorialized in KSHS *Annals of Kansas*, 198; Mrs. Lease's threats *ibid.*, 1:195; the criticism of the university *ibid.*, 1:197; and the bankruptcy of the *Daily Capital ibid.*, 1:199.

4. "Will Try It Again: Judge Williams Presides," *Topeka Daily Capital*, March 11, 1896 (description of Judge Williams).

5. "For the Fifth Time," *Topeka Daily Capital*, March 8, 1896.

6. "They Knew Hillmon," *Topeka Daily Capital*, March 12, 1896.

7. *Ibid.*

8. "What Does It Hold?" *Topeka Daily Capital*, March 14, 1896.

9. *Ibid.*

10. The scene is completely invented. It is true, however, that the phrase "Less corn, more hell!" became a rallying cry at appearances by Mrs. Lease. She often denied that she had originated the recommendation that farmers should raise less of one and more of the other, although she allowed that it was good advice.

11. "The Other Side Now," *Topeka Daily Capital*, March 17, 1896, 1.

12. *Ibid.* (Sallie's testimony); "Buchan Testifies," *Topeka Daily Capital*, March 21, 1895, 5 (Buchan's testimony).

13. "The Other Side Now," *Topeka Daily Capital*, March 17, 1896, 1.

14. "How Tall Was He?" *Topeka Daily Capital*, March 18, 1896.

15. "Story of Two MDs," *Topeka Daily Capital*, March 19, 1896.

16. *Ibid.*

17. "Evidence Piled Up," *Topeka Daily Capital*, March 20, 1896.

18. "Wanted: The Truth," *Topeka Daily Capital*, March 25, 1896.

19. "Wait for a Witness," *Topeka Daily Capital*, March 27, 1896.

20. *Ibid.*

21. "Nearing the End," *Topeka Daily Capital*, March 28, 1896.

22. *Ibid.*

23. *Ibid.*

24. "Hutchings Is Sick," *Topeka Daily Capital*, March 29, 1896.

25. "What Does It Hold?" *Topeka Daily Capital*, March 14, 1896.

26. "Arguments Begun," *Topeka Daily Capital*, March 31, 1896.

27. *Ibid.*

28. *Ibid.* (remainder of Hutchings's summation).

29. *Ibid.* (Green's summation).

30. "What's the Verdict?" *Topeka Daily Capital*, April 1, 1896.

31. *Ibid.*

32. *Ibid.*

33. "What's the Verdict?" *Topeka Daily Capital*, April 1, 1896.

34. "A Verdict, Perhaps," *Topeka Daily Capital*, April 2, 1896.

35. "Can't Get Together," *Topeka Daily Capital*, April 3, 1896.

36. *Ibid.*

37. *Ibid.*

38. "Same Old Result," *Topeka Daily Capital*, April 4, 1896.

39. *Ibid.*

40. *Ibid.*
41. *Ibid.*
42. The figures on life insurance profits are from KSHS *Annals of Kansas*, 225.
43. "Hillman Heirs Become Aggressive," *Chicago Daily Tribune*, Feb. 27, 1894, 1 (Sallie's complaint); "Mighty Is M'Nall," *Topeka Daily Capital*, March 4, 1897, 8 (Superintendent's first order); KSHS *Annals of Kansas*, 228 (refusal to renew business licenses)
44. "Warns One Company," *Topeka Daily Capital*, April 1, 1897, 1.
45. "An Insurance Damage Suit," *Los Angeles Times*, April 7, 1897.
46. Cassius G. Foster, Judge, Circuit Court of the United States, District of Kansas, "Hillmon v. Insurance Cos., In re Webb McNall, Opinion," April 12, 1897, Records for the U.S. Circuit Court for the District of Kansas, 1st Div., Topeka, RG 21, Box 221, NARA Archive; see also "Miscellaneous: Topeka, Kan., Special," *Wall Street Journal*, April 12, 1897, 4.
47. "Web Wilder on M'Nall," *Topeka Daily Capital*, April 15, 1897, 4.
48. "The Hillmon Case Up to Date," *Topeka Daily Capital*, Aug. 17, 1897, 4.
49. "An Arrogant Official," *Leavenworth Times*, March 4, 1897, 2.
50. *Ibid.* ("arrogant official"); *Atchison Daily Globe*, Jan. 22, 1898, 2 ("blackmail"); H. Roger Grant, "Insurance Reform: The Case of Webb McNall in Kansas," *Kansas Historical Quarterly* 36 (1970): 65 ("widespread bipartisan support"); Letter to Webb McNall from "A Policyholder," April 1, 1897, in KSHS, Kansas Insurance Department Correspondence, 1897, quoted *ibid.*
51. KSHS *Annals of Kansas*, 237.
52. Grant, "Insurance Reform," 67 (withdrawal of two companies); KSHS *Annals of Kansas*, 265 (Kansas Supreme Court judgment).
53. "Kansas Insurance War," *New York Times*, Jan. 22, 1898, 2.
54. "News and Comment," *Atchison Daily Globe*, Jan. 21, 1898, col. D; "The Hillmon Settlement," *Emporia Daily Gazette*, Jan. 25, 1898, col. G. (James Smith's statement). The *Eagle*'s remark was repeated and attributed in "Multiple News Items," *Emporia Daily Gazette*, Jan. 24, 1898, col. C.
55. "Hillmon Case Ends," *Chicago Daily Tribune*, Jan. 22, 1898, 6 (general belief); *Atchison Daily Globe*, Jan. 22, 1898, 2.
56. *Ibid.*
57. "Hillmon Claim Settled," *Lawrence Daily Journal*, Jan. 21, 1898.
58. "Affidavit of Sallie E. Smith," Feb. 12, 1898, Records for the U.S. Circuit Court for the District of Kansas, 1st Div., Topeka, RG 21, Box 221, NARA Archive; C.F. Hutchings, "Letter to Hon Geo. J. Barker and Hon. J.W. Green," Feb. 4, 1898, *ibid.*; "News and Comment," *Atchison Daily Globe*, Feb. 5, 1898, col. C.
59. "Affidavit of C. F. Hutchings," May 7, 1898, Records for the U.S. Circuit Court for the District of Kansas, 1st Div., Topeka, RG 21, Box 221, NARA Archive; John A. Williams, Judge, Circuit Court of the United States for the District of Kansas, First Division, Order Continuing Trial, May 9, 1898, *ibid.*
60. KSHS *Annals of Kansas*, 265; "Mrs. Hillmon Wins," *Atchison Daily Globe*, Jan. 21, 1898, col. A (company permitted to resume business); "Victory for Mr. M'Nall," *Emporia Daily Gazette*, Jan. 22, 1898, col. G ("widely predicted"); *Atchison Daily Globe*, Jan. 22, 1898, 2; "Mutual Life Drops Suit in Kansas," *New York Times*, May 26, 1898, 7 (permitted to resume business).
61. Grant, "Insurance Reform," 72.

NOTES TO CHAPTER 8

1. "Hillmon Fraud Comes Up for Sixth Trial," *Leavenworth Times*, Oct. 15, 1899, 4
2. "The Sixth Trial," *Leavenworth Evening Standard*, Oct. 6, 1899.
3. "Atwood's Attitude in the Hillmon Case," *Leavenworth Times*, Oct. 17, 1899, 6.
4. *Ibid.*
5. *Ibid.*
6. "Hillmon Case On," *Leavenworth Evening Standard*, Oct. 16, 1899.
7. Prior Dickey is identified as "a colored man," and P.G. Lowe is addressed as "Senator," in "Isham and Barker Close for Defense," *Leavenworth Times*, Nov. 18, 1899, 4. Lowe is identified as a member of the State Senate from Leavenworth in KSHS *Annals of Kansas*, 52.
8. "By Conspiracy," *Leavenworth Times*, Oct. 18, 1899, 4
9. *Ibid.*
10. *Ibid.*
11. 'Taking of Evidence in Hillmon Case Begins," *Leavenworth Times*, Oct. 19, 1899, 4.
12. *Ibid.*
13. *Ibid.*
14. *Ibid.*
15. "Five Depositions in the Hillmon Case," *Leavenworth Times*, Oct. 20, 1899, 4.
16. This proffered testimony is described in *Connecticut Mutual Life Ins. Co. v. Hillmon*, 107 F. 834, 839 (1903).
17. "Five Depositions in the Hillmon Case," *Leavenworth Times*, Oct. 20, 1899, 4.
18. *Ibid.*
19. "Brown Declared He Saw Hillmon Kill His Man," *Leavenworth Times*, Oct. 21, 1899, 4.
20. *Ibid.*
21. "Brown's Statement to Buchan Ruled Out," *Leavenworth Times*, Oct. 22, 1899, 4.
22. "Mrs. Hillmon's Evidence to Be Finished Today," *Leavenworth Times*, Oct. 25, 1899, 4.
23. "Mysterious Silence of Alva Baldwin Broken," *Leavenworth Times*, Oct. 26, 1899, 4.
24. *Ibid.* A Charles C. Emery would later testify for the defense that he had asked Alva Baldwin, at about the time of the inquest, how he could account for the difference in height between John Hillmon and the corpse, and Alva had said he could not. "Walters Left Wichita with Hillmon and Brown," *Leavenworth Times*, Nov. 5, 1899, 4.
25. "Mysterious Silence of Alva Baldwin Broken," *Leavenworth Times*, Oct. 26, 1899, 4 (direct testimony);"A Demurrer Filed," *Leavenworth Times*, Oct. 27, 1889, 4 (cross-examination); "Claims Walters Was in Leavenworth in May 1879," *Leavenworth Times*, Nov. 14, 1899, 4 (rebuttal testimony).
26. "A Demurrer Filed," *Leavenworth Times*, Oct. 27, 1899, 4.
27. *Ibid.*
28. The transcript is authentic, from the NARA Archive. "By the court. I desire to say this . . . " from unlabeled typewritten transcript of the 1899 trial, Boxes 224–25, RG 21, NARA Archive, page numbers unavailable. The scene preceding it is invented, but conforms in general to Judge Hook's description in the transcript of what has occurred, and to the timing of matters as reported contemporaneously.
29. Unlabeled typewritten transcript of the 1899 trial, Box 224–25, RG 21, NARA Archive, 668A–668E.

30. *Ibid.*
31. *Ibid.*
32. *Ibid.*
33. "A Demurrer Filed," *Leavenworth Times*, Oct. 27, 1899, 4; "Attempt Bribery," *Lawrence Evening Standard*, Oct. 26, 1899.
34. "A Demurrer Filed," *Leavenworth Times*, Oct. 27, 1899, 4.
35. Harmon's "Gleed," 81–85.
36. "A Demurrer Filed," *Leavenworth Times*, Oct. 27, 1899, 4.
37. "Demurrer to Plaintiffs Evidence Overruled," *Leavenworth Times*, Oct. 28, 1899, 4.
38. *Ibid.*
39. The fourth trial featured as an exhibit John Hillmon's enlistment papers, said to be dated September 1864. "The Hillmon Trial," *Topeka Daily Capital*, Feb. 16, 1895, 6. Hillmon was born in January 1848. The testimony of Mrs. Corkadel is recorded in "Mrs. Corkadel Says She Was Engaged to Hillmon," *Leavenworth Times*, Oct. 31, 1899, 4; and of Mrs. Nichols in "Damaging Evidence by John Hillmon's Sister," *Leavenworth Times*, Nov. 1, 1899, 4.
40. "Damaging Evidence by John Hillmon's Sister," *Leavenworth Times*, Nov. 1, 1899, 4.
41. *Ibid.*
42. "Hillmon Trial," *Lawrence Evening Standard*, Oct. 28, 1899.
43. "W.J. Buchan Tells of J. H. Brown's Statement," *Leavenworth Times*, Nov. 3, 1899, 6.
44. *Ibid.*
45. "On the Track of Walters," *Leavenworth Times*, Nov. 4, 1899, 8. The reference to Dreyfus occurs in "Walters Left Wichita with Hillmon and Brown," *Leavenworth Times*, Nov. 5, 1899, 4.
46. *Ibid.*
47. "The Hillman Horror," *Lawrence Standard*, April 10, 1879, 1.
48. "Brown and Hillmon Were Seen in Wichita," *Leavenworth Times*, Nov. 7, 1899, 4.
49. "Trying to Shut Out Conspiracy Evidence," *Leavenworth Times*, Nov. 9, 1899, 4.
50. *Ibid.*; "Brother and Sister Swear It Was Walters," *Leavenworth Times*, Nov. 11, 1899, 6.
51. "Walters' Last Letter to His Sweetheart," *Leavenworth Times*, Nov. 10, 1899, 4.
52. *Ibid.*
53. "Brother and Sister Swear It Was Walters," *Leavenworth Times*, Nov. 11, 1899, 6.
54. *Ibid.* The contents of the letters are described in 1899 Transcript, 1791–94.
55. "Brother and Sister Swear It Was Walters," *Leavenworth Times*, Nov. 11, 1899, 6.
56. "Evidence for Defense Ends with Mrs. Walters," *Leavenworth Times*, Nov. 12, 1899, 4.
57. *Ibid.*
58. The newspaper story is authentic. "Claims Walters Was in Leavenworth in May 1879," *Leavenworth Times*, Nov. 14, 1899, 4. The preceding scene is invented, but conforms to contemporary descriptions of the events in the courtroom. As always, the thoughts and reflections of the characters are imagined.
59. *Ibid.*
60. *Ibid.*
61. *Ibid.*
62. *Ibid.*
63. "Ready for Arguments in the Hillmon Case," *Leavenworth Times*, Nov. 15, 1899, 4.
64. *Ibid.*

65. *Ibid.*

66. *Ibid.*; see T. A. McNeal, *When Kansas Was Young* (Topeka: Capper Publishers, 1922), 91–92.

67. "Ready for Arguments in the Hillmon Case," *Leavenworth Times*, Nov. 15, 1899, 4.

68. "Mrs. Hillmon Would Not Get a Dollar of Money," *Leavenworth Times*, Nov. 16, 1899, 4.

69. *Ibid.*

70. *Ibid.*

71. "Simmons' Testimony a Footless Fancy," *Leavenworth Times*, Nov. 17, 1899, 4.

72. *Ibid.*

73. *Ibid.*

74. *Ibid.*

75. *Ibid.*

76. "Isham and Barker Close for Defense," *Leavenworth Times*, Nov. 18, 1899, 4.

77. *Ibid.*

78. "Simmons' Testimony a Footless Fancy," *Leavenworth Times*, Nov. 17, 1899, 4.

79. *Ibid.*

80. "Isham and Barker Close for Defense," *Leavenworth Times*, Nov. 18, 1899, 4.

81. *Ibid.*

82. *Ibid.*

83. "Simmons' Testimony a Footless Fancy," *Leavenworth Times*, Nov. 17, 1899, 4.

84. *Ibid.*

85. *Ibid.*

86. "Ready for Arguments in the Hillmon Case," *Leavenworth Times*, Nov. 15, 1899, 4.

87. "The Jury Out," *Lawrence Evening Standard*, Nov. 18, 1899.

88. "Gives Her $33,102," *Leavenworth Times*, Nov. 19, 1899, 4.

89. "A Just Verdict," *Lawrence Evening Standard*, Nov. 20, 1899.

90. "Motion for a New Trial Was Overruled," *Leavenworth Times*, Nov. 21, 1899, 4.

91. "Mrs. Hillmon Wins Suit," *Chicago Daily Tribune*, Nov. 19, 1899, 2.

92. *Ibid.*

93. "Hillmon Case Is Done For," *Topeka Daily Capital*, July 5, 1903, 5.

NOTES TO CHAPTER 9

1. Judy Crichton, *America, 1900: The Turning Point* (New York: Henry Holt, 1998), 9, 27, 50, 73.

2. Deborah Blum, *Ghost Hunters: William James and the Search for Scientific Proof of Life after Death,* (New York: Penguin, 2006), 91–92, 309–10, 222–23.

3. *Ibid., passim.*

4. Crichton, *America, 1900*, 6.

5. *Connecticut Mutual Life Ins. Co. v. Hillmon*, 107 F. 834 (1903).

6. *Chicago Tribune*, Aug. 8, 1900, 1; *New York Times*, Aug. 8, 1900, 10.

7. *Connecticut Mutual Life*, 107 F. 834.

8. "Notes of Insurance Interests," *New York Times*, Aug. 11, 1900, 9.

9. "Famous Insurance Case Turns This Way," *Los Angeles Times*, June 28, 1901, 2.

10. "Not Known Here," *Los Angeles Times*, June 28, 1901, 2.

11. "News of the Court: United States Supreme Court," *Chicago Daily Tribune*, Nov. 15, 1902, 11.

12. *Connecticut Mutual Life v. Hillmon*, 188 U.S. 208 (1903).
13. "Hillmon Insurance Case Ended after 24 Years," *Chicago Daily Tribune*, July 1, 1903, 4 (report of settlement, claim by Hutchings that Sallie received money in settlement); "No Concessions by Company," *Chicago Daily Tribune*, July 4, 1903, 15 (claim that no money was paid to Sallie).
14. Later Dennis and Paul supplied me with some articles showing that this technique is regarded as scientifically valid for the identification of human remains, although a positive identification is only possible if all but one subject can be ruled out, and the site is one of a "closed disaster"—that is, it can be shown that all the possible subjects have been compared. See, for example, Todd W. Fenton, Amber N. Heard, and Norman J. Sauer, "Skull Photo Superimposition and Border Death: Identification through Exclusion and the Failure to Exclude," *Journal of Forensic Science* 53 (Feb. 2008): 34. Dennis's own report is available at "A Digital Photographic Solution to the Question of Who Lies Buried in Oak Hill Cemetery," *Hillmon Case*, accessed Feb. 11, 2011, http://www.thehillmoncase.com/results.html, a website maintained by the author. Other references and more photographs may also be seen there.
15. This scene is entirely invented. Walters's cough is compatible with Arthur Simmons's testimony, and that of several other witnesses who said Walters was ill when he worked with them near Lawrence in 1878 and 1879. I have done some investigation into nineteenth-century postmarks, or cancellations as enthusiasts call them. It does not appear that in 1879 they were uniform or intricate, nor that it would have been difficult to simulate one. Local postmasters often ordered their own cancellation stamps from commercial companies that manufactured and sold them. Kenneth L. Gilman, ed., *The New Herst-Sampson Catalog: A Guide to Nineteenth-Century United States Postmarks and Cancellations* (North Miami: D.G. Philips, 1989), especially the unpaginated material preceding the table of contents, and pp. 128–29.
16. *Shepard v. United States*, 290 U.S. 96 (1933).
17. All details of the case of Angelo Inciso are from *United States v. Pheaster*, 544 F.2d 353 (9th Cir. 1976). In 1977, skeletal remains identified as those of Larry Adell were found in a shallow grave near Desert Hot Springs, California. "Remains May Be Kidnap Victim's," *Los Angeles Times*, Nov. 20, 1977, B1.
18. Mrs. Piper did live in her father-in-law's house in Beacon Hill in 1903, and held sittings there under the observation of the Australian researcher Richard Hodgson, for which she charged a dollar. The descriptions of her trance states match his reported observations. The origins of Sallie's wedding ring are as she described them in the third trial. Otherwise, the scene is entirely imagined.

INDEX

The index begins with the *Hillmon v. Mutual Life Insurance Company et al.* trials in chronological order. Other subject entries follow thereafter.

Hillmon, John Wesley *(continued)*: brother
(*see* Hillmon, William); brother-in-
law (*see* Nichols, W.W.); Brown, John,
relationship with, 7–8, 24, 51–52, 76,
86–88; Brown's accounts of accidentally
shooting, xx, 11, 15, 18, 86–88, 106, 203,
239–240, 262; burial, xvii–xviii, 21, 77;
business complaints against, 6; cattle
business, 5–6; childhood, 4; Connecticut
Mutual Life Insurance Company, 31;
Corkadel, Annette, 280; as "Coyote Bill,"
200; death, site of his presumed, *179*;
death, suspicions about his reported,
8, 76; the decedent, alleged alternative
identifications of (*see* Burgess or Berkley
or Burgis, Joe; "Colton"; Lowell, Mrs. M.
L., brother of; Nichols, Frank; Walters,
Frederick Adolph; Willey, Mr.); DNA
analysis, 92–94, *185*; employee, former
(*see* Brown, John); engagement to Sallie,
204; Franklin, J.H., 165–167; Grasshopper
Springs, Kansas, 4, 339n2; Green, James
Woods, 166, 201, 212, 243; hair color, 110,
153; hands, 120, 123, 127–128, 132, 150–151,
207, 269, 353n68; hands/scars, 120; headstone for, 317–319; Heely, Patrick, 242;
height, 30–31, 97–98, 105, 110, 119–120,
121, 125, 132, 141, 150, 151, 207–209, 210–
212, 223, 232, 239, 242, 265, 283; insurance
fraud, 76, 307; insurance policies bought
by, beneficiary of, 80; insurance policies bought by, lien on, 74, 111; insurance
policies bought by, number and magnitude, 8, 31, 76–77, 154; insurance policies
bought by, premium for, 51, 77–78, 80,
84, 110; insurance policies bought by,
purchase of, 80–81, 162; insurance policies bought by, Sallie's rights to proceeds
of, 123; intentions, 327; journal of, 139,
163; journey to western Kansas, first, 7,
51–52, 118–119; journey to western Kansas,
second, 8, 24, 52, 113–114; Judson, Arthur,
3, 97–98, 110; killing of, accidental, xx,
8, 86–88; killing of, site of, xx; male
descendent (*see* Hillmon, Leray); marriage certificate, *179*, 339n4; marriage to
Mexican woman, reported, 200; marriage

to Sallie, 6, 23, 245, 340n18; McNeal, T.E.,
76; Medicine Lodge, Kansas, 7; mole, 269;
murder confession, reported, 200; New
York Life Insurance Company, 31; nose,
102–104; occupations, 5–6; Patterson,
Dr., 265; photographs of, *69, 211*, 313–318;
profile, 103; promissory notes, 219; pseud-
onym, alleged, 53; Quartzville mine, 5, 7;
Quinn, Candice, 2; Selig, A.L., 31; sister
(*see* Nichols, Mary Elizabeth); smallpox
vaccination, 21–22, 52, 97, 119–120, 121,
139, 340n18; Stewart, J.H., 119; teeth, 27,
29, 96–97, 98, 112–114, 120, 124, 138, 139,
140, 142, 150, 151, 207, 208–209, 213, 281;
teeth, plaster cast/mold of, 138, 190, 263;
tintypes of, 31–32; Travelers Insurance
Company, 154; traveling companion (*see*
Brown, John); trunk belonging to, 243,
260, 266; Walters, Frederick, alleged
murder of, xxiv–xxv; Walters, Frederick
compared to, 96, 102–103, 121, 313–318;
wealth, 141; wedding ring, 340n18; Wheat,
Lysander, 143; in Wichita, 71; Wiseman,
Theodore ("Major"), 31

Hillmon, Leray (John Hillmon's great
nephew): disinterment of grave number
555, 92, 213–215; genealogy, 94–96; photograph of, *185*; Y chromosome, 257

Hillmon, Mary Elizabeth (John's sister; first
trial witness), 123

Hillmon, Sallie Quinn (plaintiff): first trial,
82–86, 96–98, 109–112, 117–118, 136, 213,
343n1; second trial, 137–138, 139–140,
142; third trial, 148–149, 159, 164, 340n18;
fourth trial, 202–203, 204; fifth trial, 238–
239; sixth trial, 269; affidavit by, 82–83;
appearance, 186–187; author's position
on, 301; Bailey and Smith's funeral parlor,
3, 16, 21, 23, 338n1, 340n11; Baldwin, Levi,
118; Borgalthaus, E.O., 73, 82, 149; Brown,
John, in affidavit by, 53, 59; Brown, John,
Leavenworth meeting, 73–76; Brown,
John, letter from, 12, 15, 54, 116; Brown,
John, relationship with, 81; Brown,
Reuben, 108, 109; Buchan, W.H., 73–75,
110–112, 115, 117–118, 128, 148–149, 294;
Buchan, W.H., letters to, 118, 148–149, 152;

ABOUT THE AUTHOR

Marianne Wesson, Mimi to her friends, teaches evidence and related subjects at the University of Colorado Law School. She is the author of best-selling and prize-winning legal novels including *Render Up the Body*, *A Suggestion of Death*, and *Chilling Effect*. She lives in a Colorado mountain valley with her husband, llamas, dogs, and visiting wildlife.